HOW TO DRAW REPTILES and MAMMALS

An Educational Guide

EARL R. PHELPS

HOW TO DRAW REPTILES and MAMMALS

An Educational Guide

By Earl R. Phelps

Copyright © 2015 by Earl R. Phelps

All rights reserved. No part of this book may printed or published in any form or by any means without permission in writing from the author.

Published by
Phelps Publishing
P.O. Box 22401
Cleveland, Ohio 44122

Library of Congress Catalog Number: 2014919072
ISBN 978-1-887627-08-5

Printed in the United States of America.

Cover design and illustrations by Earl R. Phelps

Visit our web site at www.phelpspublishing.com

Table of Contents

Table of Contents

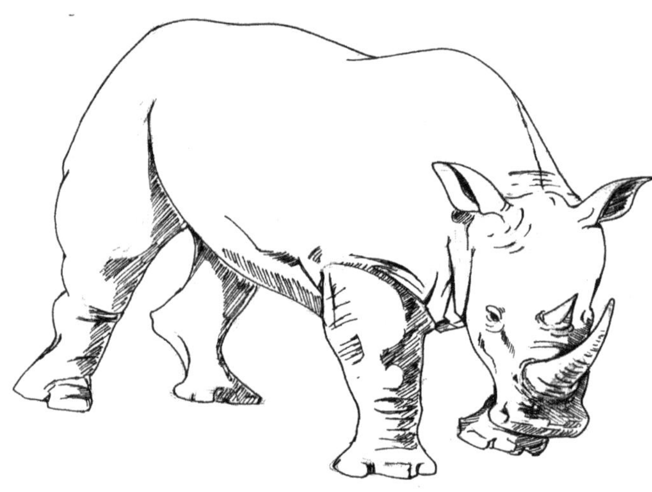

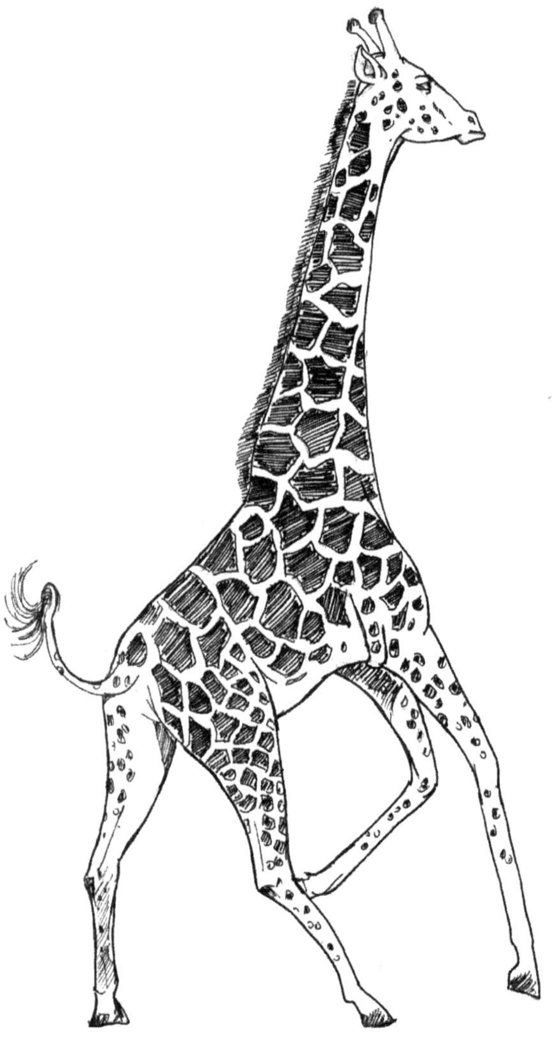

Introduction

Those of you who have great interest in reptiles and mammals will surely enjoy this new book. As a child growing up in Cleveland, my mother would take me and my brother to visit our grandmother in Macon, Georgia I had only one brother at the time, now I have two. During one of my summer visits while I was taking a nap, I saw a baby snake outside of the window on the branch of a brush. I became excited and jump out of the bed and ran outside. The snake was still there, I then proceeded to try and catch the snake. The baby snake glided from one branch to another with the swiftness of ease. I was surprised on have fast it was. I finally caught the snake and put it in a paper bag to show my mother and ask her could I take it back to Cleveland as a pet. You can probably guess what her answer was. One person said it was a baby rattlesnake, someone else said it was probably a rat snake. I believe it was the later, I didn't see a rattler on that snake. As you may have guessed, I returned to Cleveland without the snake.

I've always had a interest in reptiles, especially snakes. This is the first book of its kind, to my knowledge on instructing you on how to draw the different reptiles and mammals of the world. When one speaks of reptiles, you tend to think of snakes and lizards, but there are many different species outside of this group. Through I titled part of this book about learning how to draw reptiles, I have included a few amphibians. This would include the several difference frogs I illustrated in this book.

Amphibians are small creatures with water-permeable skin, which restricts them to damp habitats. All species require water foe breeding, and lay waterborne eggs. These develop into tadpoles which eventually change into adult form in the water. This metamorphosis is characteristic of amphibians. Unlike amphibians, reptiles have dry, scaly skin, and have no need for water for breeding. Reptiles may have live young, or lay eggs, and the offspring produced are generally miniatures of the adults, and undergo no metamorphosis.

What are Mammals? Any vertebrate of the class Mammalia, having the body more or less covered with hair, nourishing the young with milk from the mammary glands, and, with the exception of the egg-laying monotremes, giving birth to live young.

This book is a conbination of two of my prevously books, "*How to Draw Spectacular Reptiles*" and "*How to Draw Magnificent Mammals*" it will not only focus on teaching you on how to draw the most interesting reptiles and mammals in the universe, but will give you some educational information about each species.

In this book, like in my previous books, I've created many step-by-step illustrations showing you how to draw these dynamic reptiles and mammals of the world. This book isn't wordy because as most of us know, a picture is worth a thousand words. so this book must contain over a million invisible words. As you learn from this book I want to give you a guide line tip. When I draw the creature's body, most of the time I'll start with the head then proceed to draw the neck, other parts of the figure and so forth. On some occasions depending on how I plan to position the figure, I would draw that part of the anatomy first.

To truly become good at anything in life, you have to study, visualize, and perform, in other words, practice, practice, and more practice, ain't nothing to it, but to do it!

Let's get busy!

Earl R. Phelps
Cleveland, Ohio

REPTILES

I first started drawing the head and then I preceded to draw the lines to show the shape of the whole Diamondback Rattle snake.

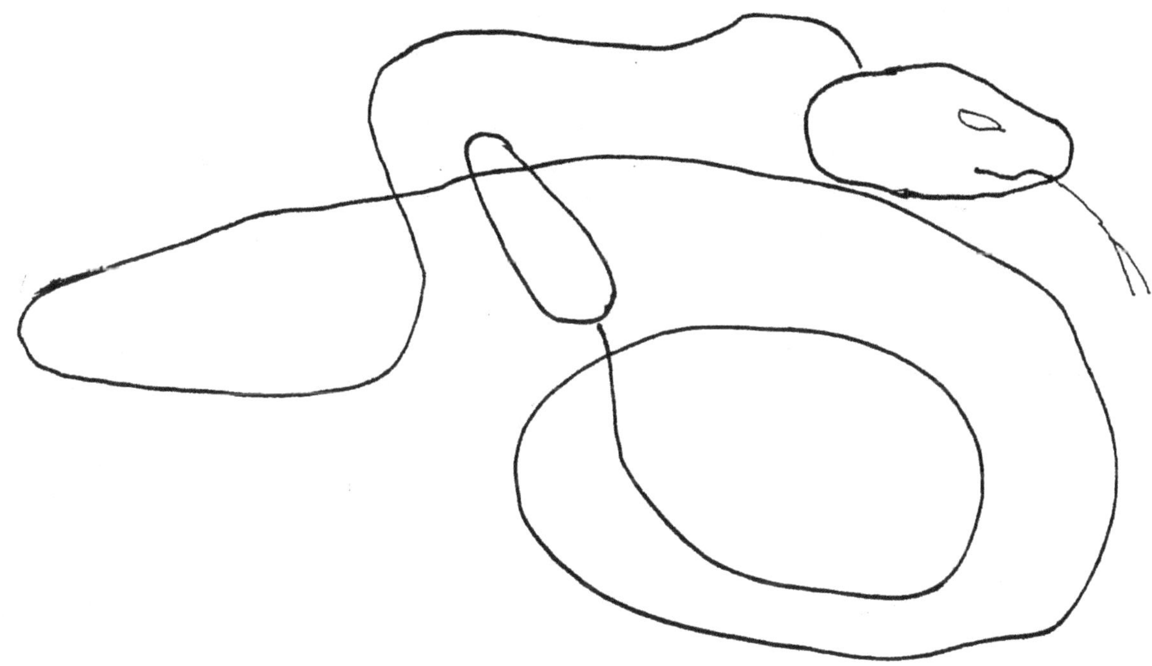

Now, I've filled out the snake's body in drawing in more detail to the head, tongue and rattler, and indicating where any shadows would be.

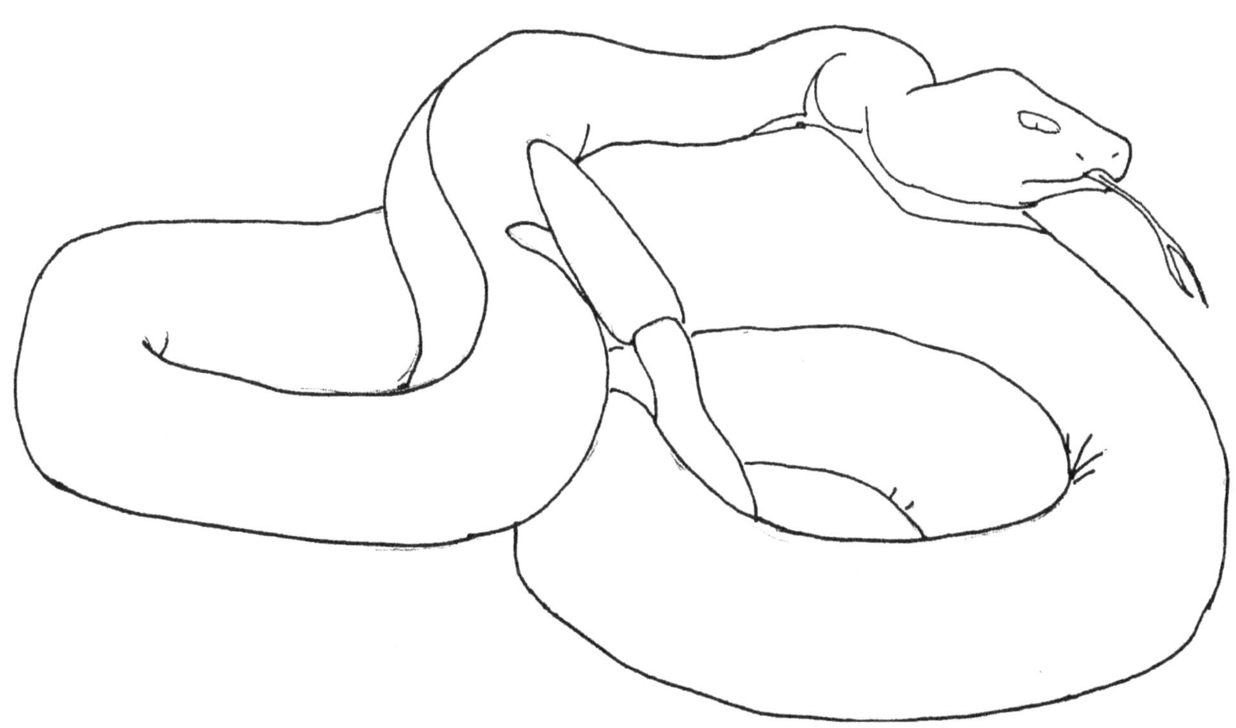

EASTERN DIAMOND RATTLESNAKE

EASTERN DIAMONDBACK RATTLESNAKE
Largest of all rattlesnakes, this magnificent create ranks as one of the biggest venomous snakes in the world. Known to have reached eight feet in length and weigh in excess of 25 pounds, today this species no longer reaches such dimensions. Diamondbacks resides in sparsely populated stretches of palmetto and turkey oak forest or pine flatlands in the southeastern U.S. Habitat destruction and persecution for hides and meat have combined to drastically reduce population of this snake. Large adults prefer cottontail rabbits as prey, but any small mammal will due. Because of its size and potent venom, the Eastern Diamondback is a dangerous snake, and bites to humans can be serious. Offspring can measure as much as 15 inches at birth.

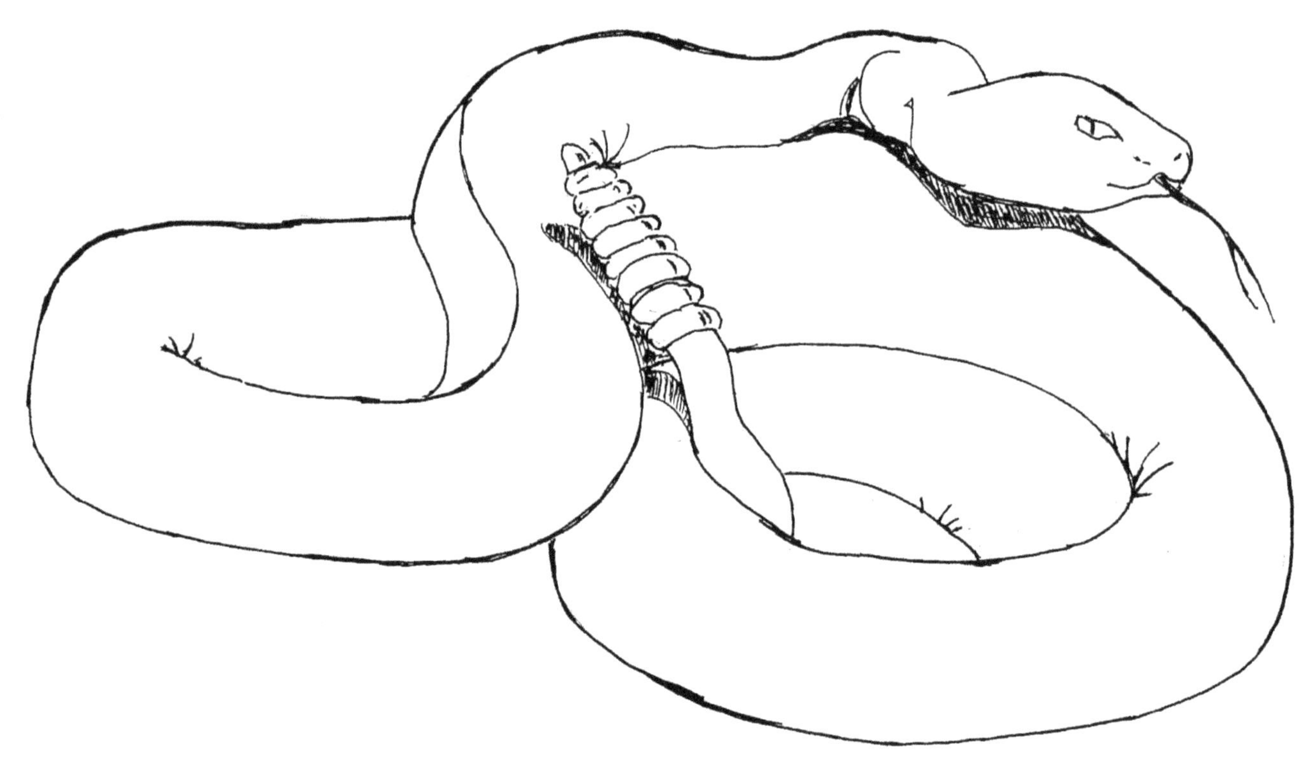

Let's try another snake, because they're easy to draw which makes for a good start for drawing reptiles. Just as before I started with the head and a curvy line for the body contour. Then I start drawing in some details, such as the eye, the fullness of the body, then erasing any unneeded lines.

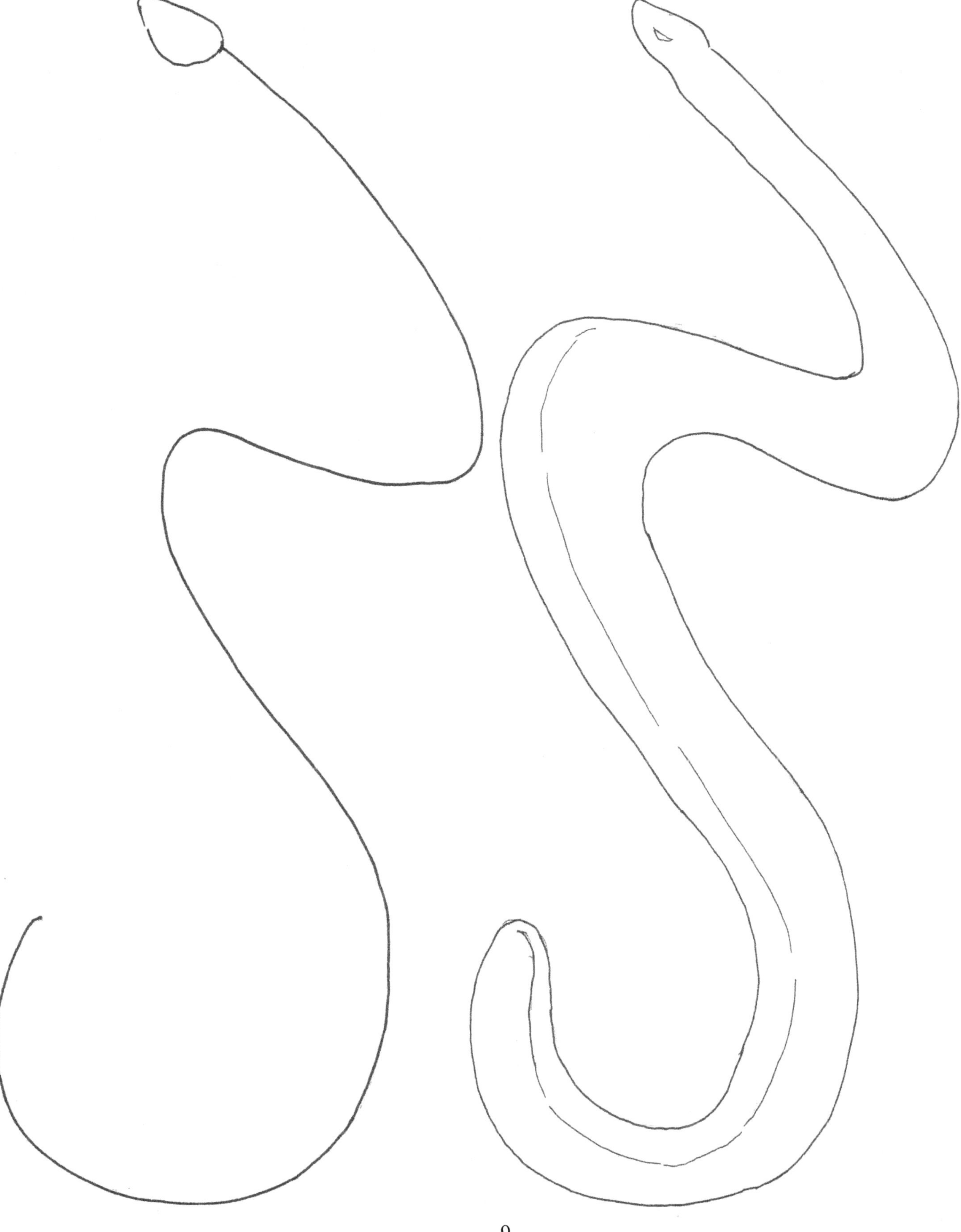

SEA SNAKE

SEA SNAKE
Common name applied to any of numerous aquatic mostly ovoviviparous, poisonous snake. They are usually 4 to 5 feet in length but some species attain a length of 8 to 9 feet. Sea snakes are not equipped with gills and rise frequently to the surface of the water for air. They are able to remain under water for several hours, however, obtaining disolved oxygen from water which they swallow and eject.

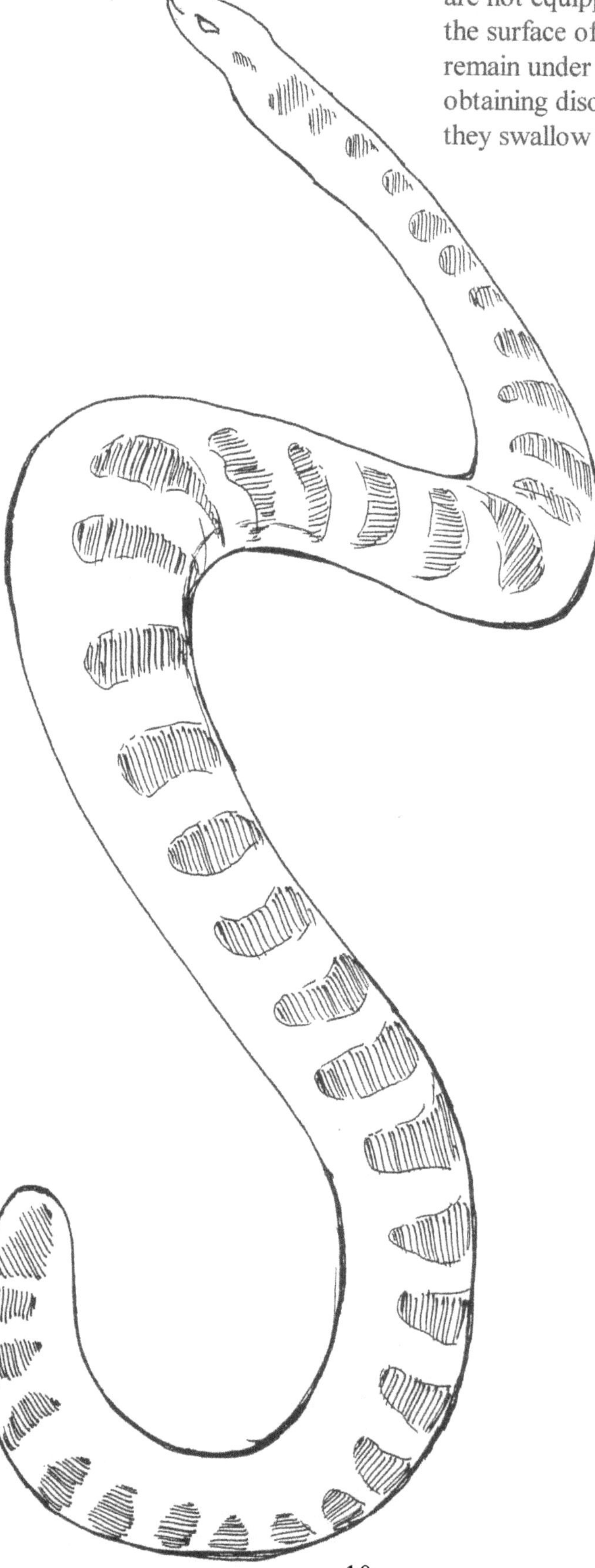

I started drawing the head first. I usually start with head first, but you don't have too all the time. Then the torso (middle body), then legs, feet and tail to construct the lizard for final details.

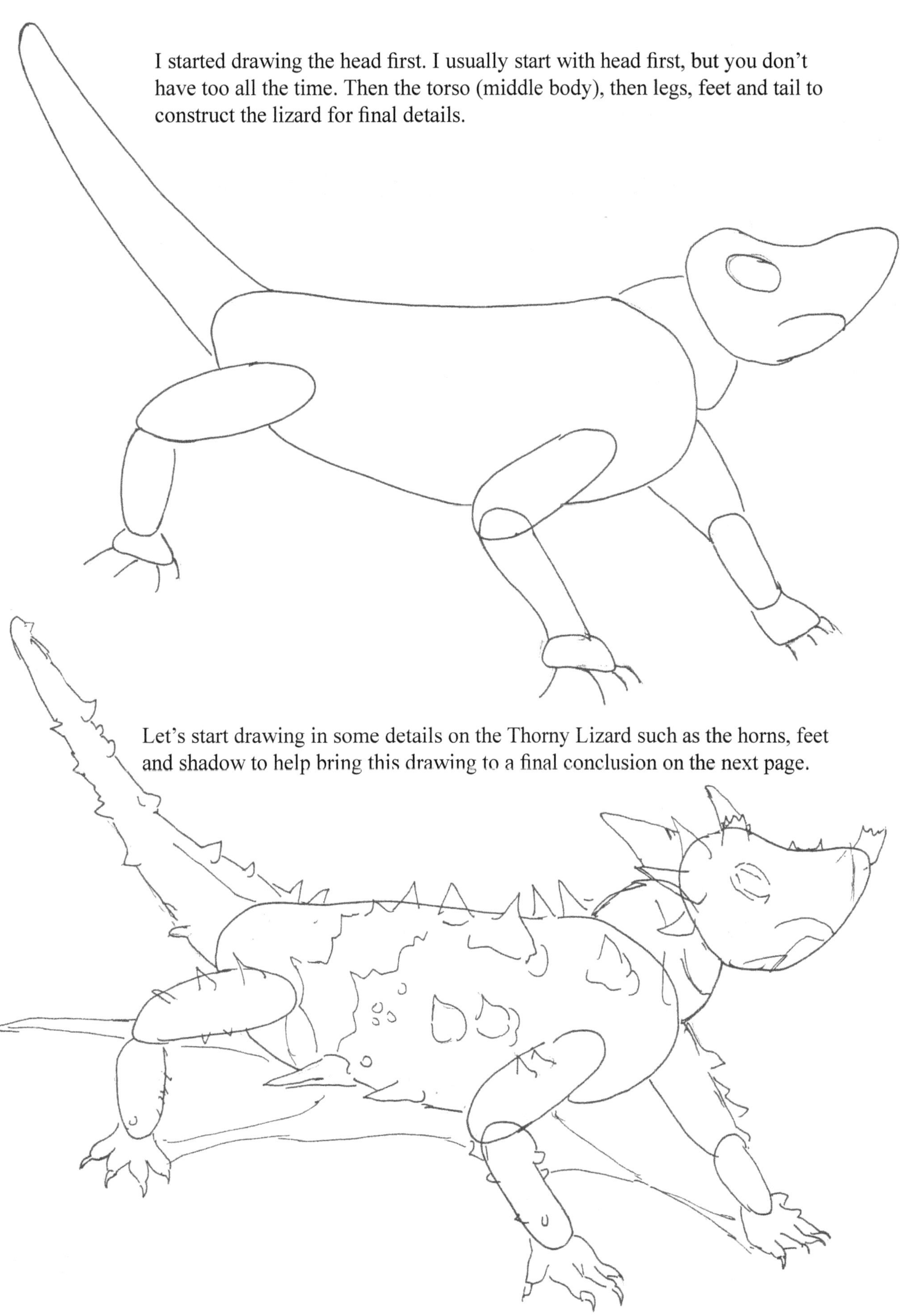

Let's start drawing in some details on the Thorny Lizard such as the horns, feet and shadow to help bring this drawing to a final conclusion on the next page.

THORNY DEVIL

THORNY DEVIL. A most bizarre looking lizard. Thorny Devils, despite their name and intimidating appearance, are gentle creatures that feed on ants. A Thorny Devil can ingest up to 5,000 black ants at meal, lapping them up with its tongue. Adapted for life in the hostile desert of inland Australia, this eight-inch reptile can alter its color and pattern to match its surroundings. Thorny Devils drink by collecting condensed water on their skin and funneling it on the corners of the mouth.

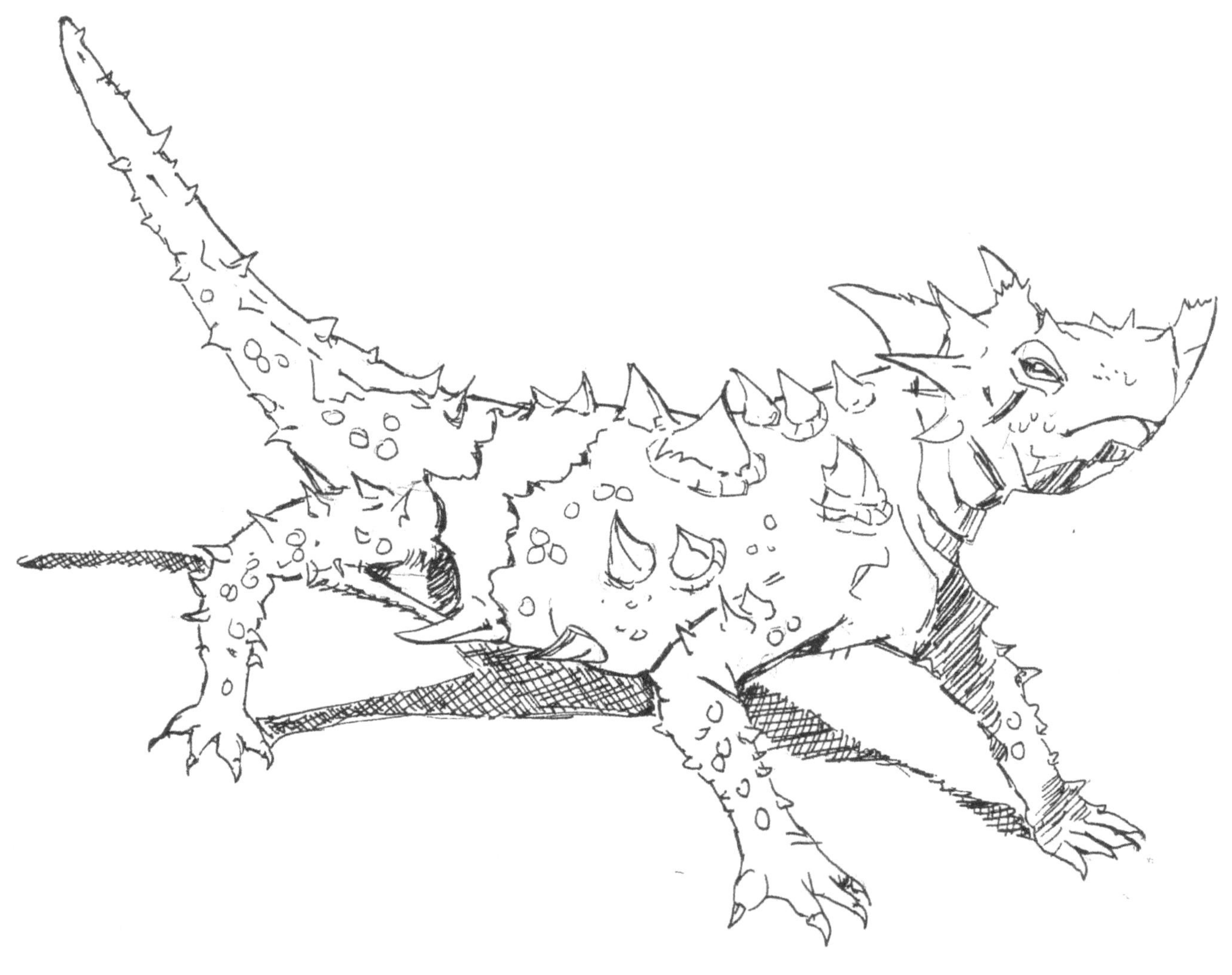

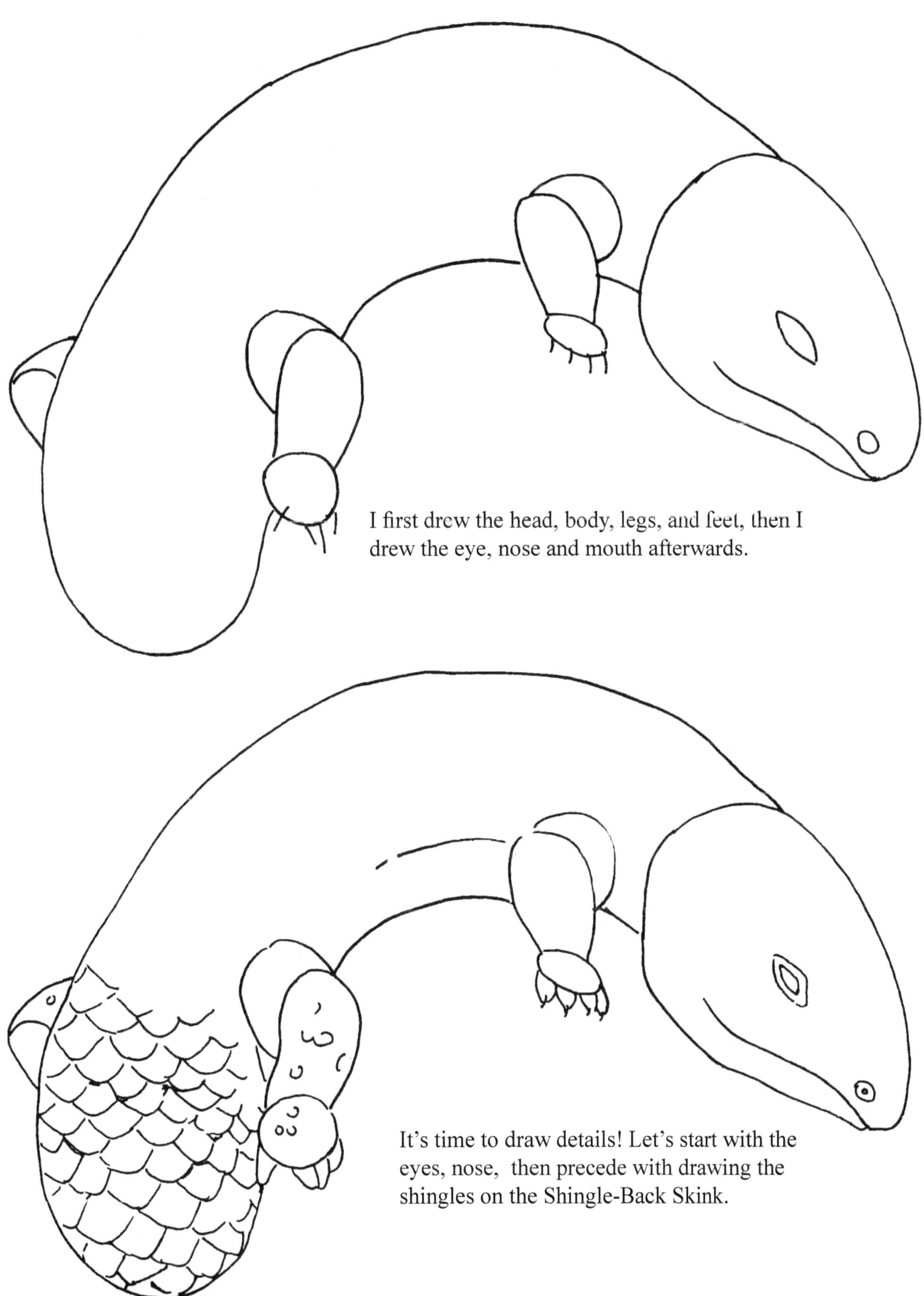

I first drew the head, body, legs, and feet, then I drew the eye, nose and mouth afterwards.

It's time to draw details! Let's start with the eyes, nose, then precede with drawing the shingles on the Shingle-Back Skink.

SHINGLE-BACK SKINK

This unique 15-inch reptile is often seen crossing roads in the Australian Outback. Because of its distinctive demeanor, and peculiar shape, Australians have a number of names for the Shingle-back. Among others it is known as "Sleepy lizard, "Bob-tail", Double-ender", and "Stump-tailed". This reptile ranges through South Australia, Victoria, New South Wales, and Queensland. Shingle-backs occupy a wide variety of habitat, both open areas and woodland. They feed on insects, fruits, mollusks, flowers, and berries. When times are good and there is plenty of food available, the animal stores fat reserves in its tail.

SHINGLE-BACK SKINK

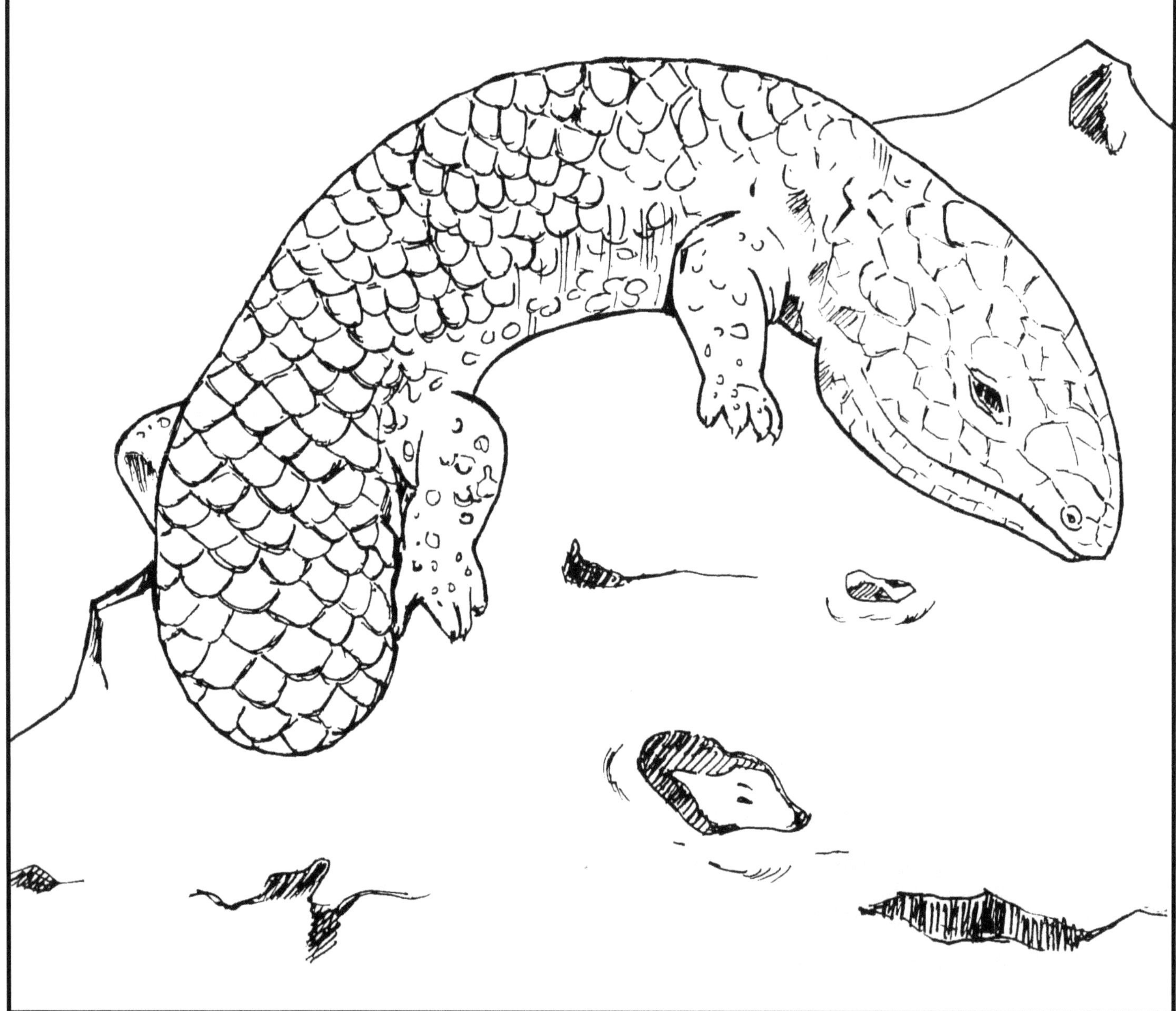

You guessed right, I started with the head again, then the torso,the body, legs and feet. Drew in the eye, nose, mouth and tongue of this gigantic lizard known as the Komodo drasgon.

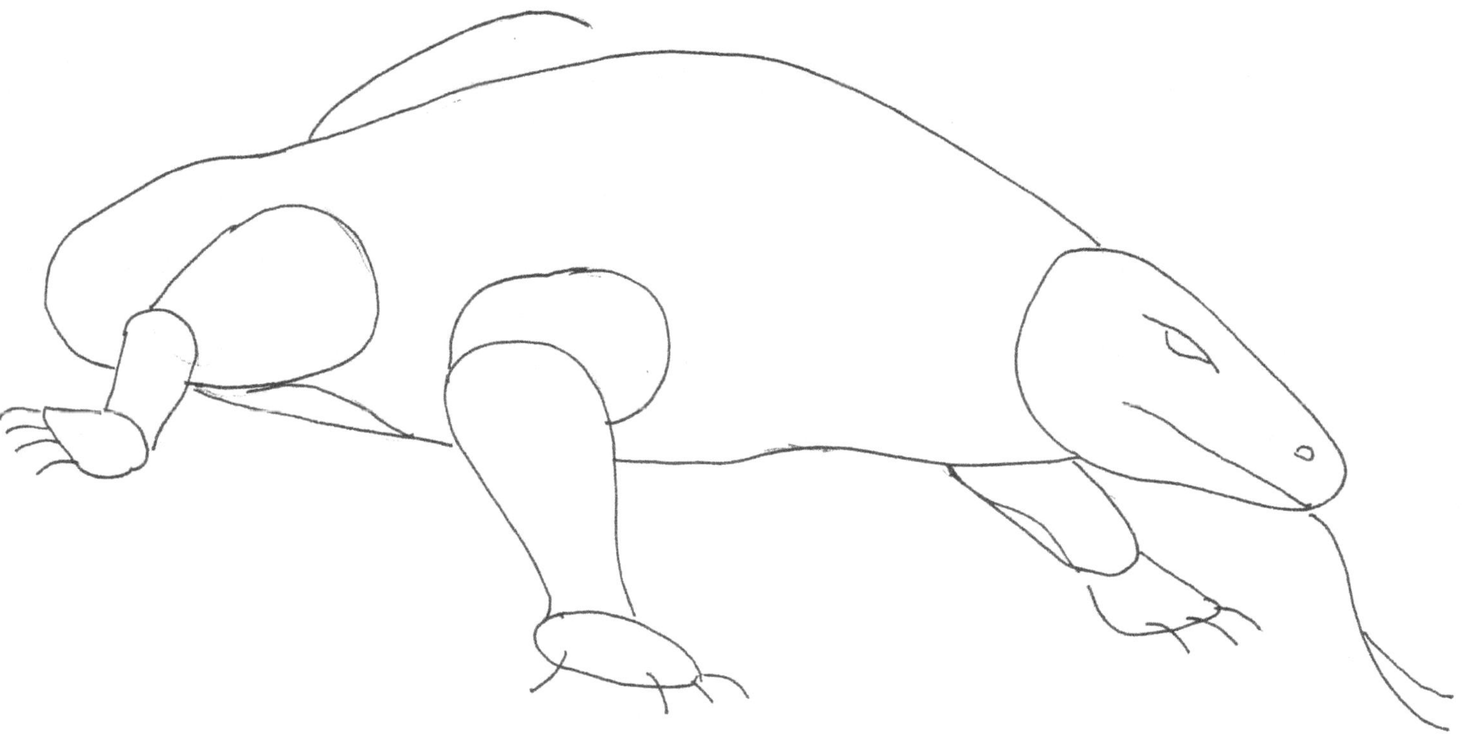

You can draw in the details, as you can see I have started with the large veins, tongue, and legs and feet to bring this to a completion on the next page.

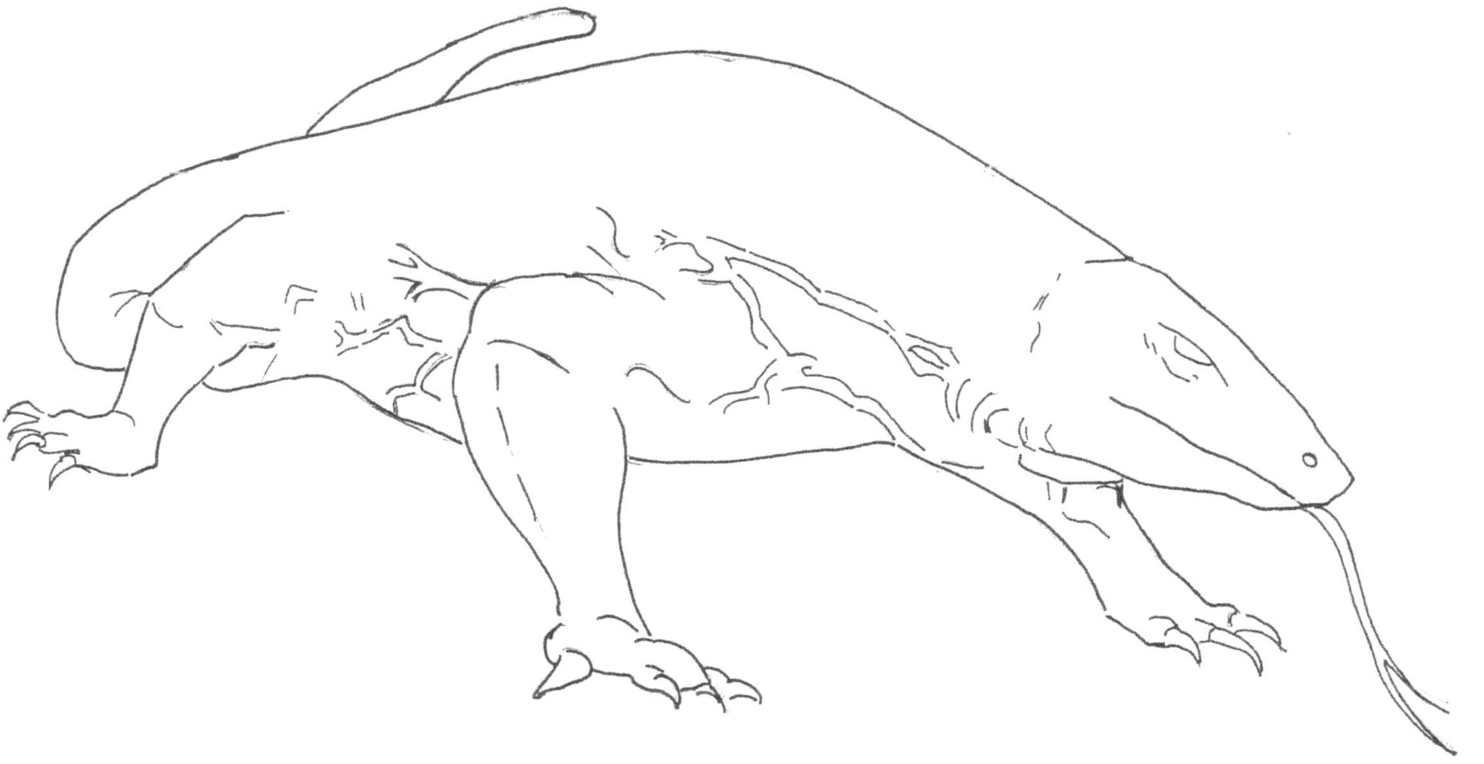

KOMODO DRAGON

KOMODO DRAGON is found on the Indonesian islands of Komodo, Rintja, Padar, and Flores. This gigantic reptile's habitat is in woodland thickets, forest fringes and clearings. Adults may measure more than 10 feet in length and weigh more than 310 pounds, and are thus the largest living lizard.

The Komodo Dragon is a strong and fearsome predator, which, on the islands where it lives, virtually occupies those ecological niches left vacant by large carnivorous mammals. To attack and kill the wild pigs, deer, and birds on which it feeds, the reptile uses its powerful, curved claws and strong jaws with shark-like teeth. Victims are usually taken by ambush. Those, which are bitten and escape, are carefully trailed using its tongue to pick up chemical signals given by off by the prey. Despite their size they are quite agile and good tree climbers and swimmers. Females lay clutches of about 18 eggs per year.

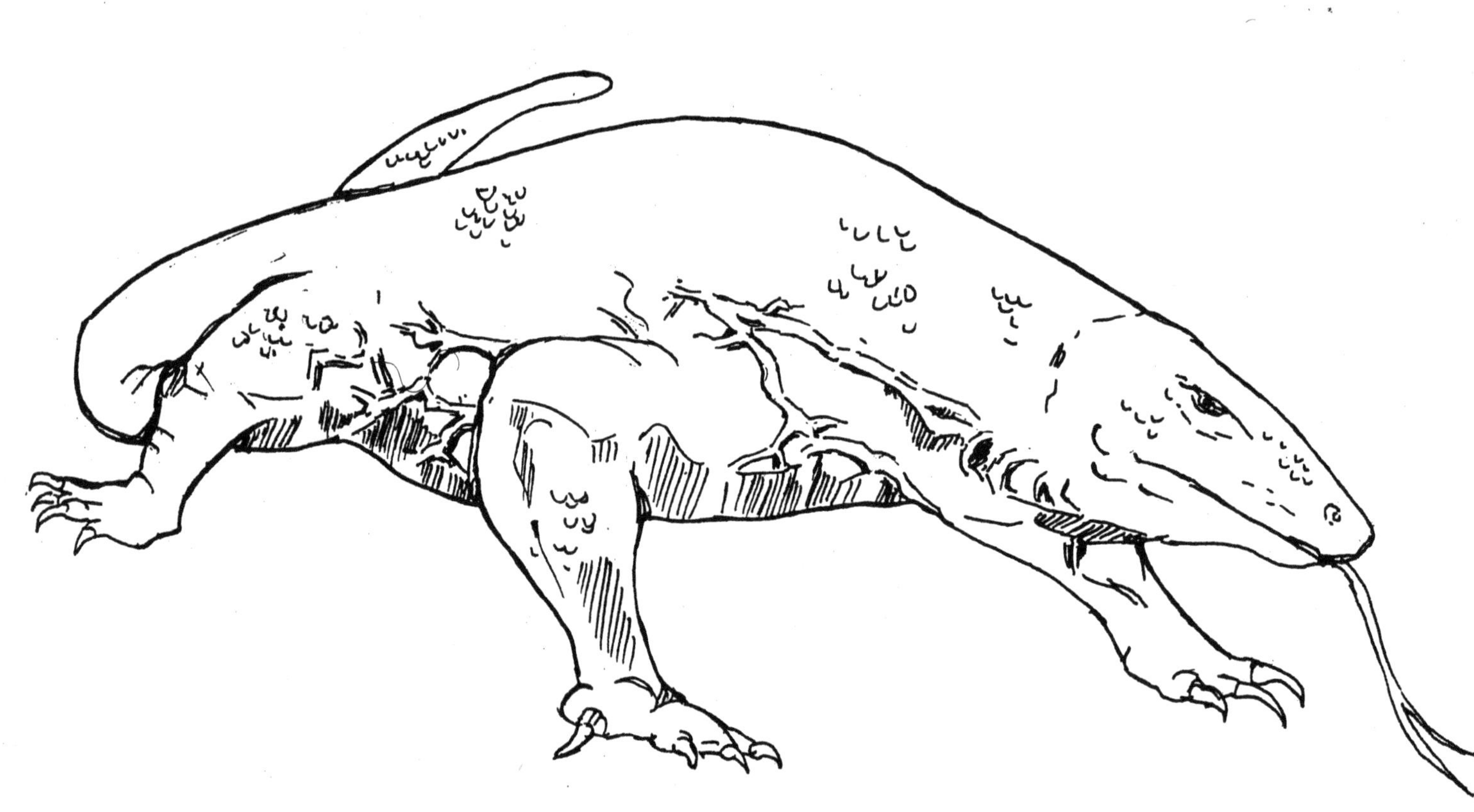

Here is an unusual reptile named the Ajolote, no it's not a snake. Let's start drawing to see what you come up with. Draw a circle for the head then a circular line for the contour of the body. Add the legs and draw in the lines on the head to indicate where to put the eyes, nose and mouth.

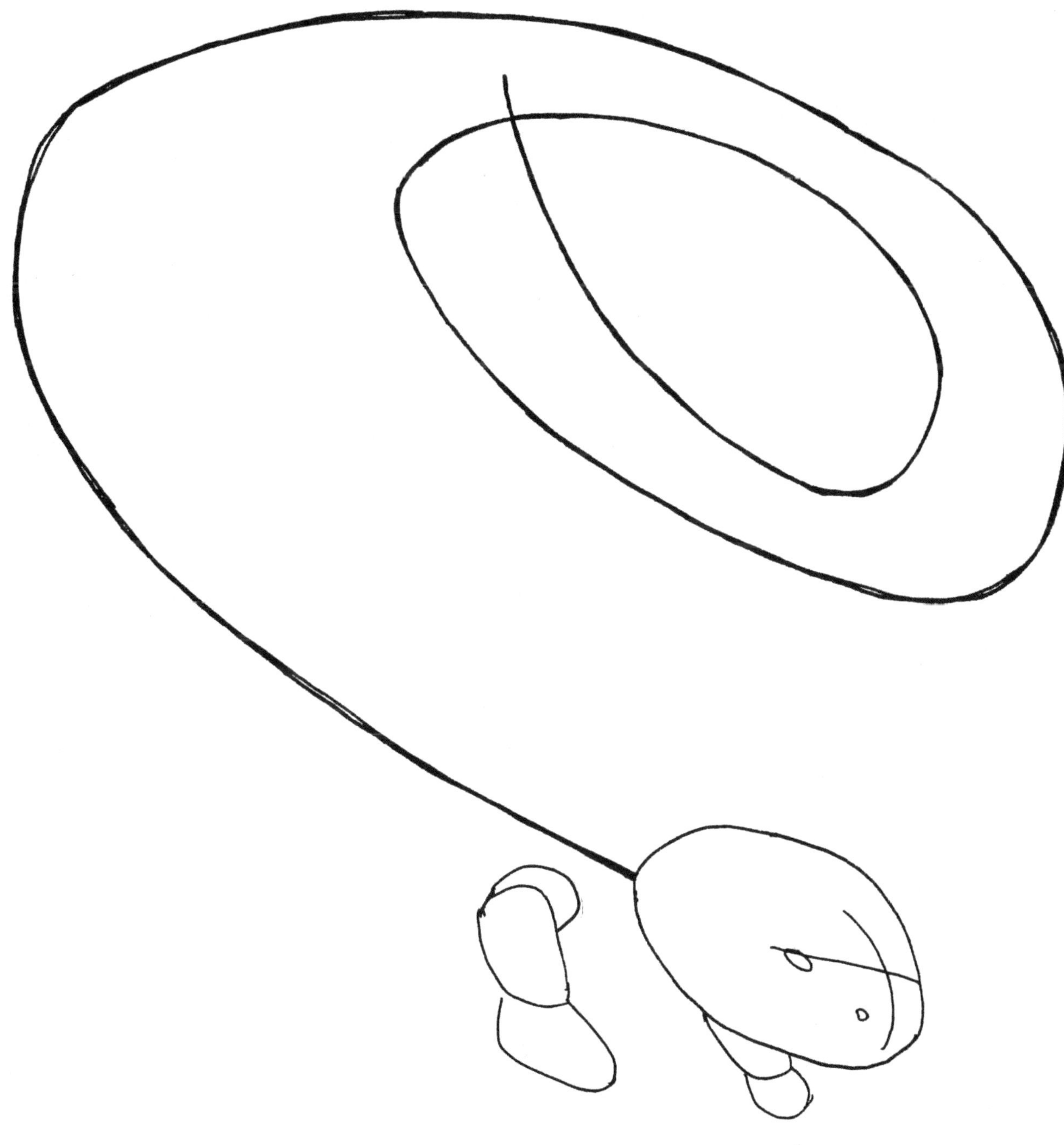

Now, you can start adding lines outside of the initial middle lines of the body to give it more form and shape. Construct the head by drawing in more detail to the nose, mouth and legs, and feet.

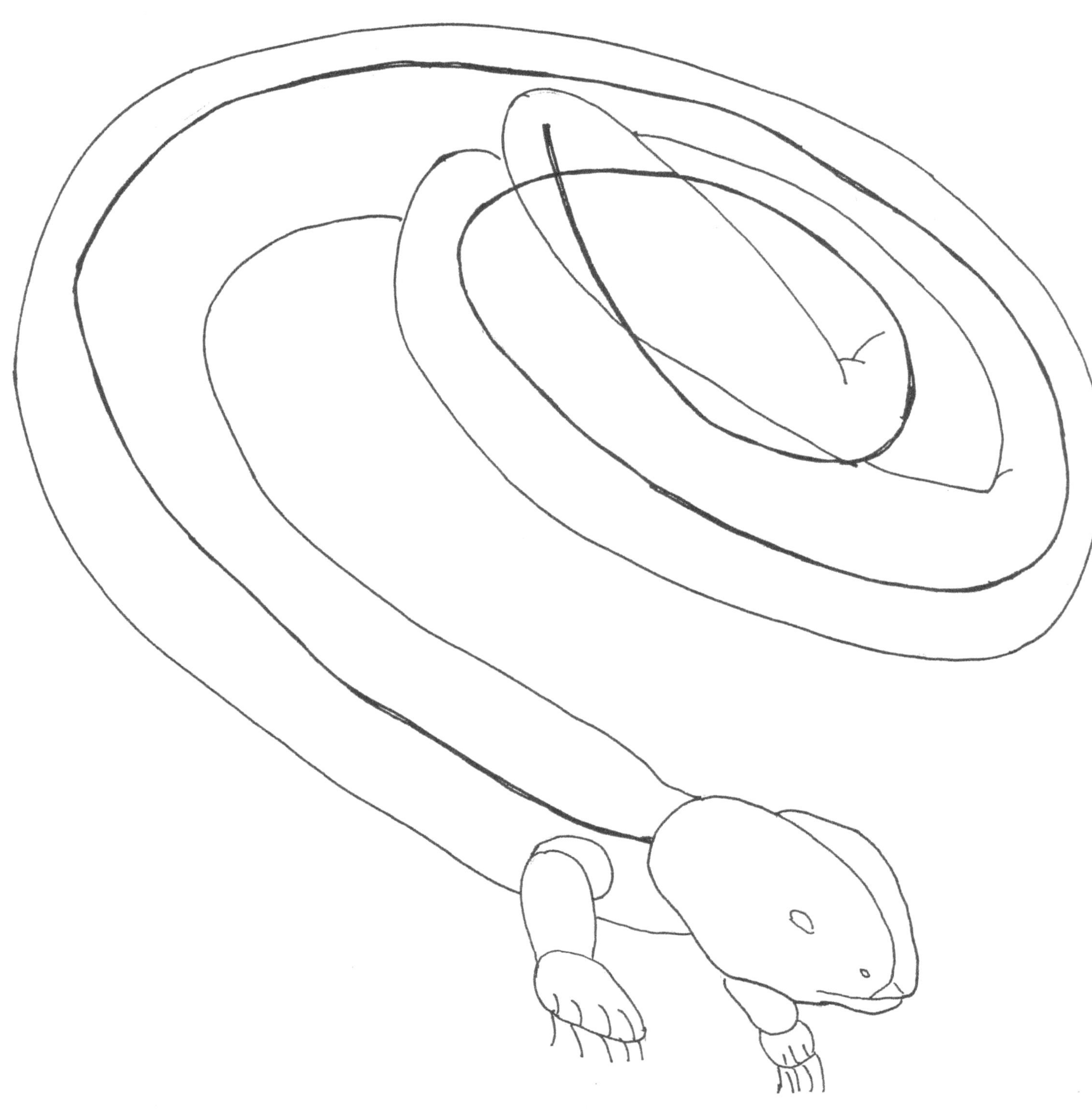

Erase all unneeded lines and this is what you have created. Basically your drawing is almost complete, it's just a matter of drawing in more details to the skin texture on the head and body as you will see on the next page.

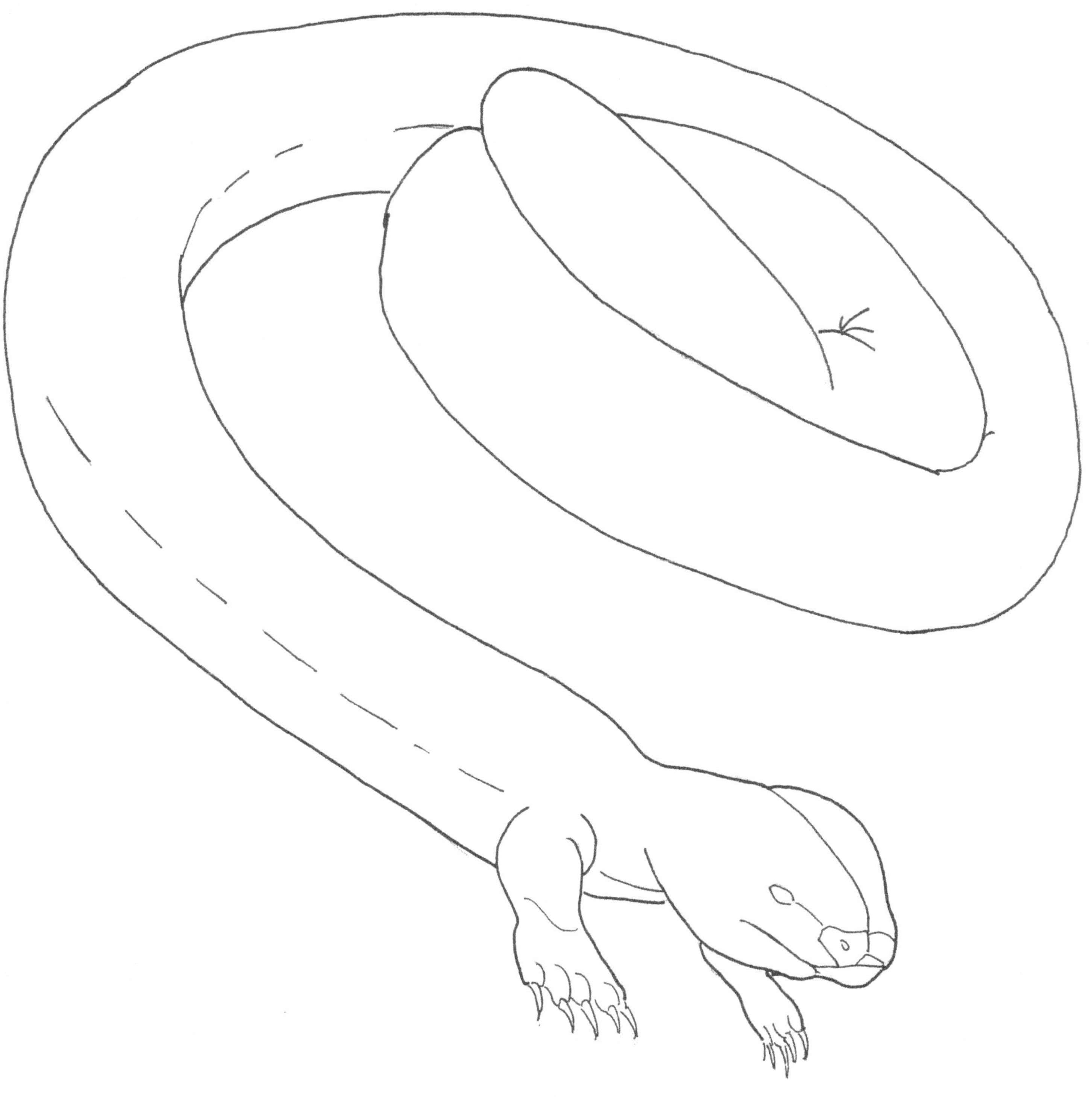

AJOLOTE

AJOLOTE

The ajolote is a Mexican reptile of the Bipes species. It and other several burrowing animals are placed in the Amphisbaenia, a group separate from lizards and snakes. This reptile has a pair of well developed front legs. In line with its burrowing habits, the skull is very solid, the eyes are small, external ears absent. The scales are arranged in rings, giving the body a wormlike appearance. One of the noticeable characters of Bipes is the hands. Bipe are the only group of amphisbaenians that possess limbs of any sort. Ajolote (Bipes biporus) coloration is light pink to white and grow up to 9.5 inches in length.

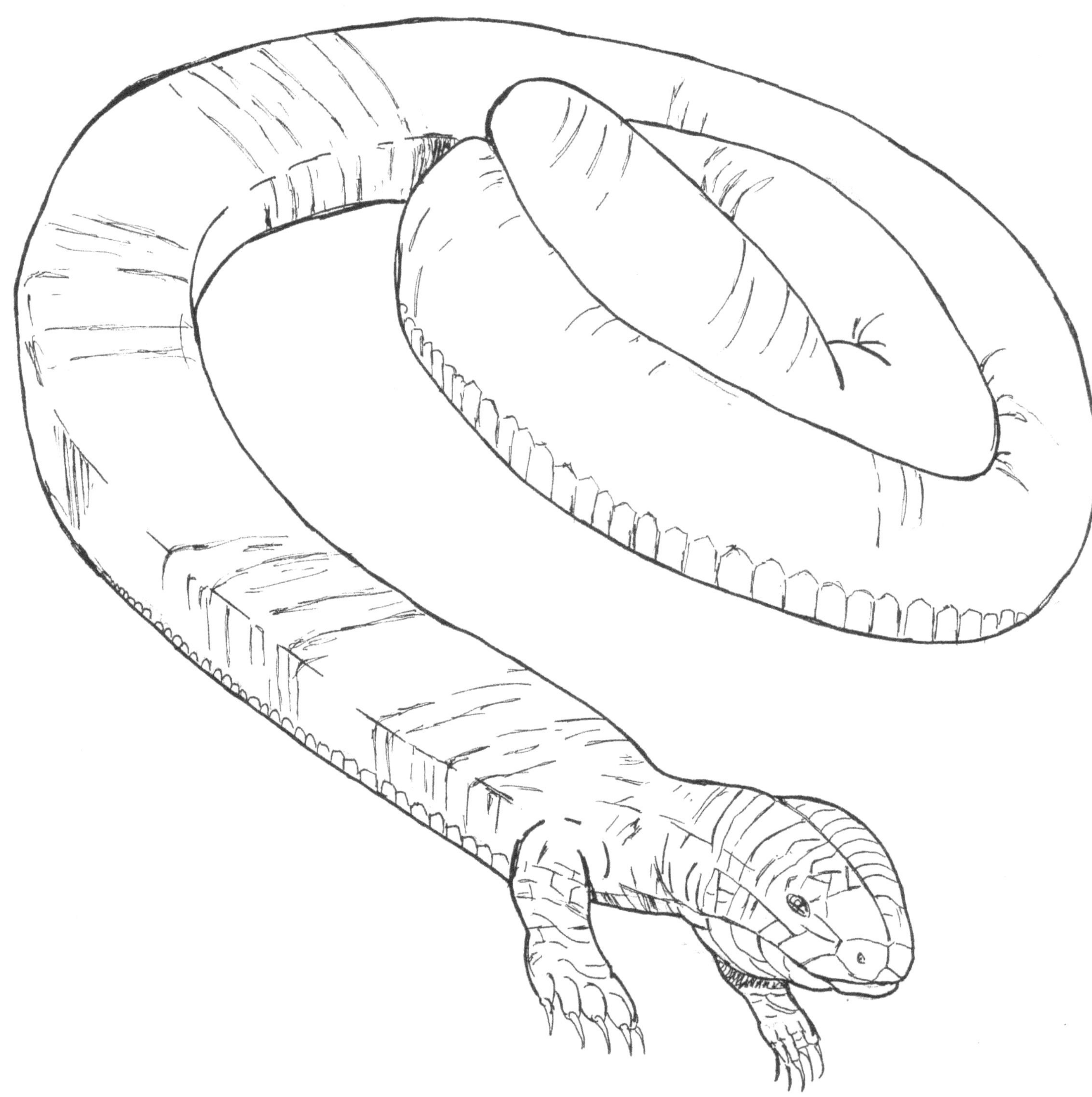

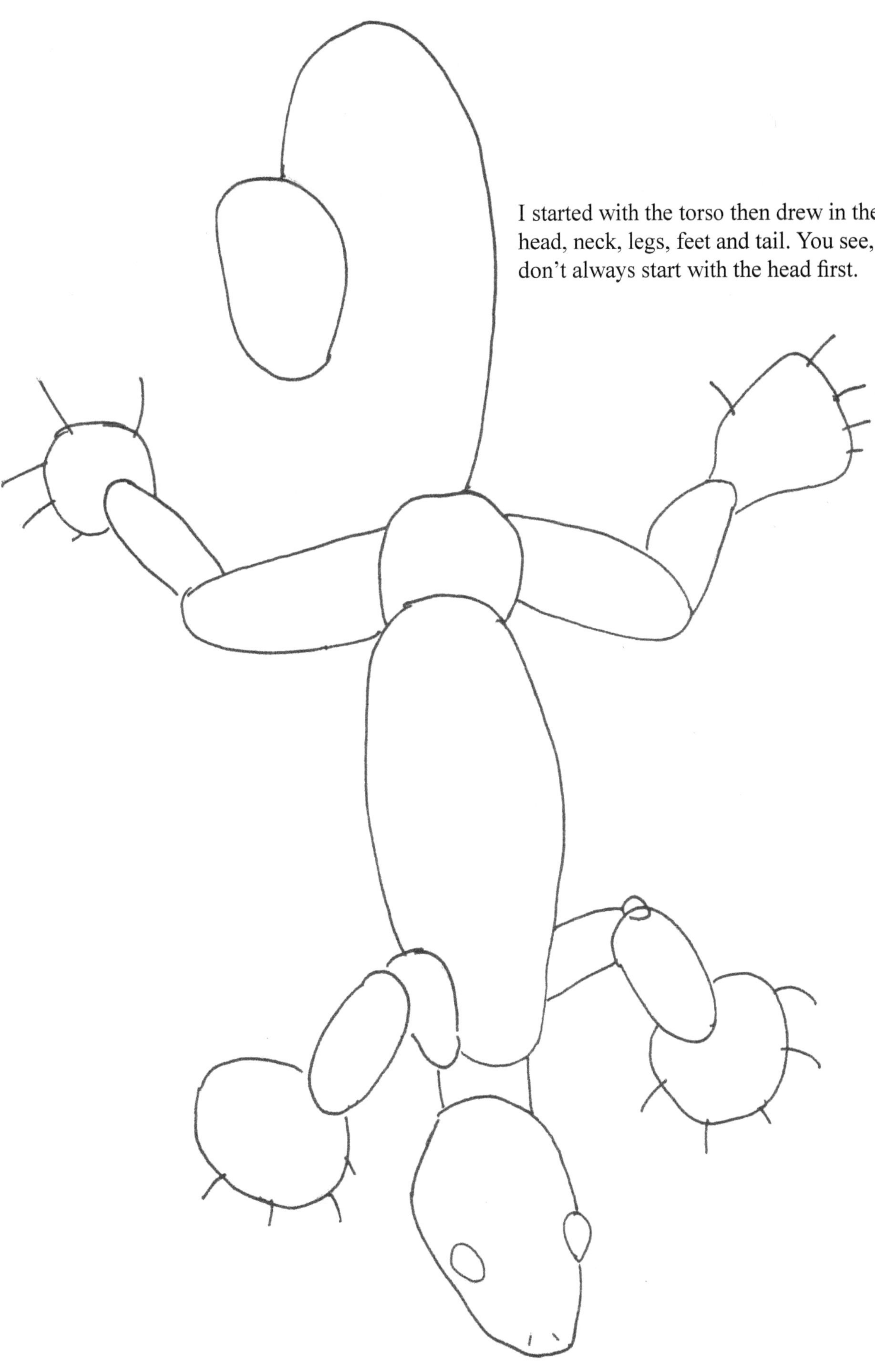

I started with the torso then drew in the head, neck, legs, feet and tail. You see, I don't always start with the head first.

Now, you can start drawing in more details on the tail, legs, feet and head. Erase any unnecessary lines.

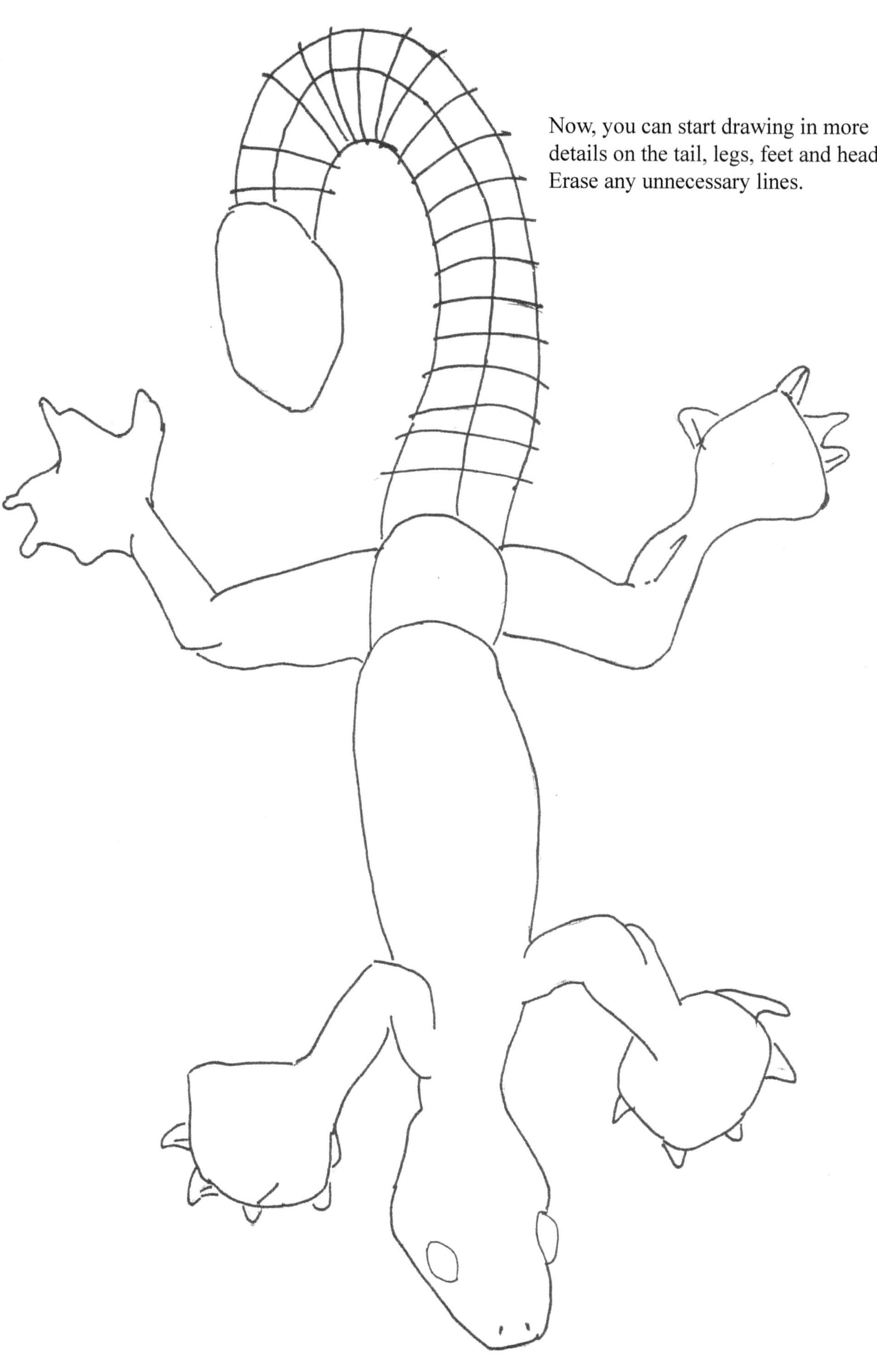

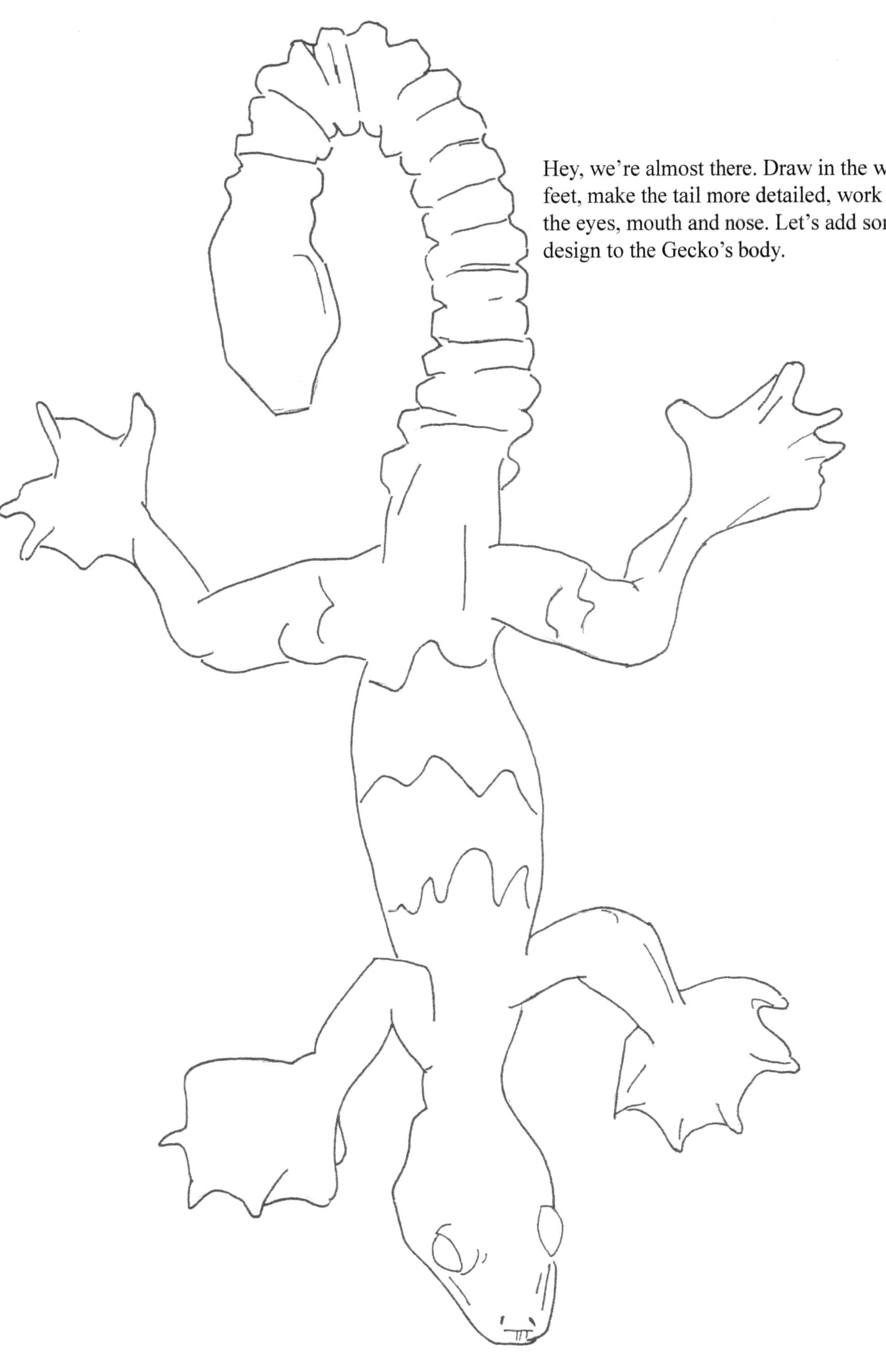

Hey, we're almost there. Draw in the web feet, make the tail more detailed, work on the eyes, mouth and nose. Let's add some design to the Gecko's body.

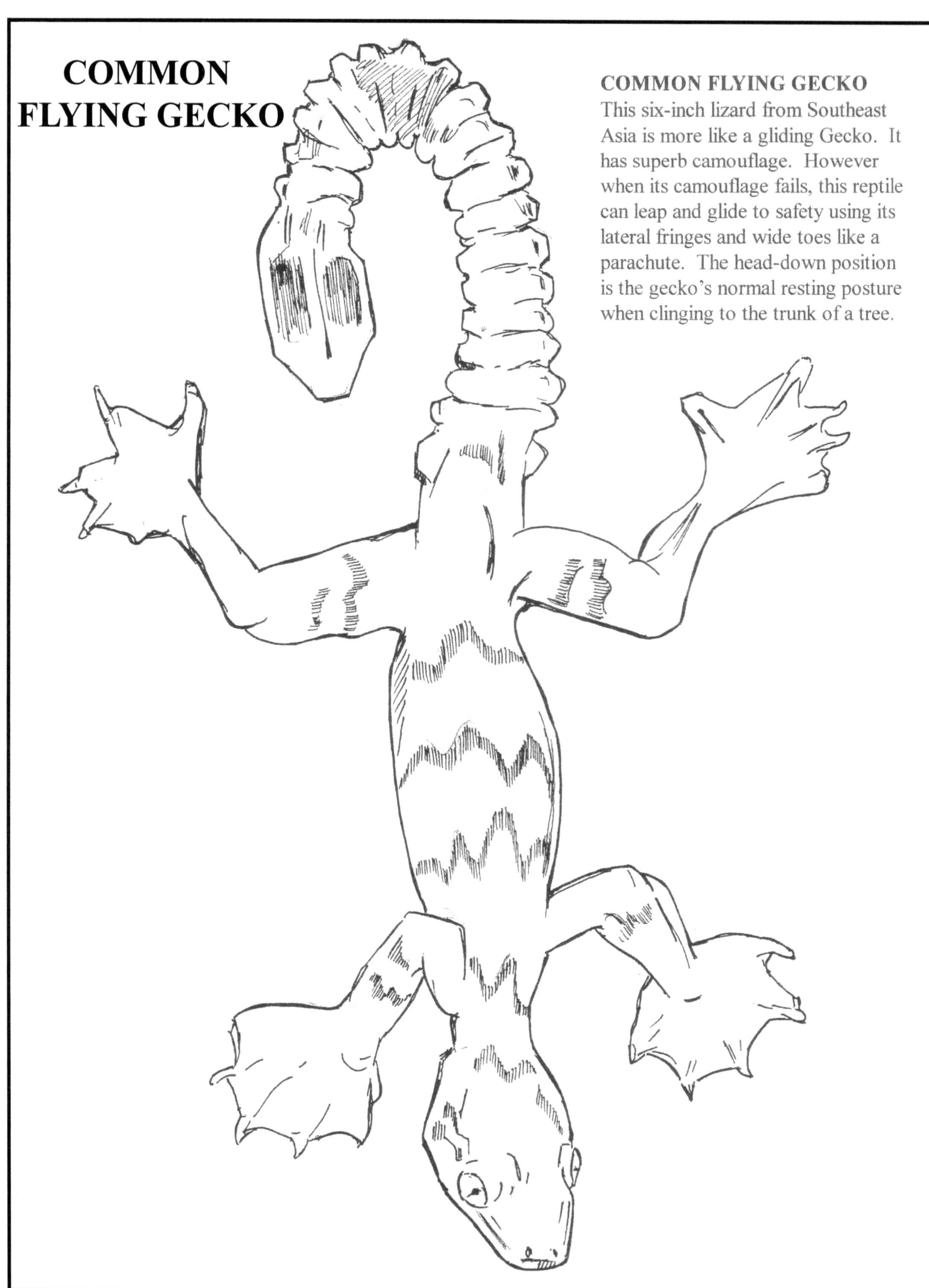

COMMON FLYING GECKO

COMMON FLYING GECKO
This six-inch lizard from Southeast Asia is more like a gliding Gecko. It has superb camouflage. However when its camouflage fails, this reptile can leap and glide to safety using its lateral fringes and wide toes like a parachute. The head-down position is the gecko's normal resting posture when clinging to the trunk of a tree.

OK, I'll give you a choice. Which part do you want to start drawing first? Head or torso, either is fine. Then draw the rest of the body parts for this Bearded Lizard. This is your construction outline to start this drawing off.

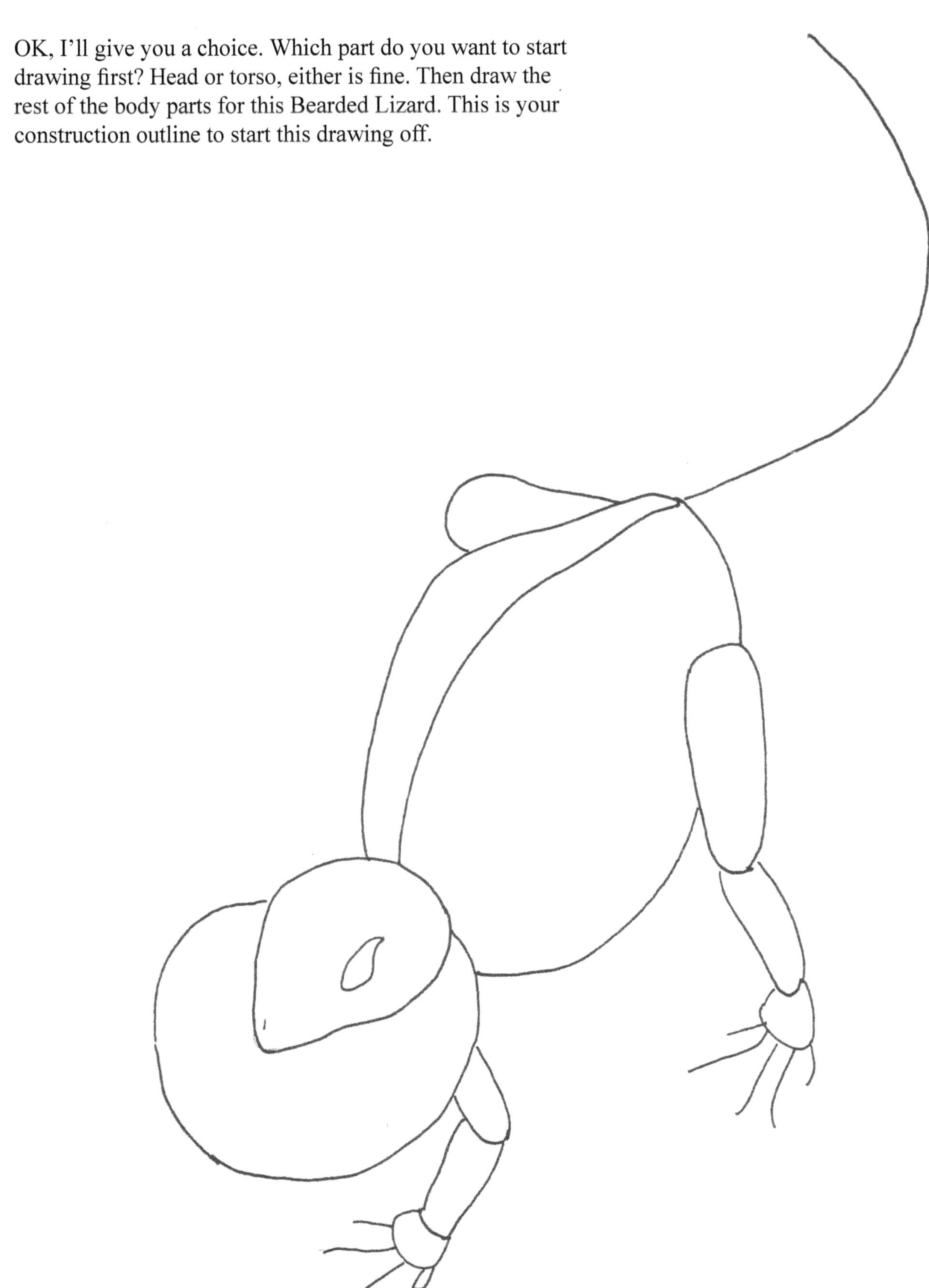

Draw another line to the tail to make it full. Draw on more to define the feet. And draw some wrinkles in the beard and neck body part of the lizard.

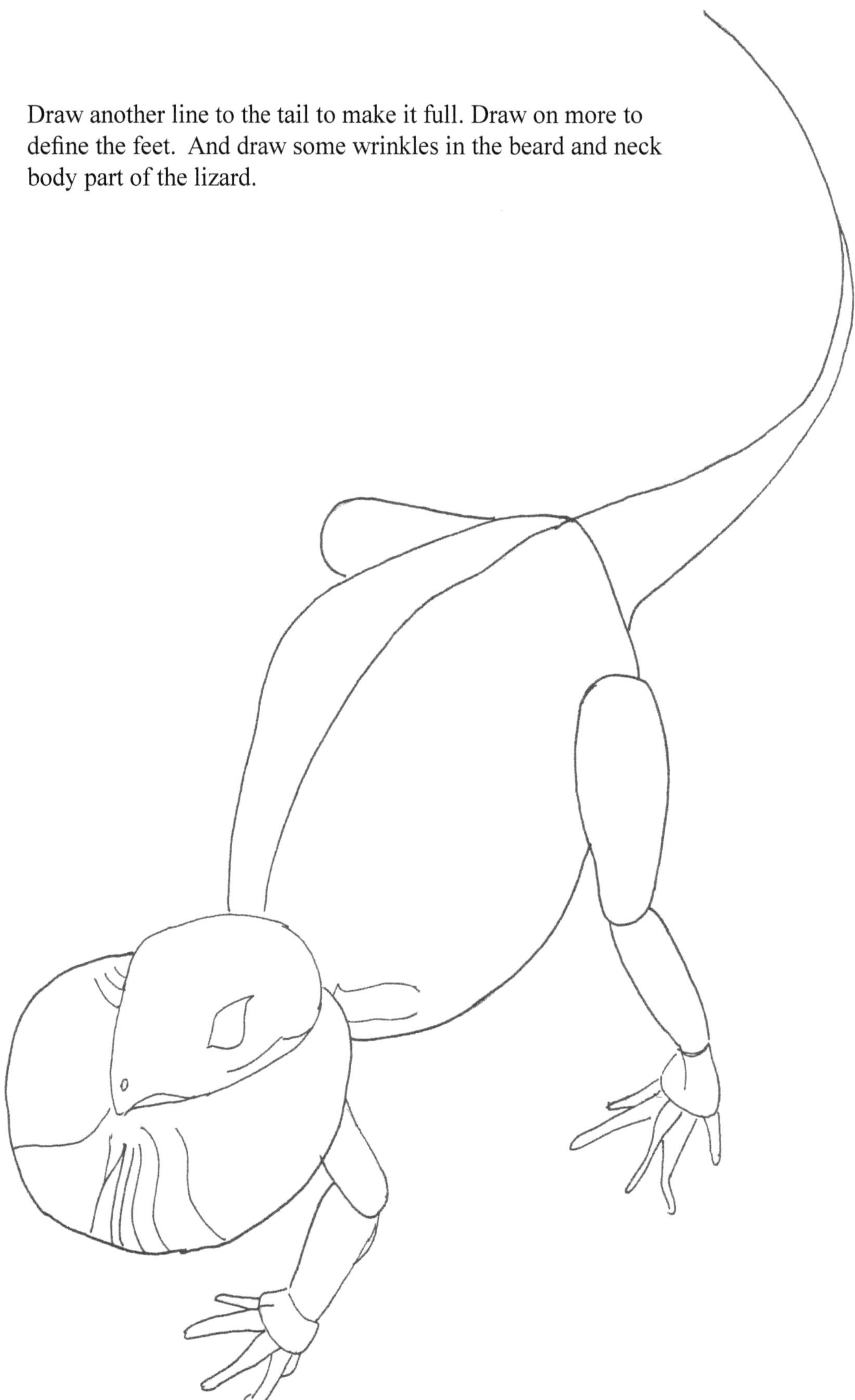

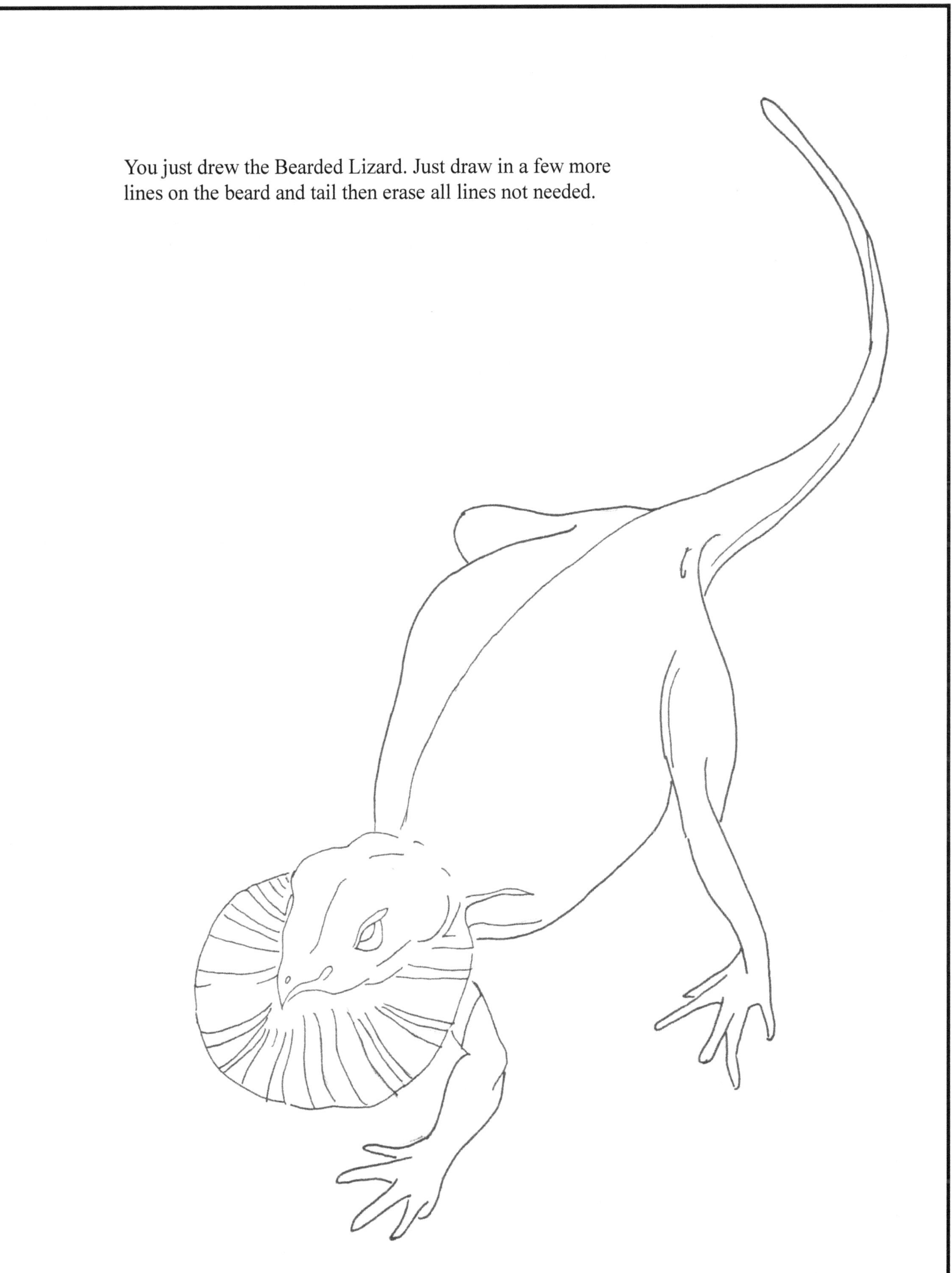
You just drew the Bearded Lizard. Just draw in a few more
lines on the beard and tail then erase all lines not needed.

BEARDED DRAGON

BEARDED DRAGON The bearded lizard can be found in Eastern Australia. This lizard has a triangular, broad flat head, with a series of large spiny scales at the corners of the mouth. This lizard is typically seen basking on stumps, fence posts, or roadways. When they have reached an optimal body temperature, they hunt for insects, flowers and soft plants. It avoids the heat of the day in deep burrows. If attacked, the bearded dragon assumes a characteristic threat posture, inflating its body, opening its mouth and hugely dilating its big, spiny throat pouch. Total length: 16-24 inches.

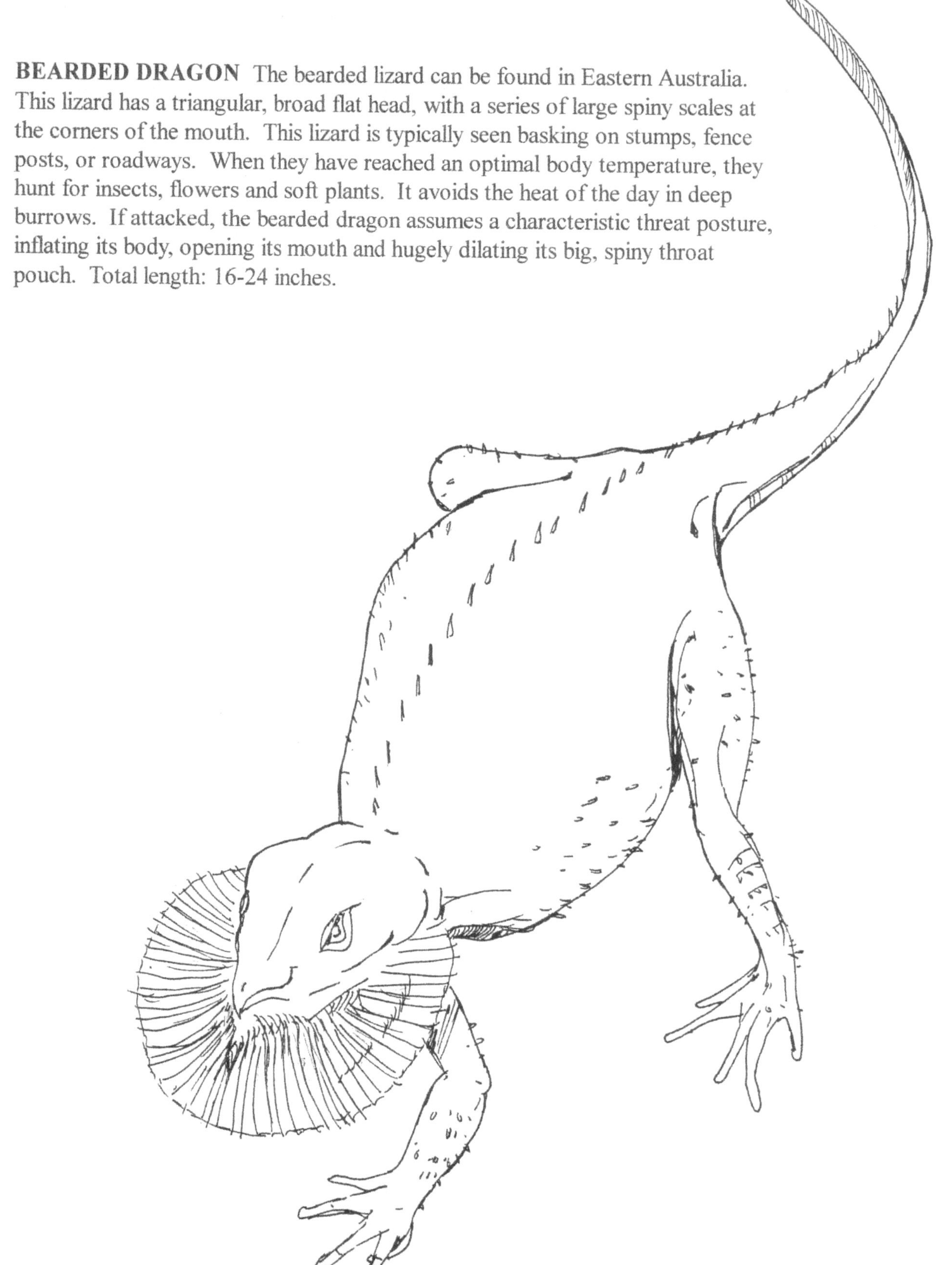

Here is a case where you again can start to draw either the shell or head of the Galapagos Tortoise first. Then proceed to draw the rest of the parts of the tortoise. This is your outline structure.

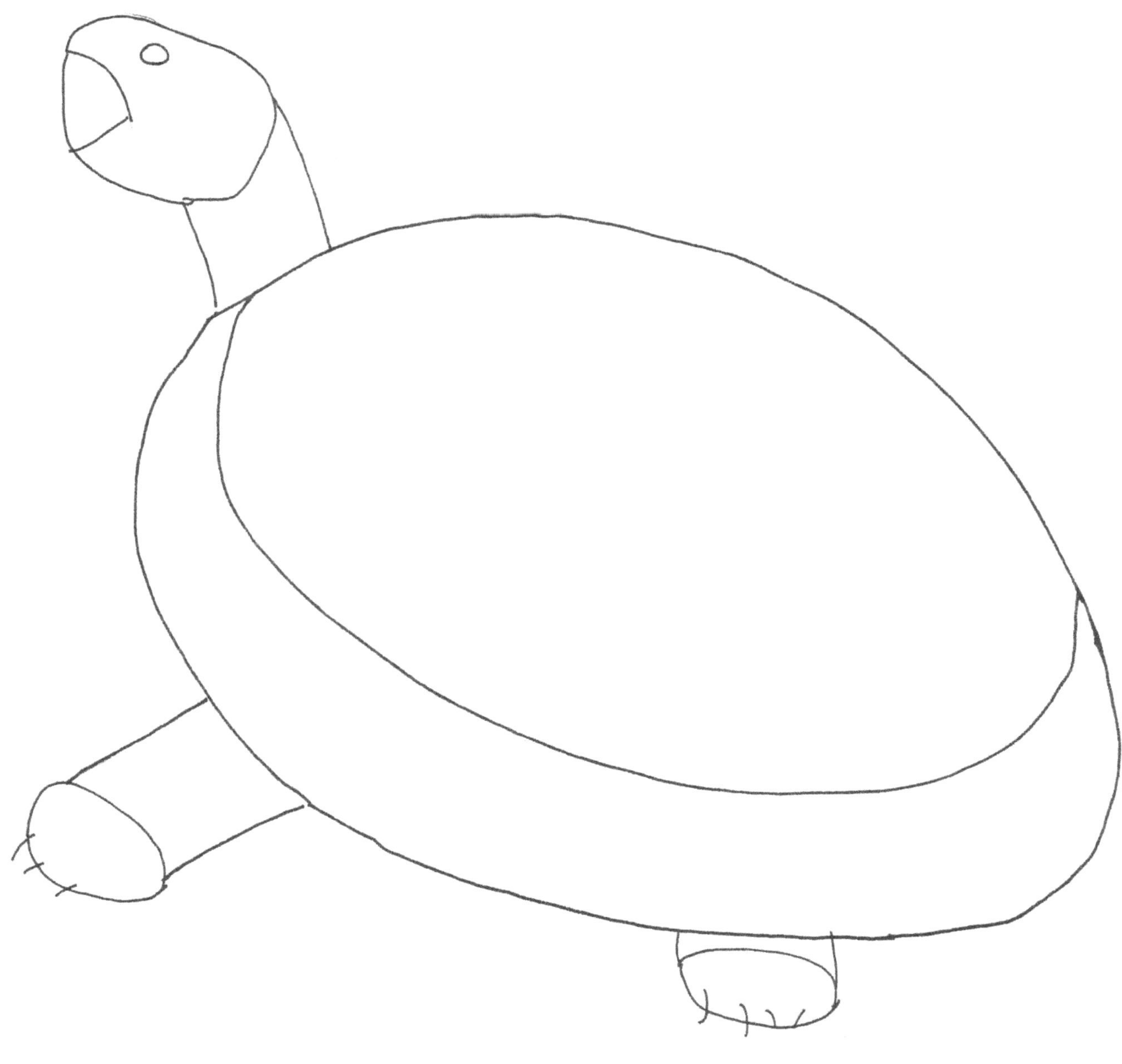

Draw in some lines to start to form the texture and shape of the shell. Draw on more lines for claws on the feet.

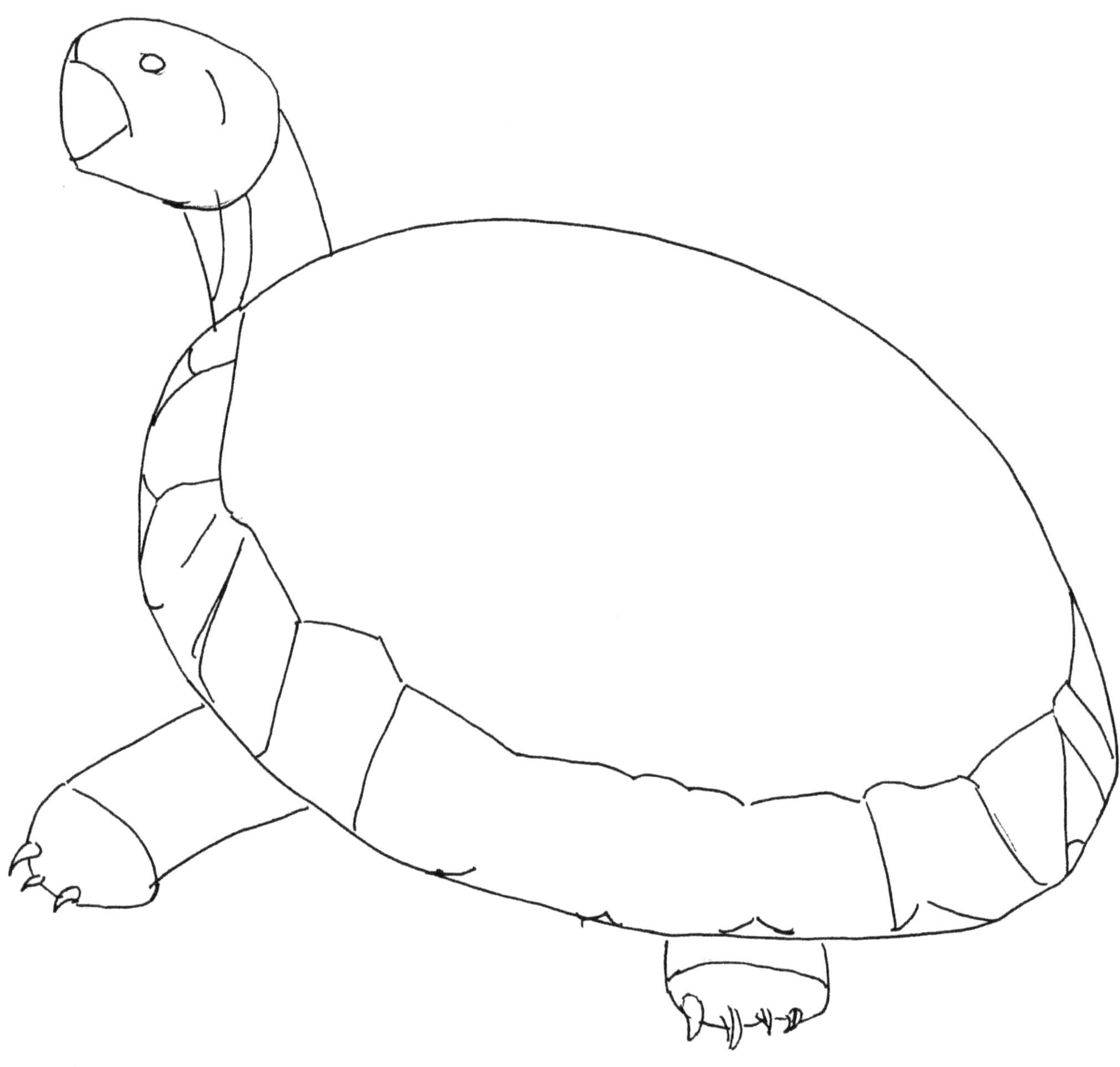

Give the beak and mouth a define shape. Draw more lines on the neck to show the stretching. Draw more lines on the shell to show a more detail, and don't forget the legs and feet. Erase any unnecessary lines. You just drew a Galapagos Tortoise. Just add some shade and detail as you will see on the next page.

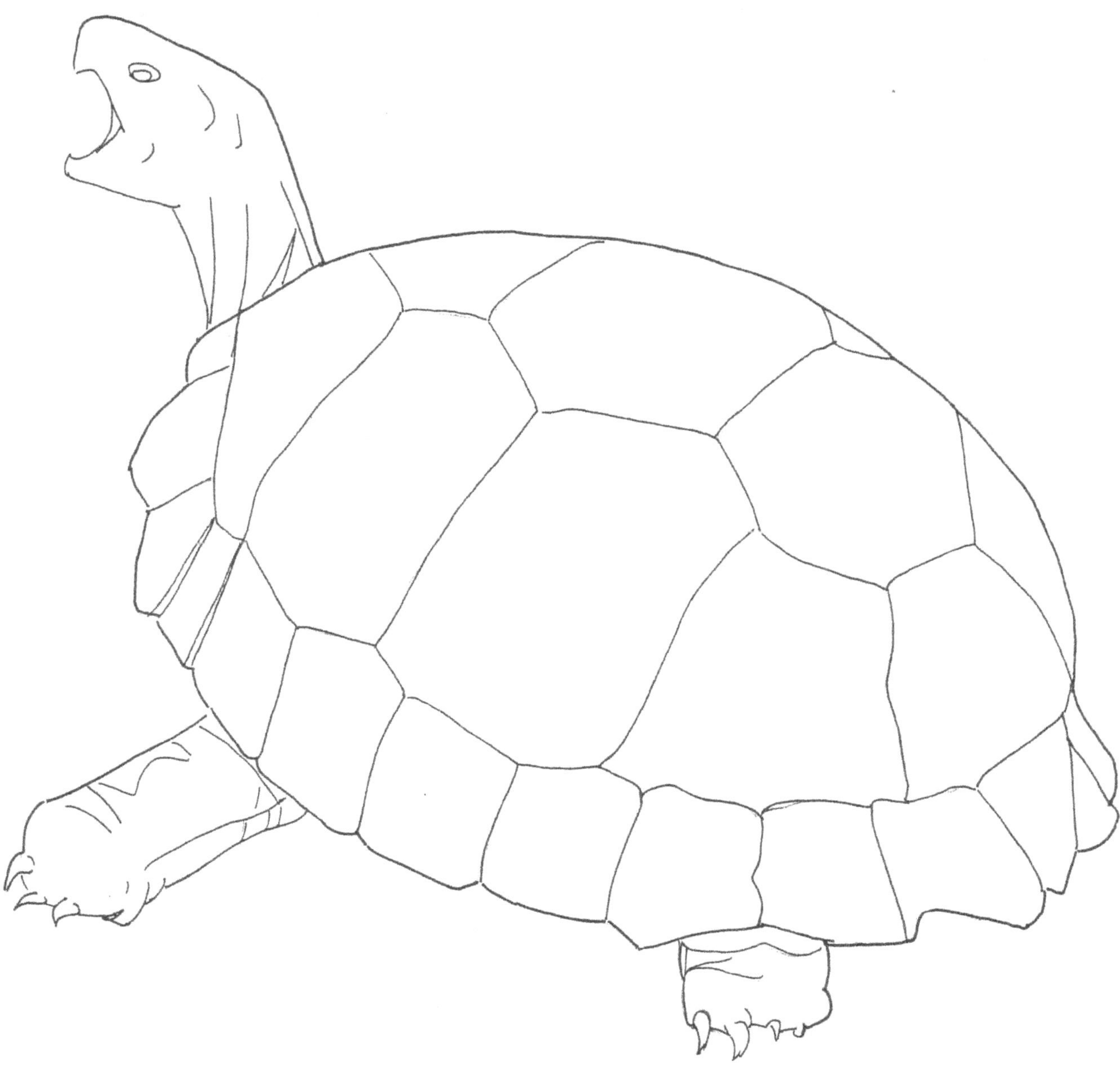

GALAPAGOS TORTOISE

GALAPAGOS TORTOISE. This gigantic tortoise has a rather small head supported by a long neck. Bony-cored scales protect the massive, columnar rear legs and elephantine forelegs. The Galapagos tortoises mainly occupy the driest and flattest parts of the islands in Ecuador, but often venture up to the volcanic highlands where there is plenty of water and vegetation. In these surroundings they bathe for long periods and feed on the fruit and flowers of various plants. The adults mate at virtually any time of year. Each female lays about 4 to 10 large eggs in a hole in the ground.

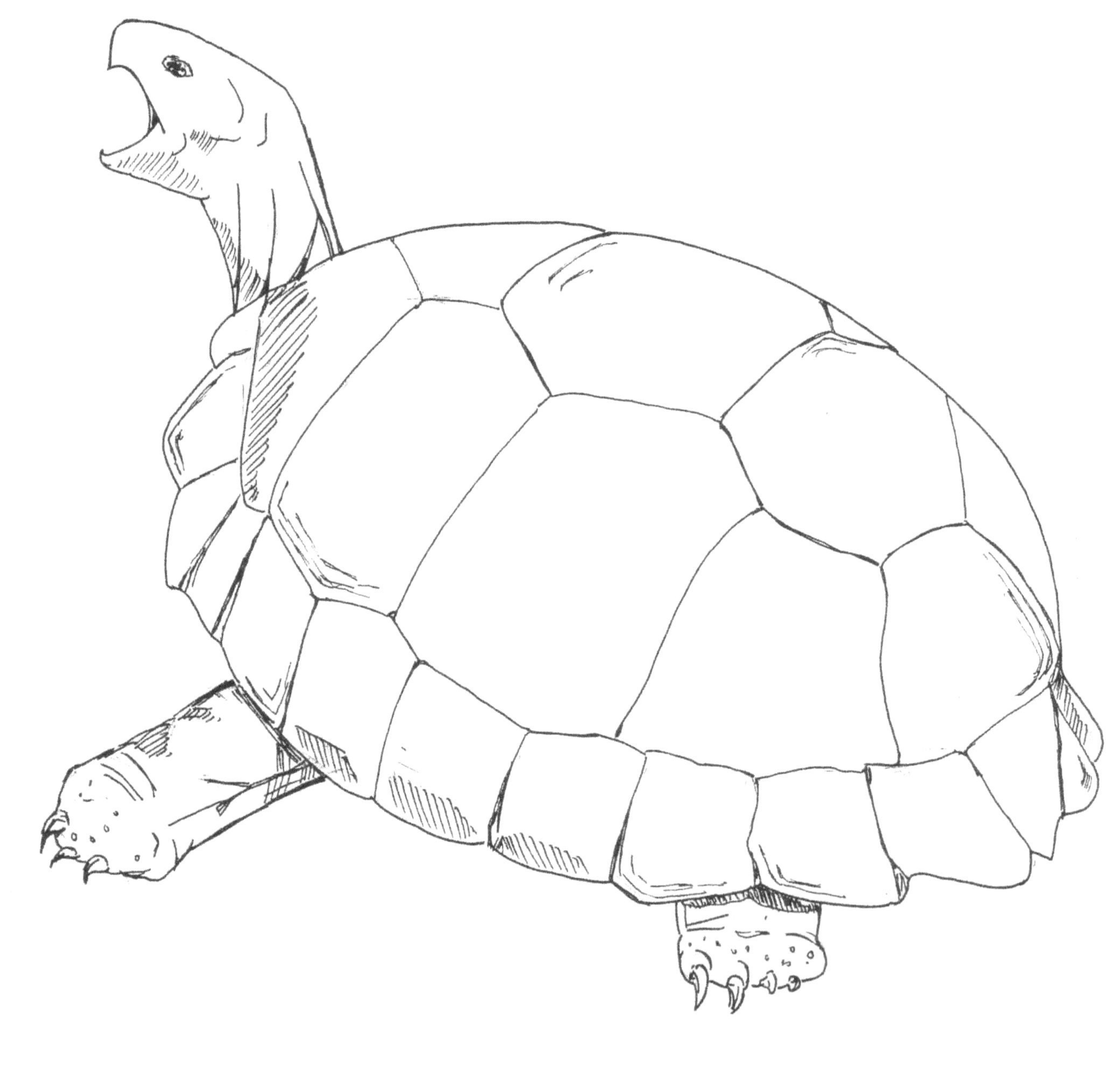

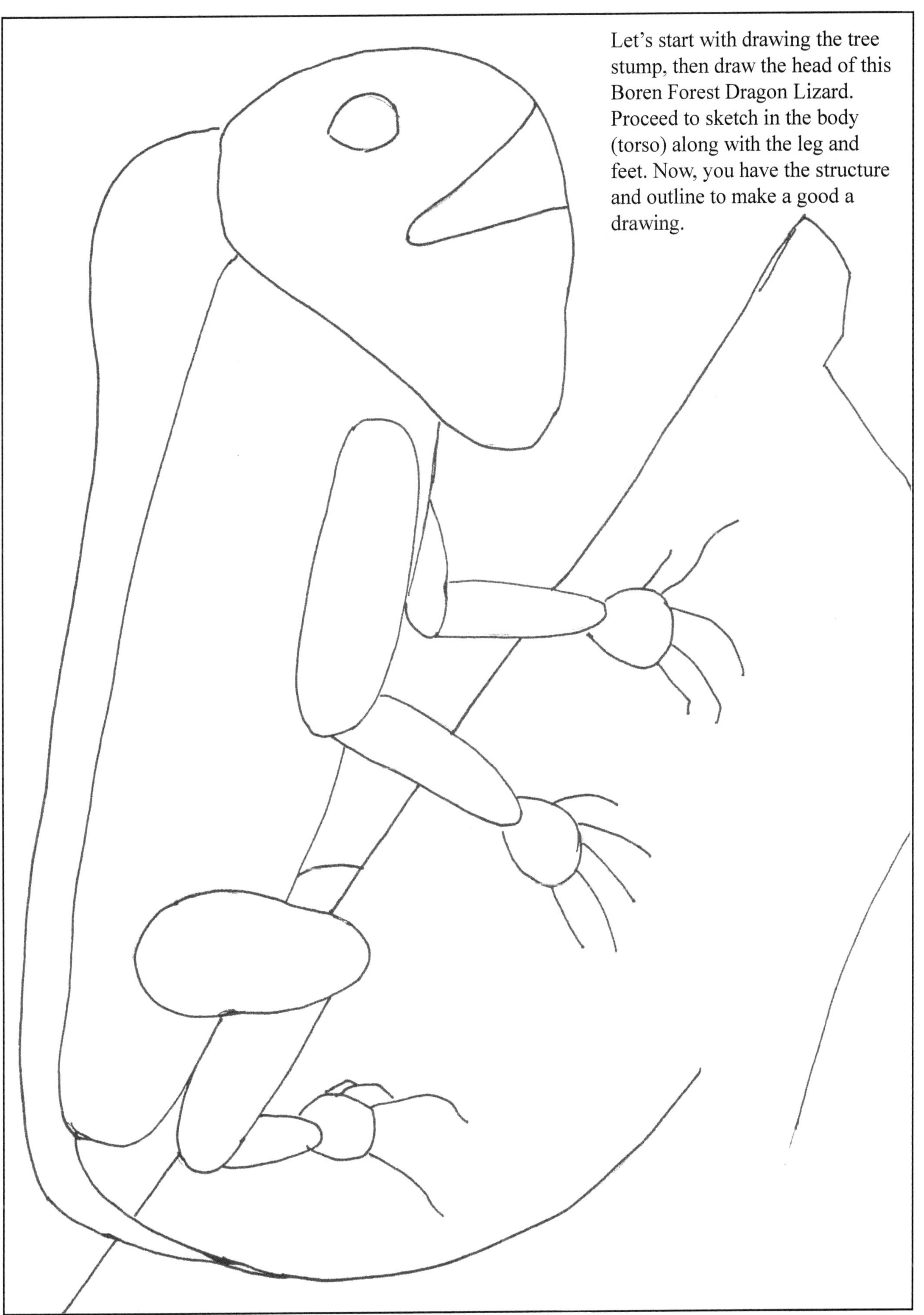

Let's start with drawing the tree stump, then draw the head of this Boren Forest Dragon Lizard. Proceed to sketch in the body (torso) along with the leg and feet. Now, you have the structure and outline to make a good a drawing.

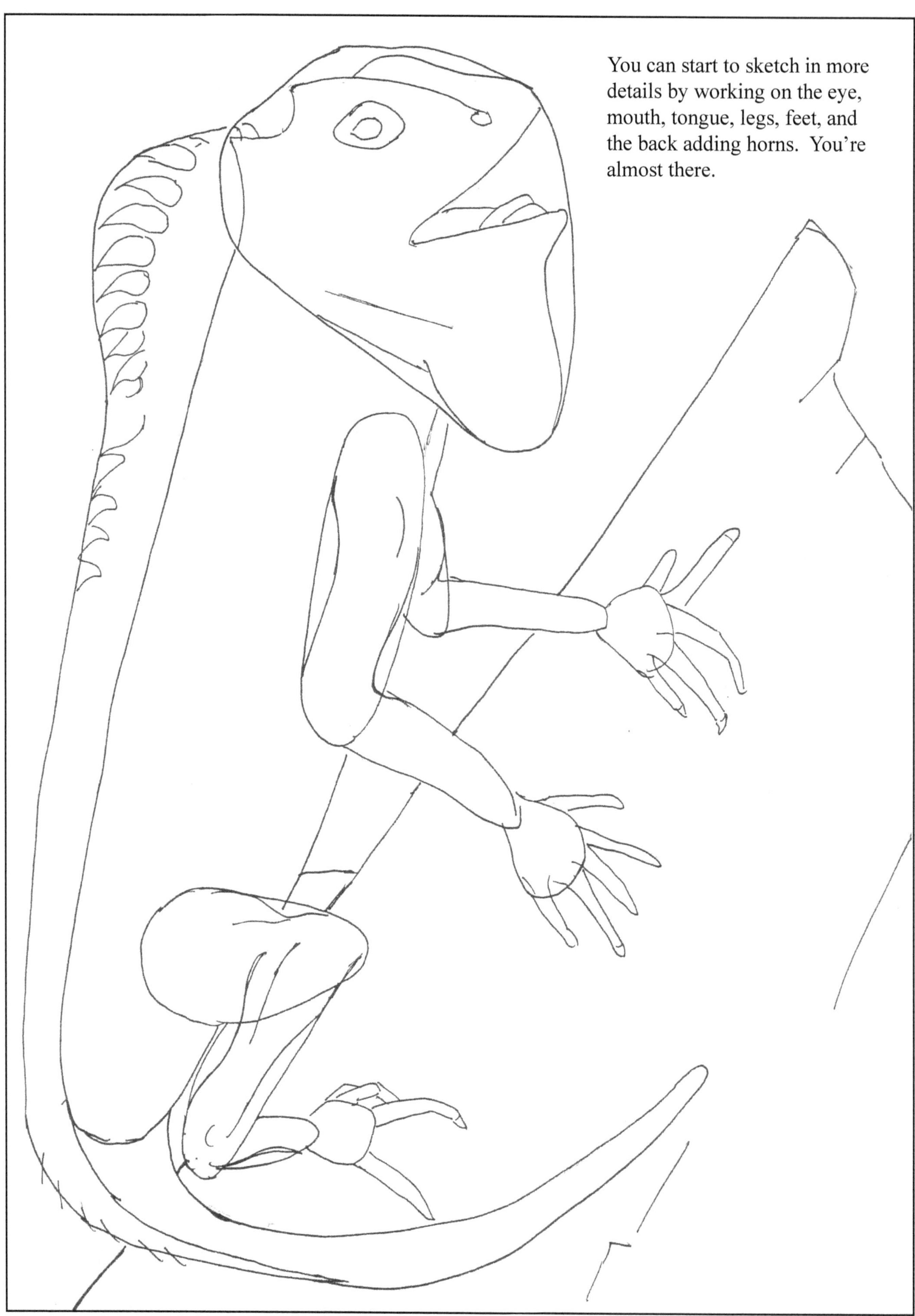

You can start to sketch in more details by working on the eye, mouth, tongue, legs, feet, and the back adding horns. You're almost there.

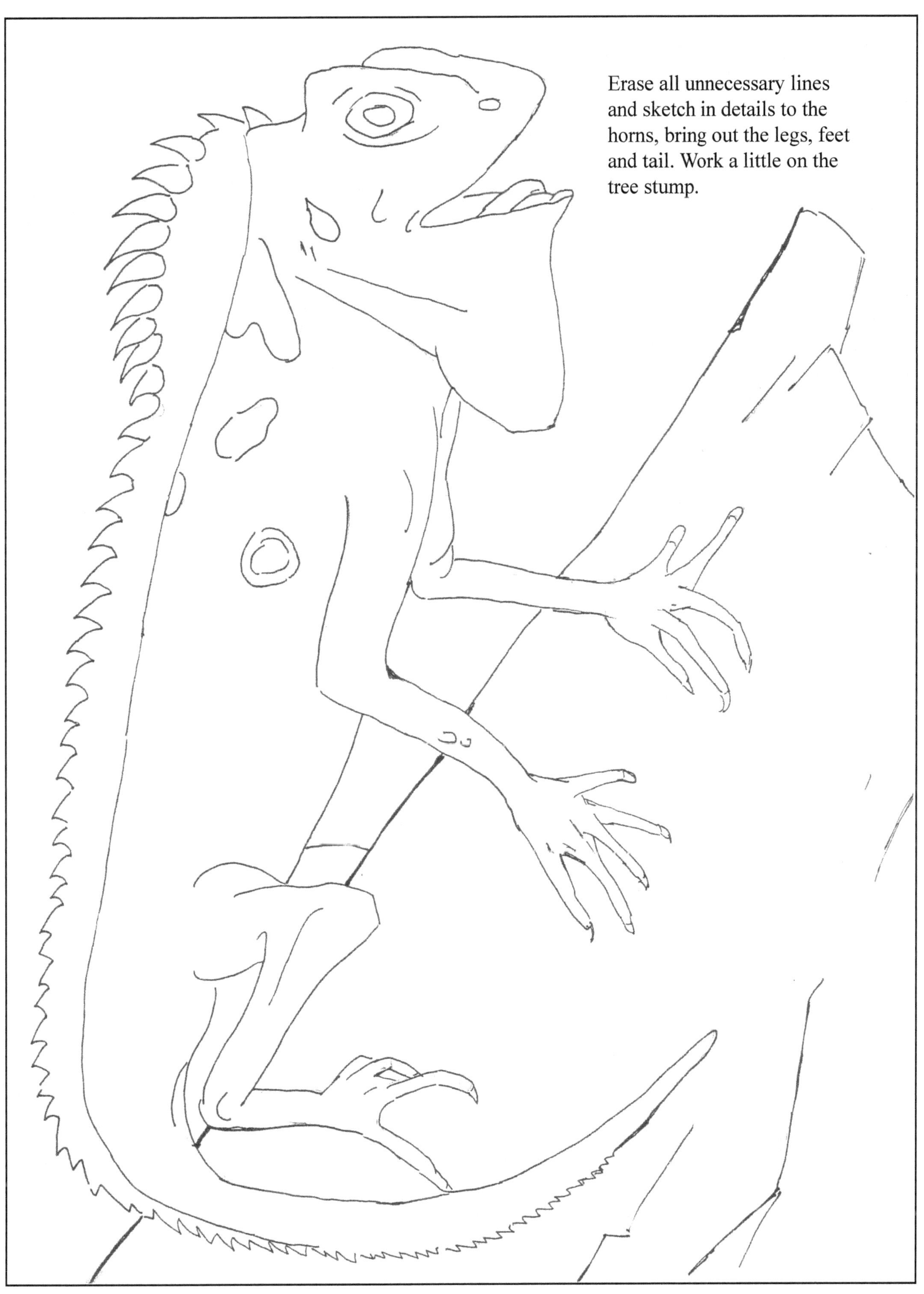
Erase all unnecessary lines and sketch in details to the horns, bring out the legs, feet and tail. Work a little on the tree stump.

BOREN FOREST DRAGON

BOREN FOREST DRAGON. This lizard is native to rainforests of Kalimantan, Borneo. It feeds on insects and is adept at climbing. Adults average about ten inches in length. When threatened, this species gapes and erects its dewlap. Females deposit their eggs in moist humus.

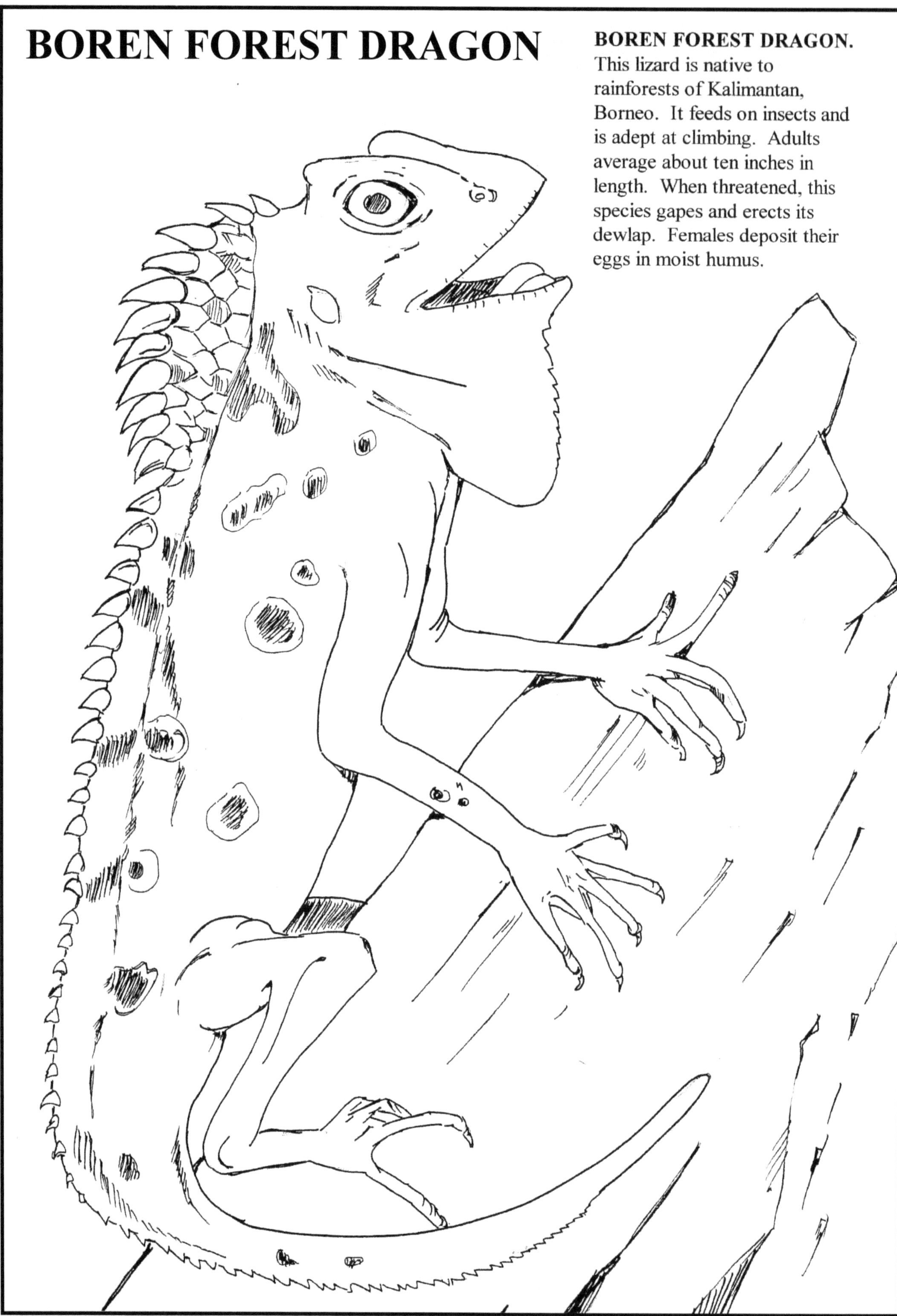

Hey, you might recognize this tortoise. It's the gigantic Galapagos Tortoise, but seen at a difference angle. The truth of the matter is that in the process of editing my book, I didn't realize I had put him in here twice, but I thought he was so interesting that I decided to keep him in and you also learn additional inhabitant facts about this creature.

Let's draw a circle for the head, two lines for his long neck. You couldn't see how long he could stretch his neck in the first drawing. Draw the shell, then draw rectangles and oval for his legs and feet. Good, you just did your ground work to get this drawing started.

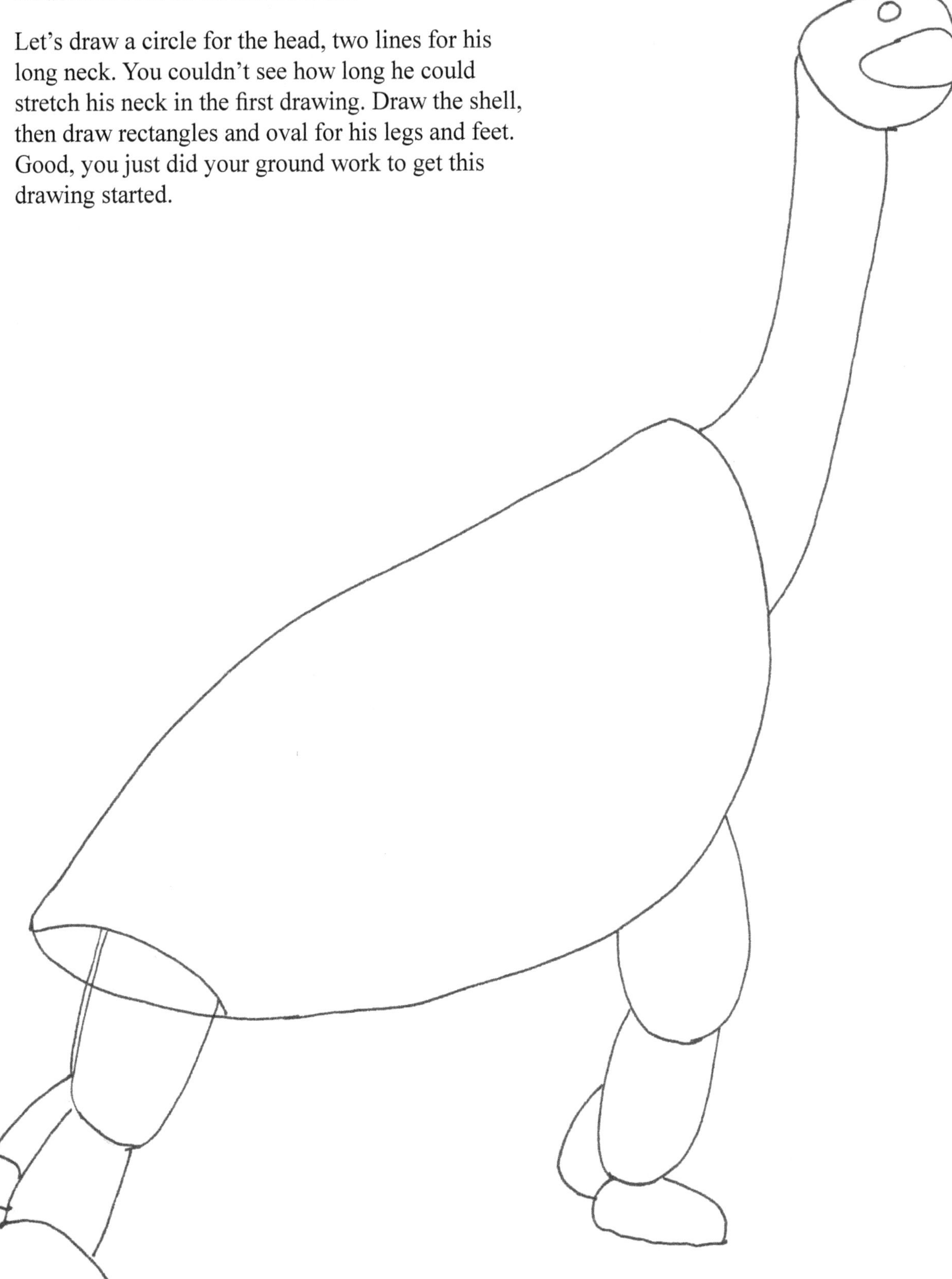

Now, you can just draw in a few contour lines on the shell, neck, leg, feet and mouth to give more definition to your drawing from the foundation you have already built.

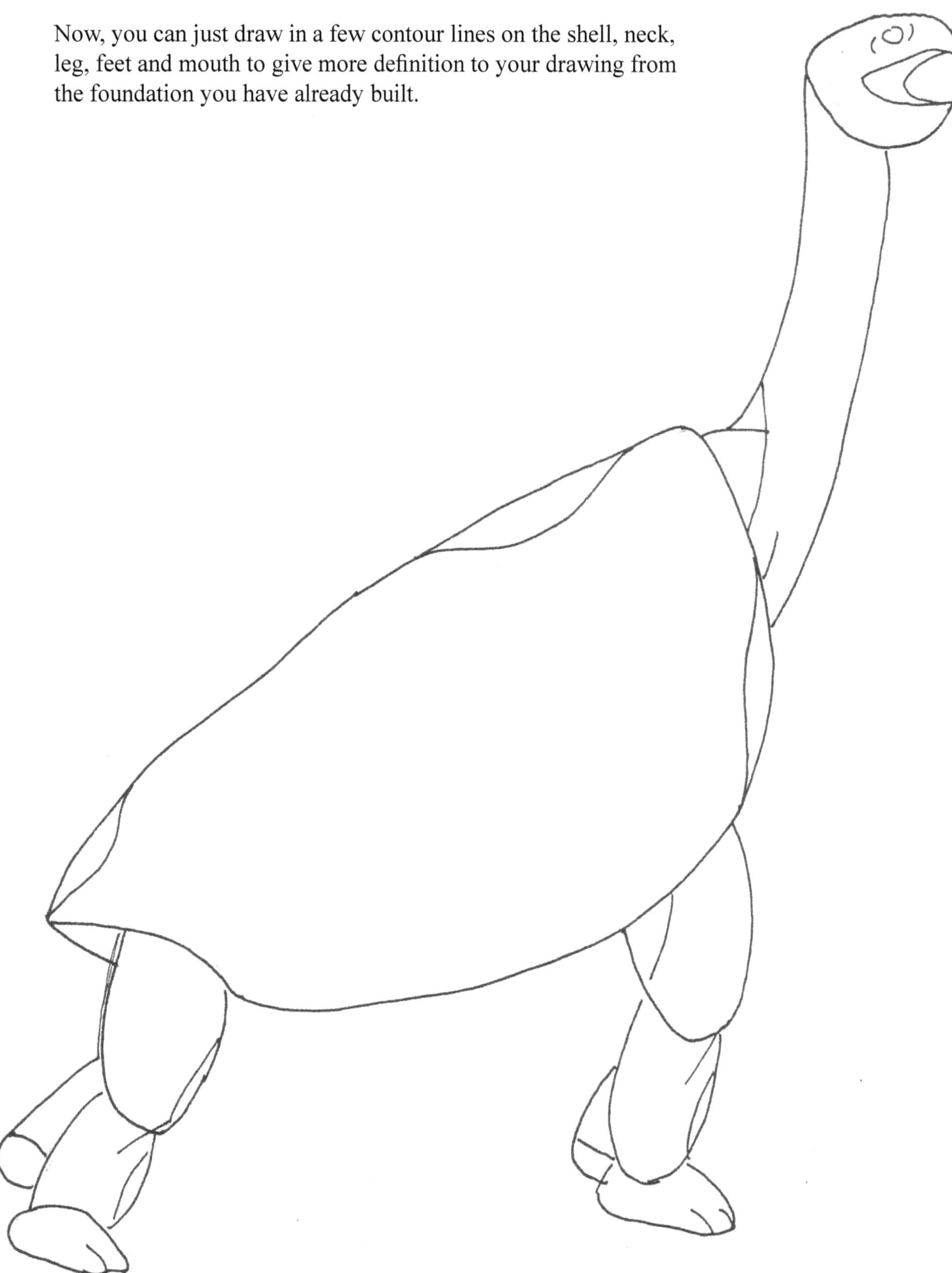

Draw some neck lines to show the extension. Don't forget to draw the shell and leg lines to give more definition to your overall drawing.

You just drew a Gigantic Galapagos Tortoise. All you need to do now is to draw in some shadows and defining lines on the head, neck, shell, legs, and feet to complete your drawing as you will see on the next page.

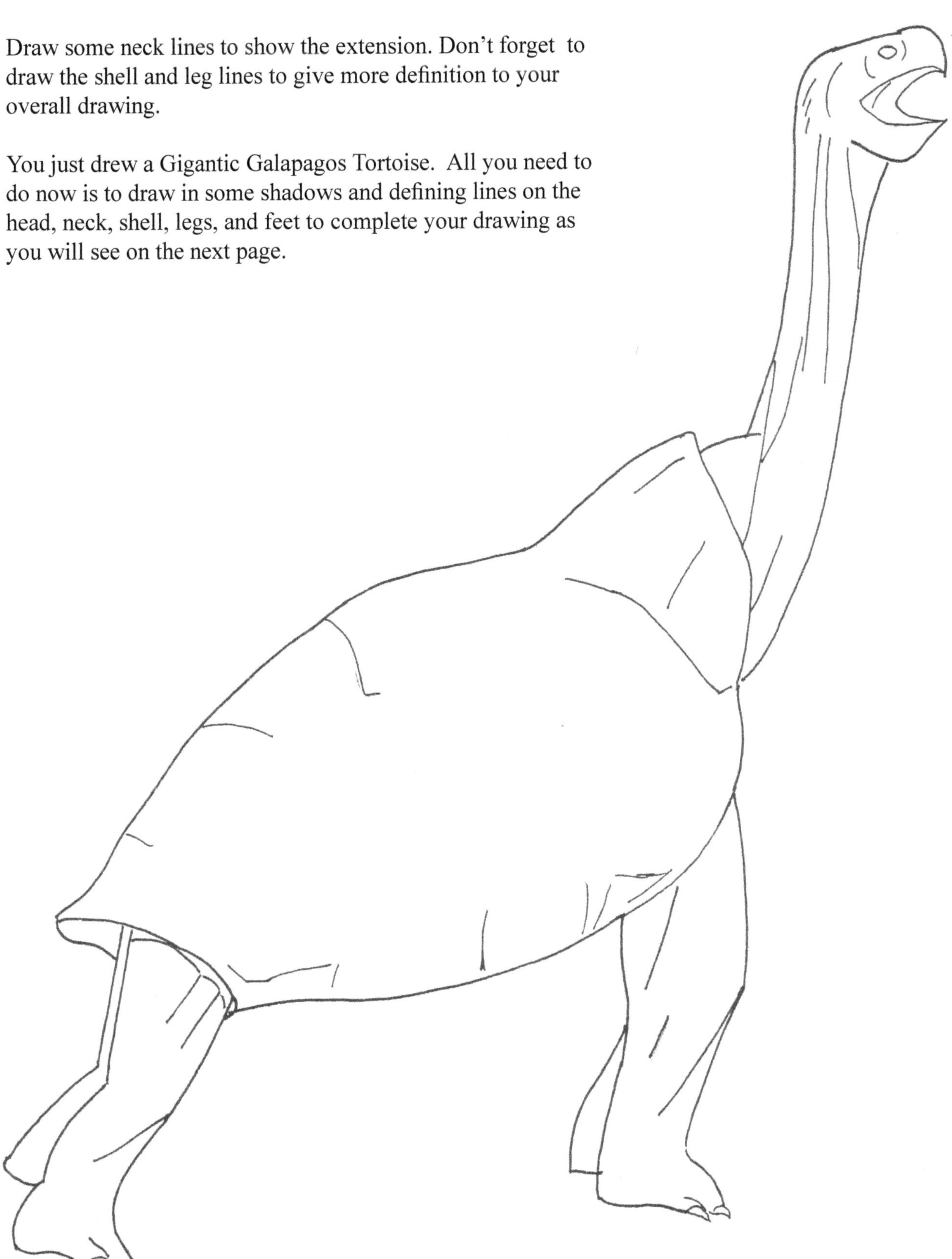

GIGANTIC GALAPAGOS TORTOISE

GALAPAGOS TORTOISE (standing in an upright position) These gigantic turtles live in Galapagos Achipelago off the coast of Ecuador. This tortoise can have a shell length of up to four feet and weights in excess of 500 pounds. Like most island creatures, these giant turtles lead a precarious existence. Historically, these giant reptiles were harvested as meat for sailors. If unmolested, the Galapagos Tortoise can live for more than 100 years.

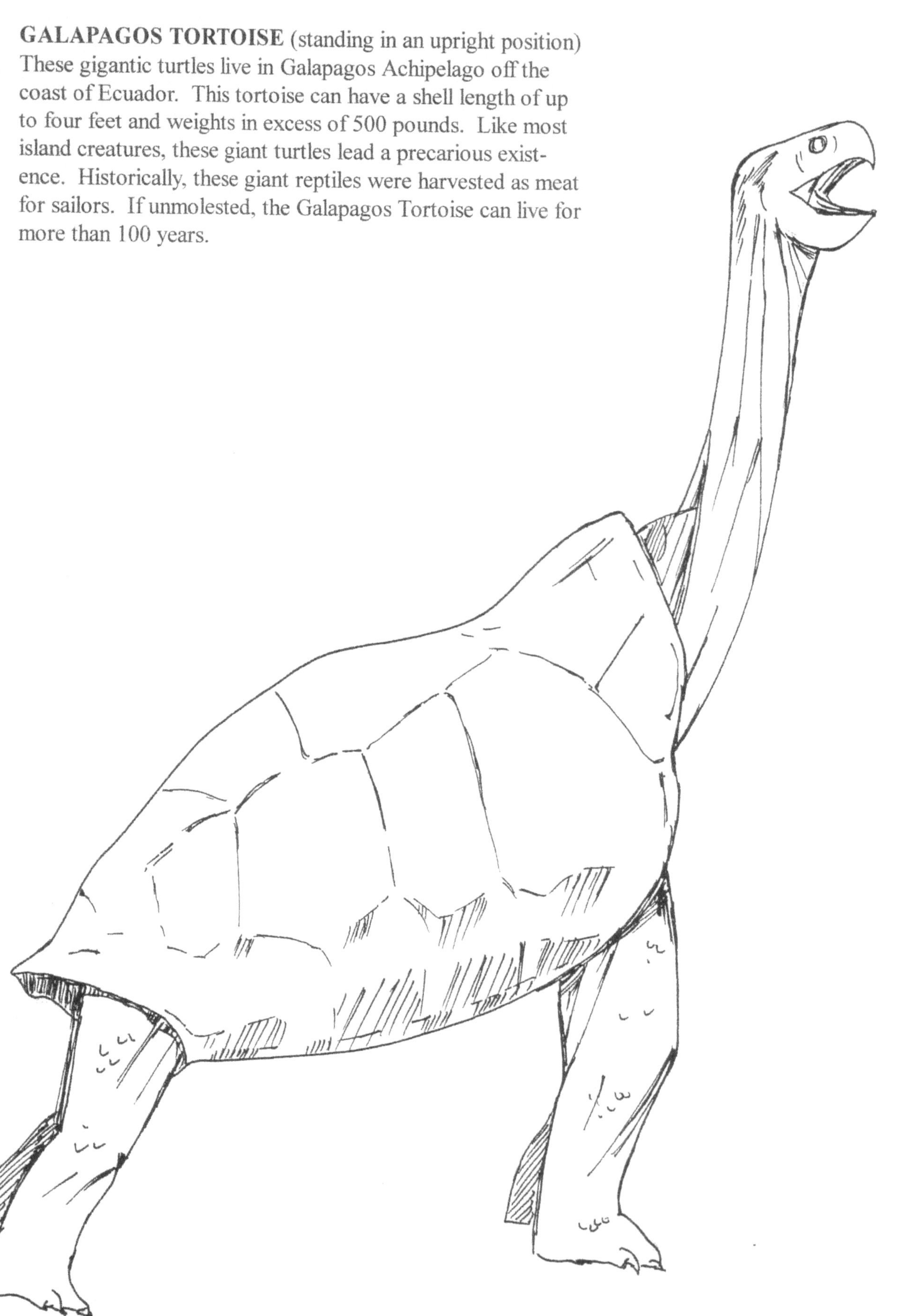

Let's create the outline structure for this drawing. Start with drawing lines for the tree limbs, a circle for the head, circular lines for the body and legs, a line for the tail. Make small lines for the lizard's mouth, eye and nose. Shoot the tongue out catching a bug for his meal.

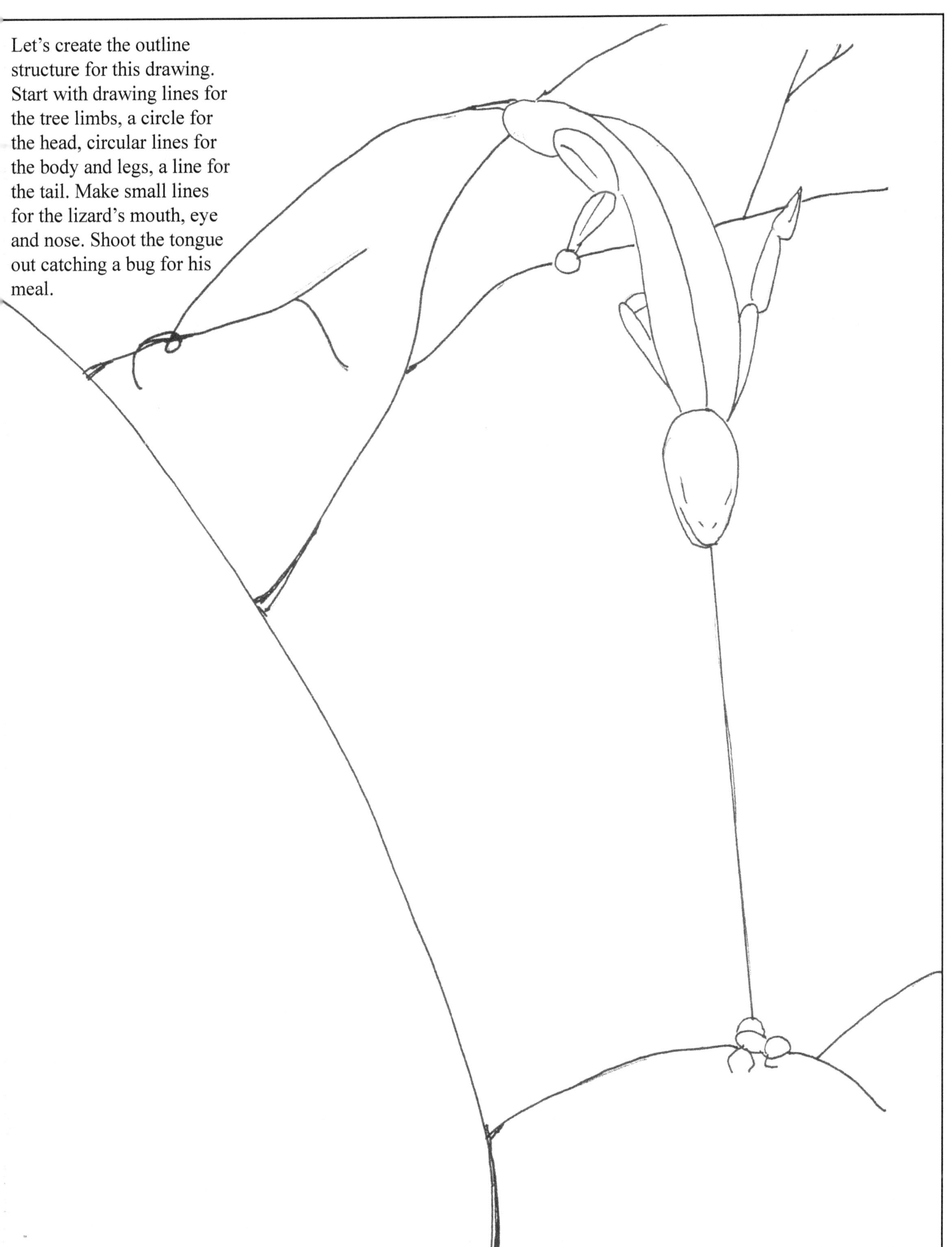

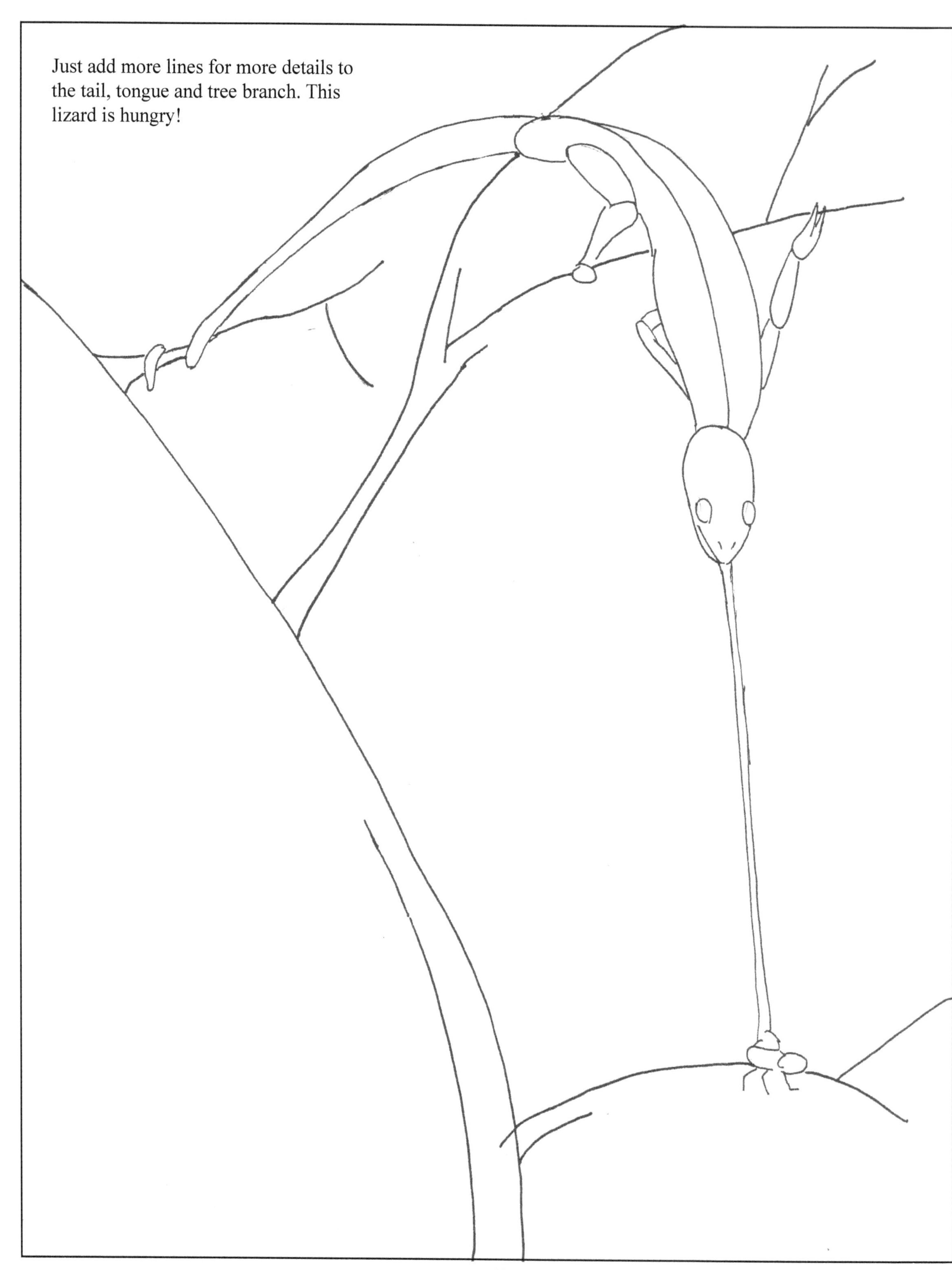
Just add more lines for more details to the tail, tongue and tree branch. This lizard is hungry!

You're almost there. Draw in more details to the tail, tree branch, add thorns on the lizard's back, form the eyes. Now, you have almost complete a good drawing of a Chameleon. Go to the next page.

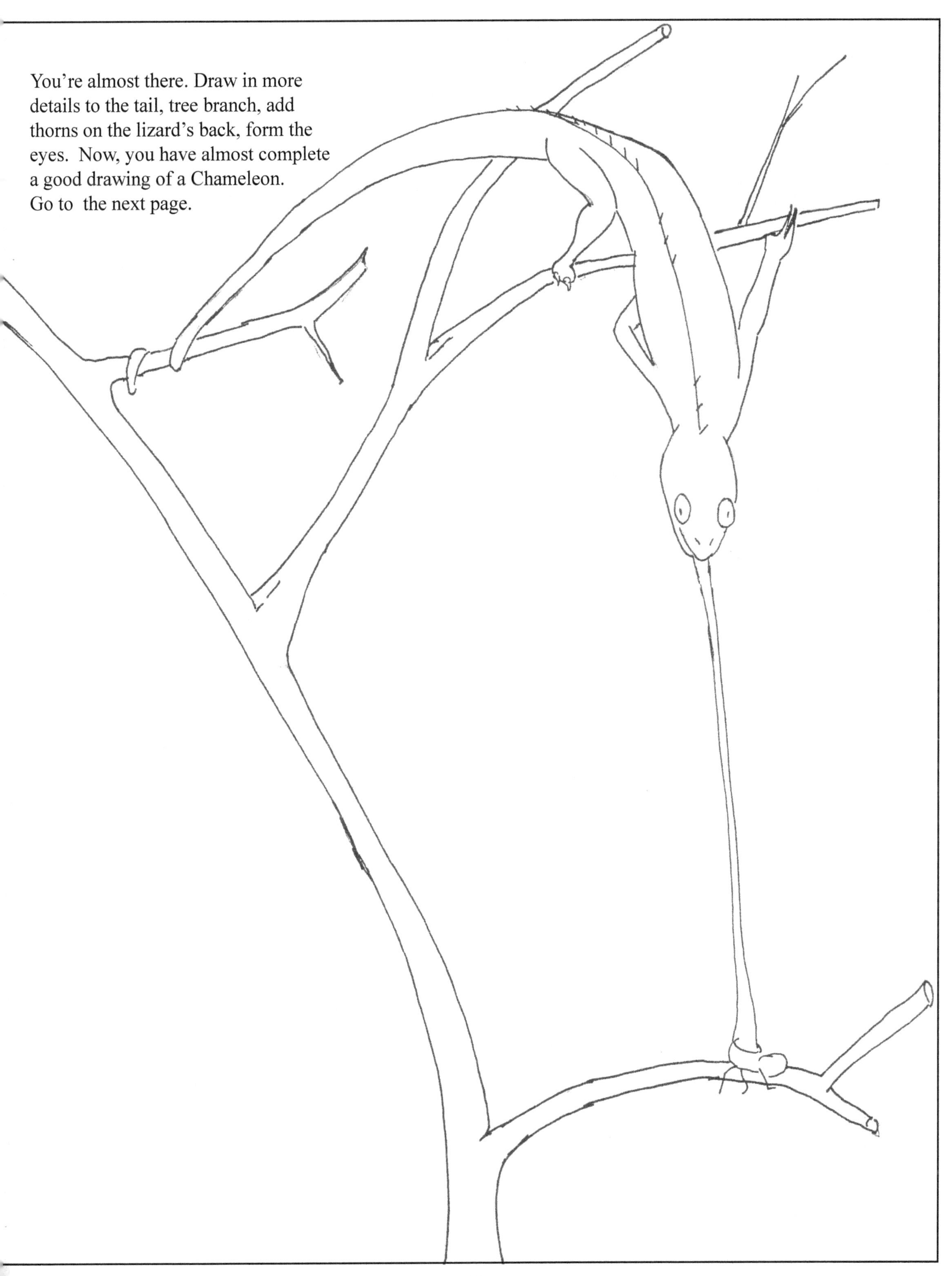

CHAMELEONS

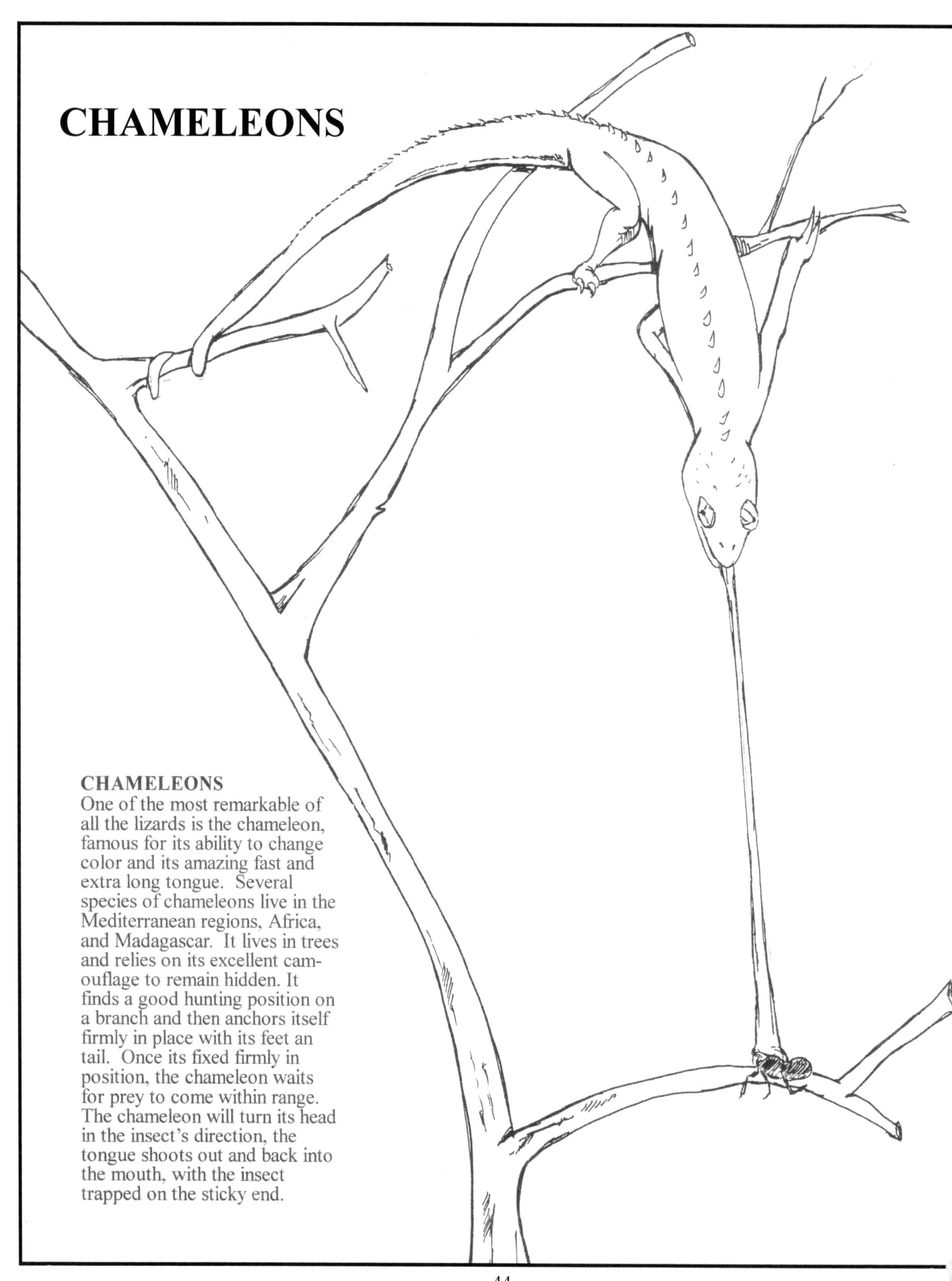

CHAMELEONS
One of the most remarkable of all the lizards is the chameleon, famous for its ability to change color and its amazing fast and extra long tongue. Several species of chameleons live in the Mediterranean regions, Africa, and Madagascar. It lives in trees and relies on its excellent camouflage to remain hidden. It finds a good hunting position on a branch and then anchors itself firmly in place with its feet an tail. Once its fixed firmly in position, the chameleon waits for prey to come within range. The chameleon will turn its head in the insect's direction, the tongue shoots out and back into the mouth, with the insect trapped on the sticky end.

As usual, I like to keep it simple. Let's begin by drawing a tree trunk with straight lines. Then draw an oblong circle for head the Boa's the head and eye. Then follow up by drawing a long zig zag line connected from the Boa's head around the tree outlining her body.

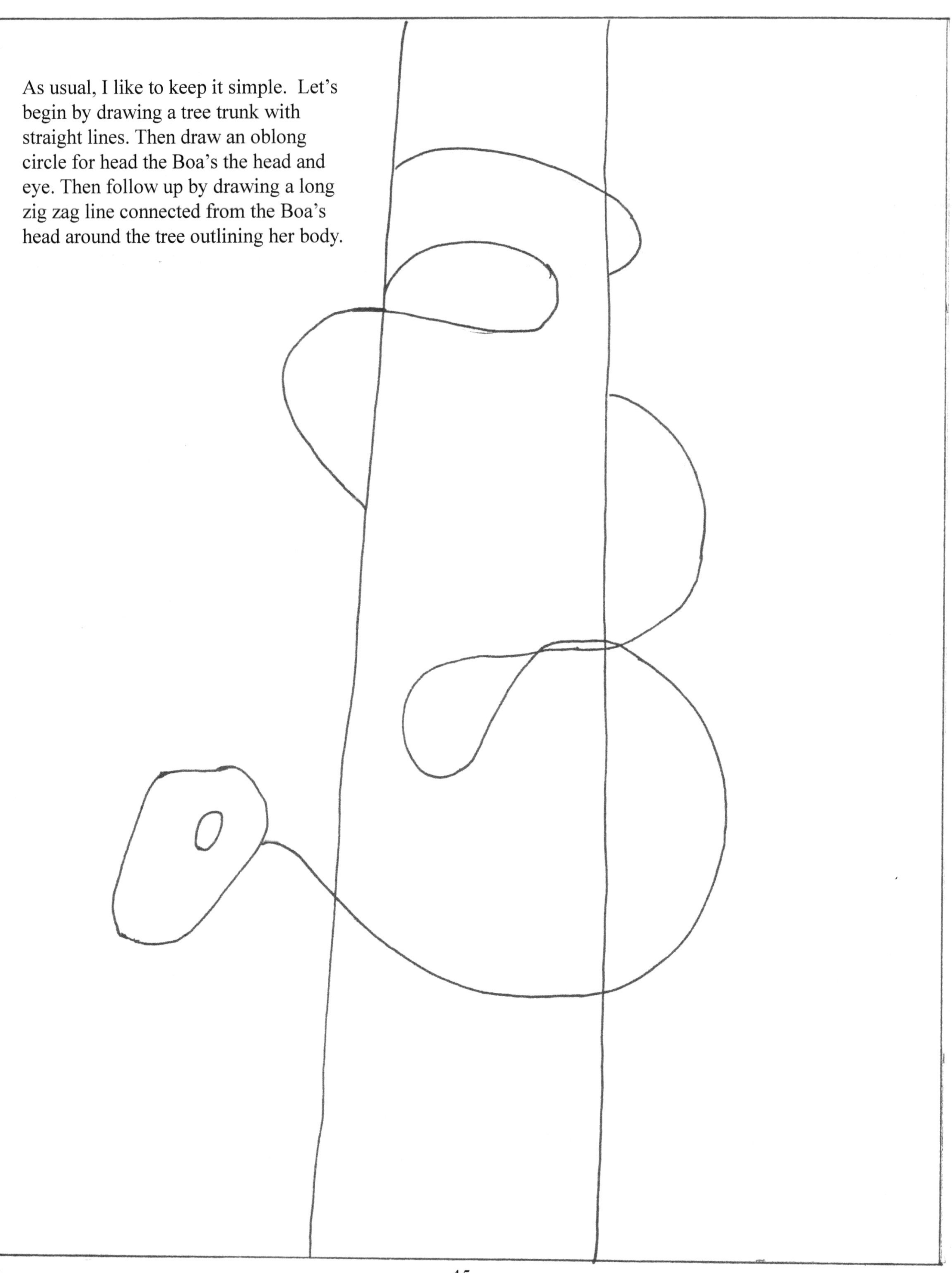

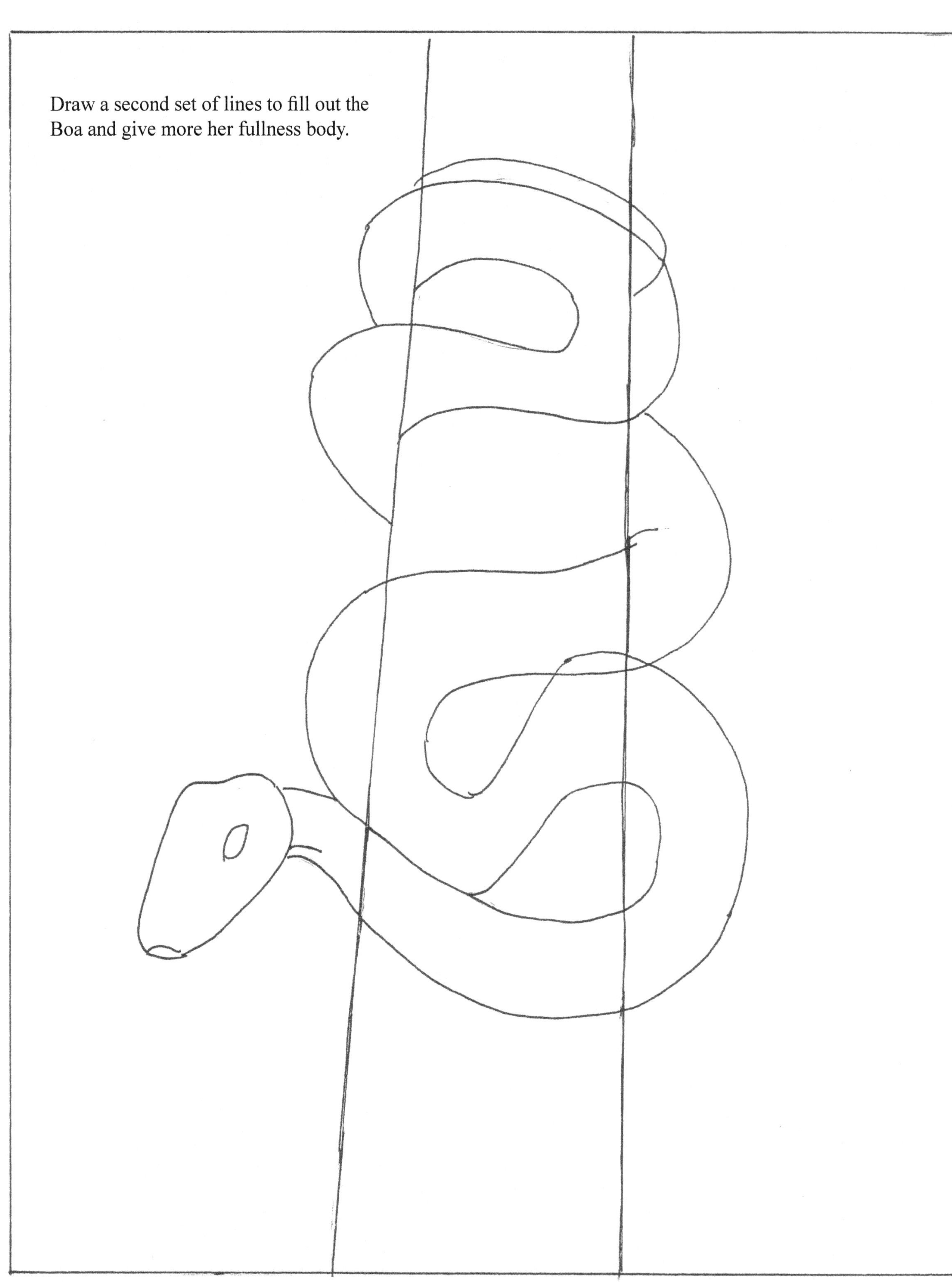
Draw a second set of lines to fill out the
Boa and give more her fullness body.

Ease all unnecessary lines. Add lines for the stomach. Draw in more definition to the eyes and mouth. Throw in some line for shadows off the tree trunk, add some lines for tree trunk bark. You're almost finish, draw in the Boa's designs on her back. See next page.

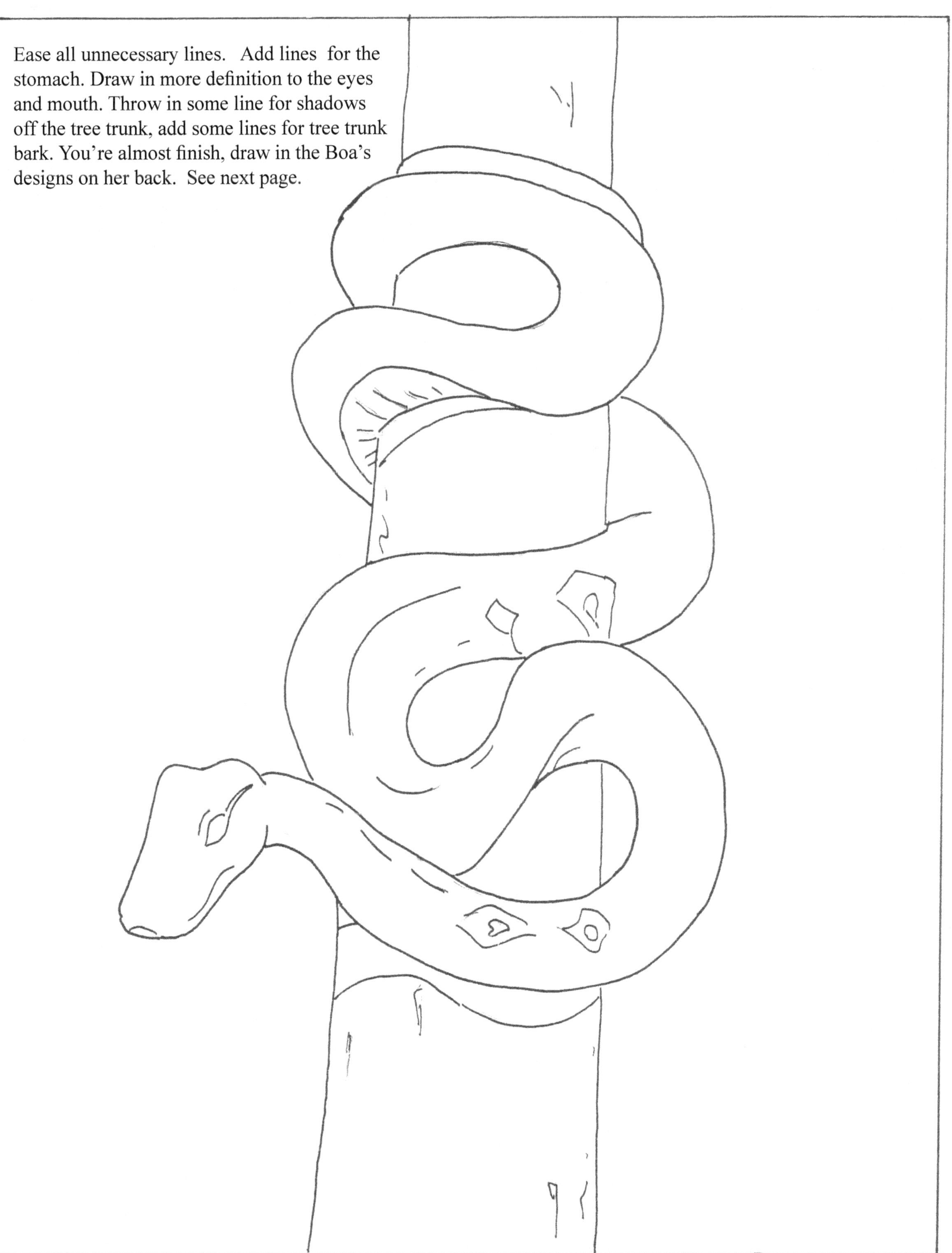

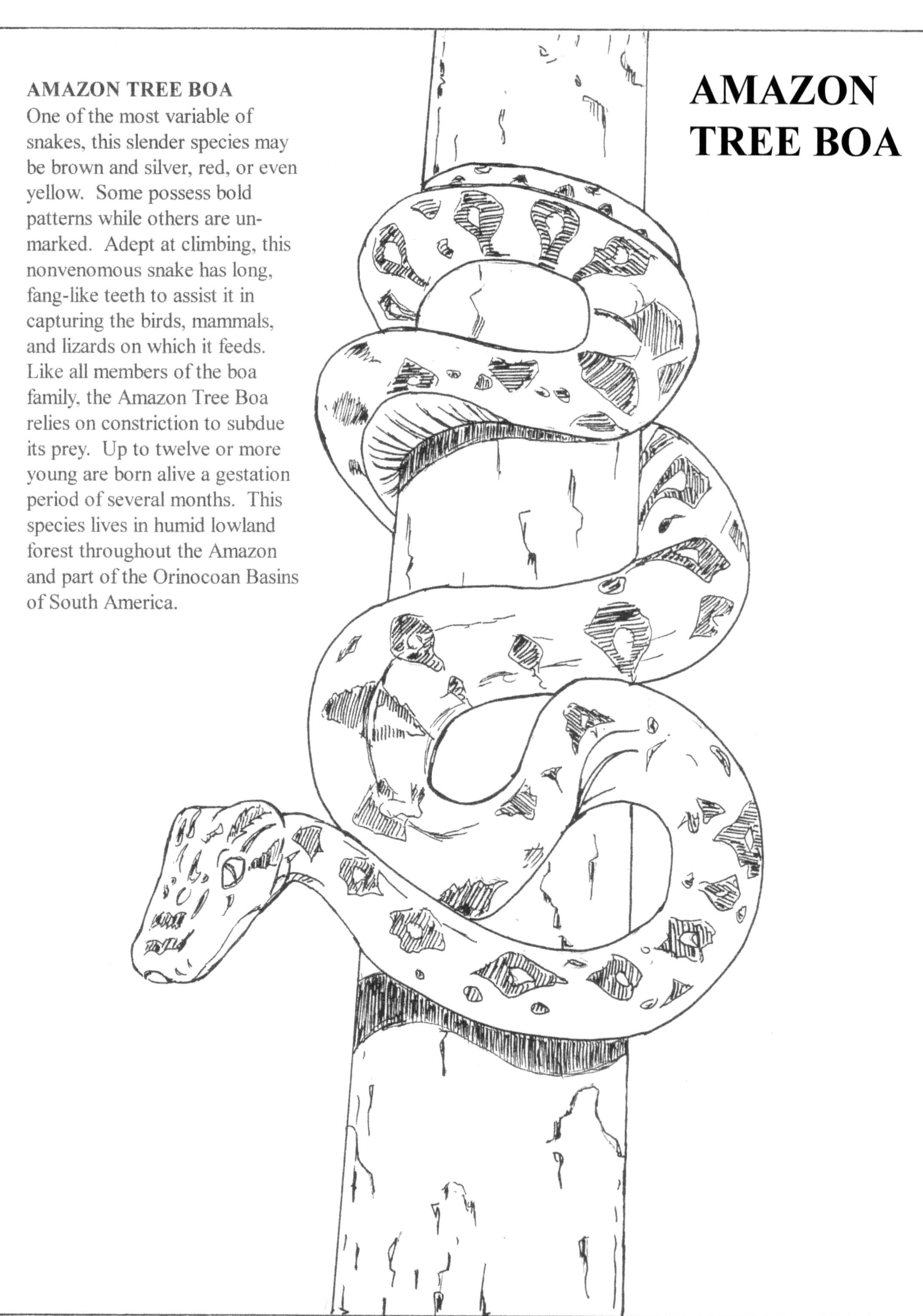

AMAZON TREE BOA
One of the most variable of snakes, this slender species may be brown and silver, red, or even yellow. Some possess bold patterns while others are unmarked. Adept at climbing, this nonvenomous snake has long, fang-like teeth to assist it in capturing the birds, mammals, and lizards on which it feeds. Like all members of the boa family, the Amazon Tree Boa relies on constriction to subdue its prey. Up to twelve or more young are born alive a gestation period of several months. This species lives in humid lowland forest throughout the Amazon and part of the Orinocoan Basins of South America.

AMAZON TREE BOA

Let's create the outline structure for this drawing. Draw a circle for the head, sketch in the eye, and then draw circular zig zag lines for the body of the snake. I got you drawing another, snake, as I always say, practice, practice and more practice.

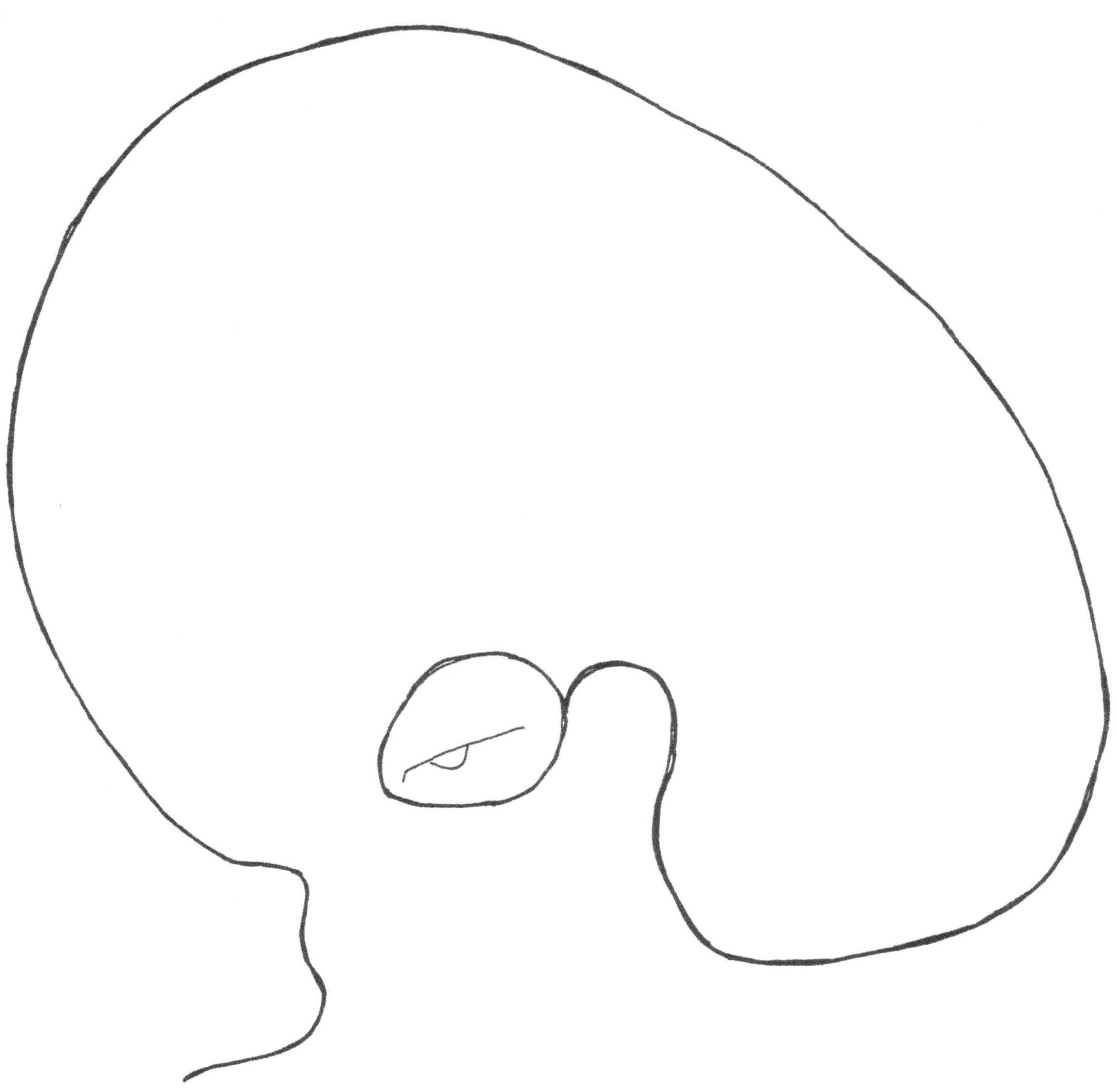

Now, add another line to form the full body of the snake. Draw in a curve line on the head indicating the form of the other eye.

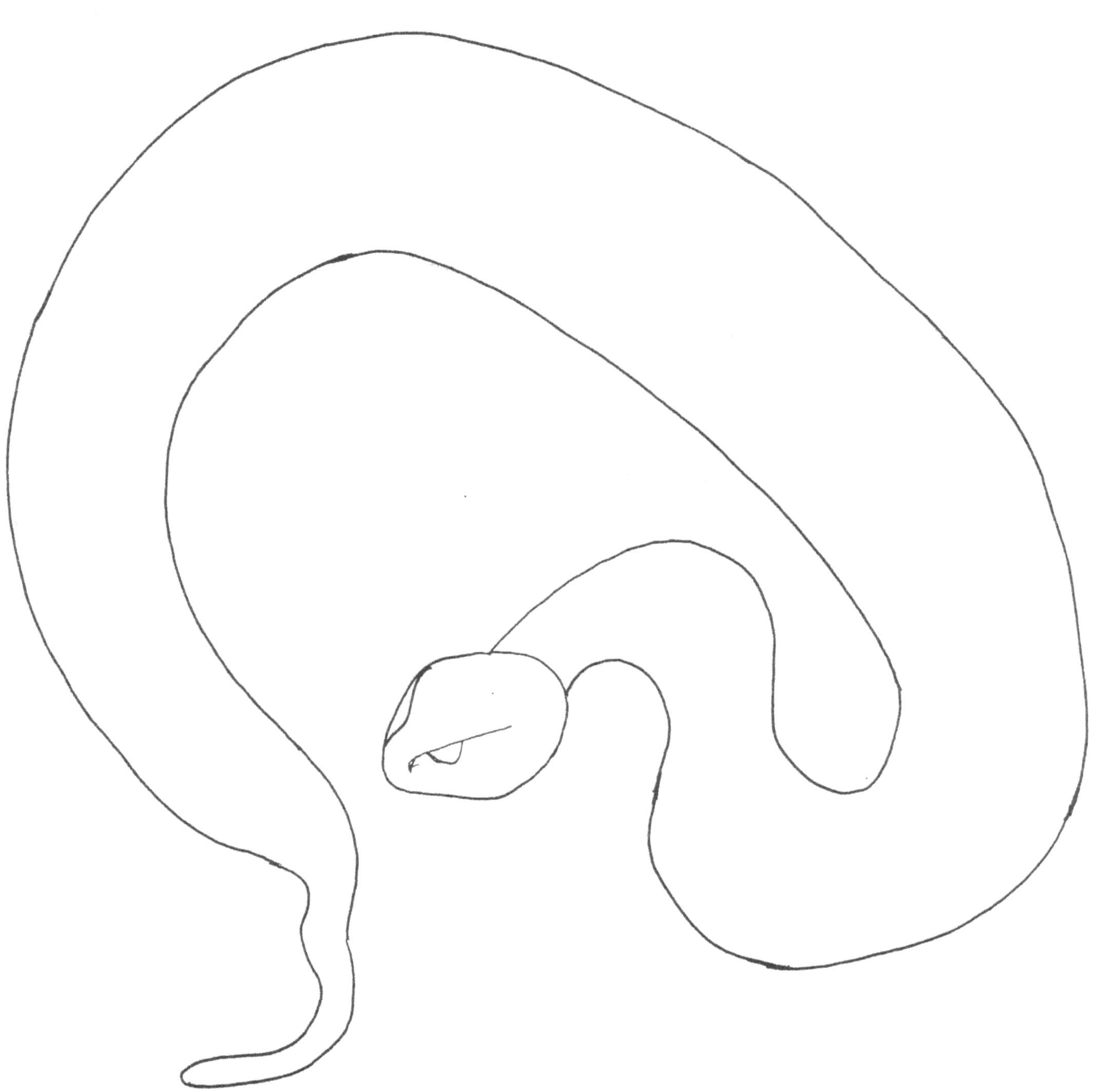

Draw in some broken lines to indicate the side of the Adder, then erase any unnecessary lines. Now, you can draw the pattern design on the Adder's body to complete your drawing as you will see on the next page.

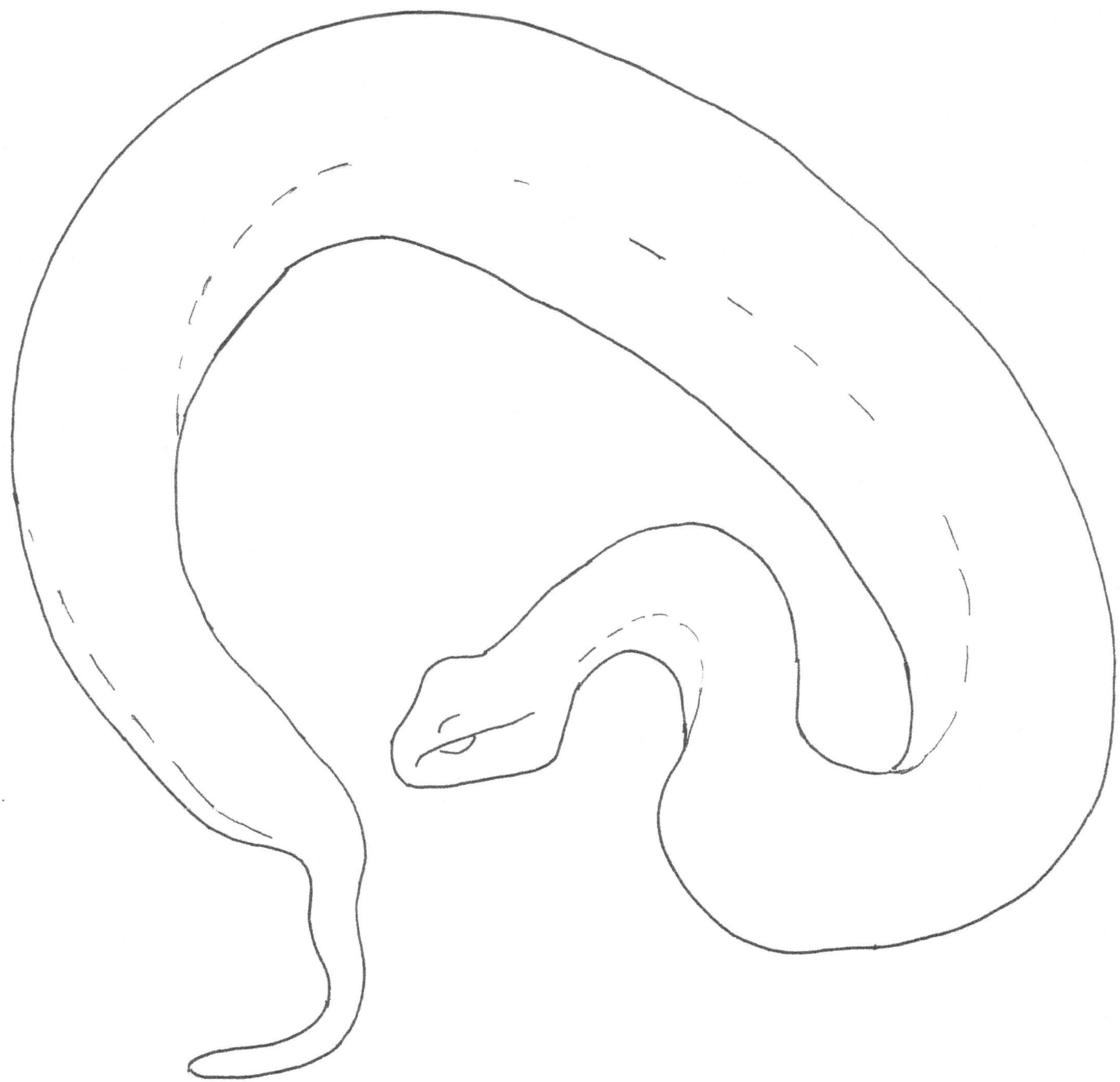

DEATH ADDER

DEATH ADDER Found in the forest, open woodlands, and semiarid scrublands of northern, eastern, and southern Australia. The viper-like species has a broad, triangular head, a short stout body, and a thin tail ending in a curved soft spine.

During the day the death adder stays hidden under decaying leaves, or half-buried in the soil, often close to trees and brushes. At dusk it emerges from its lair to hunt for lizards, small rodents, and birds. From an ambush position it will lure their prey within striking distance by twitching the tip of its distinctive tail. Their venom is extremely toxic to prey and also highly dangerous for humans. They are considered one of the world's deadliest snakes. They produce up to 20 young in a litter.

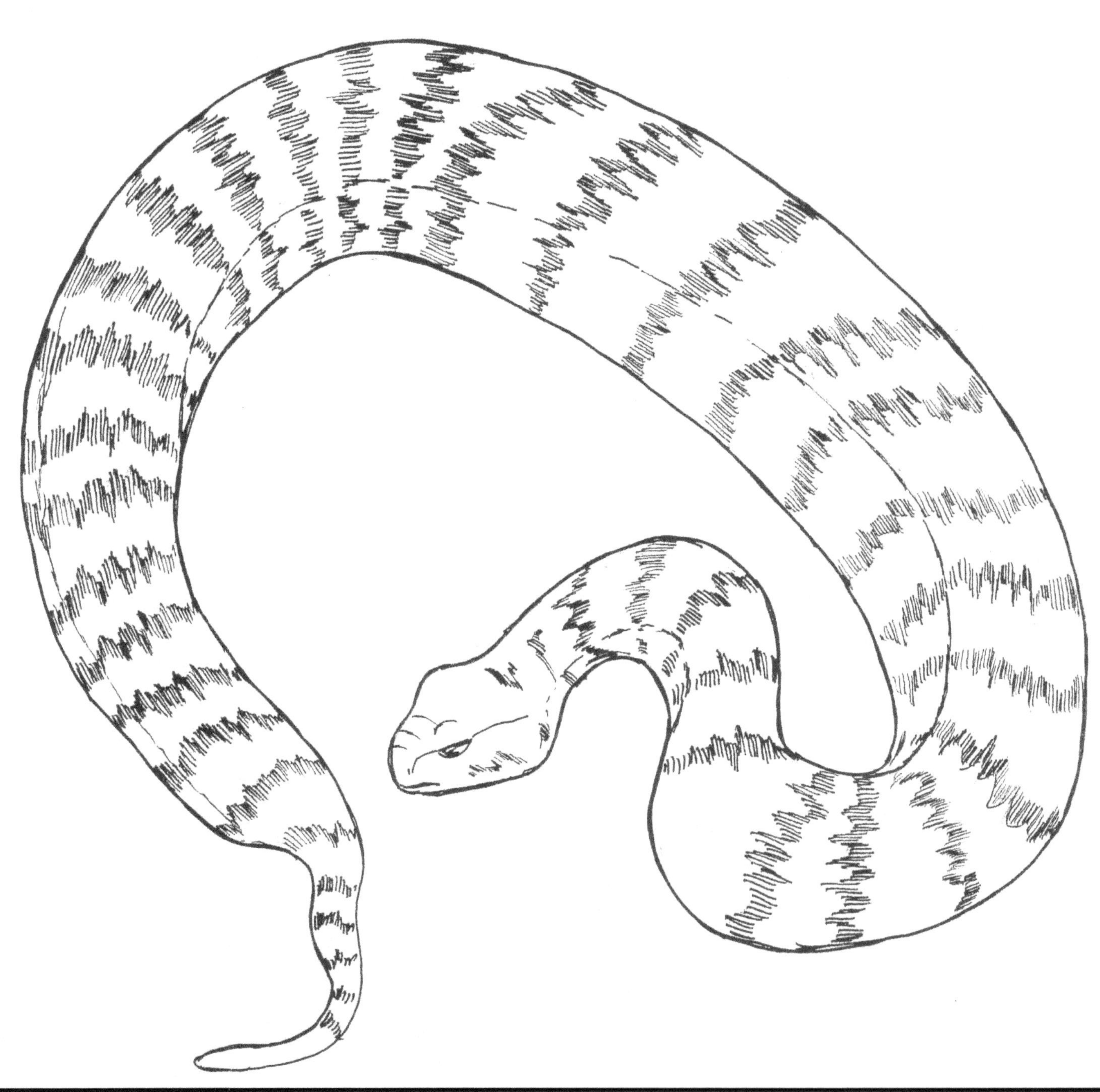

Let's start the outline of this drawing by sketching the tree log, then the draw the head, body, legs, feet and tail. Then go back add in the eye, mouth and lines for the horns of this lizard.

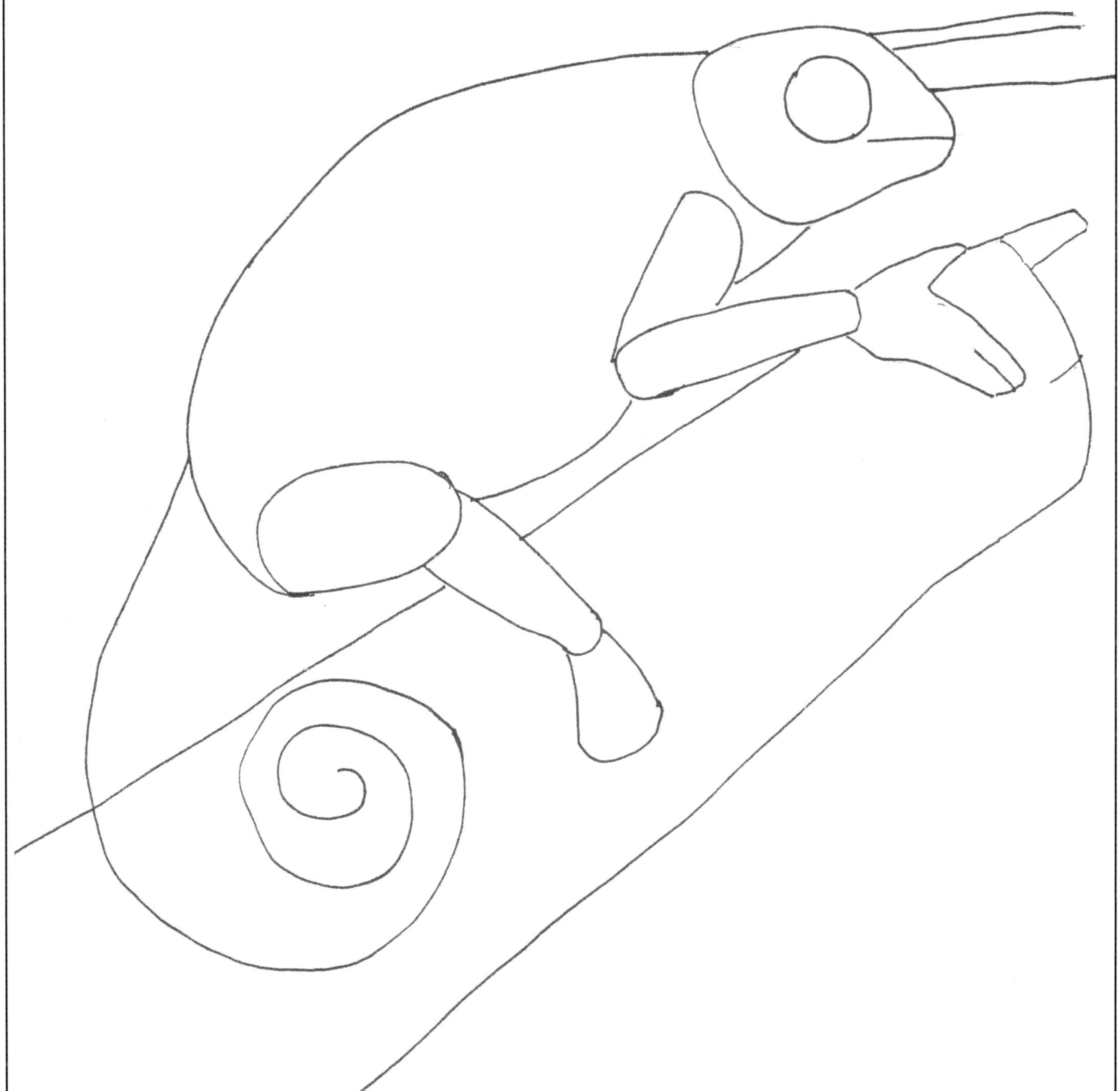

Now you can add additional lines to form the tail and horns. Draw a small circle in the middle of eye for it's pupil and erase any lines not needed.

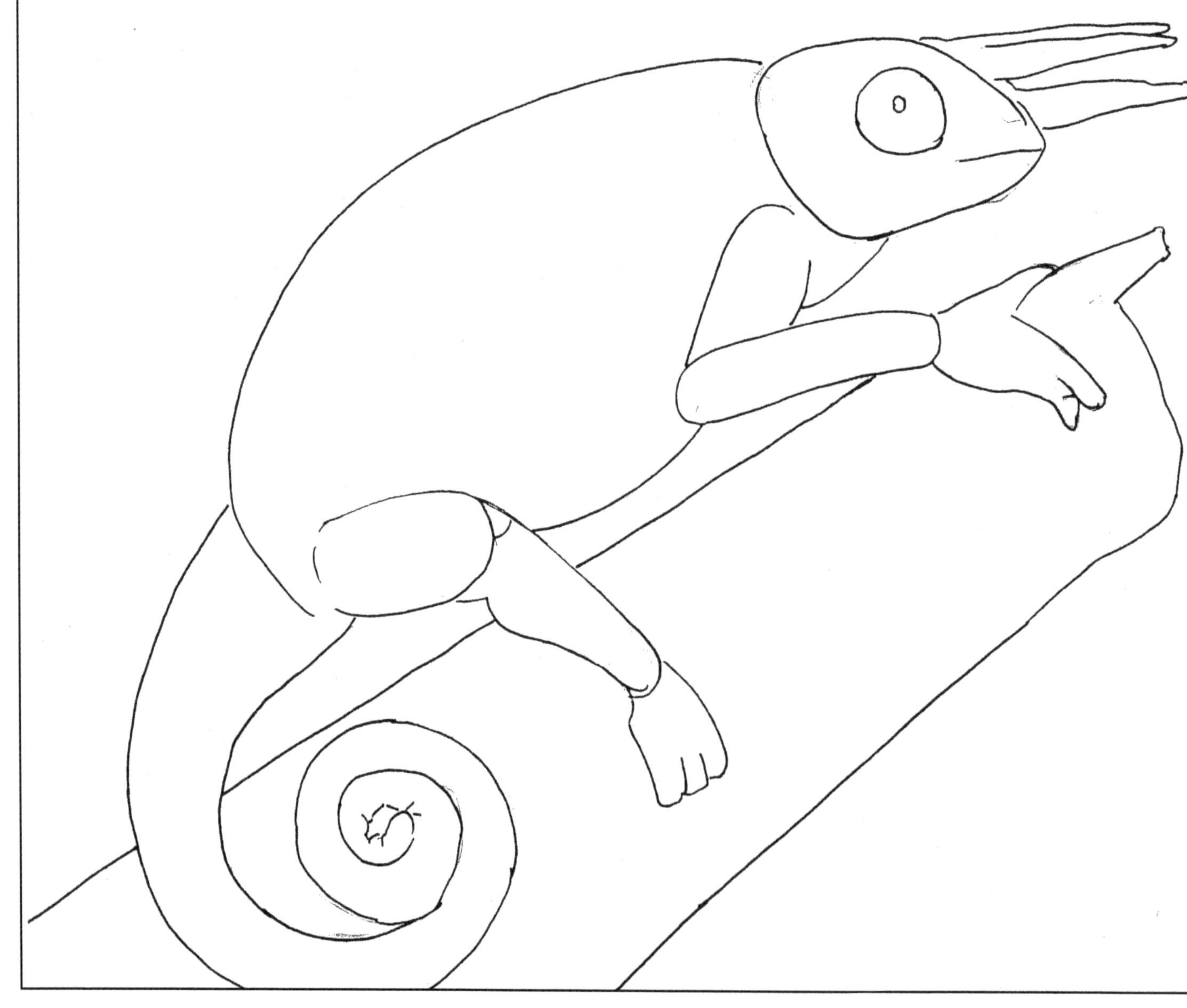

Draw more details to the eye, horns, mouth, and legs. Add some texture to the skin and erase any unnecessary lines. Continue to draw more details to the chameleon and tree log as you continue to finish your drawing as you will see on the next page.

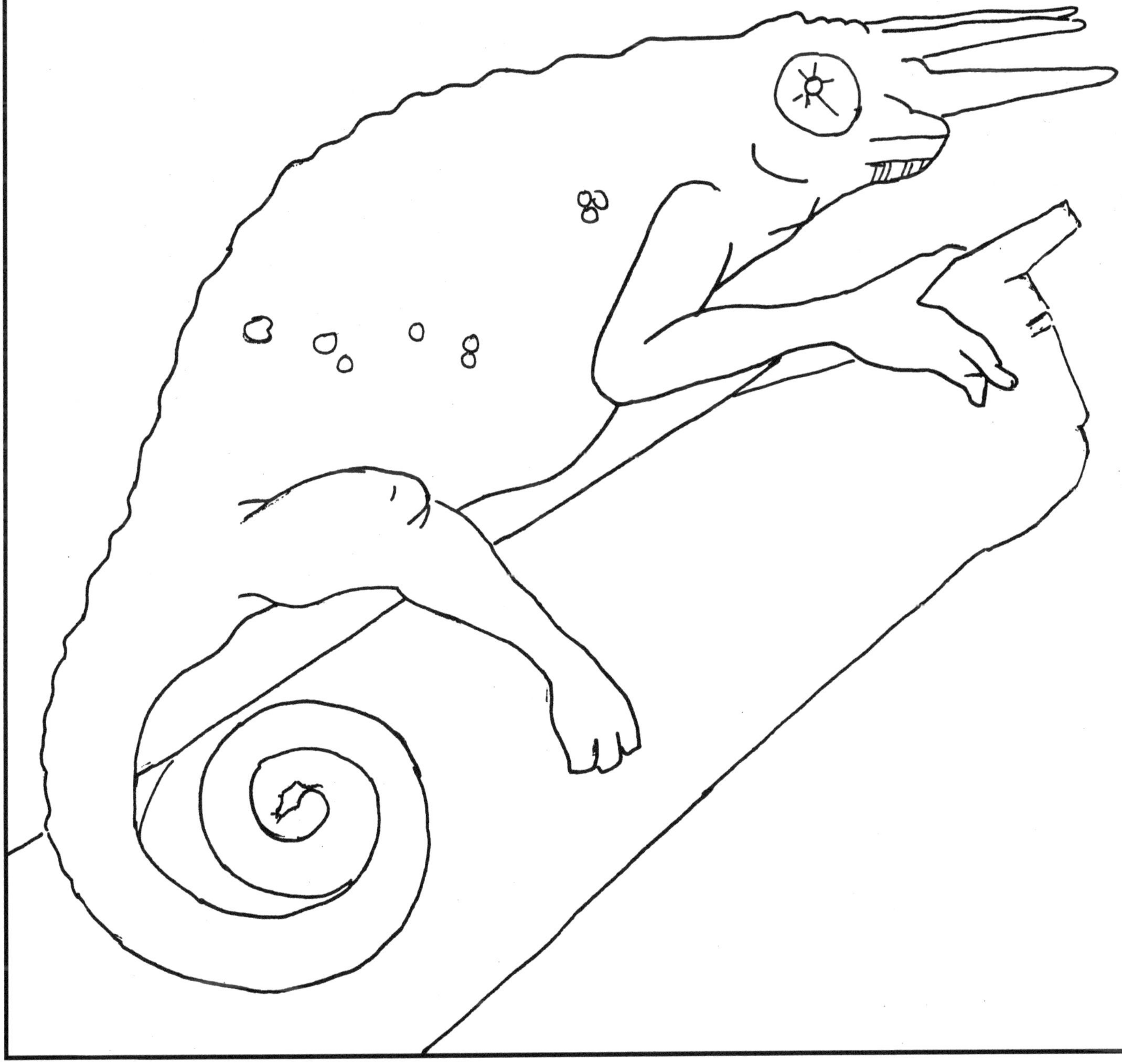

JACKSON'S CHAMELEON

JACKSON'S CHAMELEON. From East Africa introduce into Hawaii. They're habitat is mountain thickets and forests. This "three-horned" chameleon is a resident of the East African highlands and lives exclusively in trees and shrubs. It is active mainly in the morning and late afternoon, feeding on various insects. Males are markedly territorial and during the breeding season behave aggressively toward rivals, attacking with their horns. The females are ovoviviparous, hatching eggs within the body, giving birth to 7-40 young at a time.

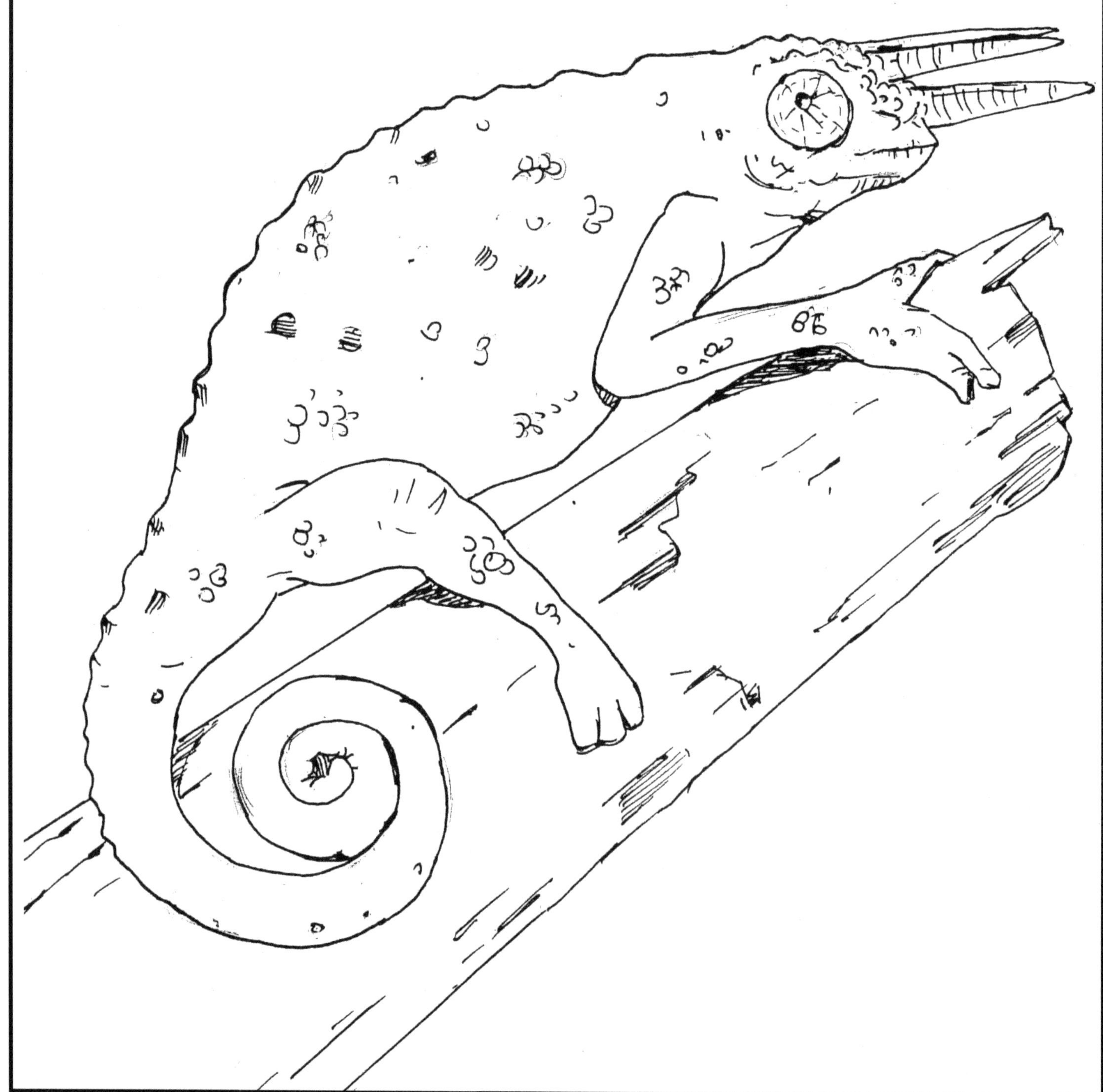

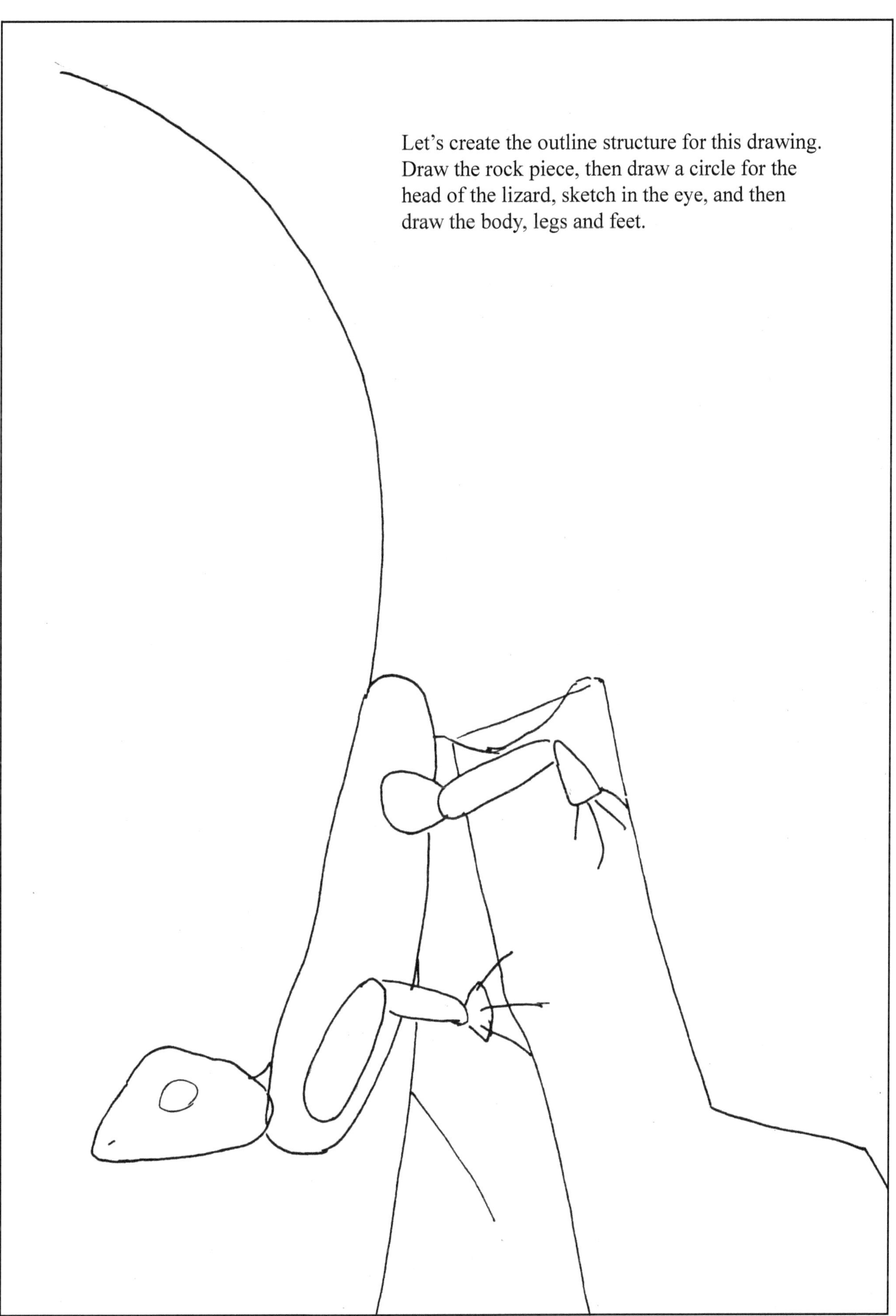

Let's create the outline structure for this drawing. Draw the rock piece, then draw a circle for the head of the lizard, sketch in the eye, and then draw the body, legs and feet.

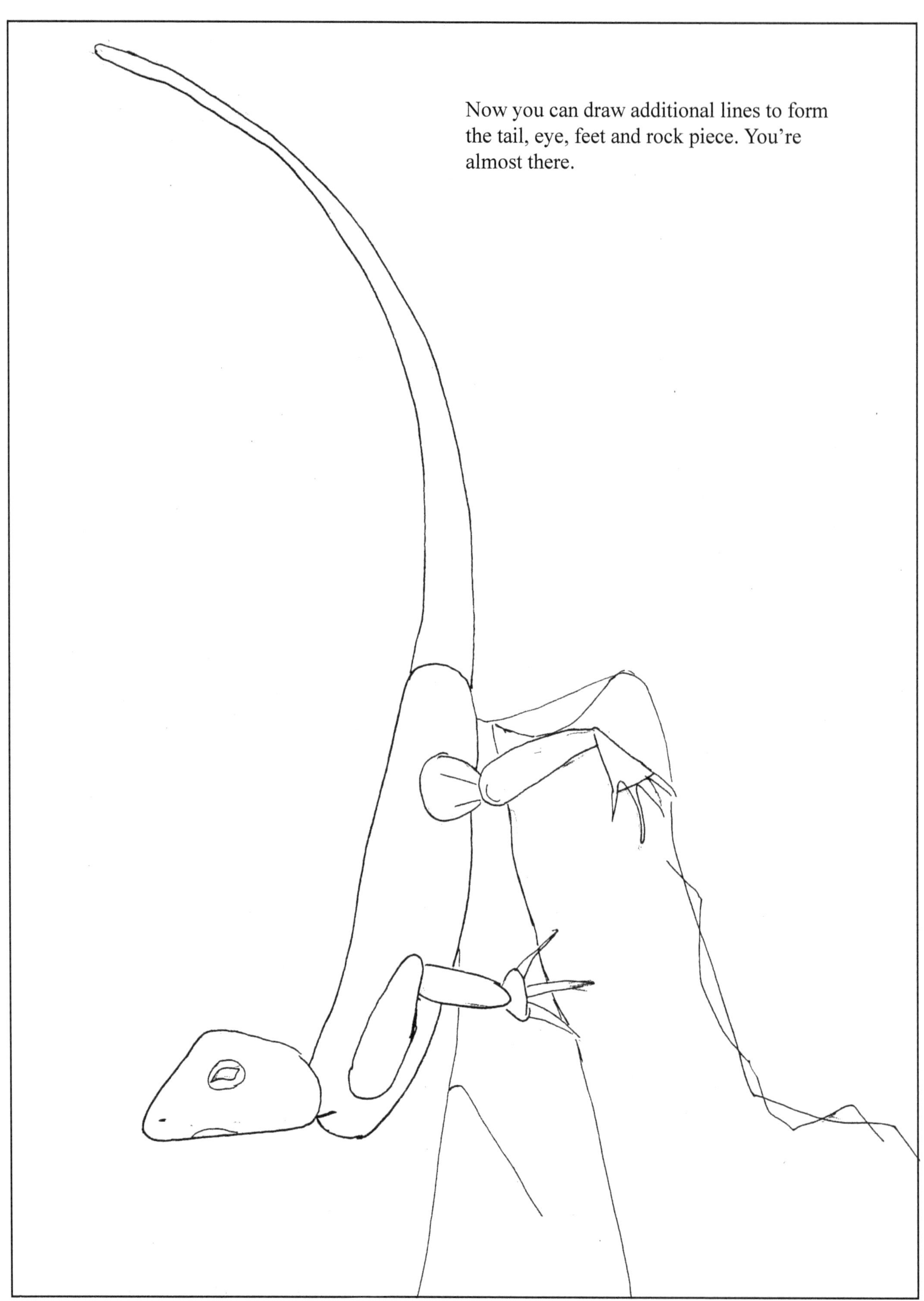
Now you can draw additional lines to form the tail, eye, feet and rock piece. You're almost there.

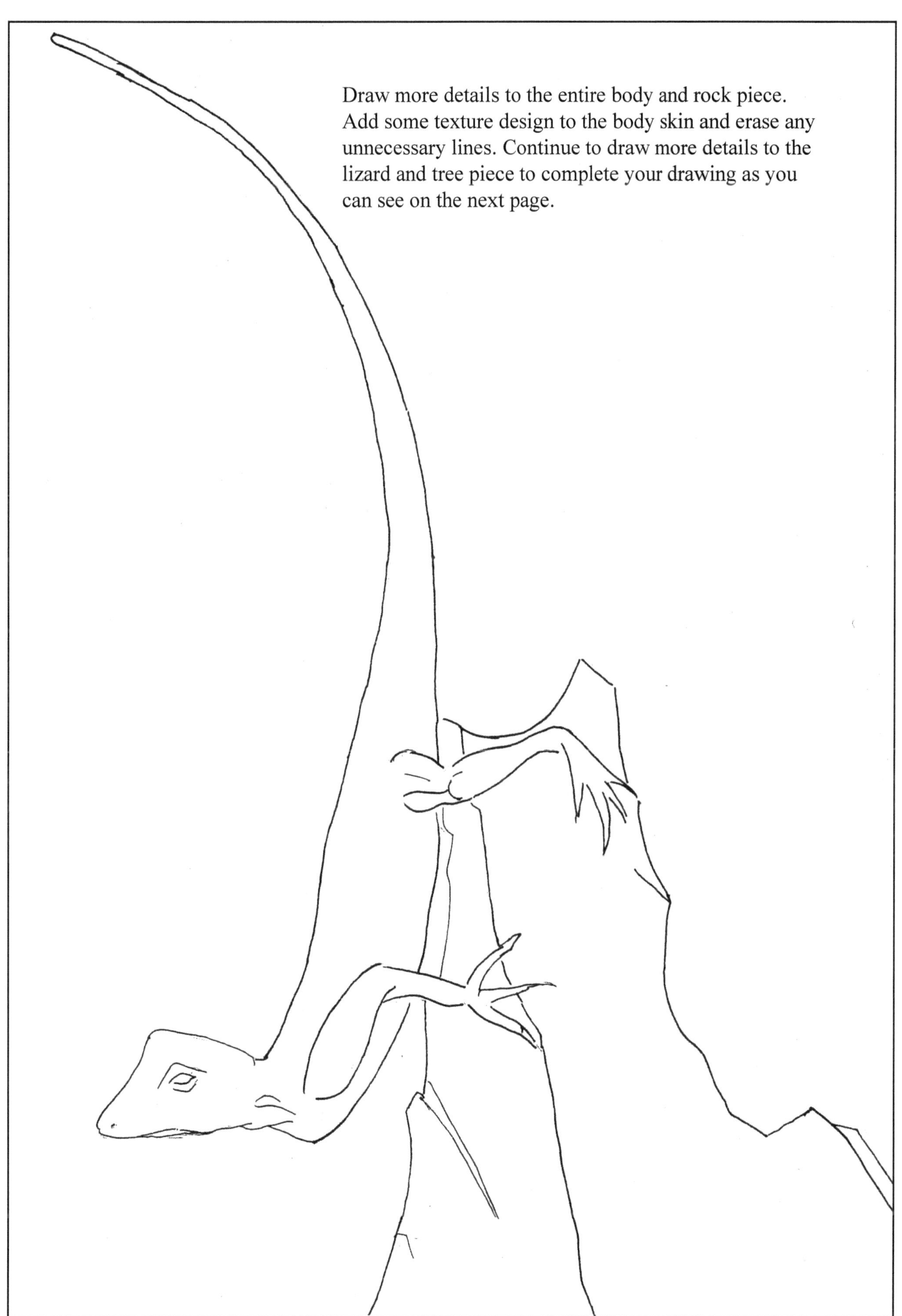
Draw more details to the entire body and rock piece.
Add some texture design to the body skin and erase any unnecessary lines. Continue to draw more details to the lizard and tree piece to complete your drawing as you can see on the next page.

INDIAN BLOODSUCKER

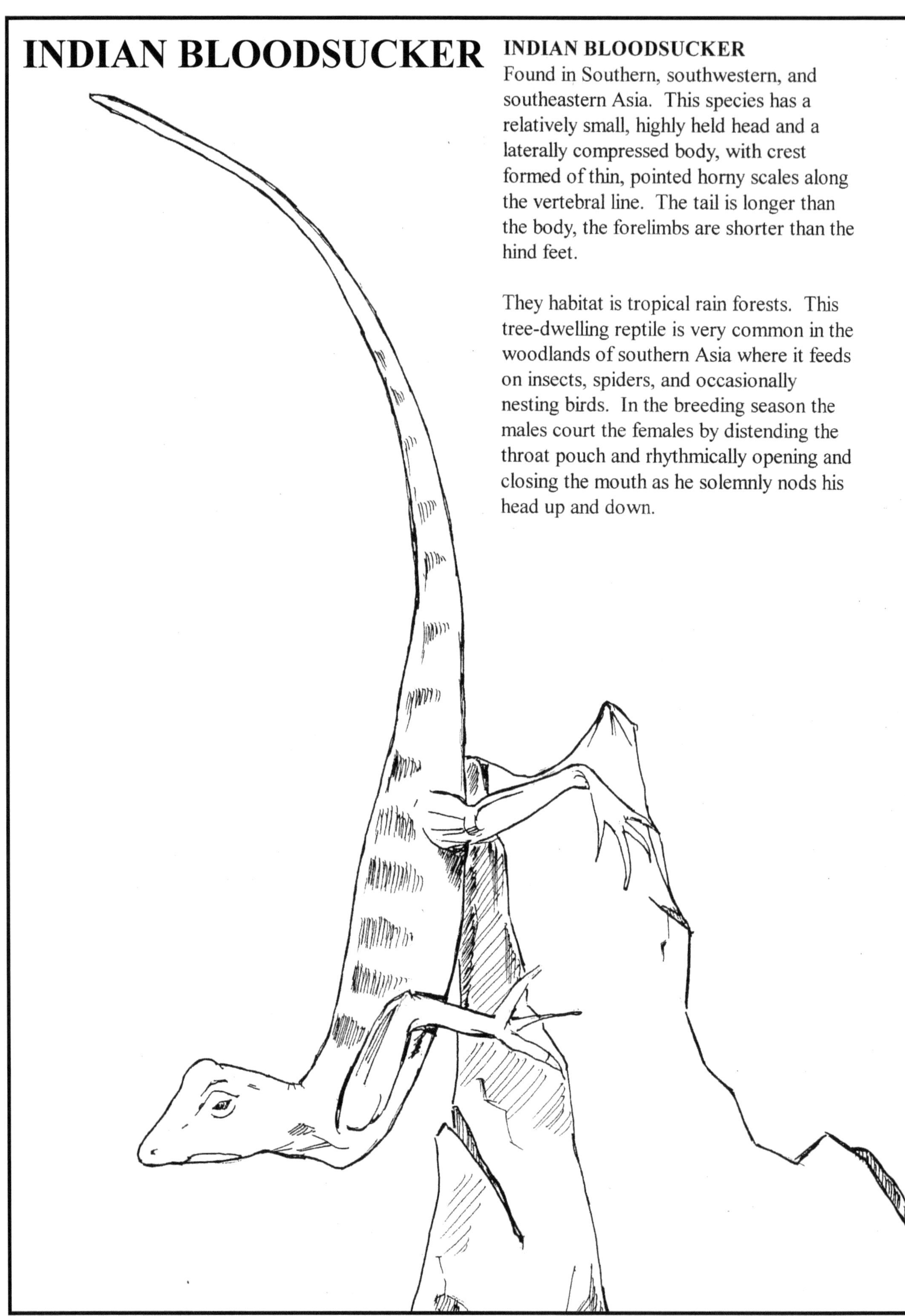

INDIAN BLOODSUCKER

Found in Southern, southwestern, and southeastern Asia. This species has a relatively small, highly held head and a laterally compressed body, with crest formed of thin, pointed horny scales along the vertebral line. The tail is longer than the body, the forelimbs are shorter than the hind feet.

They habitat is tropical rain forests. This tree-dwelling reptile is very common in the woodlands of southern Asia where it feeds on insects, spiders, and occasionally nesting birds. In the breeding season the males court the females by distending the throat pouch and rhythmically opening and closing the mouth as he solemnly nods his head up and down.

Here is a case where you again can start to draw either the shell or head of the Turtle first. Then proceed to draw the rest of the parts of the Turtle. This is your outline.

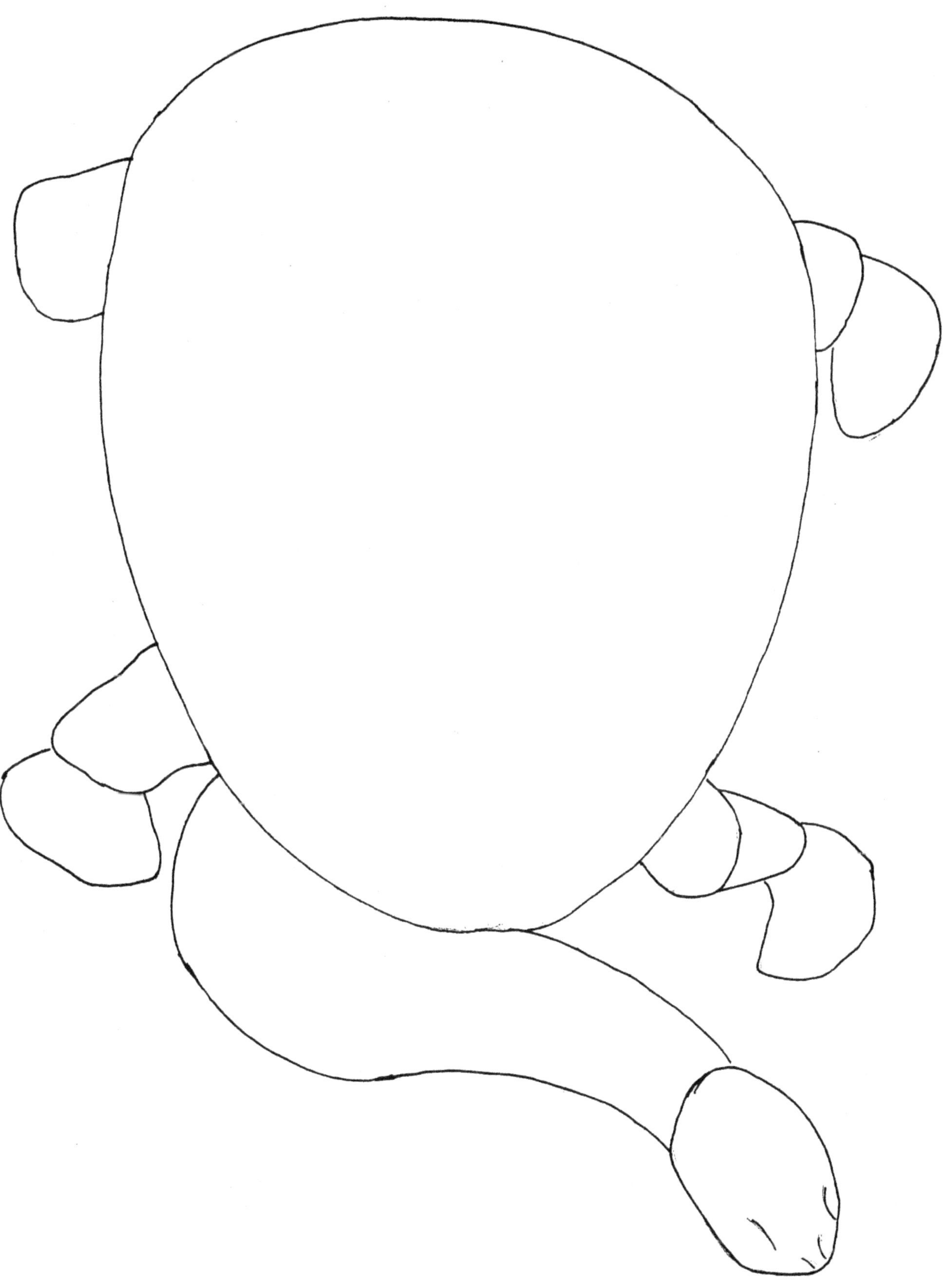

Now, you can start to draw in a few design contour lines on the shell. Then draw the neck, leg, feet and mouth to give more definition to your drawing from the outline foundation you have already built.

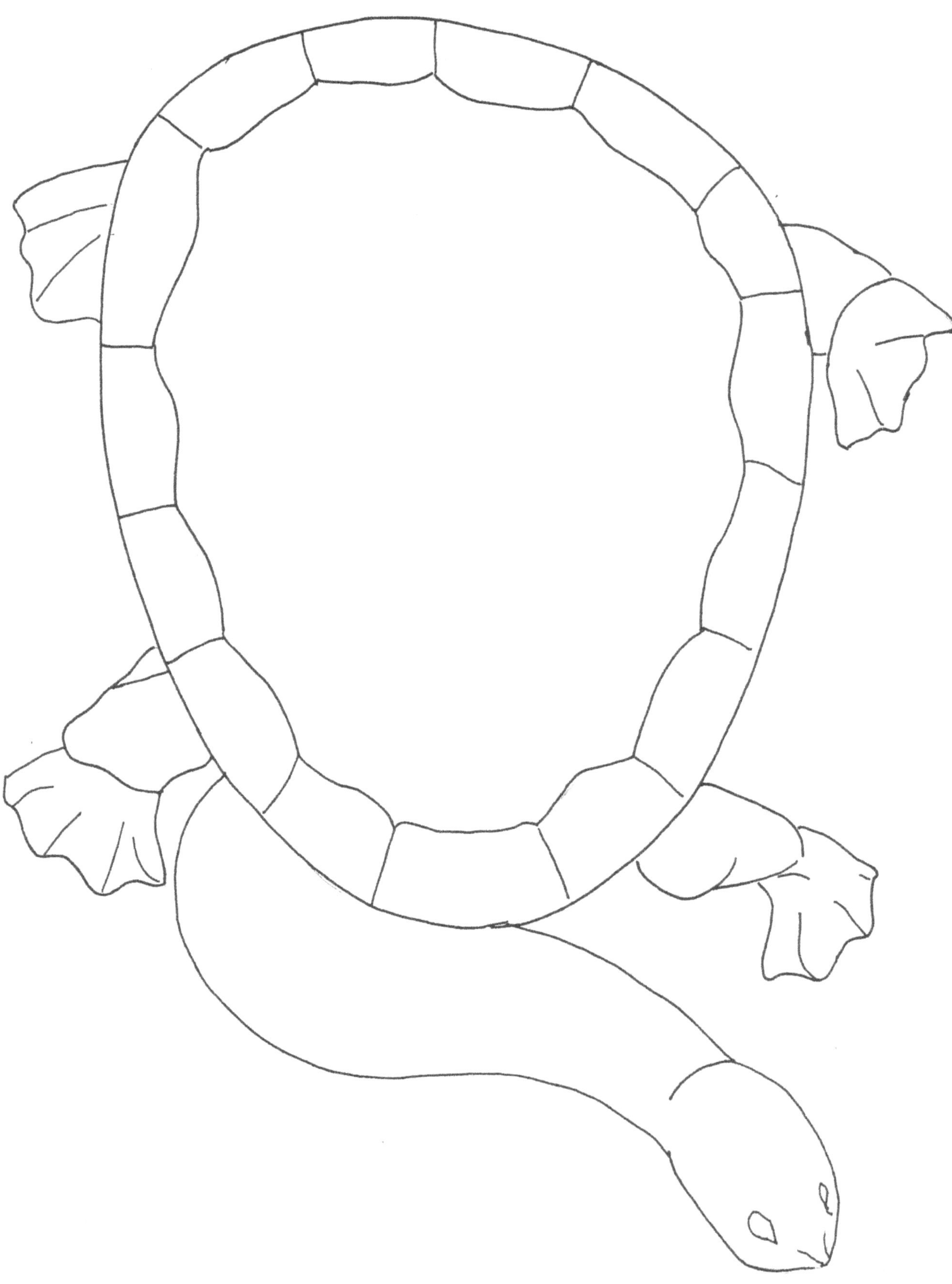

You just drew a Snakeneck Turtle. All you need to do now is to draw in some defining texture lines on the head, neck, shell, legs, and feet to complete your drawing as you will see on the next page.

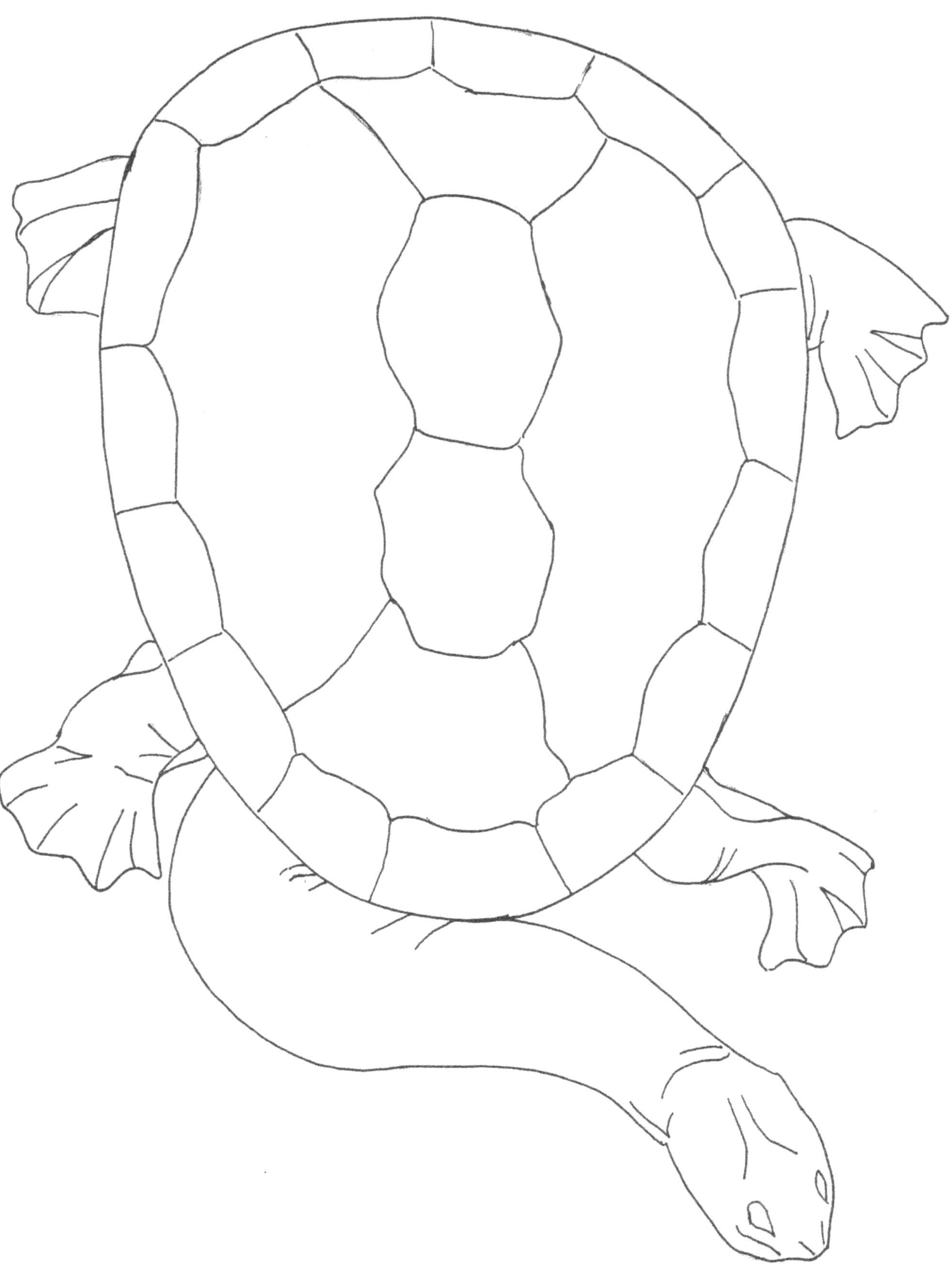

SNAKENECK TURTLE

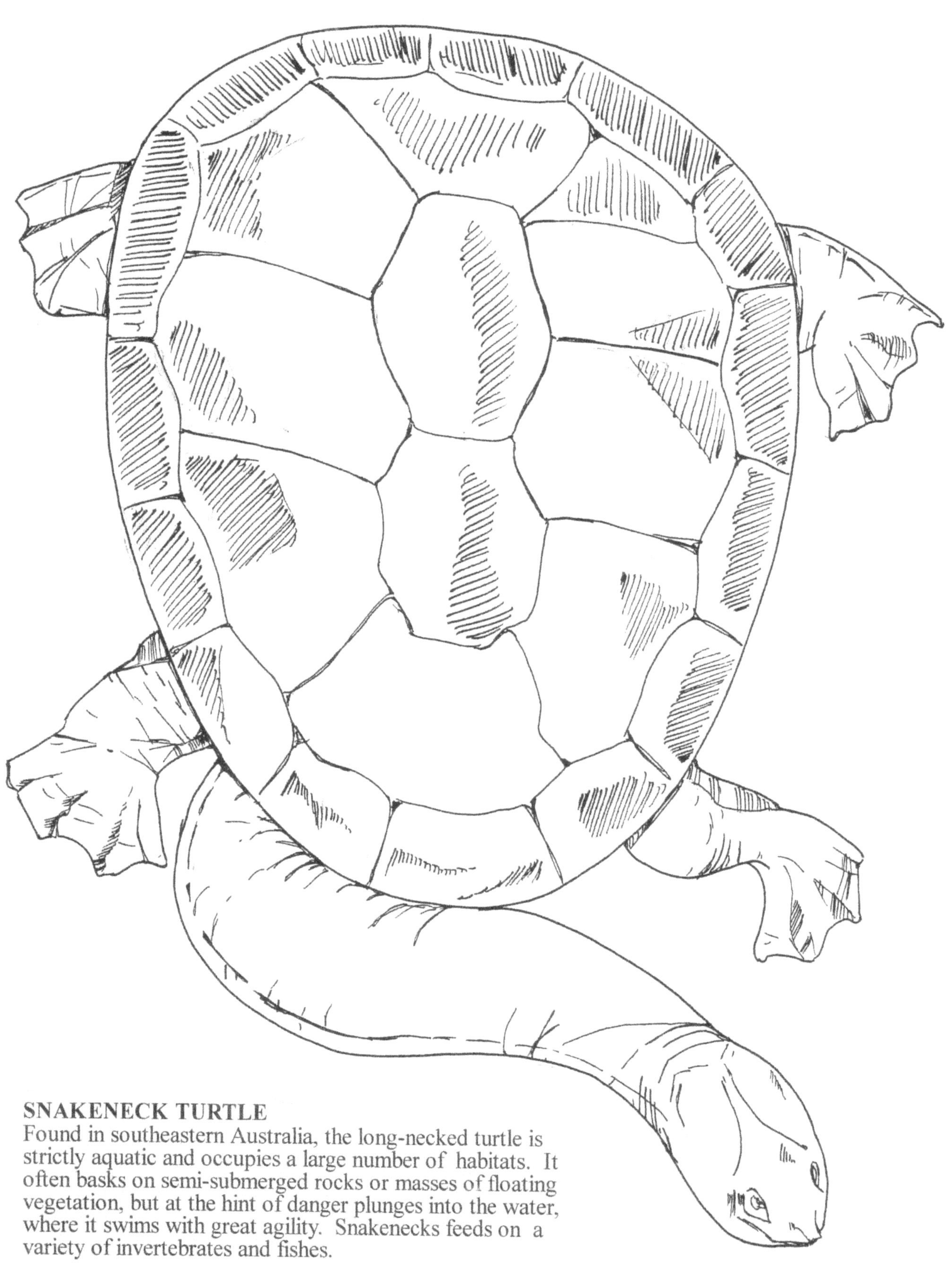

SNAKENECK TURTLE
Found in southeastern Australia, the long-necked turtle is strictly aquatic and occupies a large number of habitats. It often basks on semi-submerged rocks or masses of floating vegetation, but at the hint of danger plunges into the water, where it swims with great agility. Snakenecks feeds on a variety of invertebrates and fishes.

Let's draw the plant stem and leaf. Then proceed to draw the frog's head, body, legs, feet , then go back the head and add a circle for the eye and a line for the mouth. You have just sketch the outline construction for your drawing.

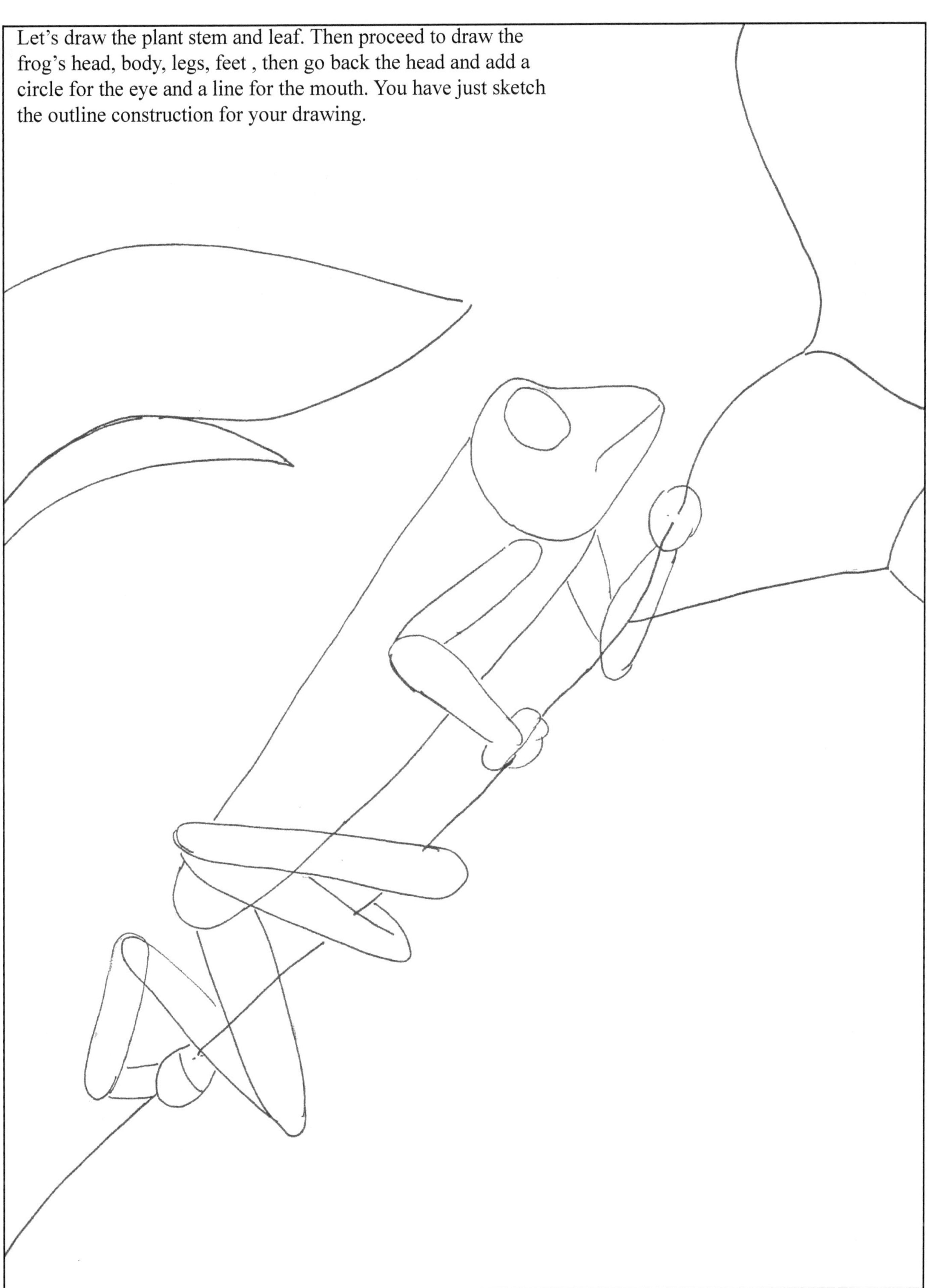

Draw in more constructive detail form to the head, body, legs, feet and plant. Then erase all lines not needed.

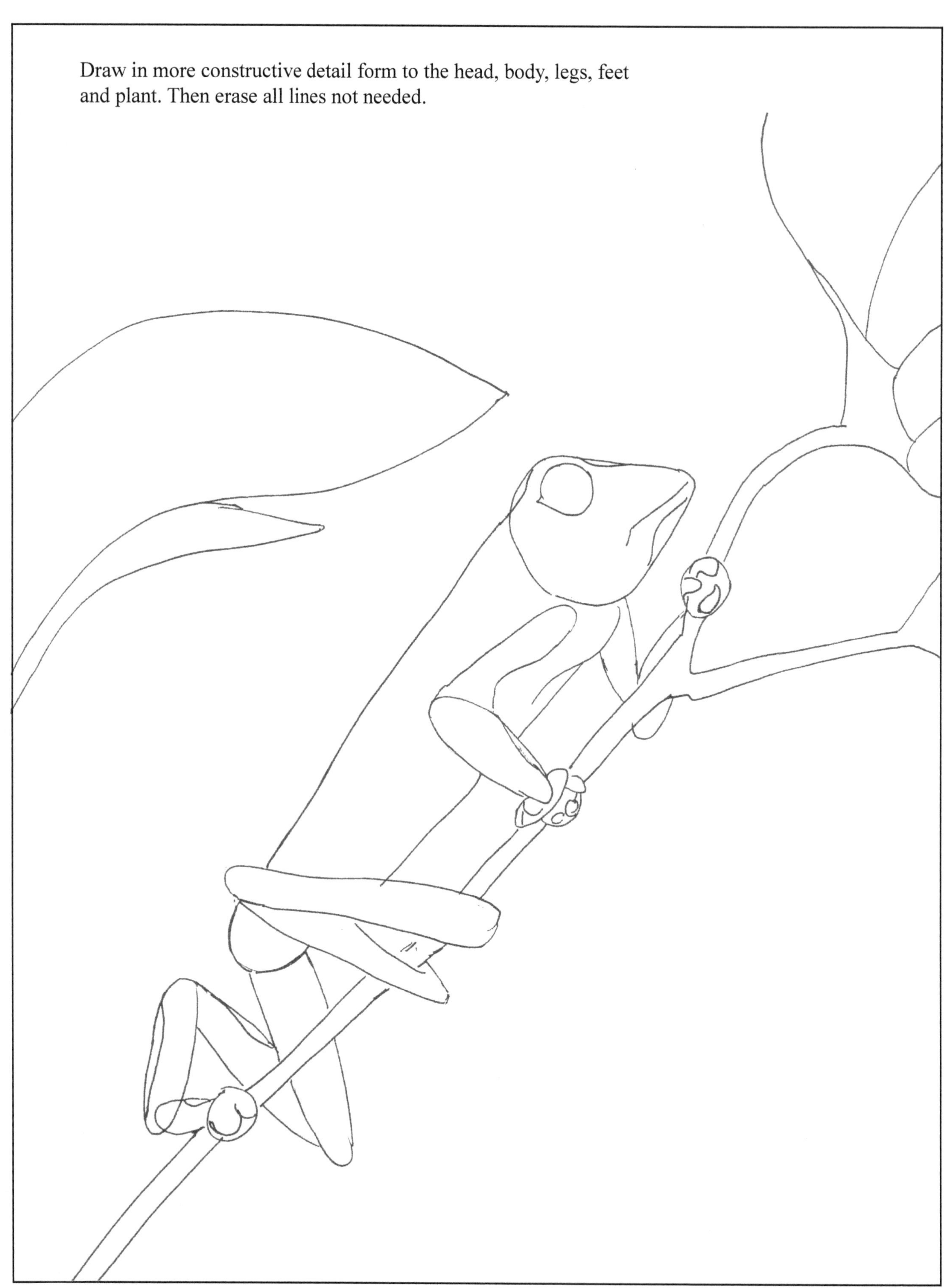

It looks like you have just drew a Leaf Frog. All you need to do now is to draw in more detail lines to create texture and depth to your drawing as you will on the next page.

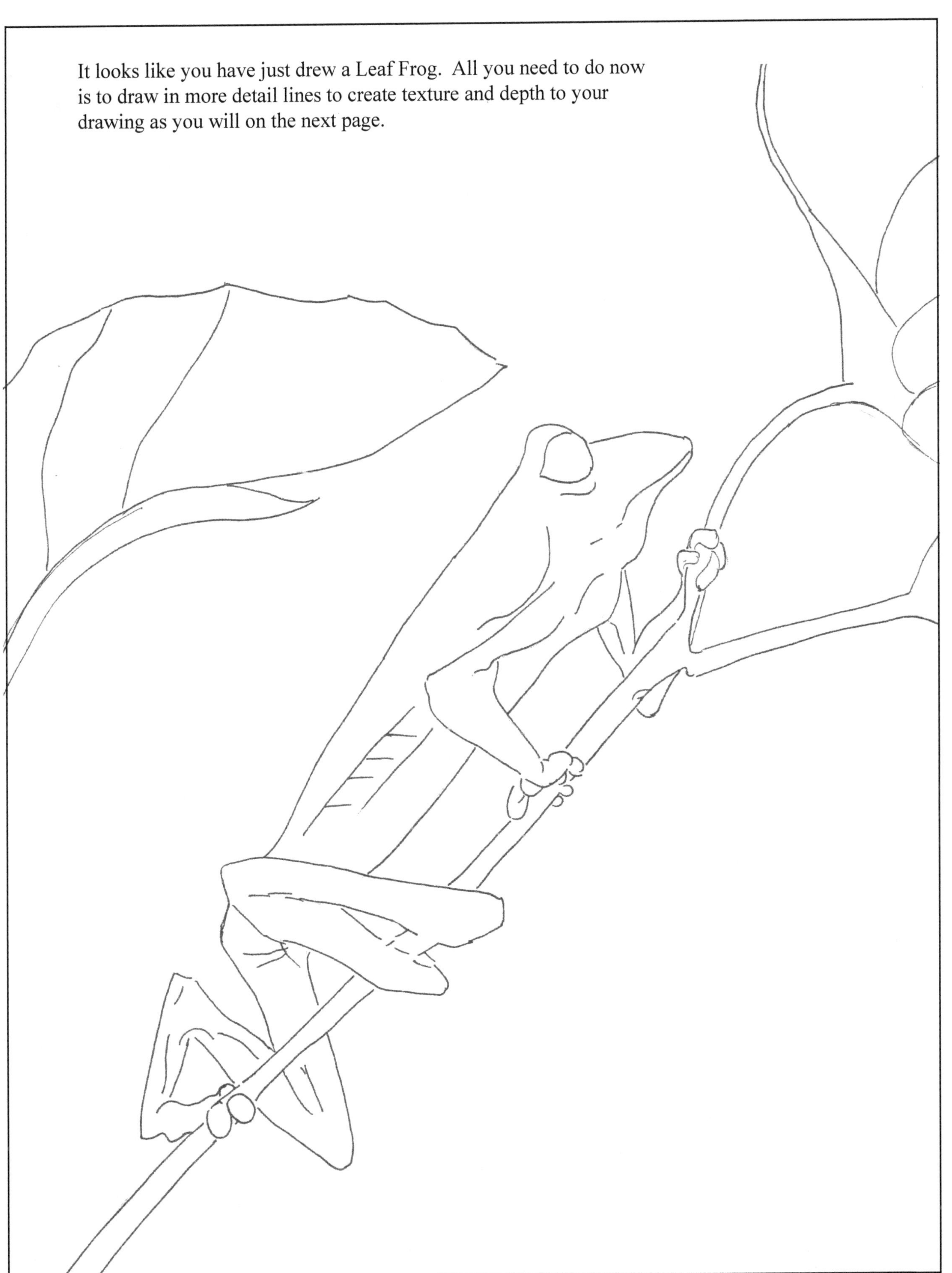

RED-EYED LEAF FROG

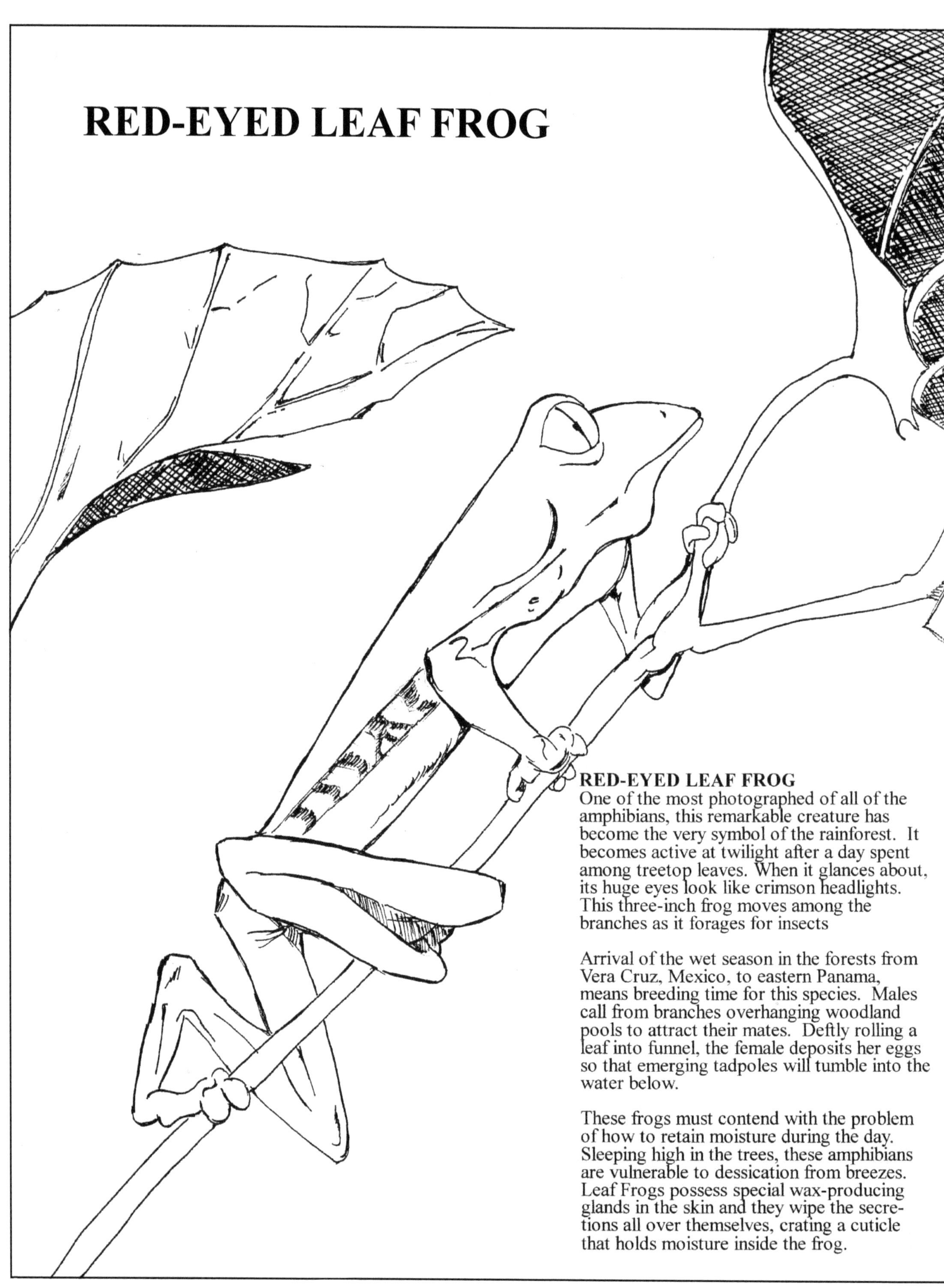

RED-EYED LEAF FROG
One of the most photographed of all of the amphibians, this remarkable creature has become the very symbol of the rainforest. It becomes active at twilight after a day spent among treetop leaves. When it glances about, its huge eyes look like crimson headlights. This three-inch frog moves among the branches as it forages for insects

Arrival of the wet season in the forests from Vera Cruz, Mexico, to eastern Panama, means breeding time for this species. Males call from branches overhanging woodland pools to attract their mates. Deftly rolling a leaf into funnel, the female deposits her eggs so that emerging tadpoles will tumble into the water below.

These frogs must contend with the problem of how to retain moisture during the day. Sleeping high in the trees, these amphibians are vulnerable to dessication from breezes. Leaf Frogs possess special wax-producing glands in the skin and they wipe the secretions all over themselves, crating a cuticle that holds moisture inside the frog.

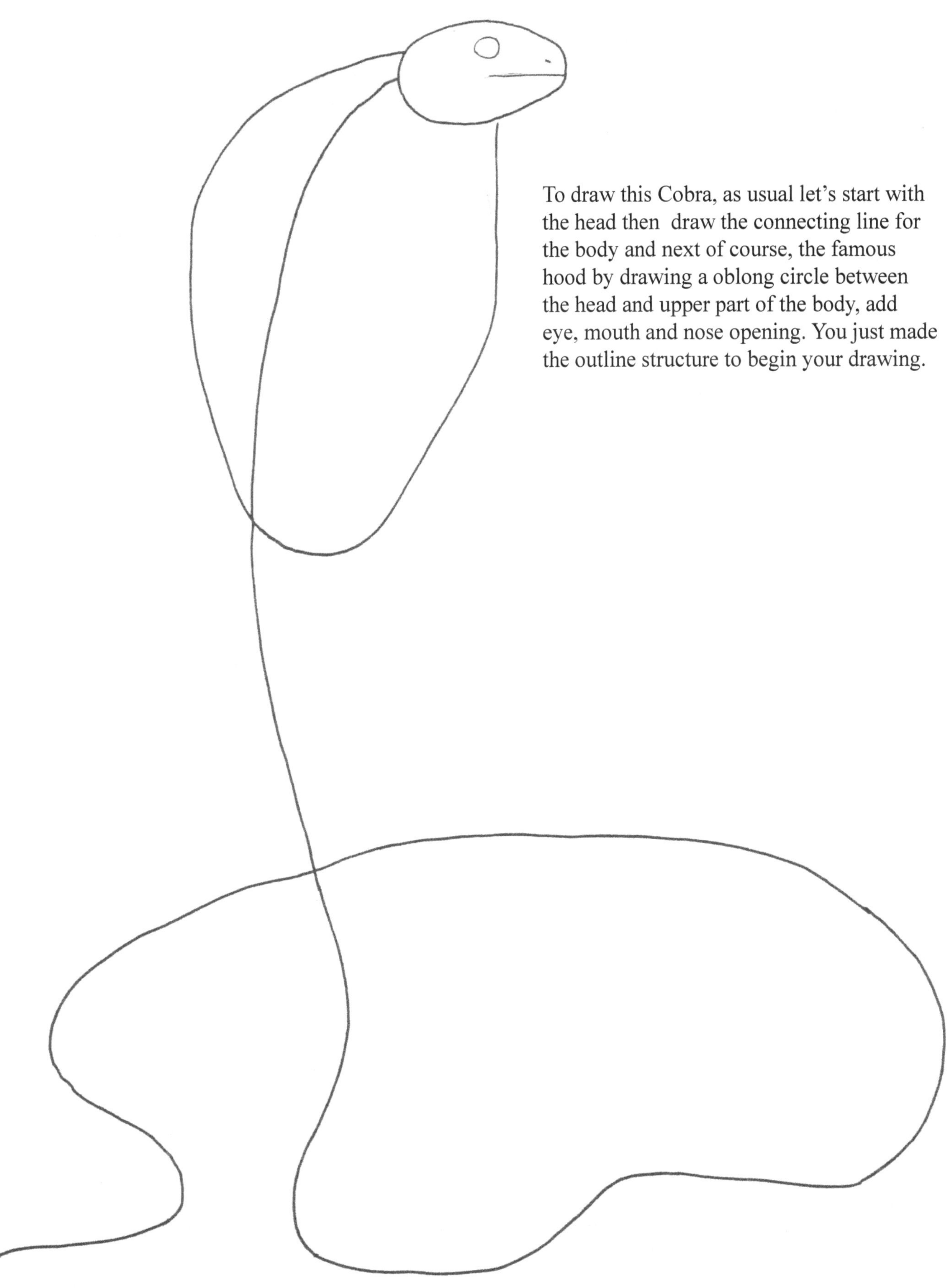

To draw this Cobra, as usual let's start with the head then draw the connecting line for the body and next of course, the famous hood by drawing a oblong circle between the head and upper part of the body, add eye, mouth and nose opening. You just made the outline structure to begin your drawing.

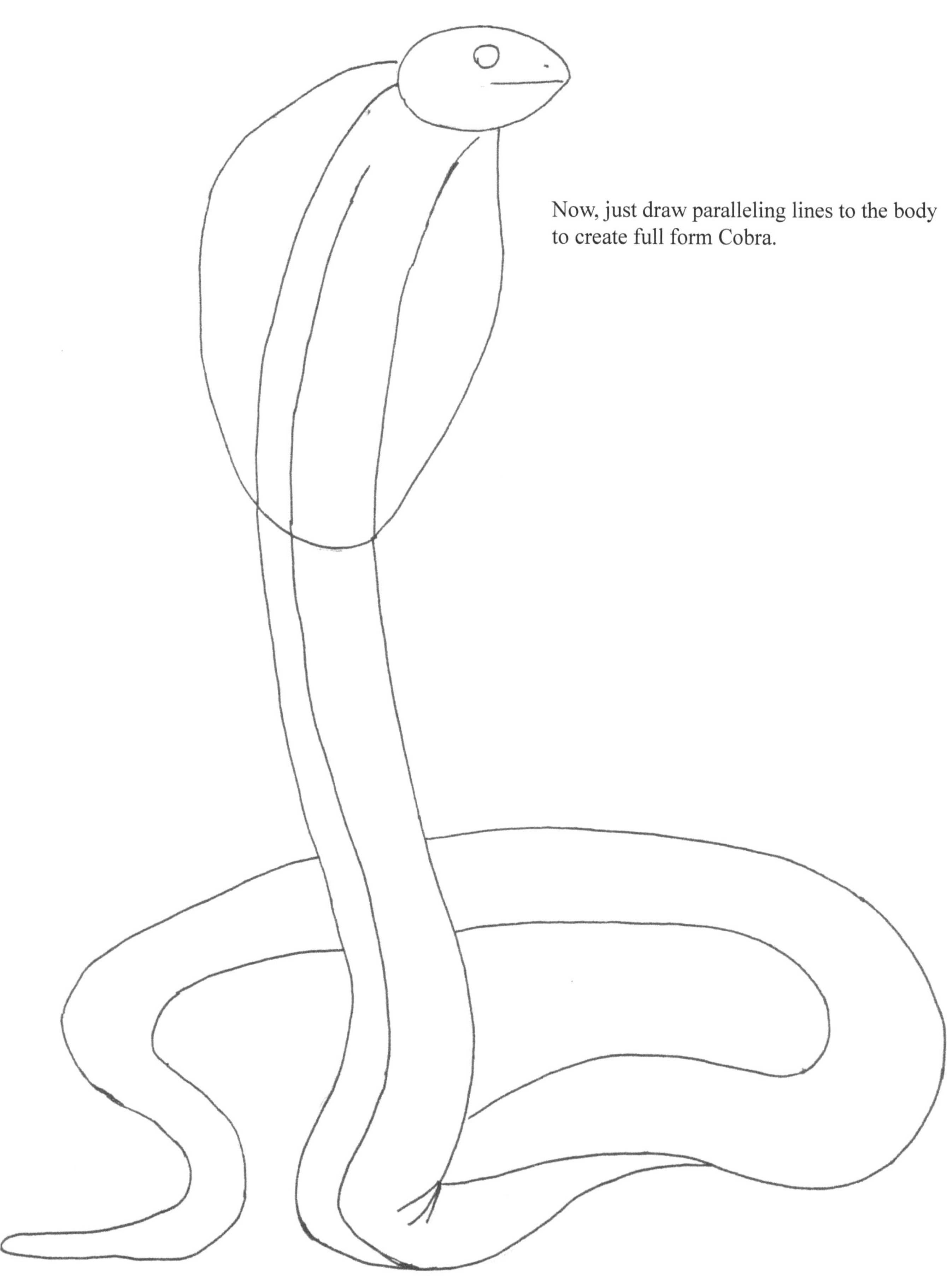

Now, just draw paralleling lines to the body to create full form Cobra.

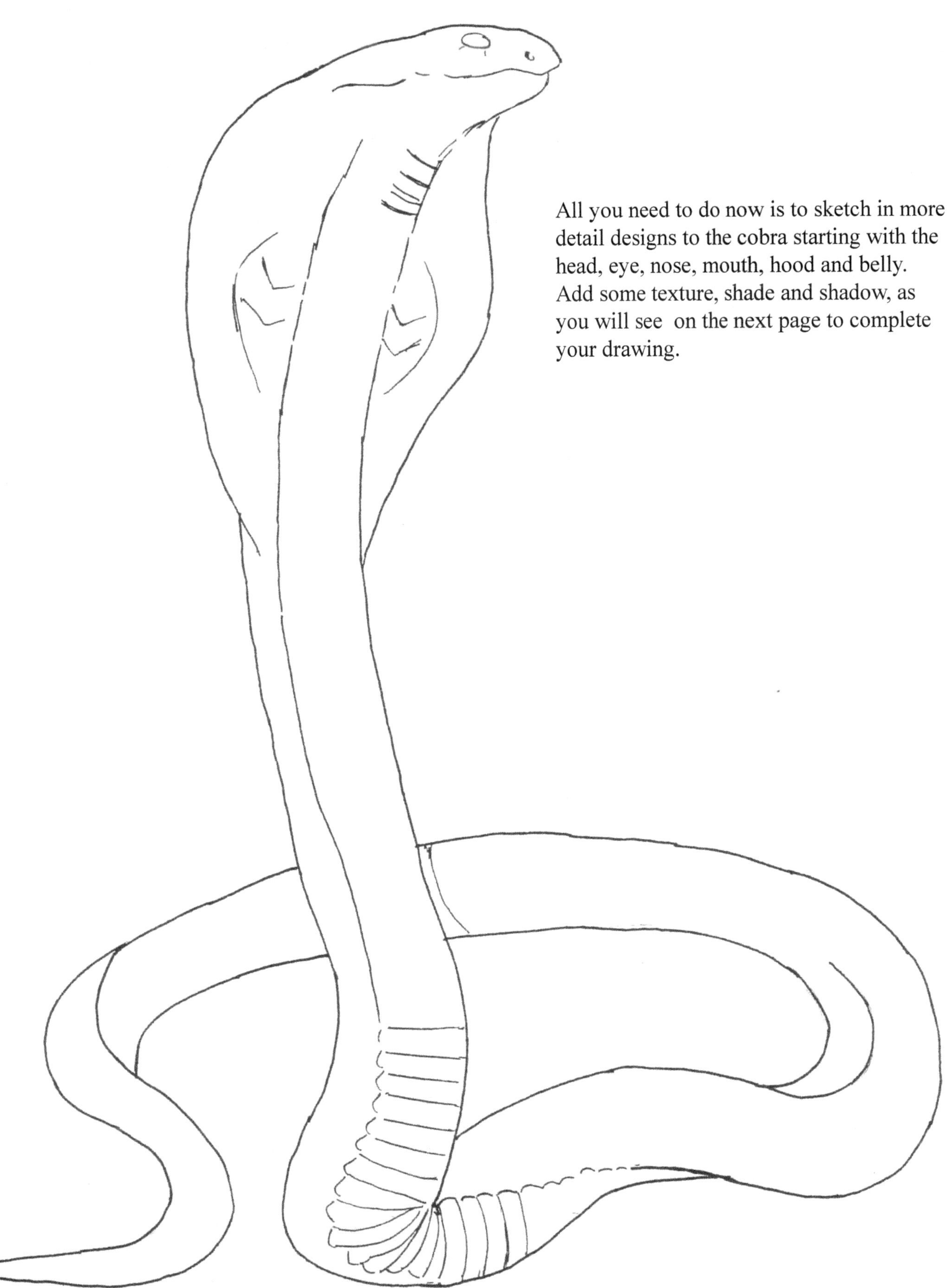

All you need to do now is to sketch in more detail designs to the cobra starting with the head, eye, nose, mouth, hood and belly. Add some texture, shade and shadow, as you will see on the next page to complete your drawing.

COMMONS COBRA

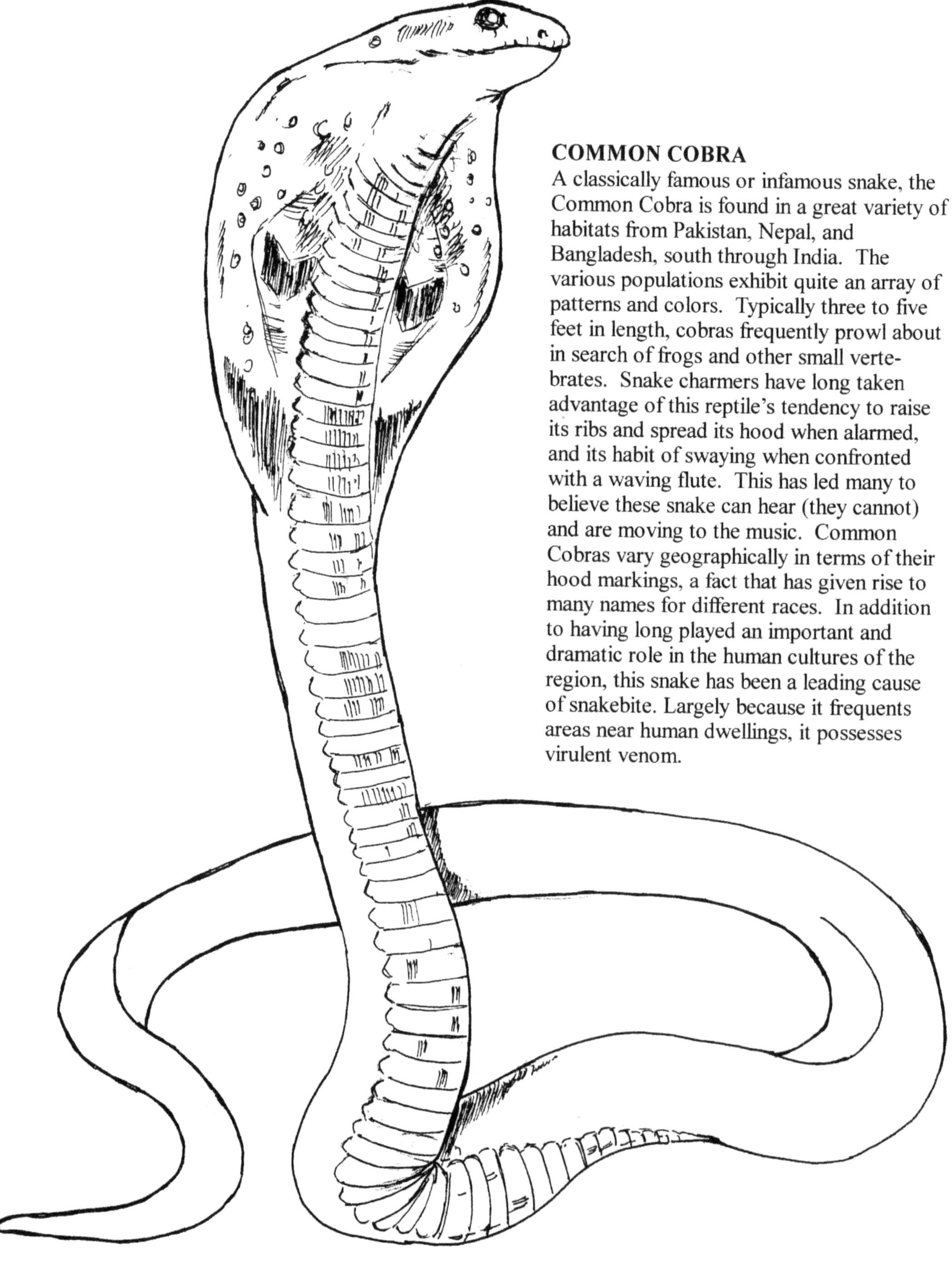

COMMON COBRA

A classically famous or infamous snake, the Common Cobra is found in a great variety of habitats from Pakistan, Nepal, and Bangladesh, south through India. The various populations exhibit quite an array of patterns and colors. Typically three to five feet in length, cobras frequently prowl about in search of frogs and other small vertebrates. Snake charmers have long taken advantage of this reptile's tendency to raise its ribs and spread its hood when alarmed, and its habit of swaying when confronted with a waving flute. This has led many to believe these snake can hear (they cannot) and are moving to the music. Common Cobras vary geographically in terms of their hood markings, a fact that has given rise to many names for different races. In addition to having long played an important and dramatic role in the human cultures of the region, this snake has been a leading cause of snakebite. Largely because it frequents areas near human dwellings, it possesses virulent venom.

Just to see have much you have learned so far, starting with this page over the next 38 pages, I want you to construct your drawing totally on your own. You do not have to always start a drawing with head. You will have the liberties to start your drawings base on what you have learned from my book. Have fun!

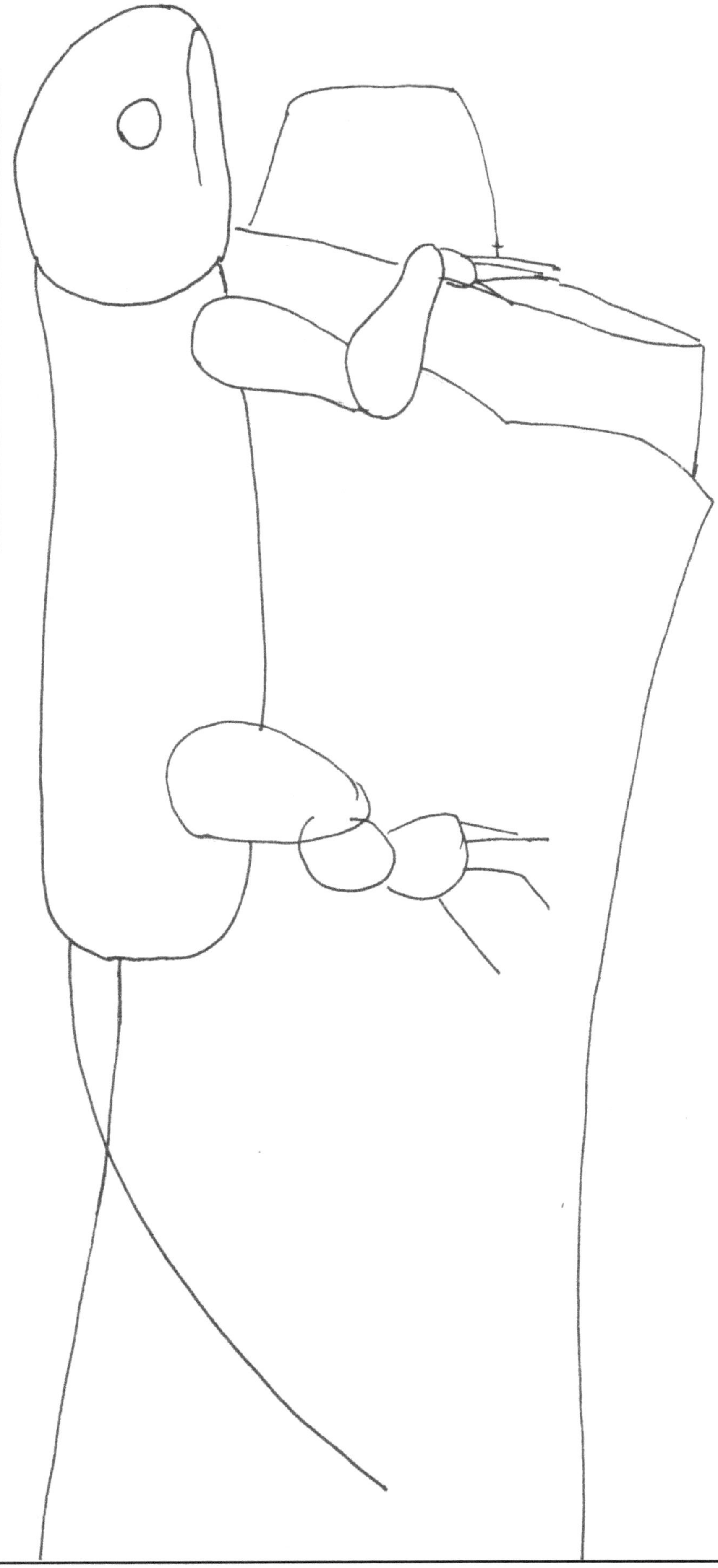

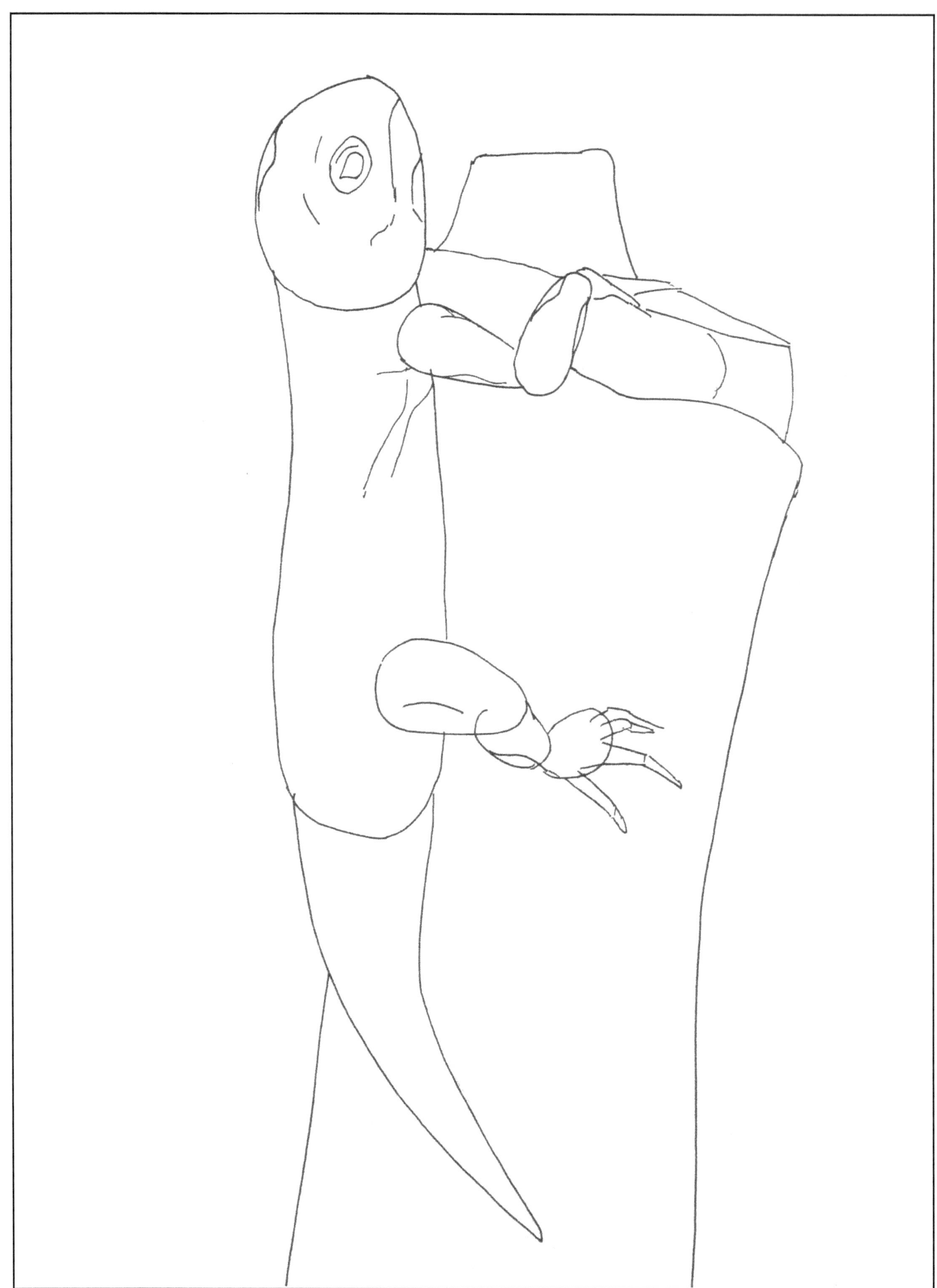

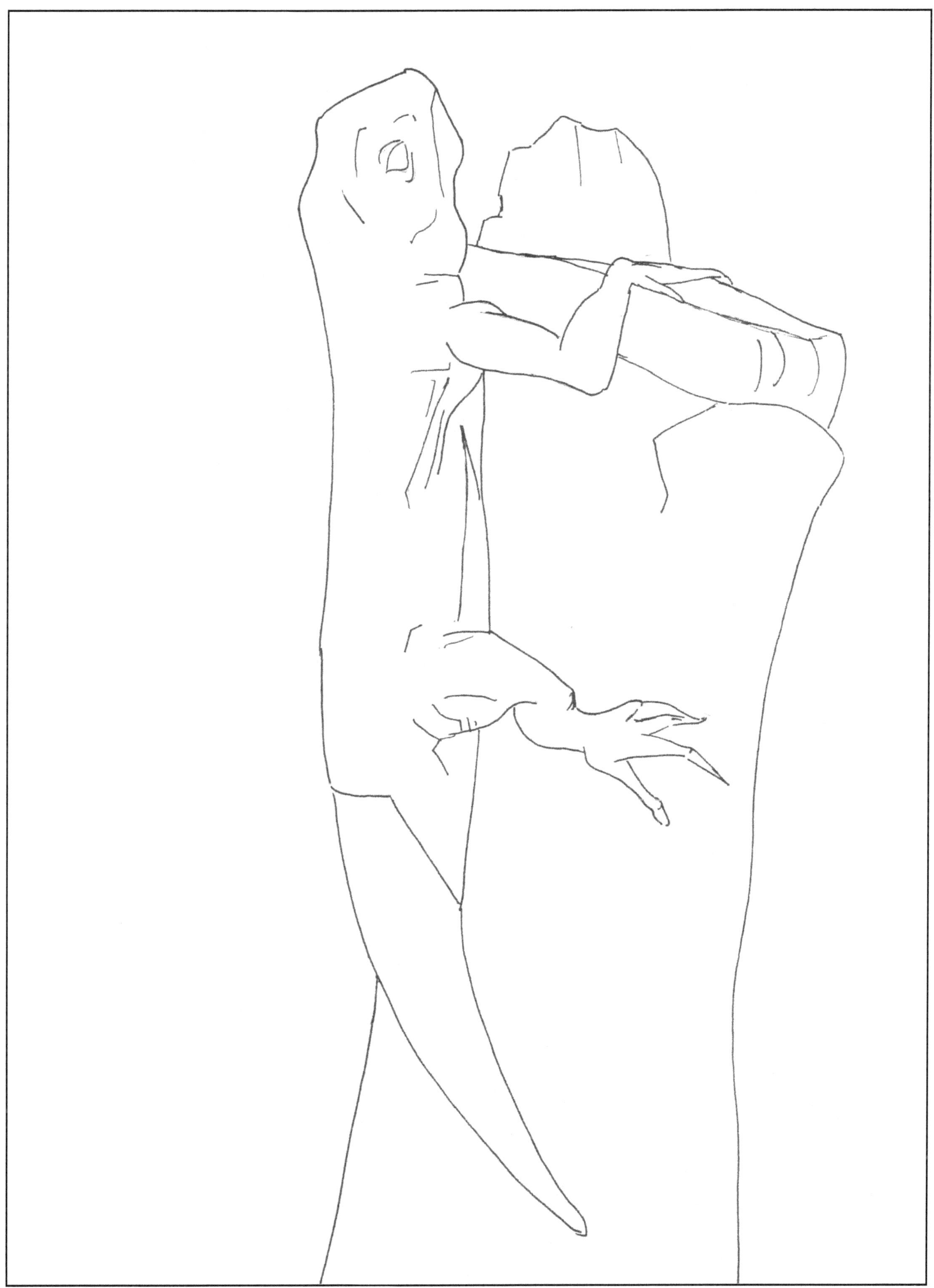

WESTERN GREEN THORNYTAIL

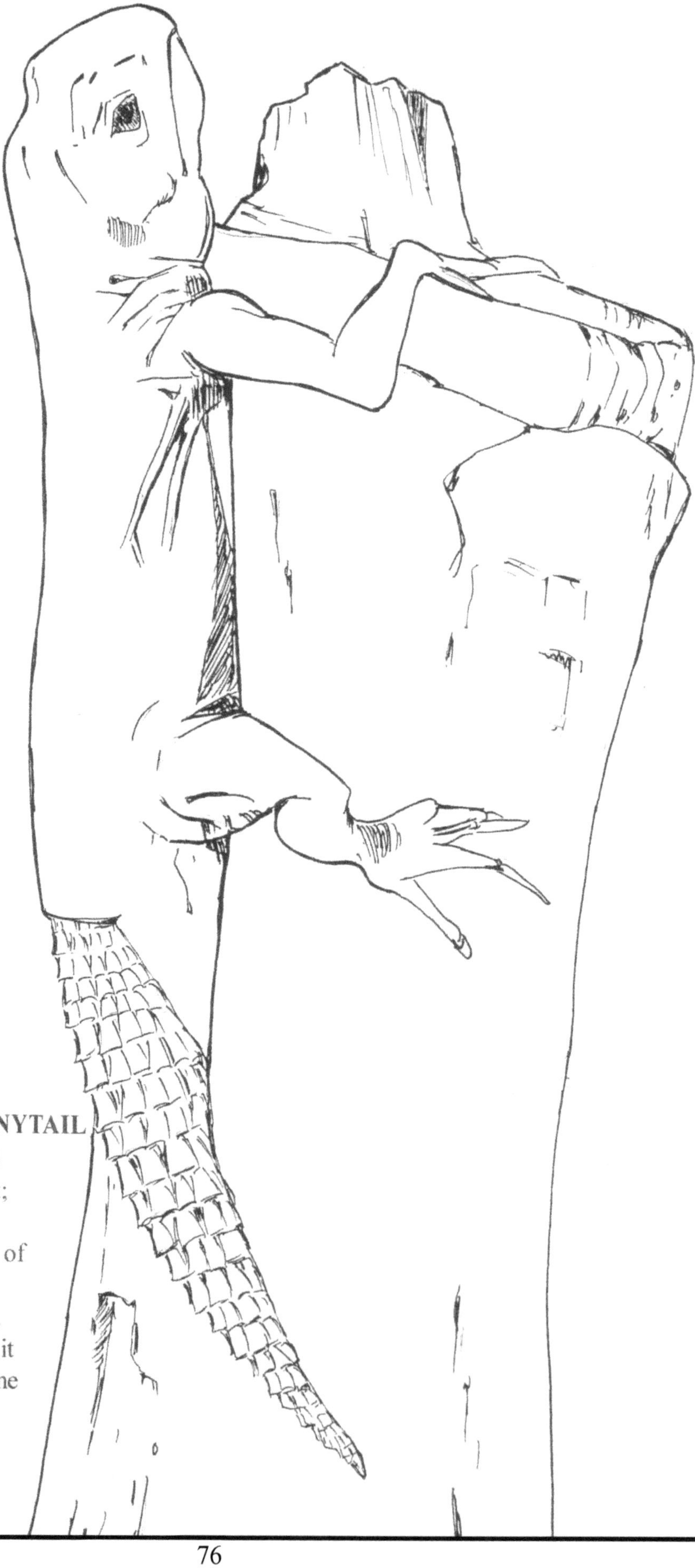

WESTERN GREEN THORNYTAIL
Humans, seldom see this lizard because of their treetop habitat; the Western Green Thornytail occupies a fairly remote sector of the Amazon Basin, in eastern Colombia, southern Venezuela, and adjacent Brazil. Although it is harmless, it is revered by some groups and feared by others as venomous.

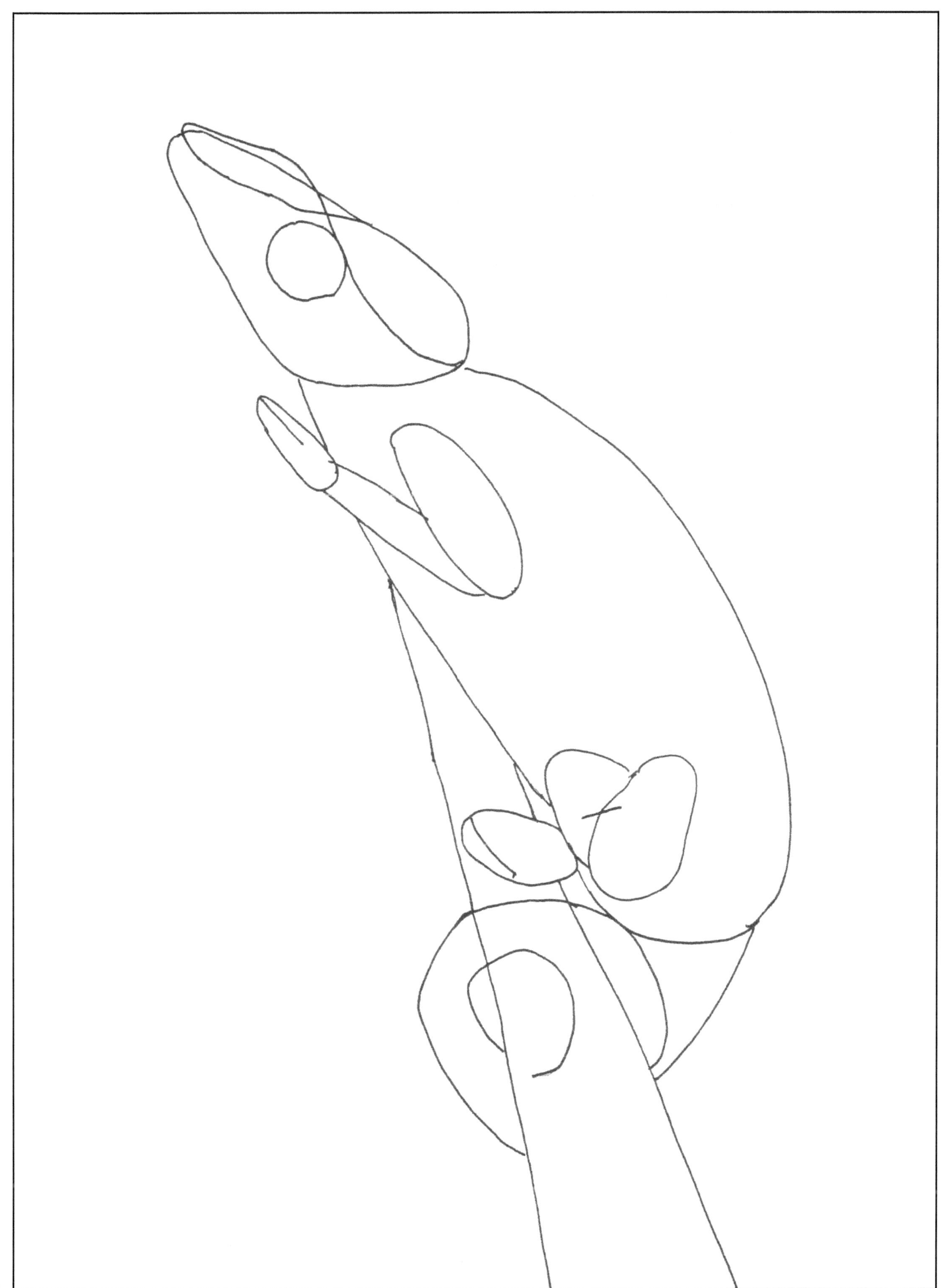

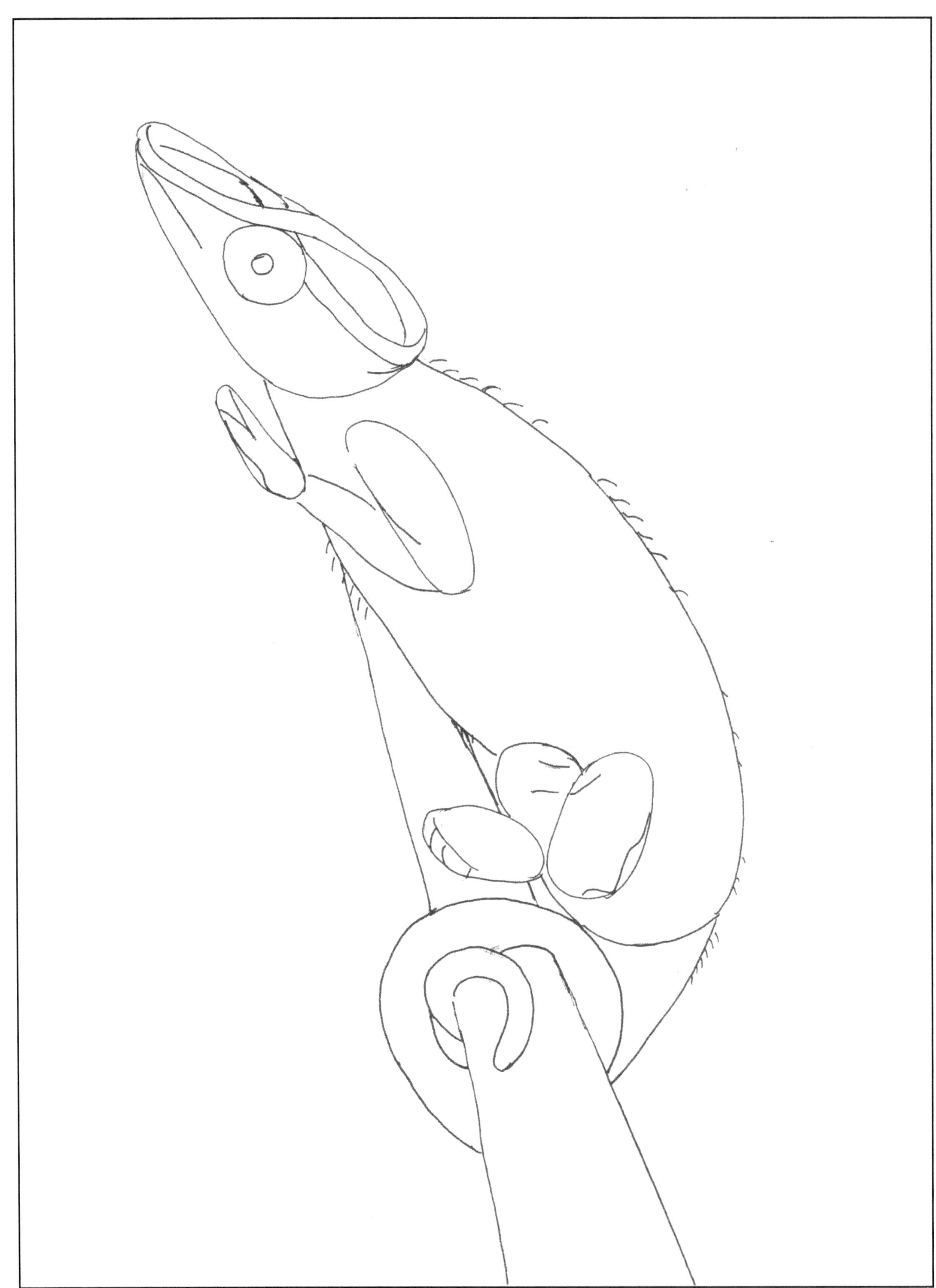

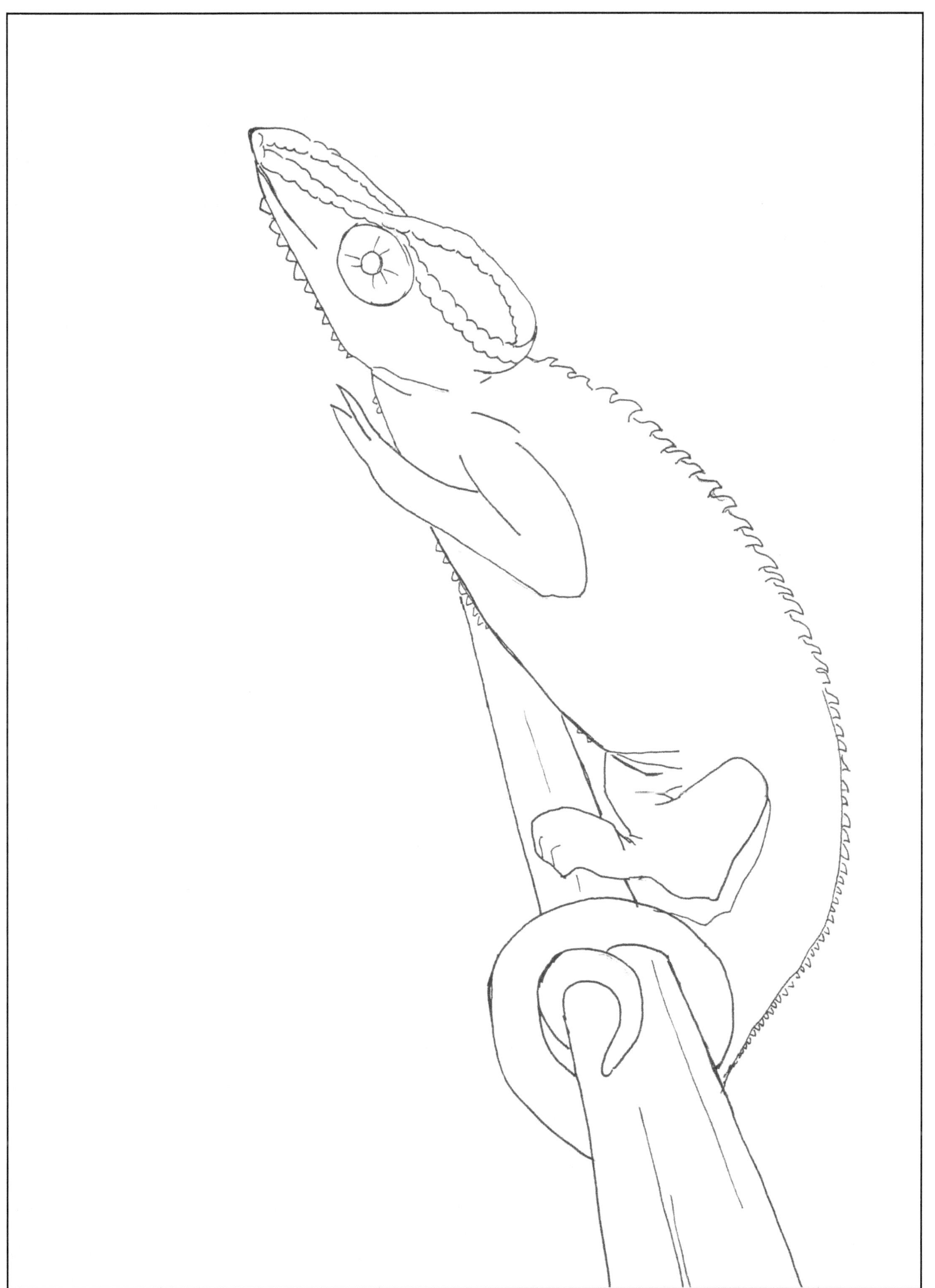

PANTHER CHAMELEON

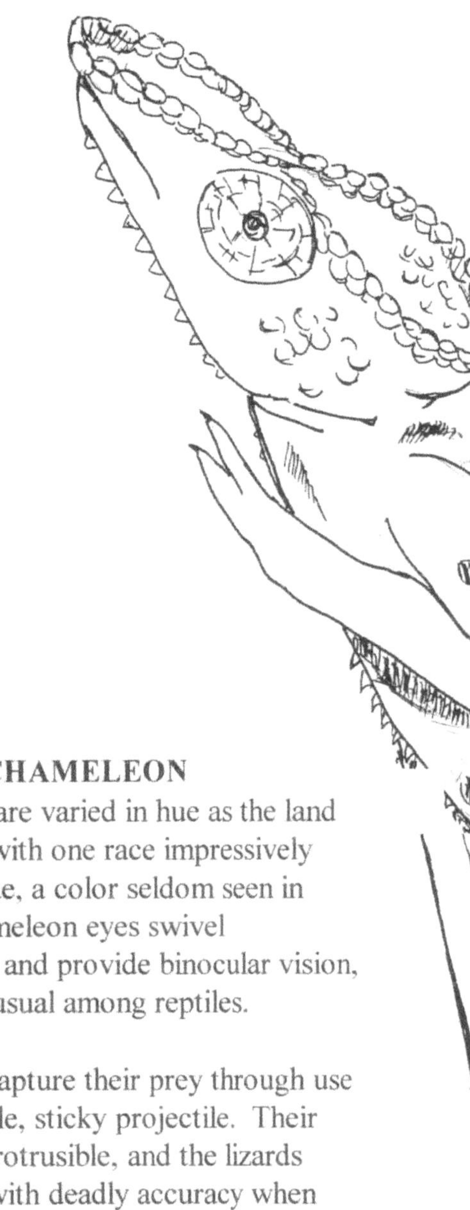

PANTHER CHAMELEON

These lizards are varied in hue as the land they occupy, with one race impressively adorned in blue, a color seldom seen in reptiles. Chameleon eyes swivel independently and provide binocular vision, something unusual among reptiles.

Chameleons capture their prey through use of a remarkable, sticky projectile. Their tongues are protrusible, and the lizards extend them with deadly accuracy when hunting for food. Swiveling both eyes in a forward direction, the chameleon can achieve nearly binocular vision, and much like someone aiming a weapon, direct its tongue at an unsuspecting insect. Upon impact, the hapless prey is drawn into the lizard's mouth.

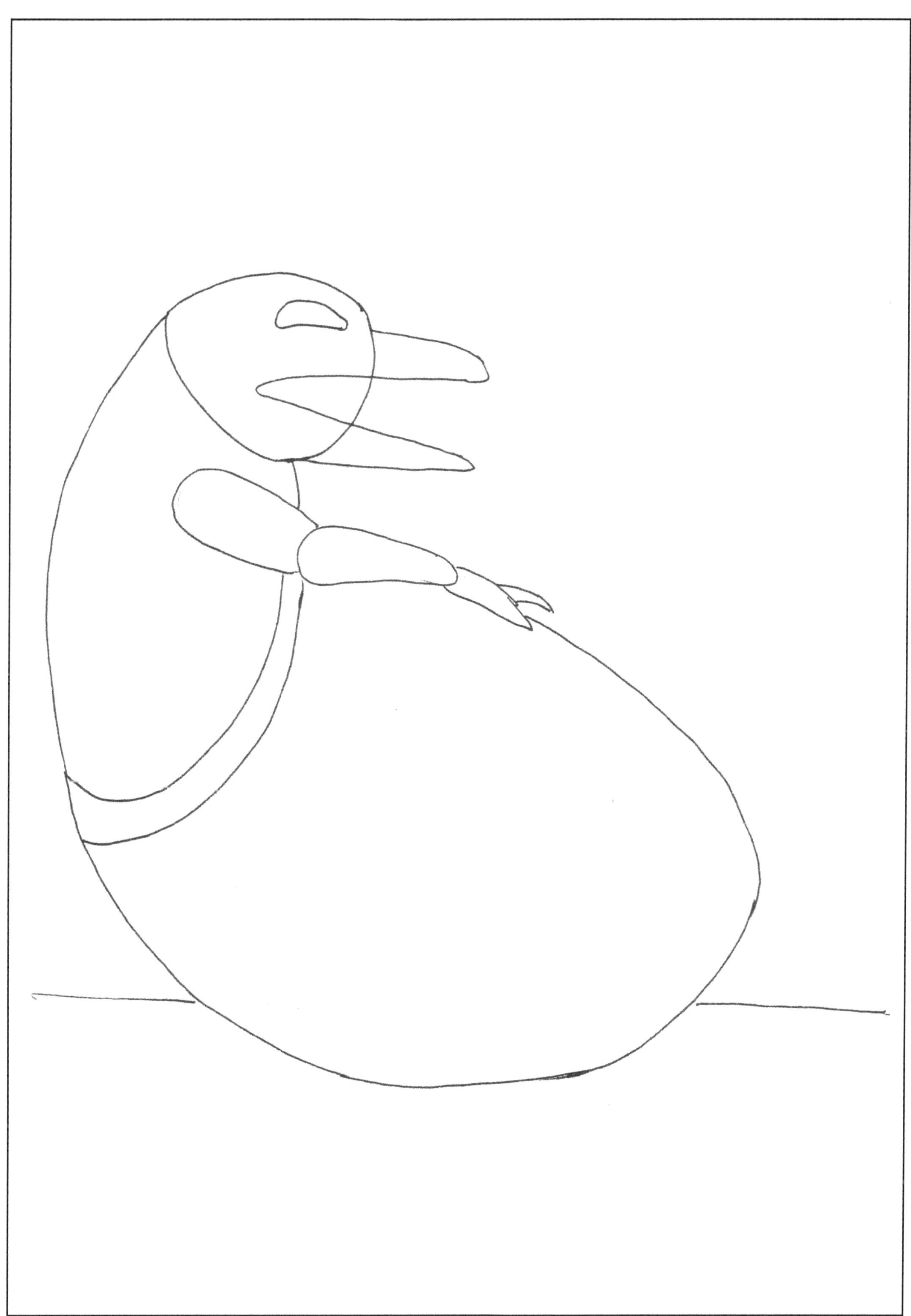

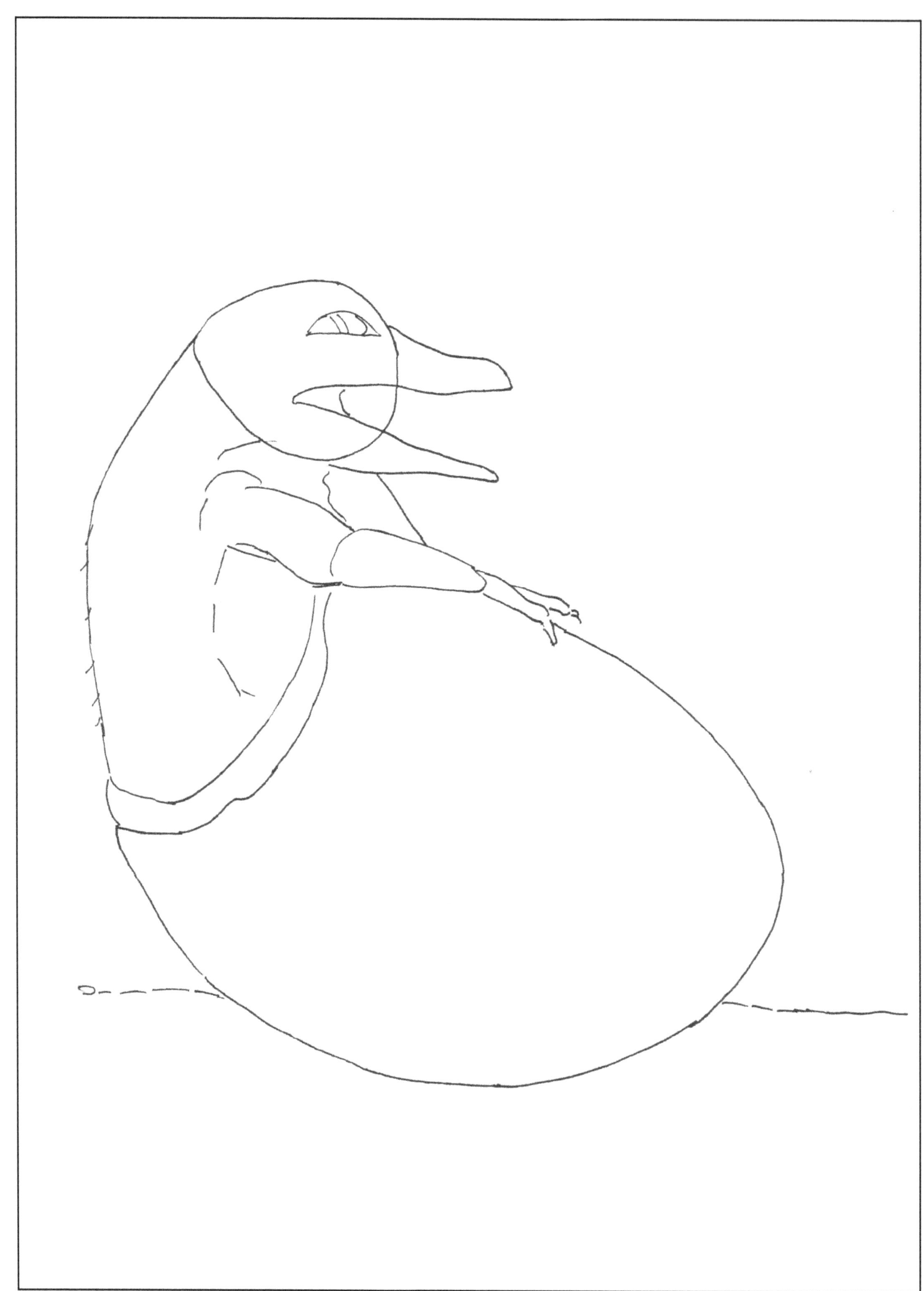

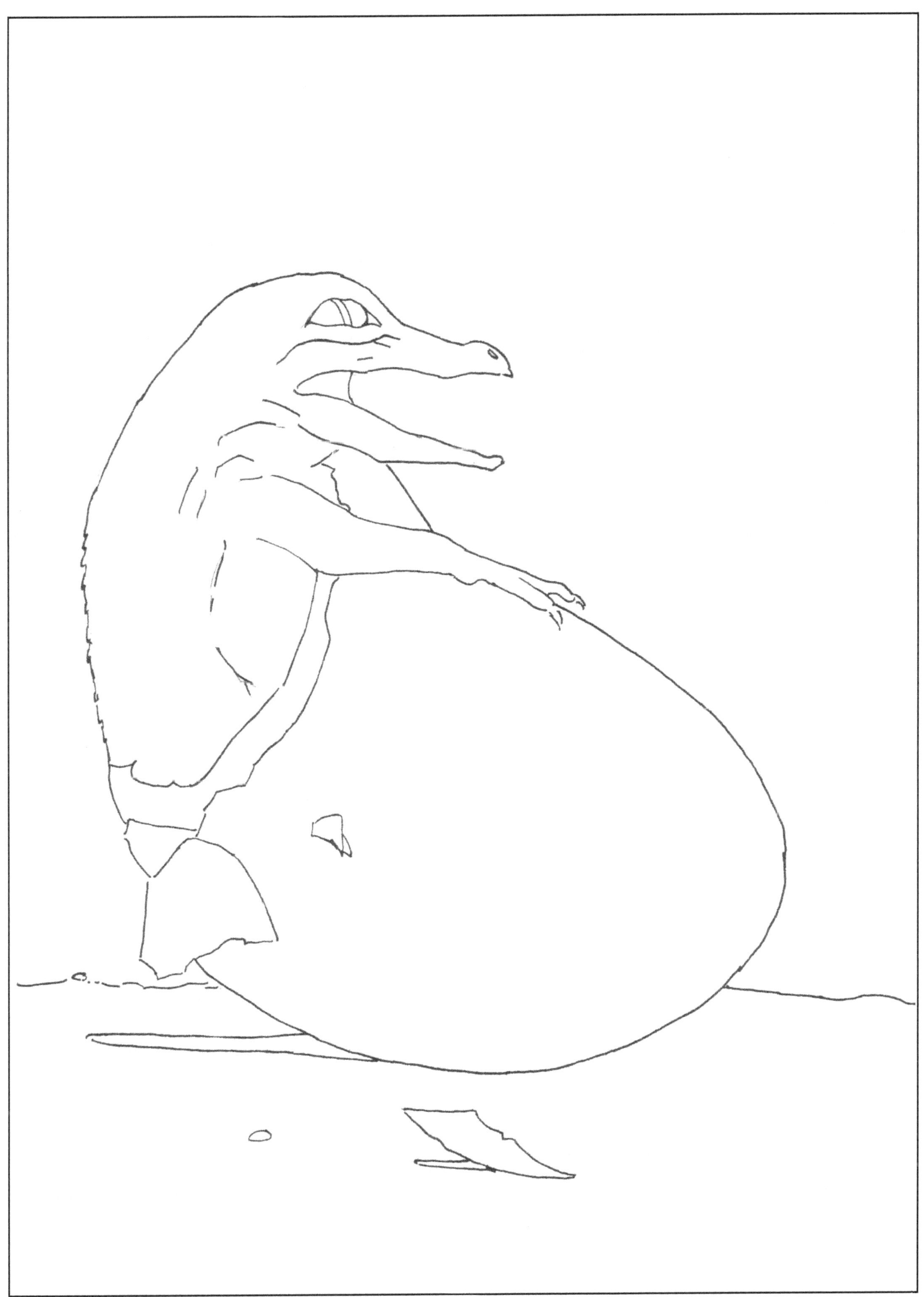

BABY ALLIGATOR

BABY ALLIGATOR

Young alligators eat insects, frogs, and small fish. The female lays her 20 to 60 eggs in an enormous mound nest of mud, near the water's edge. After the eggs hatch the mother may stay with her young for one to three years.

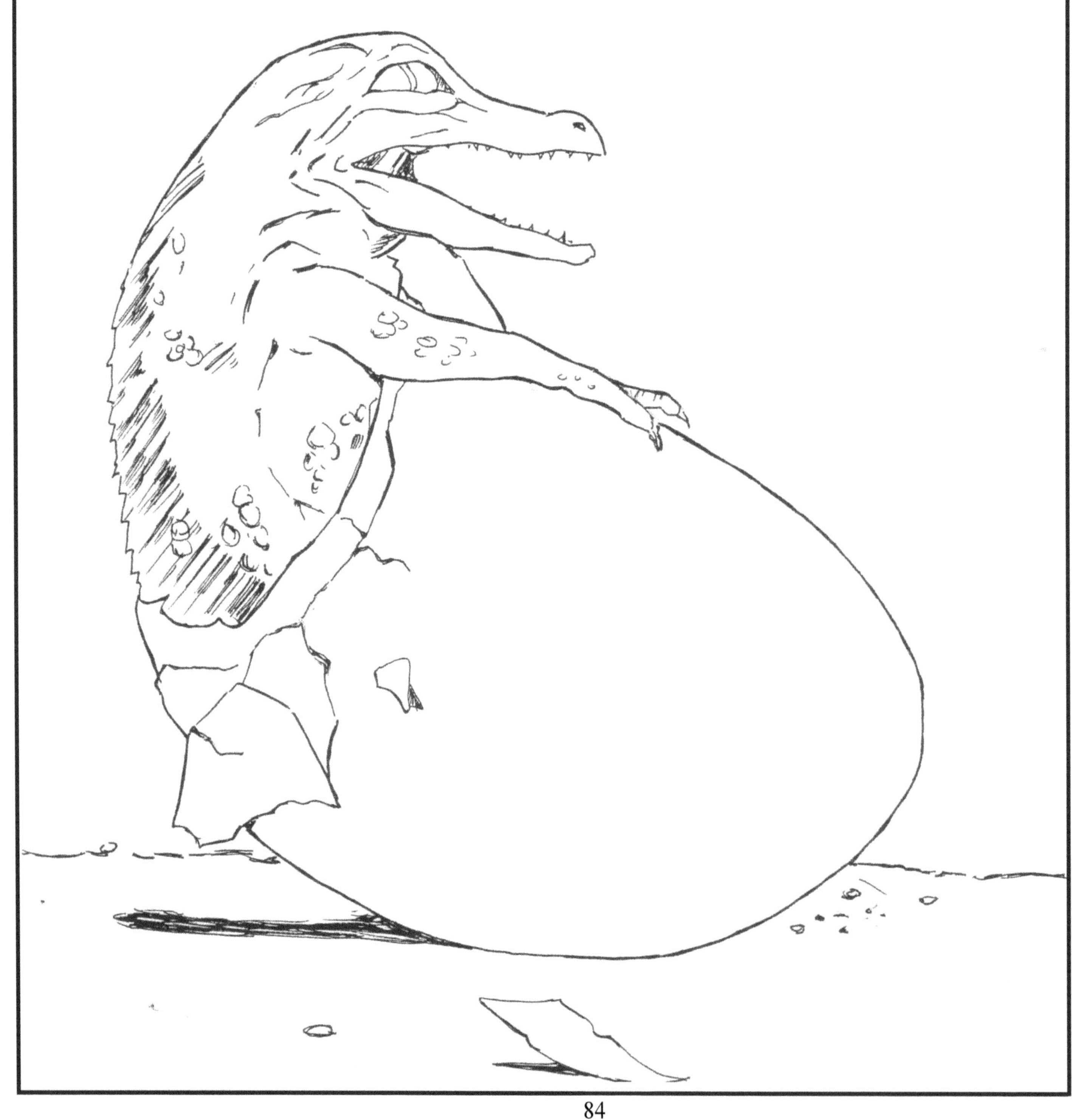

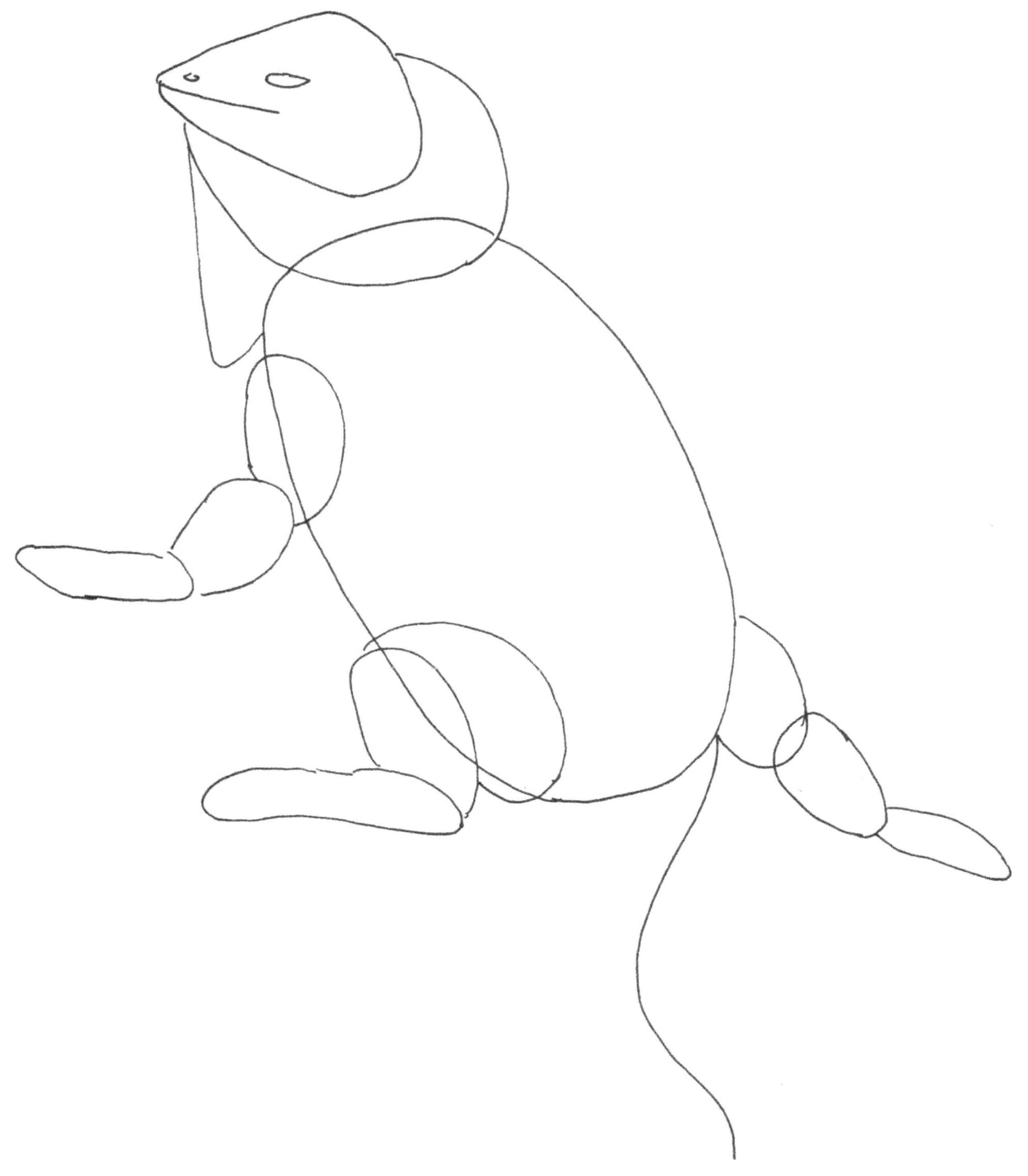

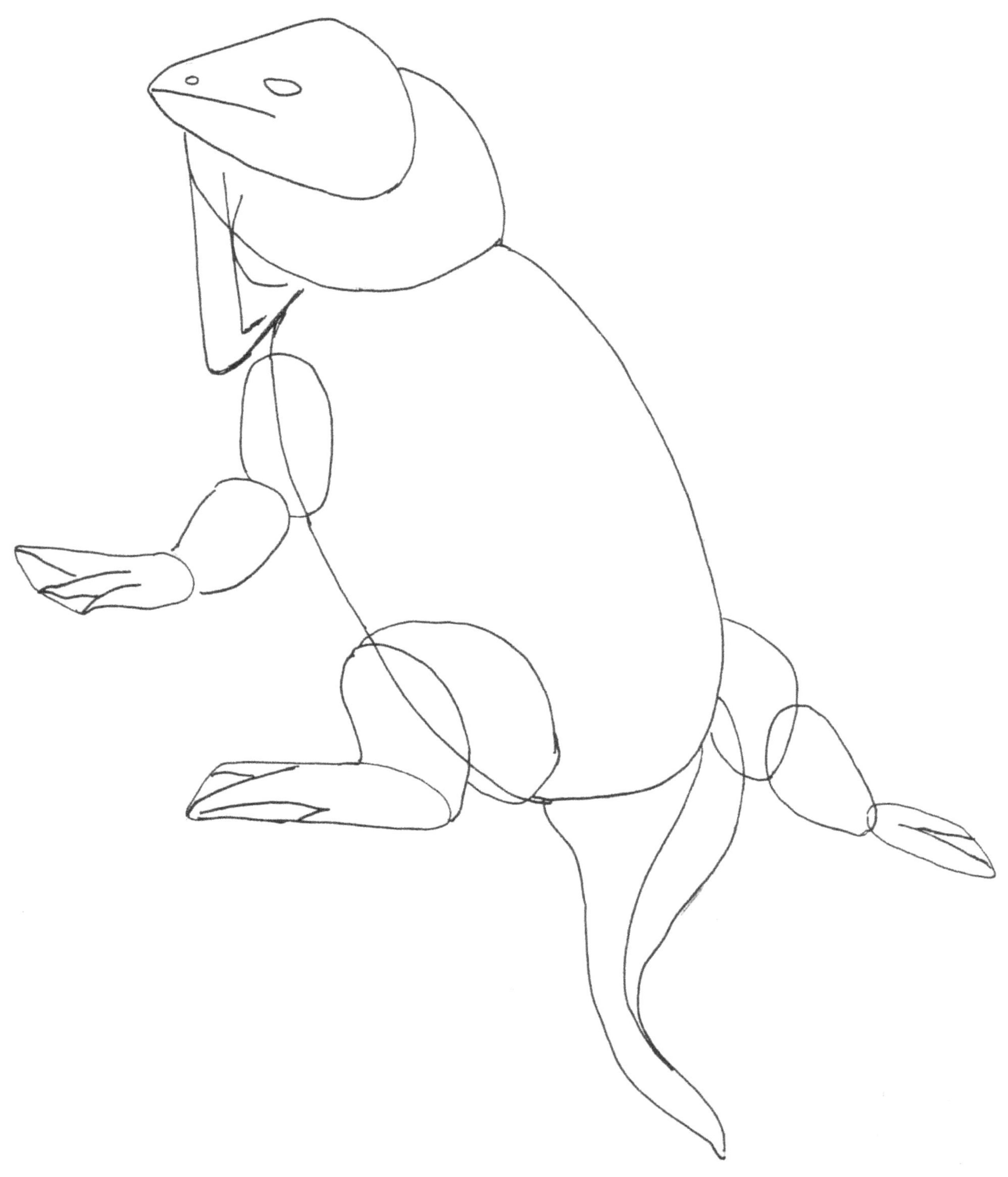

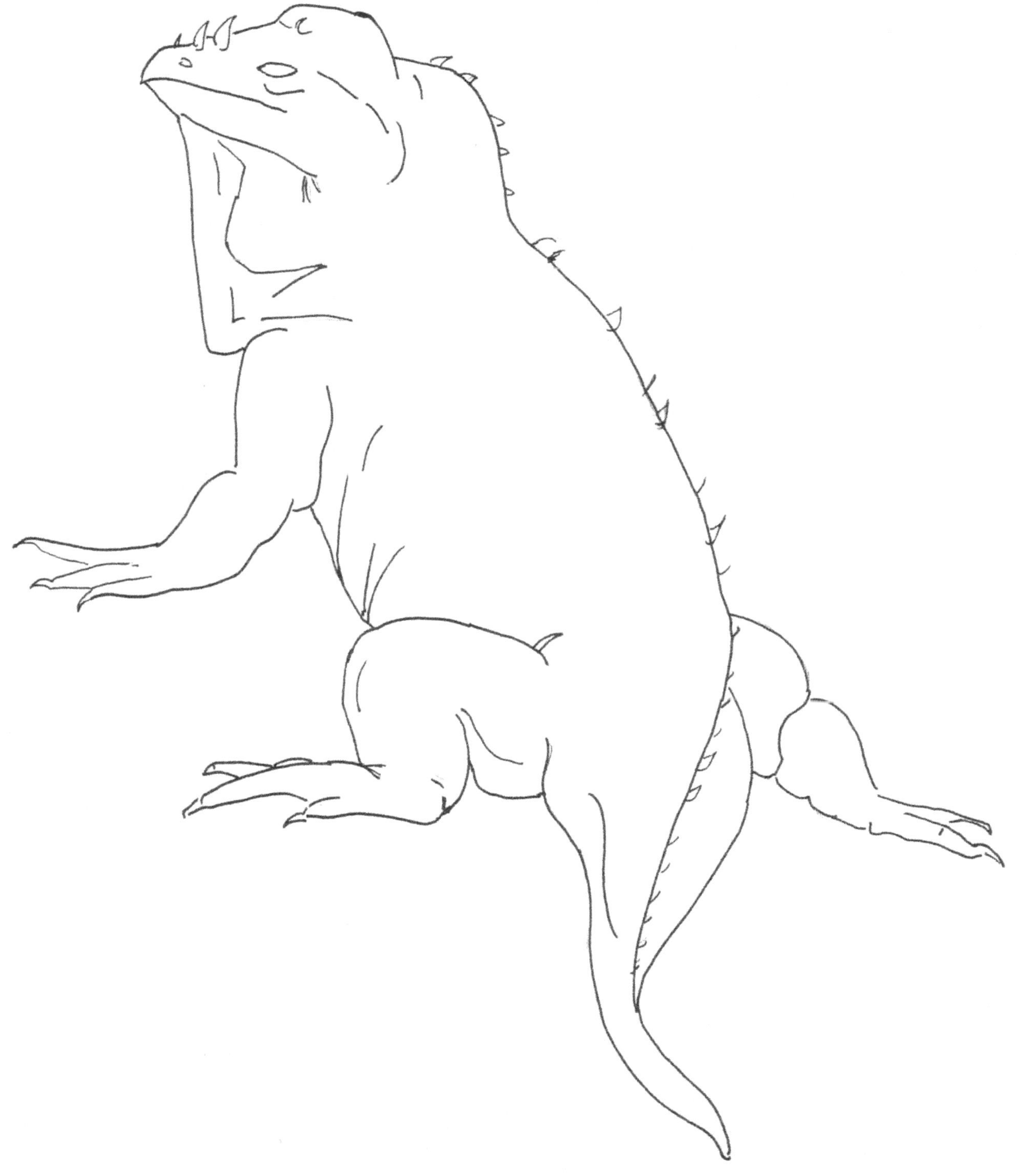

RHINOCEROS IGUANA

RHINOCEROS IGUANA
Found in Haiti and Dominican Republic, this iguana has a large, heavy head, a sturdy body, strong legs and a long tail flattened from side to side. They're habitat is dry rocky ground with cactuses and thorny bushes. The huge "rhino" iguana lives predominately in rocky zones with little vegetative cover. It is active only by day and feeds almost wholly on plants and berries. The adults are shy and quite agile, fleeing rapidly into burrows as soon as there is a hind of danger. When attacked by a predator, they nevertheless defend themselves with great determination, biting and striking the aggressor repeatedly with their strong tail. The females are egg laying, depositing 10 to 24 or more eggs while buried deep in the substrate.

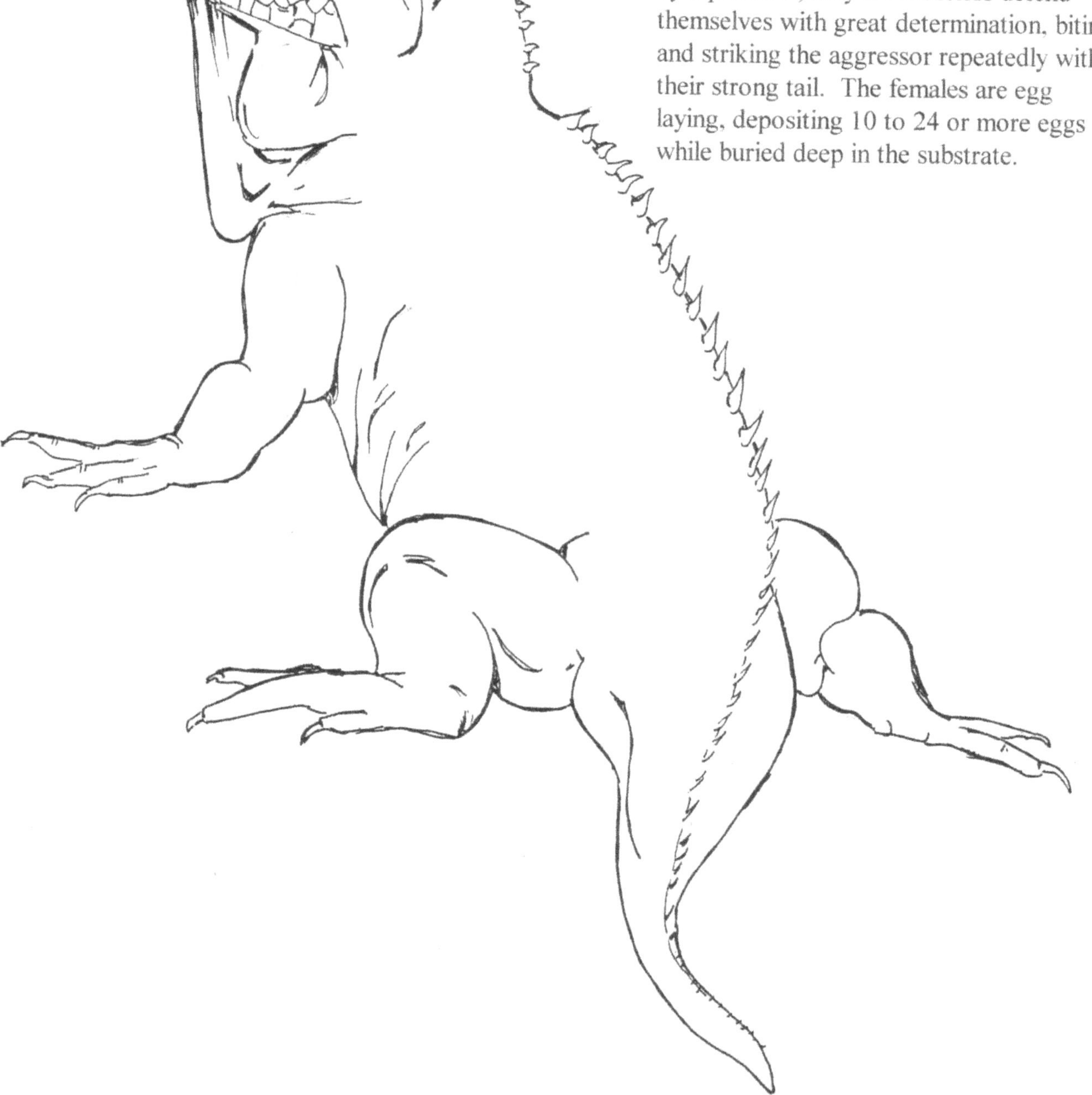

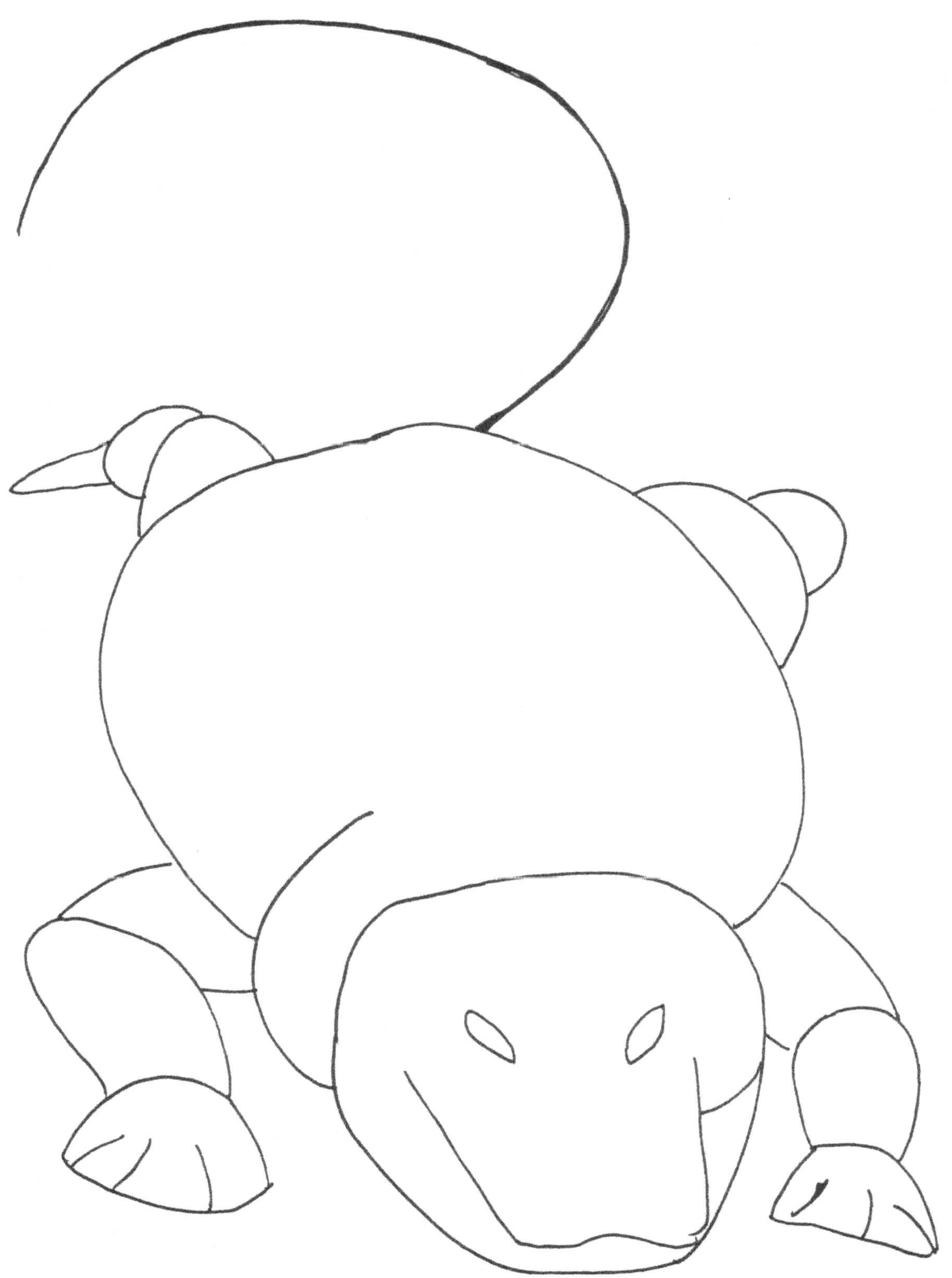

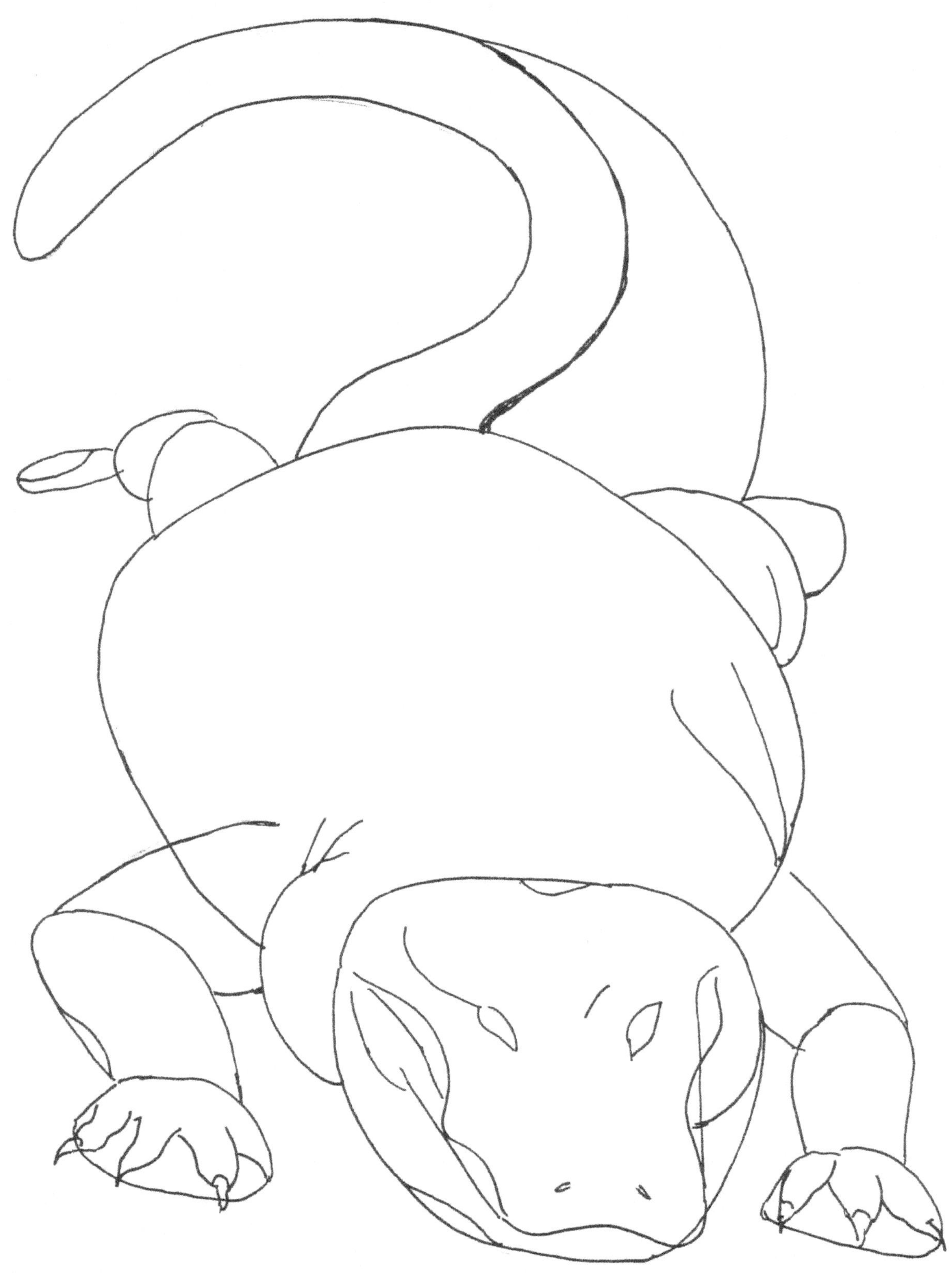

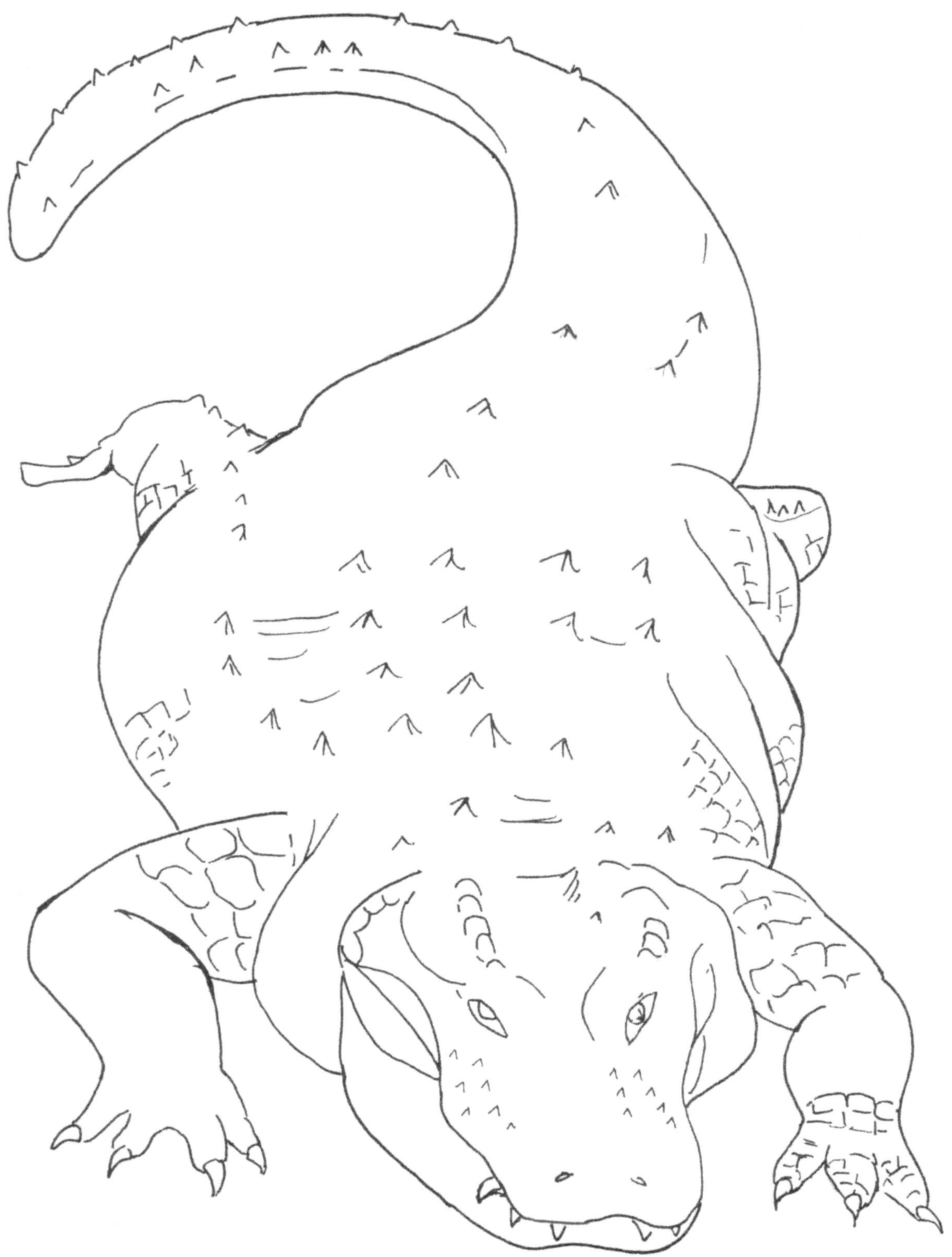

AMERICAN ALLIGATOR

AMERICAN ALLIGATOR
American Alligators are found in southeastern United States, from North Carolina to Texas. They live in extensive swampy areas, ponds, lakes and sluggish rivers, freshwater and brackish marshes. The alligator spends most of the day basking on shores or banks of rivers and lakes, often hidden in the vegetation. They may forage actively during the day or at night. Prey includes fish, turtles, snakes, mammals, and birds.

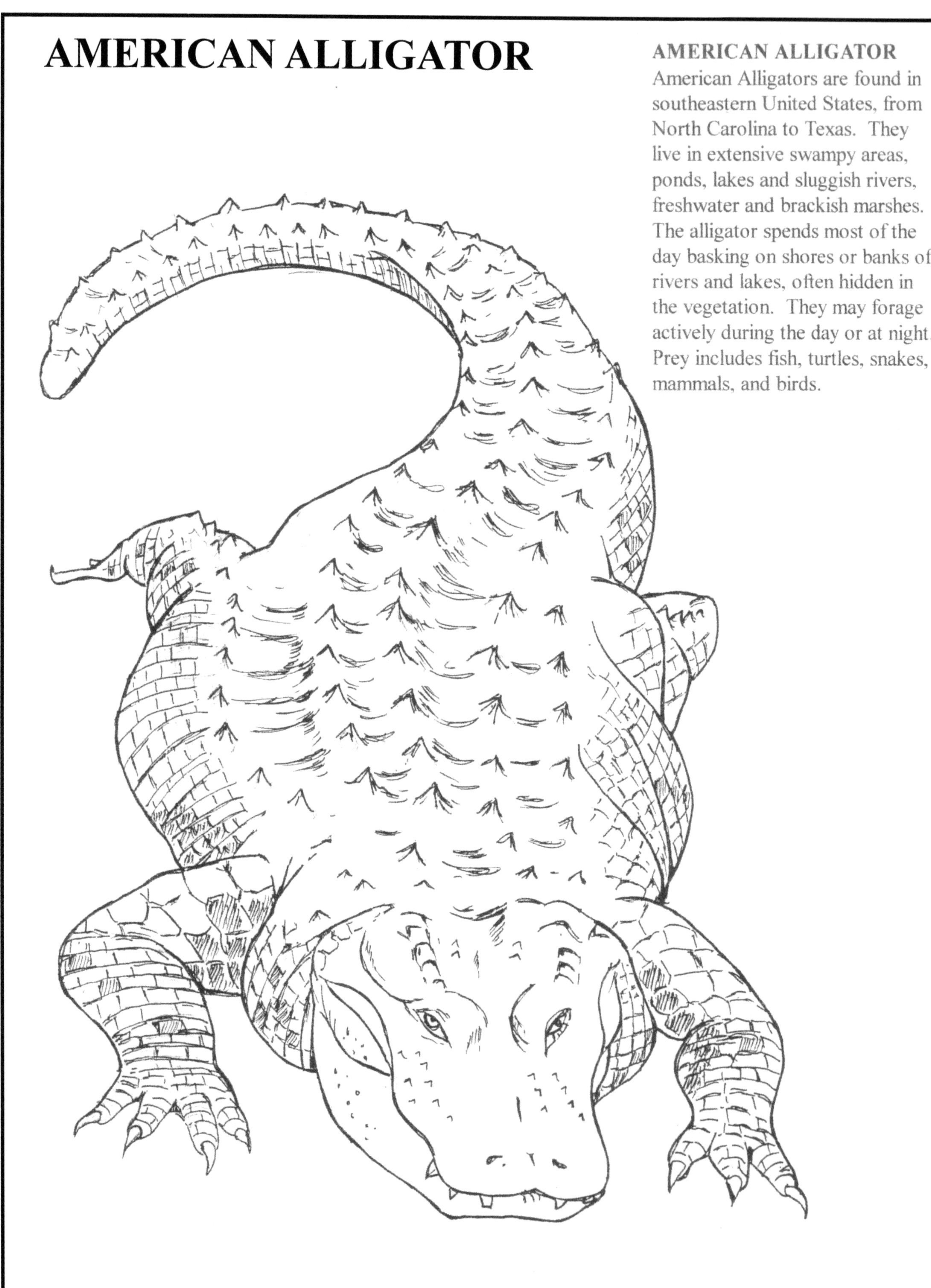

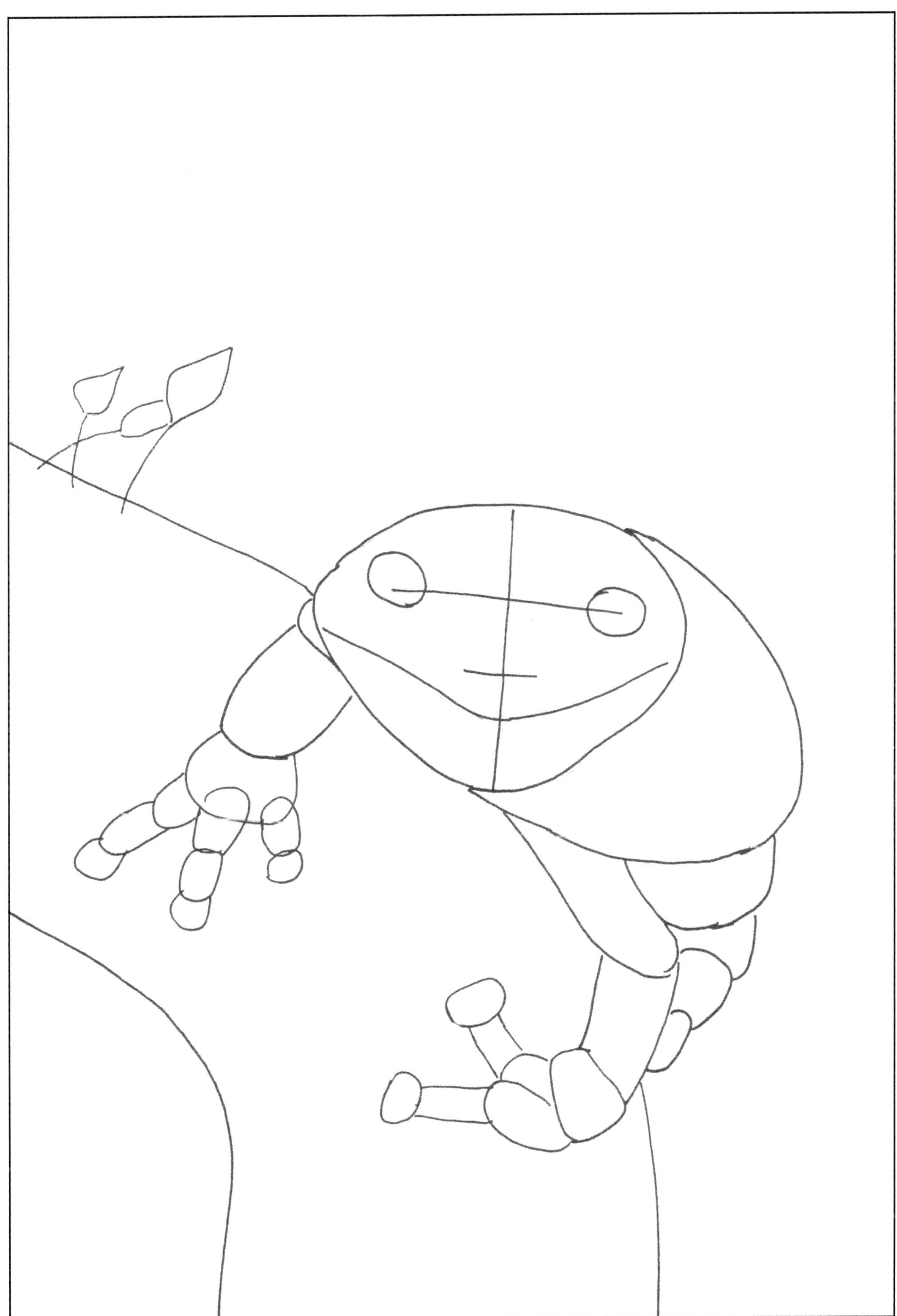

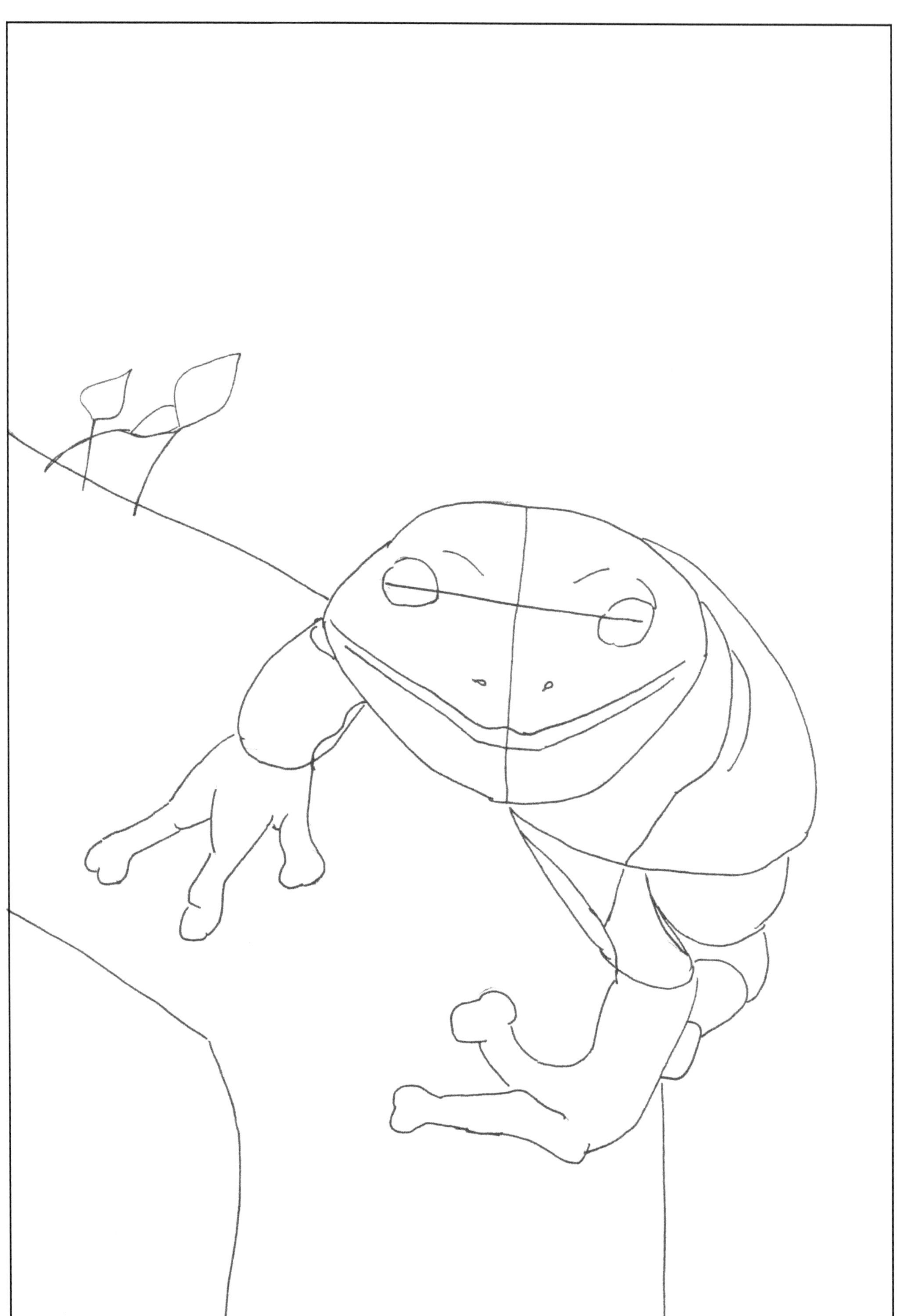

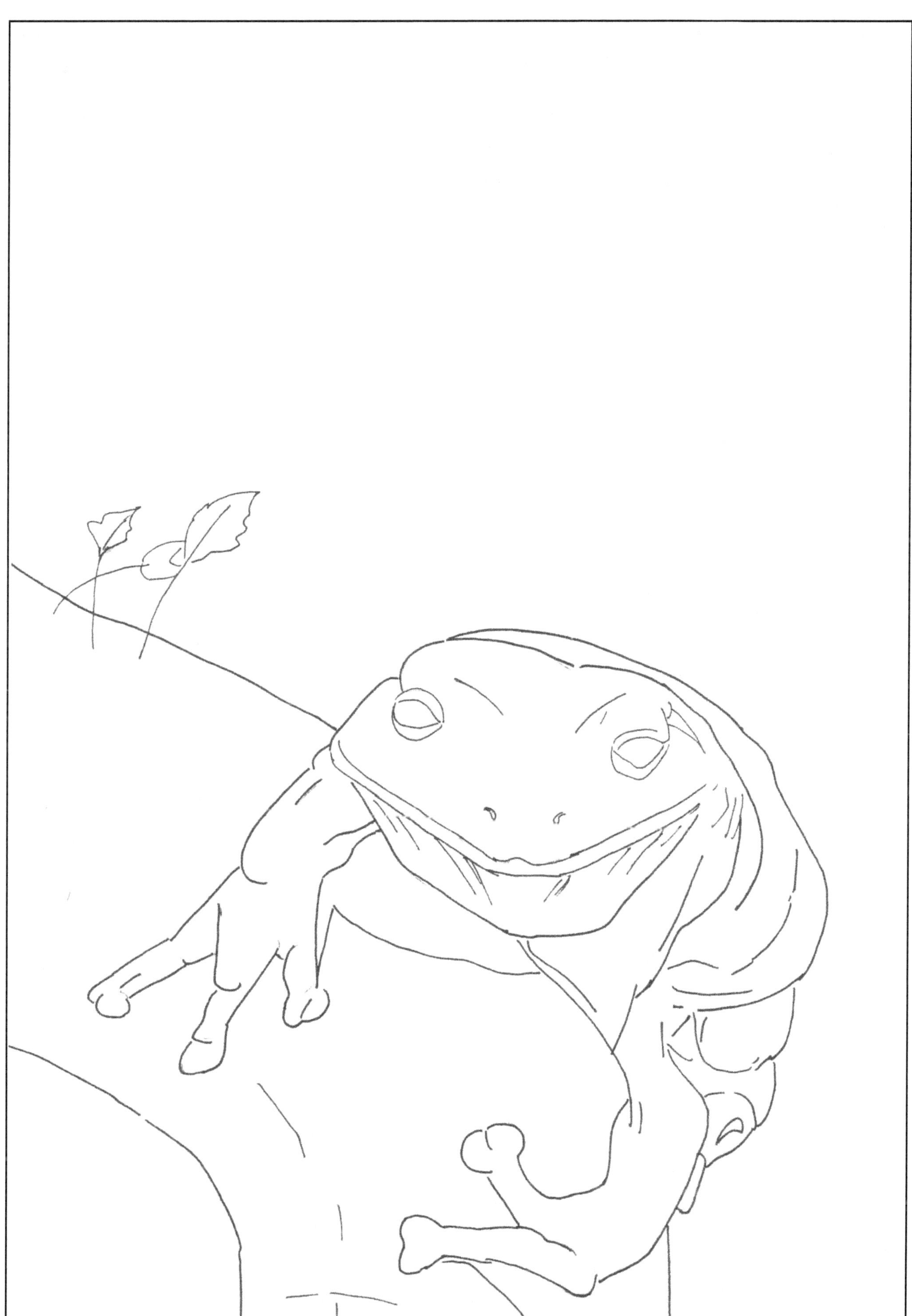

WHITE'S TREEFROG

This large plump frog is bright green above with a few small white spots on the sides. The tips of the toes have broad adhesive disks. This species is common in Australia, often found around ponds and rainwater, tanks, and sometimes in farm buildings. In the wild it spends most of its time in trees and hunts food day and night. Breeding is in the summer, the adults massing together in pools and ponds to mate and lay eggs.

WHITE TREEFROG

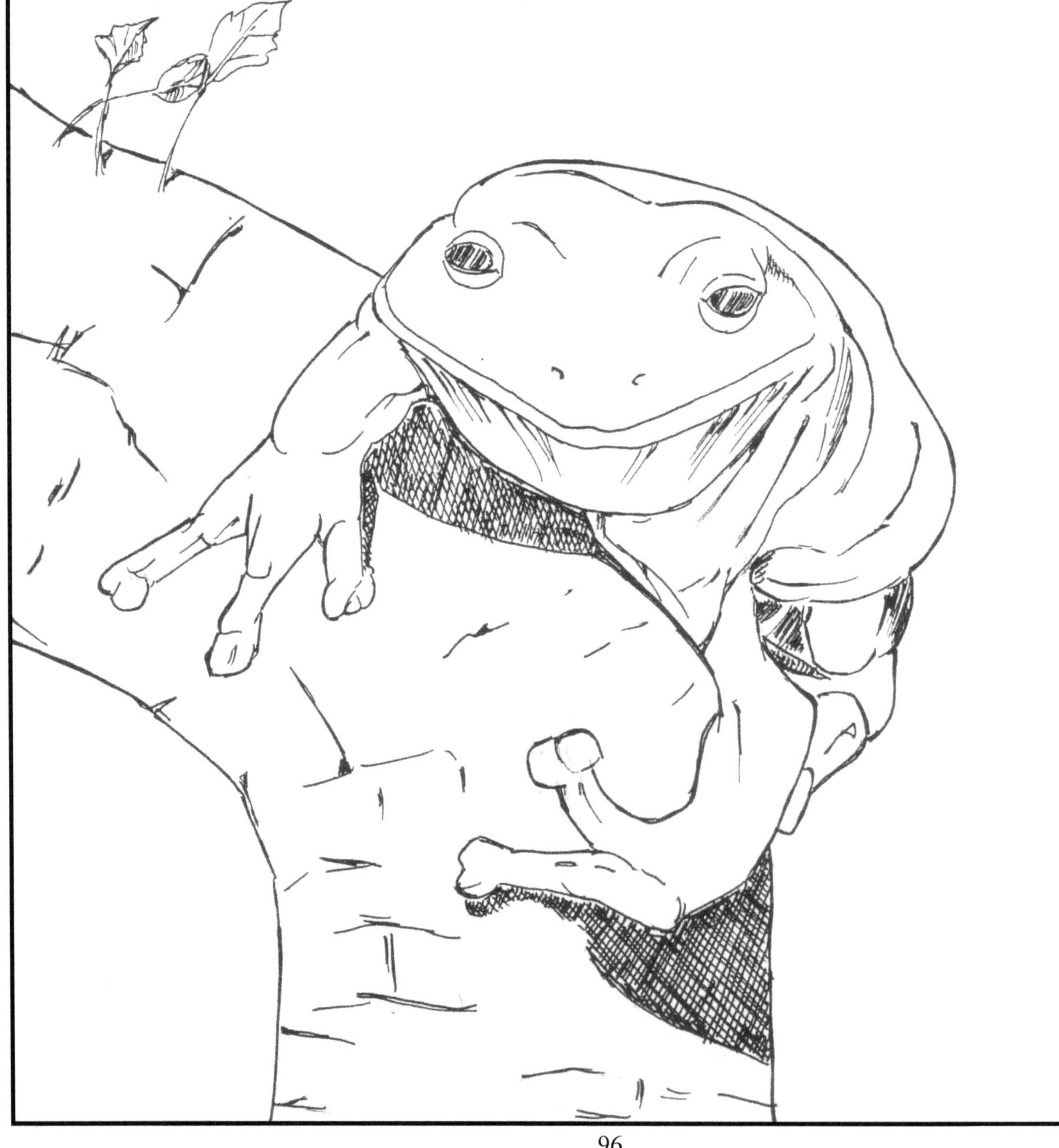

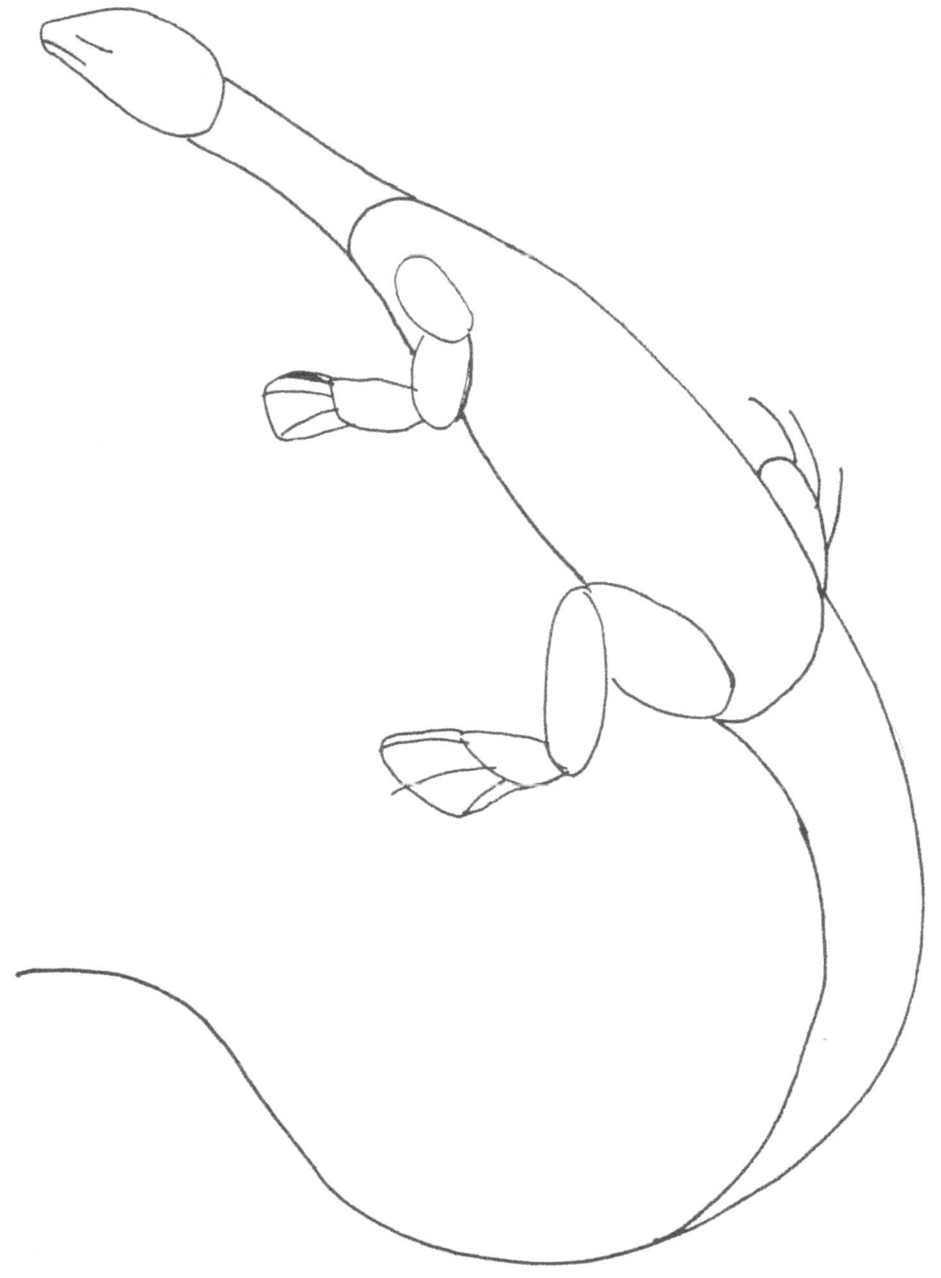

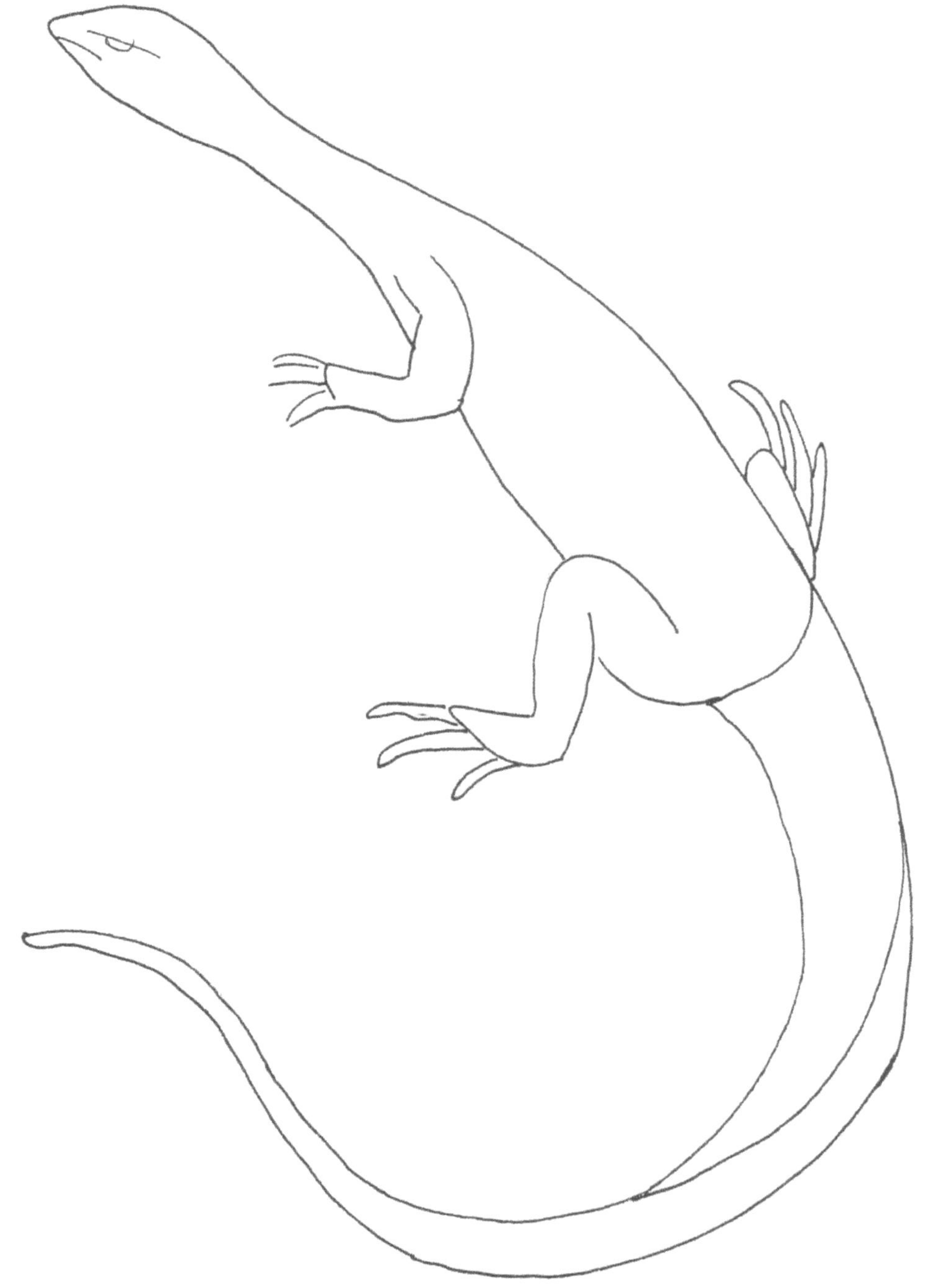

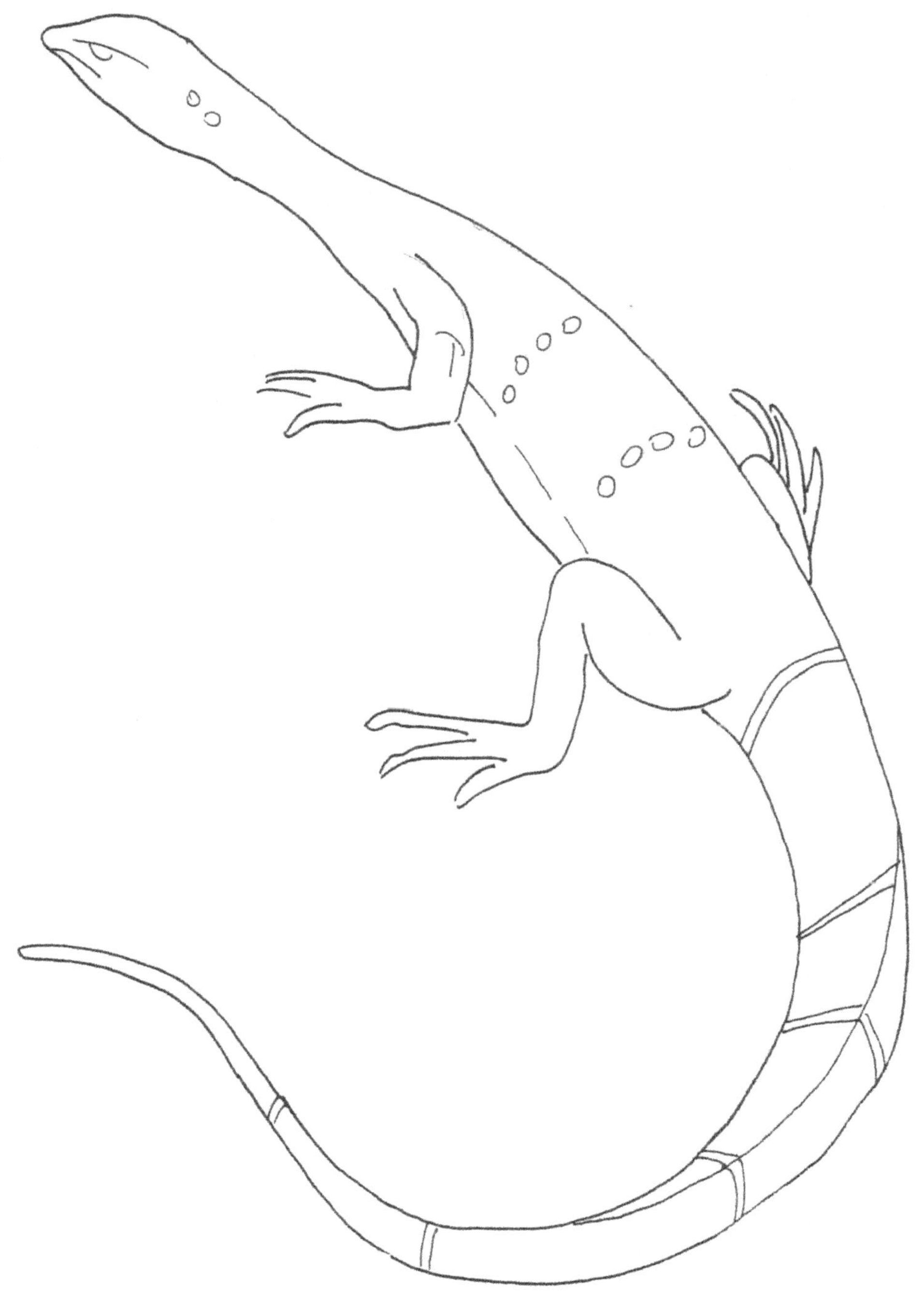

GOULD'S MONITOR

GOULD'S MONITOR

This species has a relatively flat head with small scales, very long neck and fairly slender but robust body. Coloration is variable, ranging from yellowish to dark brown or black, with numerous light and dark streaks. Found in Australia, this species inhabits a very wide variety of environments. It spends the night in deep underground burrows and is active mainly in the morning when it goes hunting for foods. It is a skillful predator, hunting birds, mammals and reptiles. The females are oviparous. Total length is 39 to 68 inches.

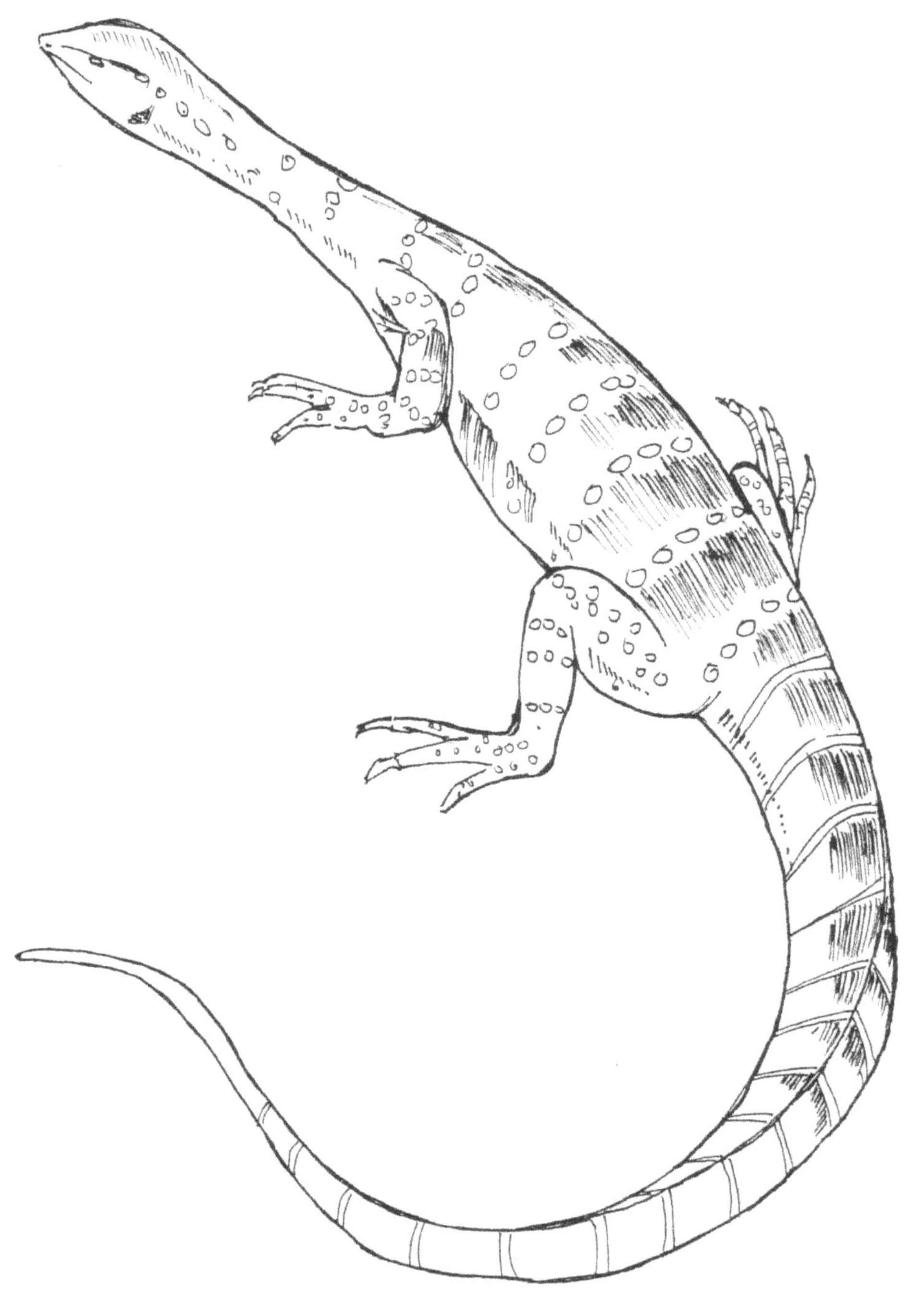

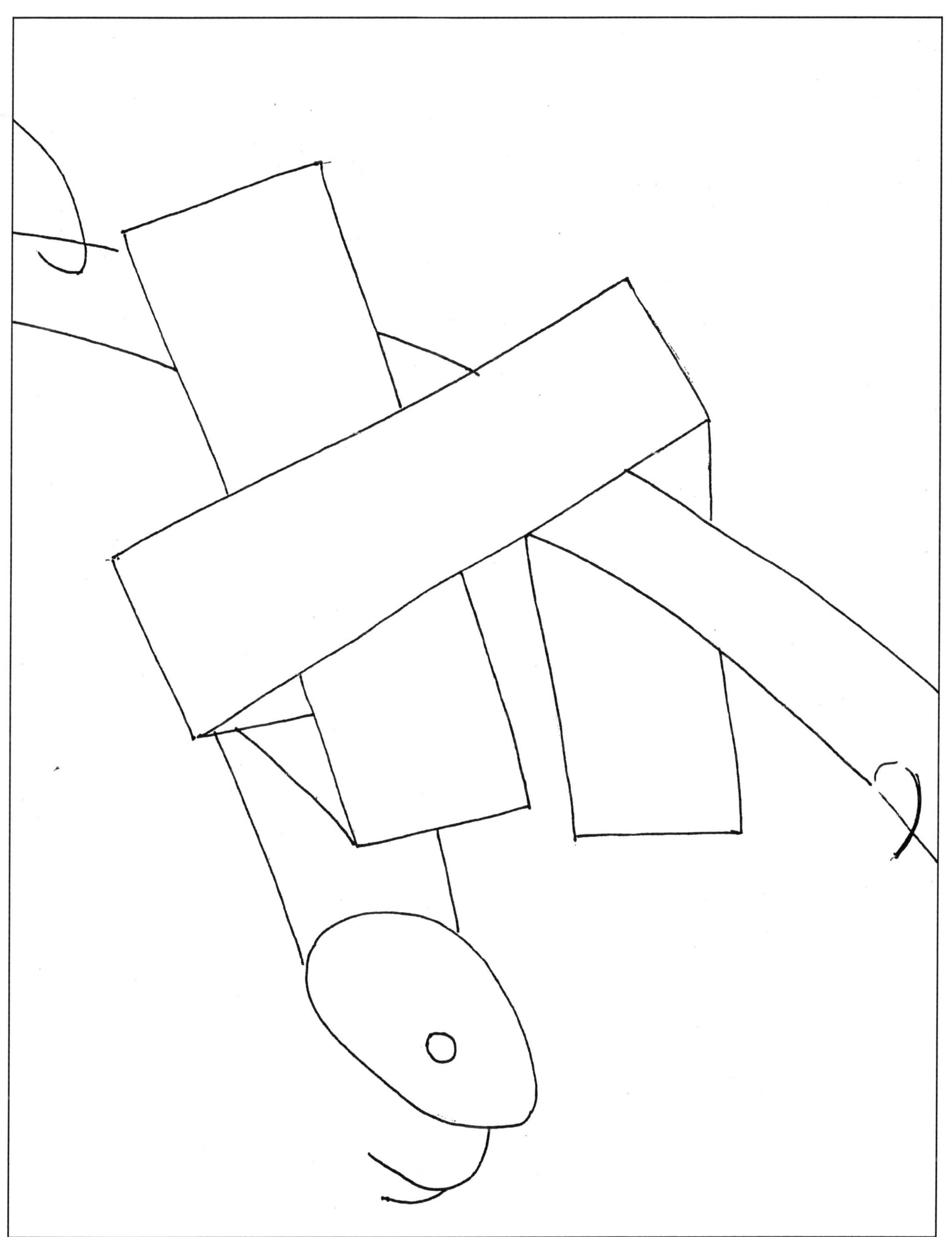

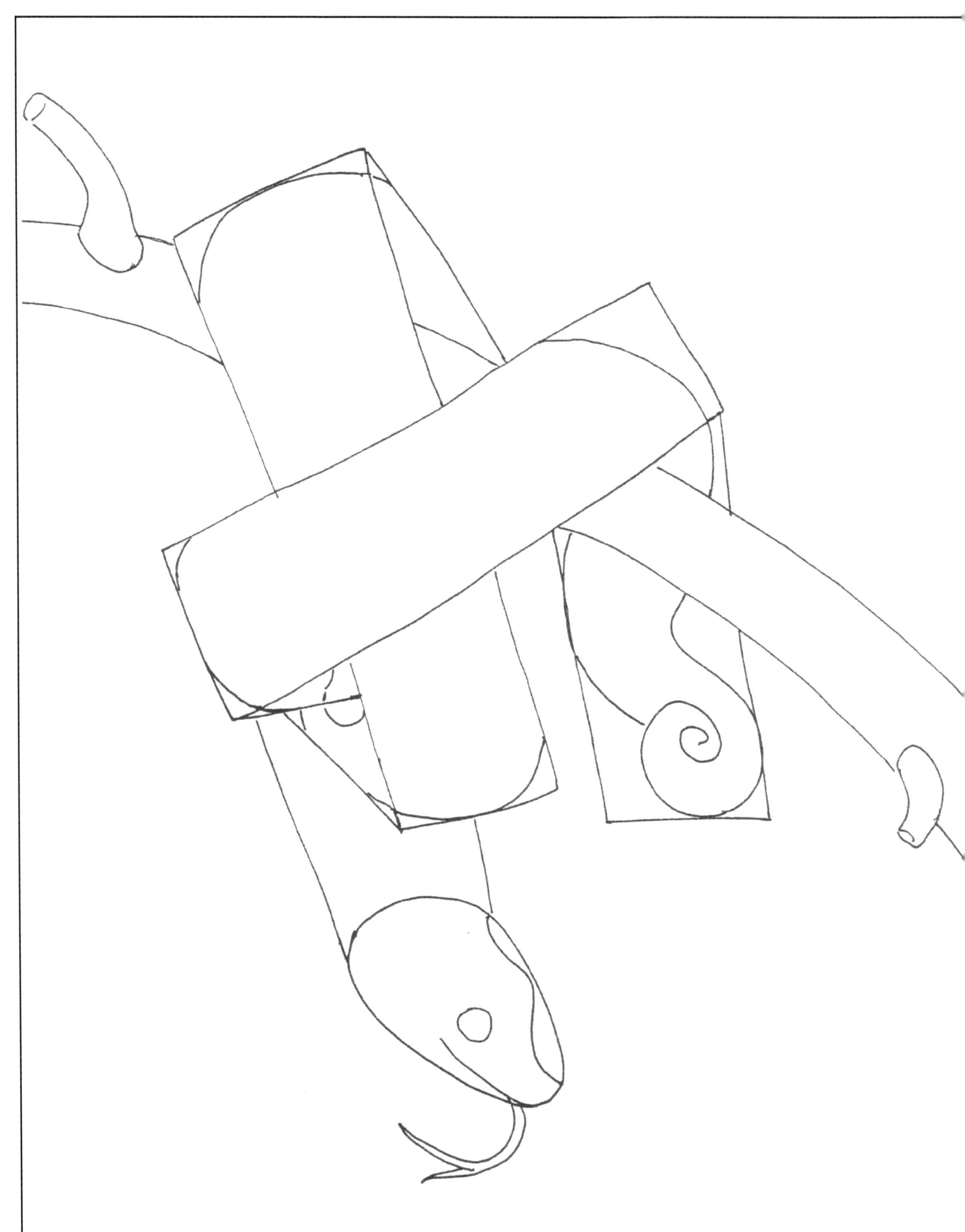

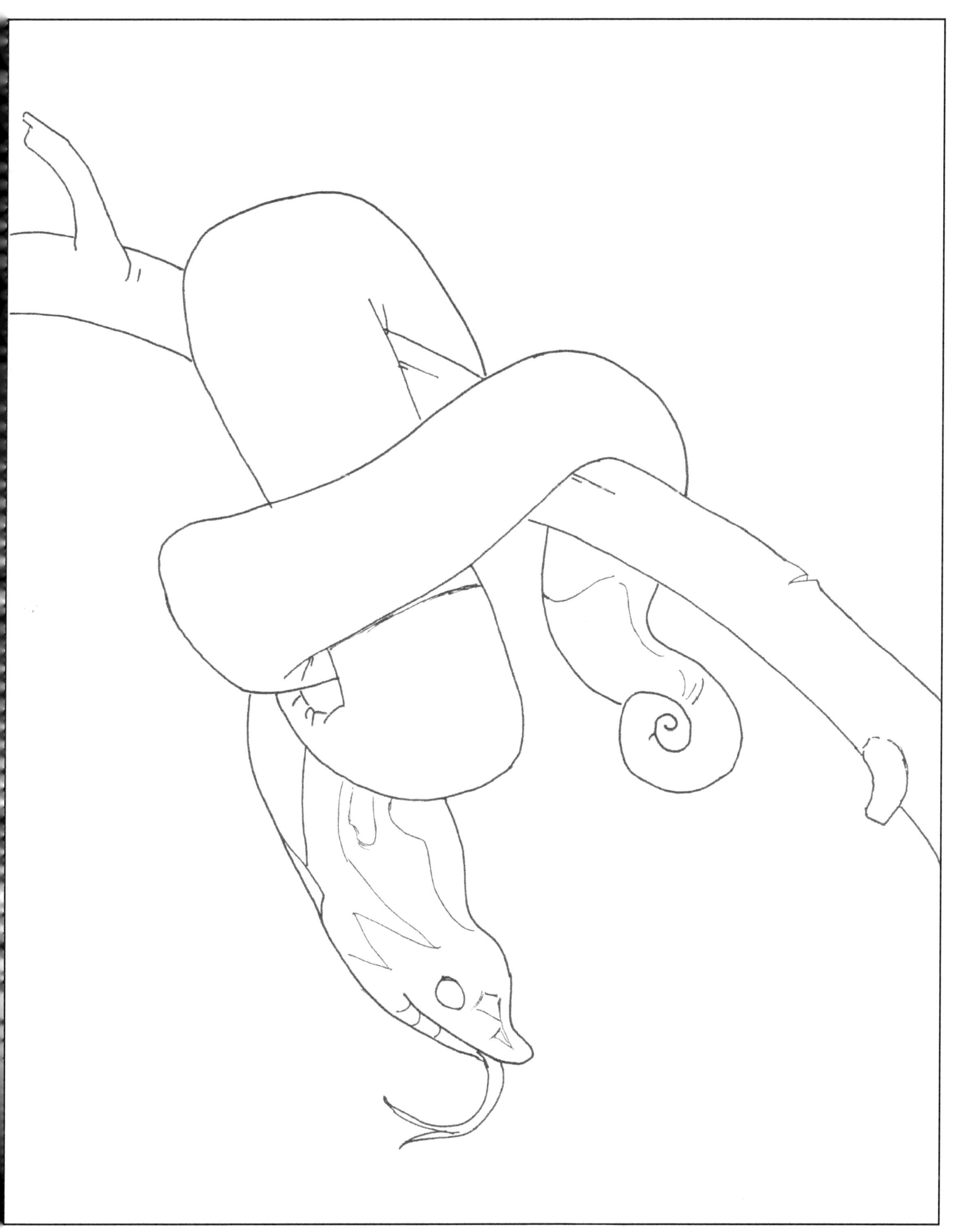

HOGNOSE SNAKE

HOGNOSE SNAKE
Thick bodied harmless North American snakes that are characterized by a flattened snout. The average length is about two feet. Although harmless, the hognose is widely feared because when under attack it assumes a threatening position if aggressive tactics fail to frighten away the intruder, the hognose pretends to be dead.

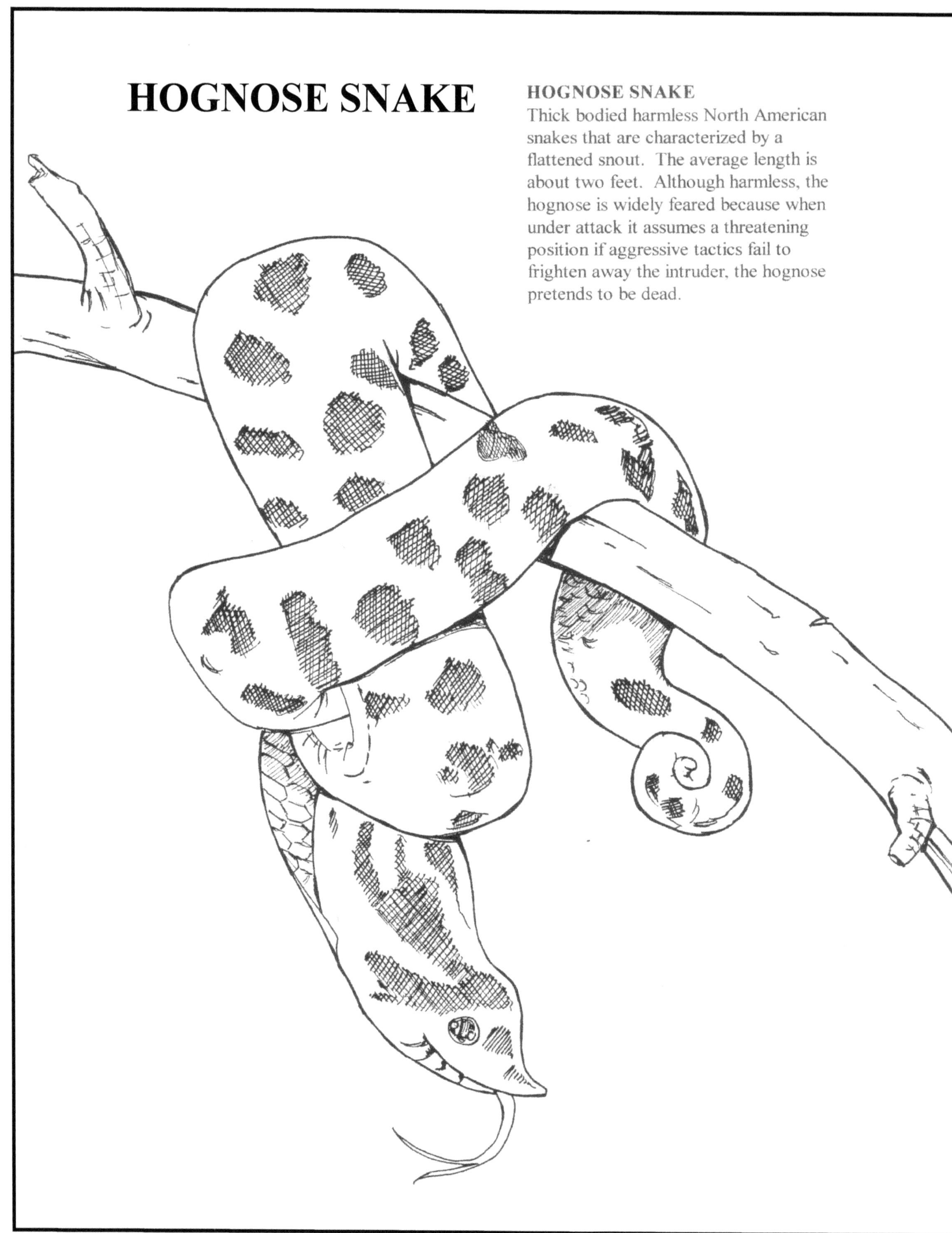

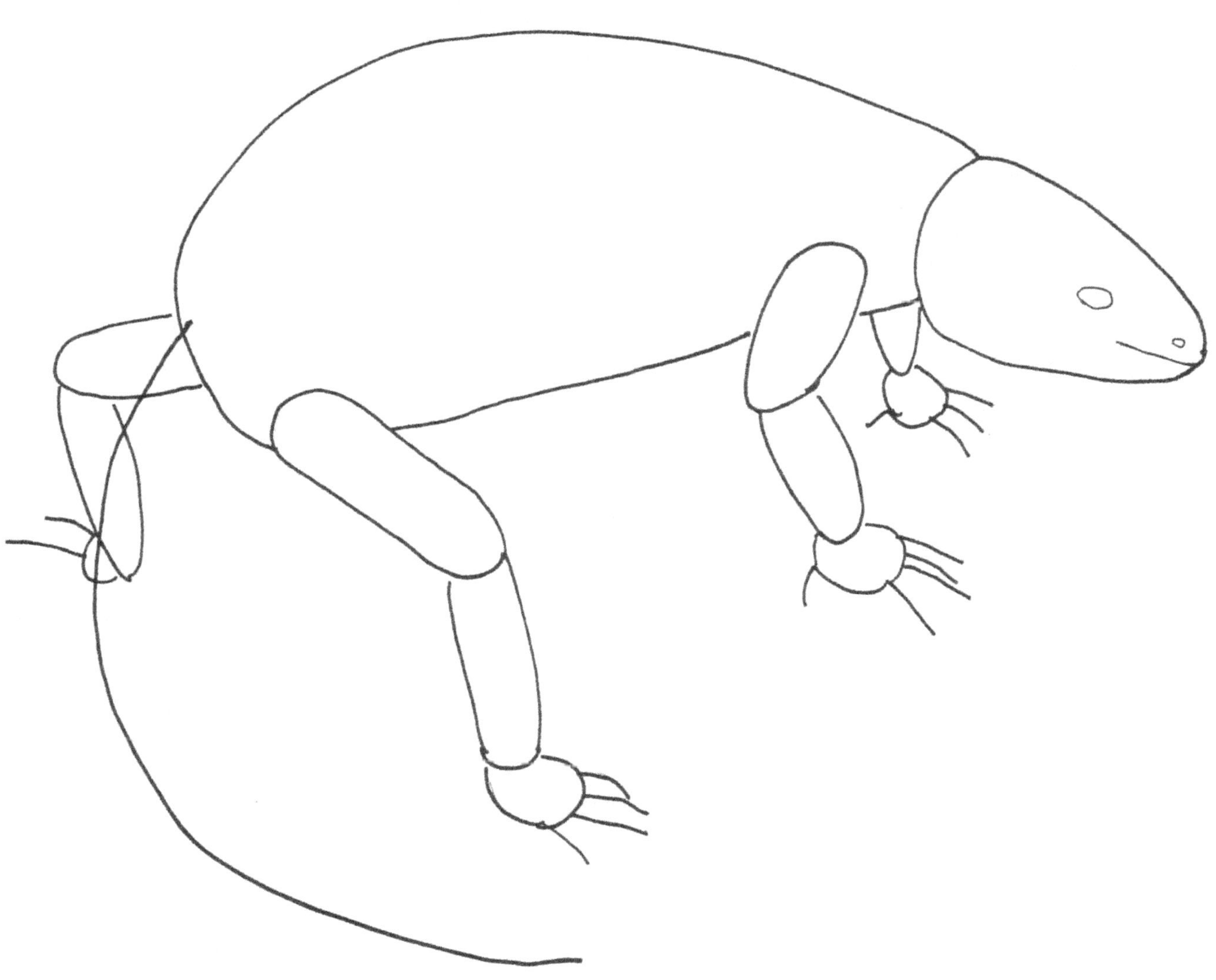

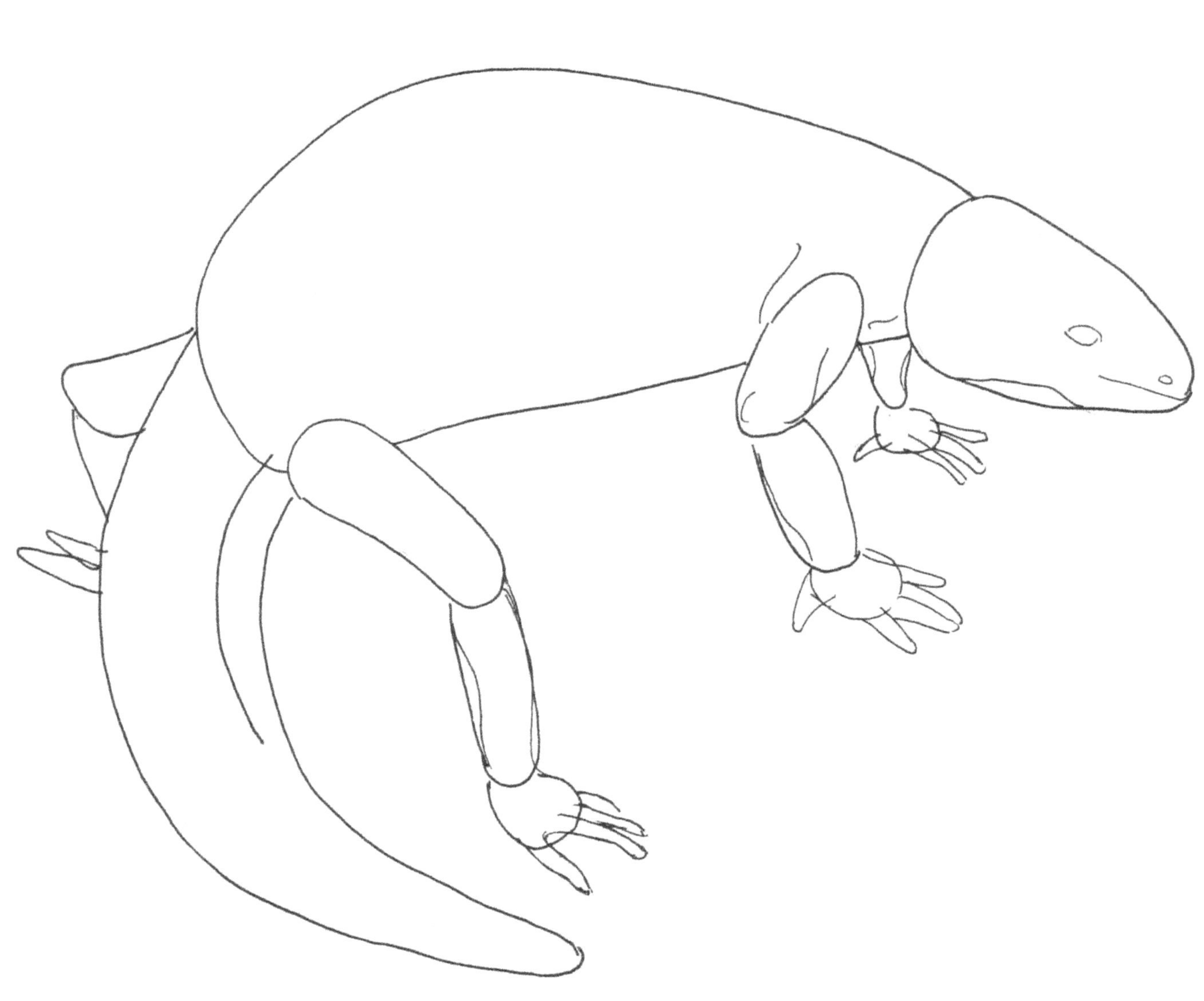

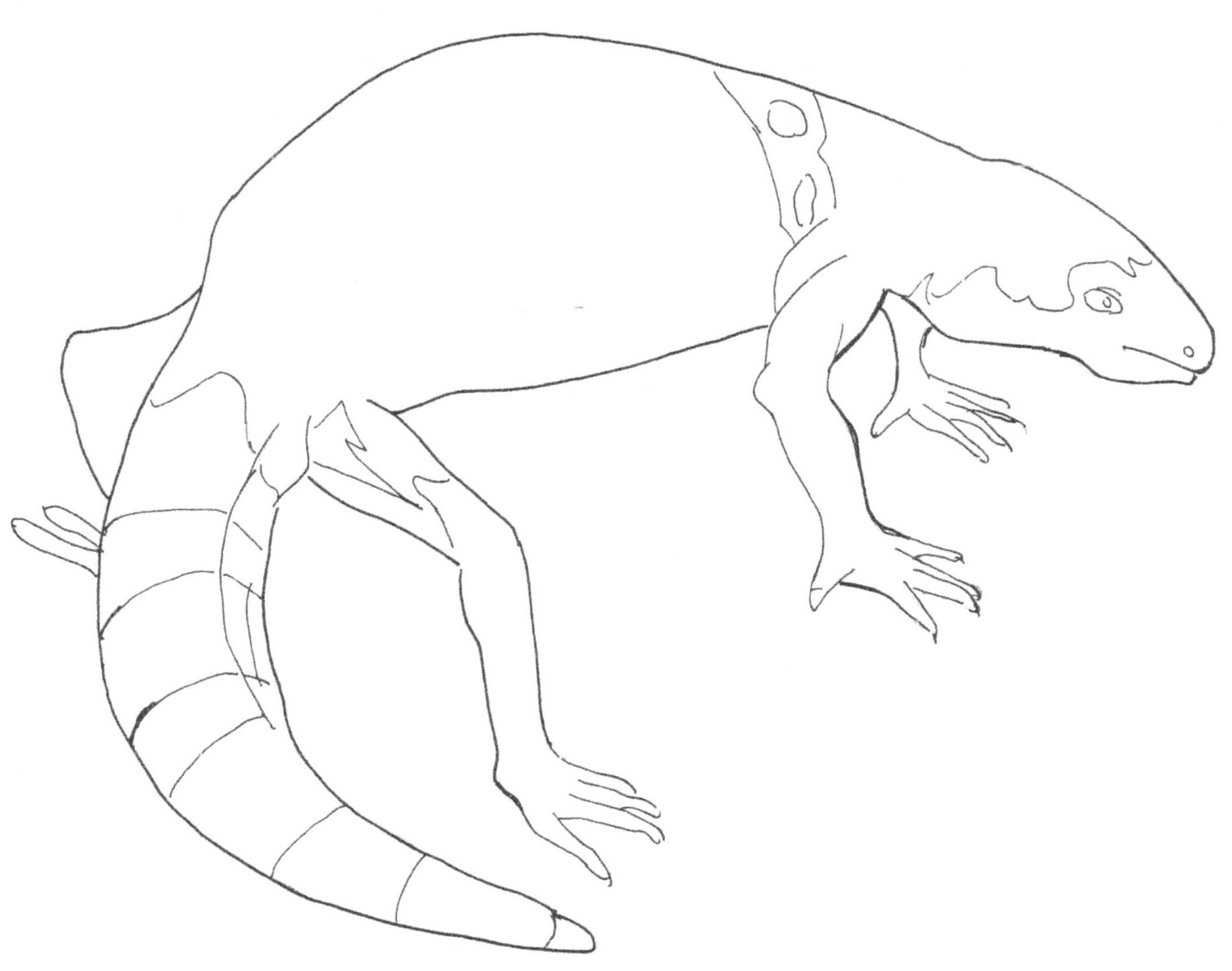

RETICULATE GILA MONSTER. Along with the Beaded Lizard of Mexico and Guatemala, the Gila Monster is the only venomous lizard. Boldly marked with pink or orange and black, at two feet in length, this species is one of the largest and most attractive lizards in the United States. Government protected, this imposing reptile has become a classic symbol of the Mojave Desert, where it lives in moist situations. Its potent venom appears to be primarily for defense, as the Gila Monster feeds on small mammals, birds, and eggs, (for which it will climb trees). If molested, this species will flee or hiss, biting only as a last resort. Few bites on humans have been document, but a bite can be a serious matter. These reptiles spend most of their time in burrows, being active primarily when high heat is not a factor. One to eight eggs are laid in the summer.

RETICULATE GILA MONSTER

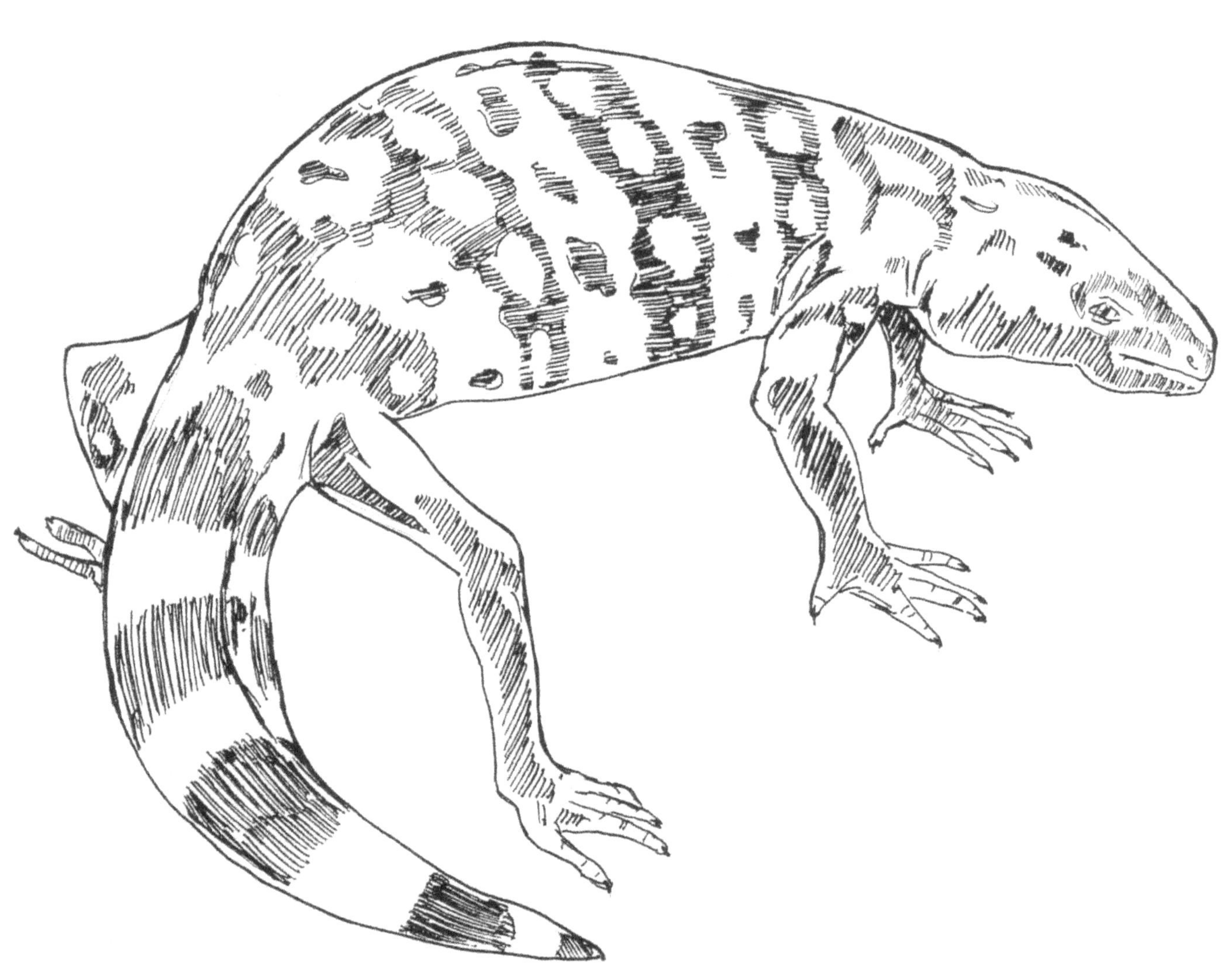

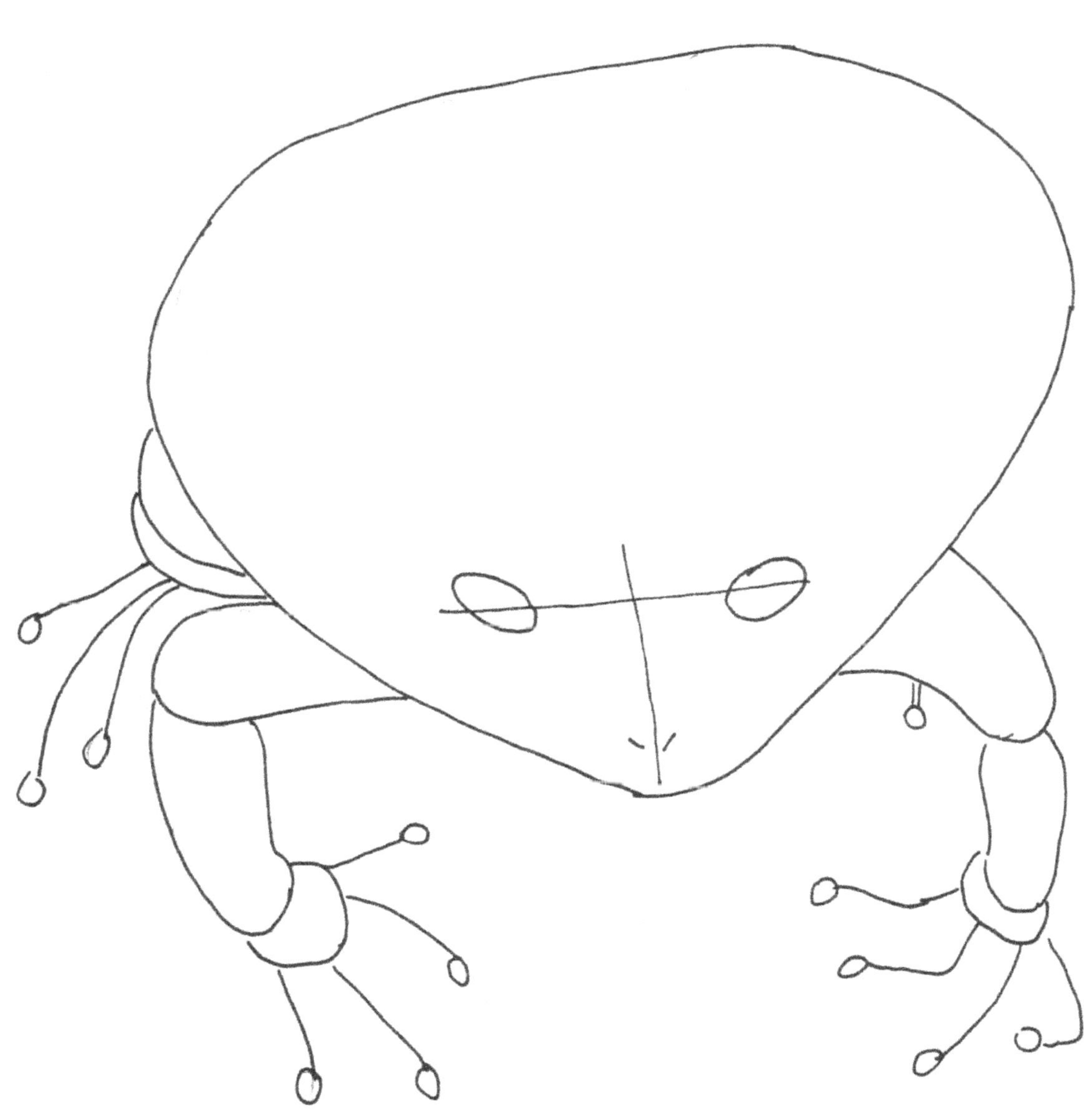

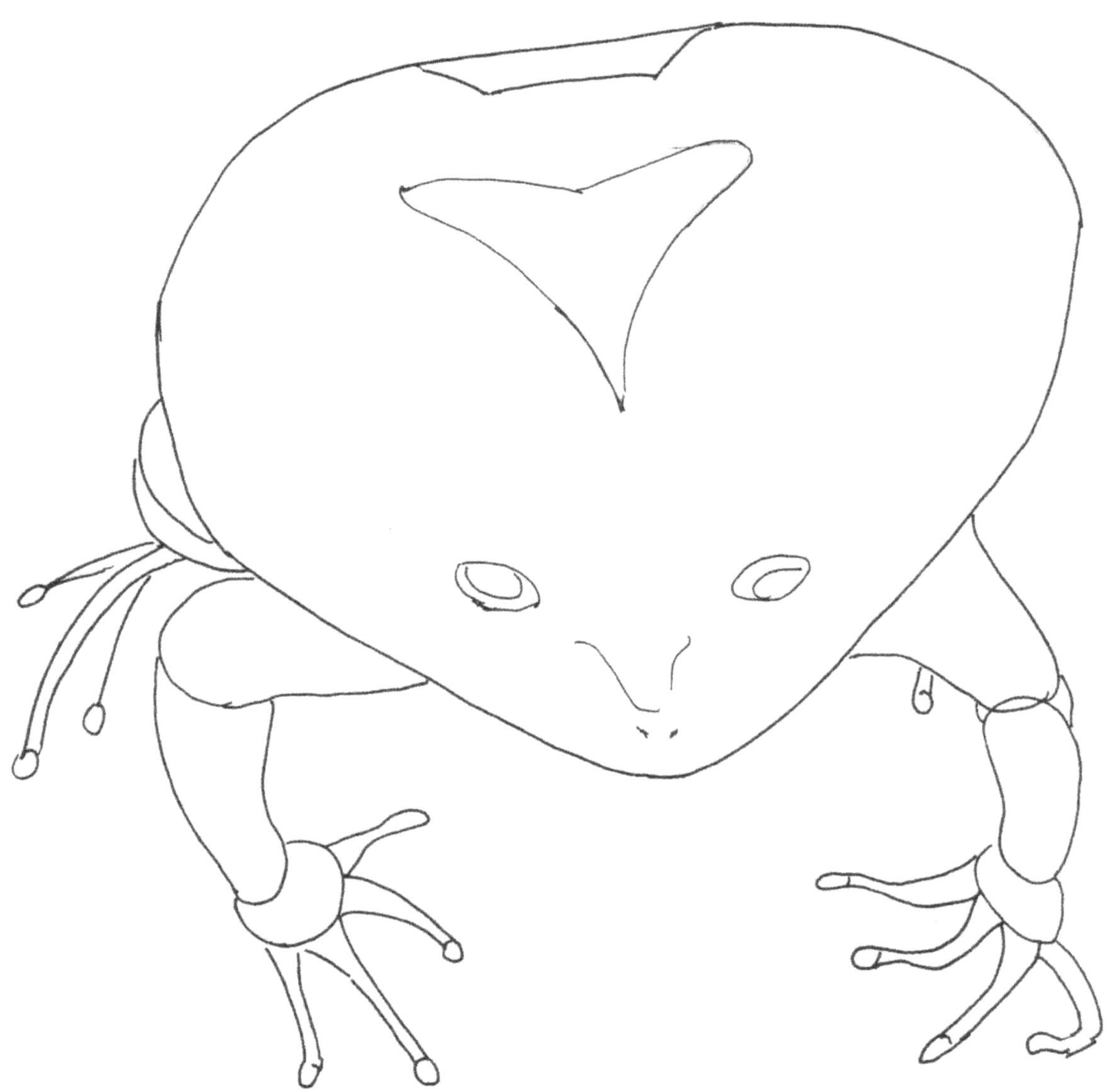

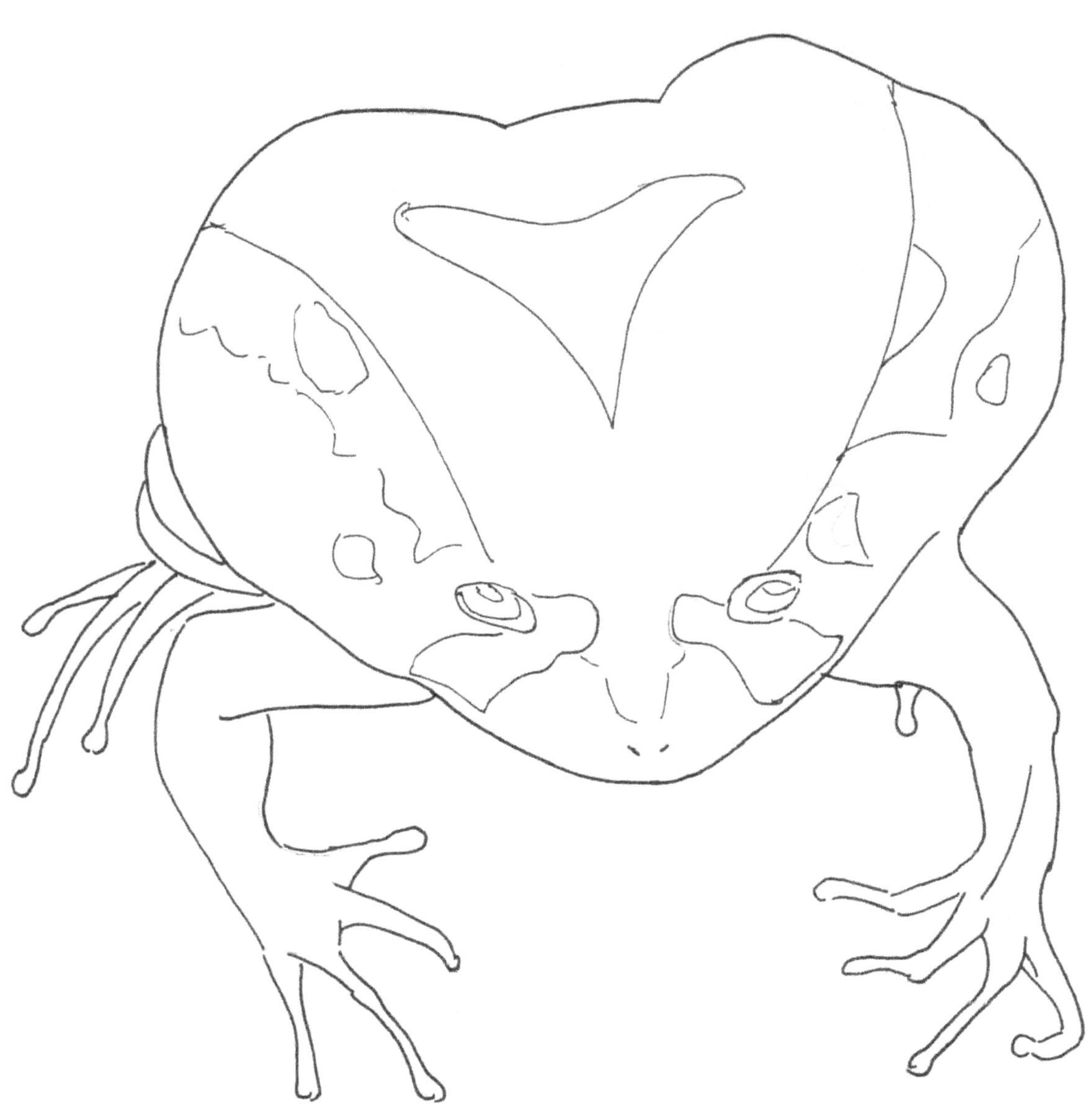

MADAGASCAR BURROWING FROG

MADAGASCAR BURROWING FROG This frog is found in the forests of southern and western Madagascar where it spends its life among the leaf litter or underground. After passing much of the year in hiding, these amphibians come forth at the onset of spring rains. Their diet consist of insects. The smaller female enter temporary pools and produce gelatinous masses containing thousands of eggs. Upon hatching, the tadpoles must mature rapidly or risk death by dehydration when the pools dry up.

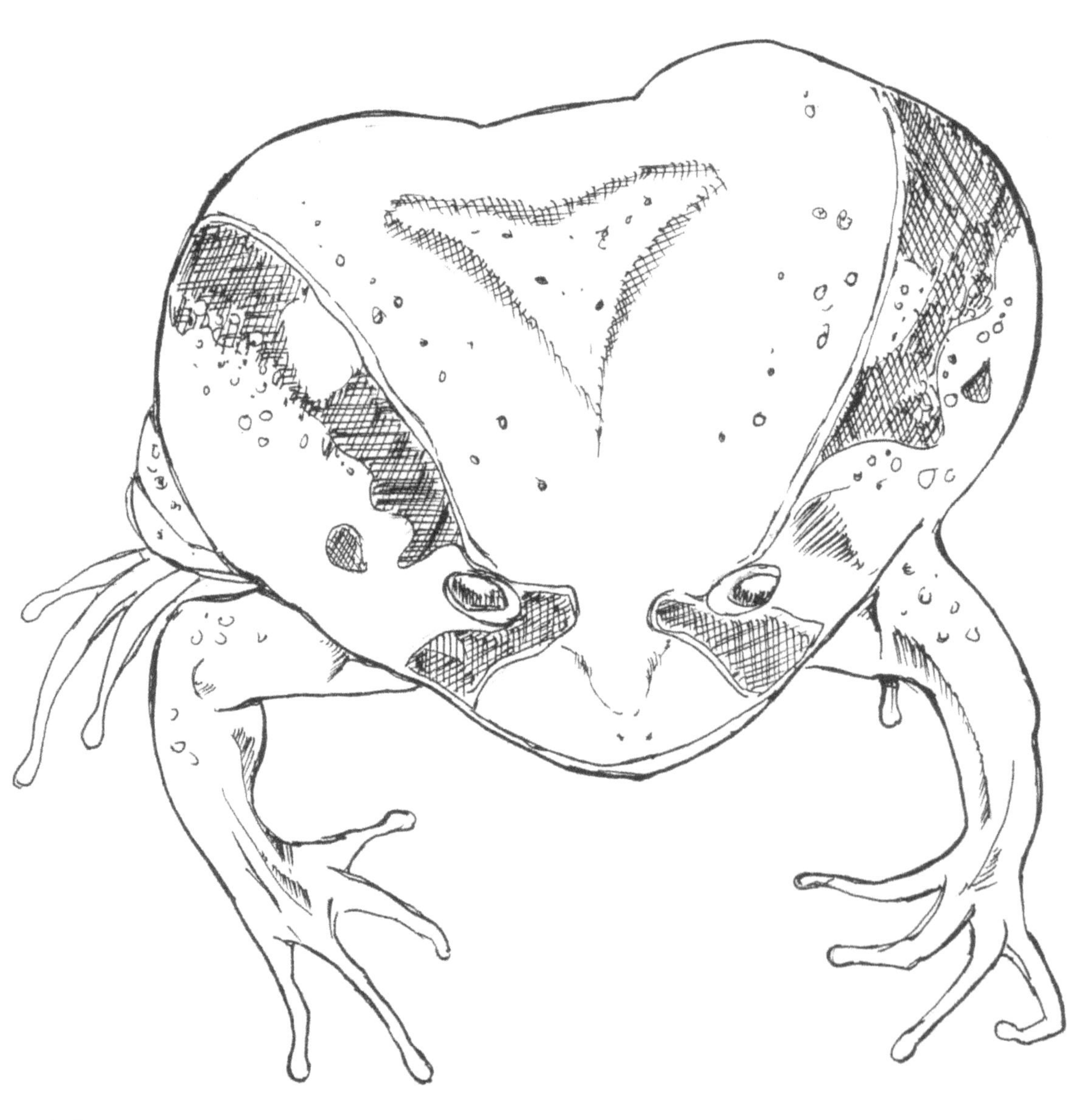

MAMMALS

I started drawing the tree limb first then proceeded with drawing an outline of the Two-toed Sloth's head, torso (middle part of the body), neck, arms and claws.

Note: The torso is the trunk of a body less head and limbs.

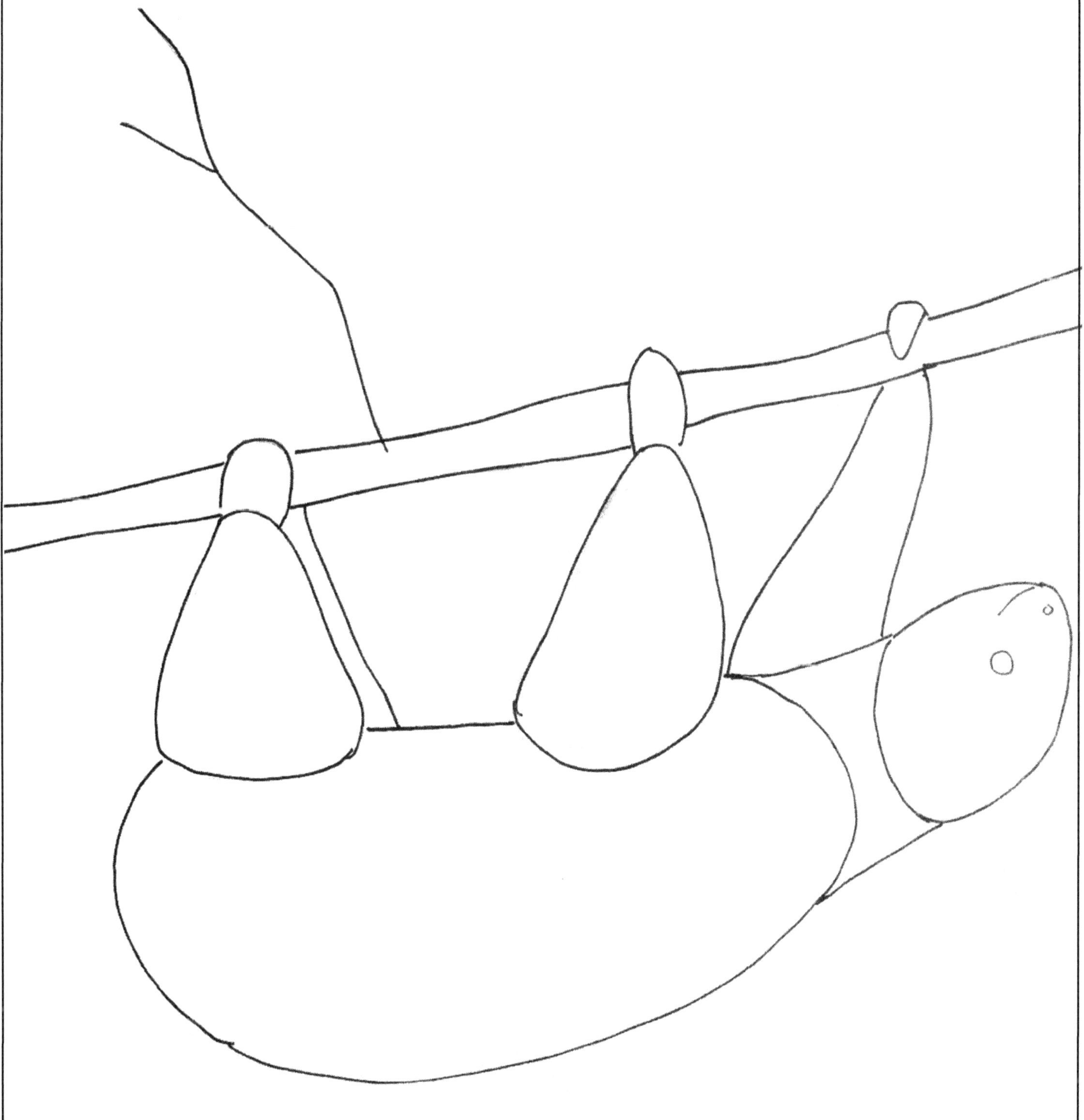

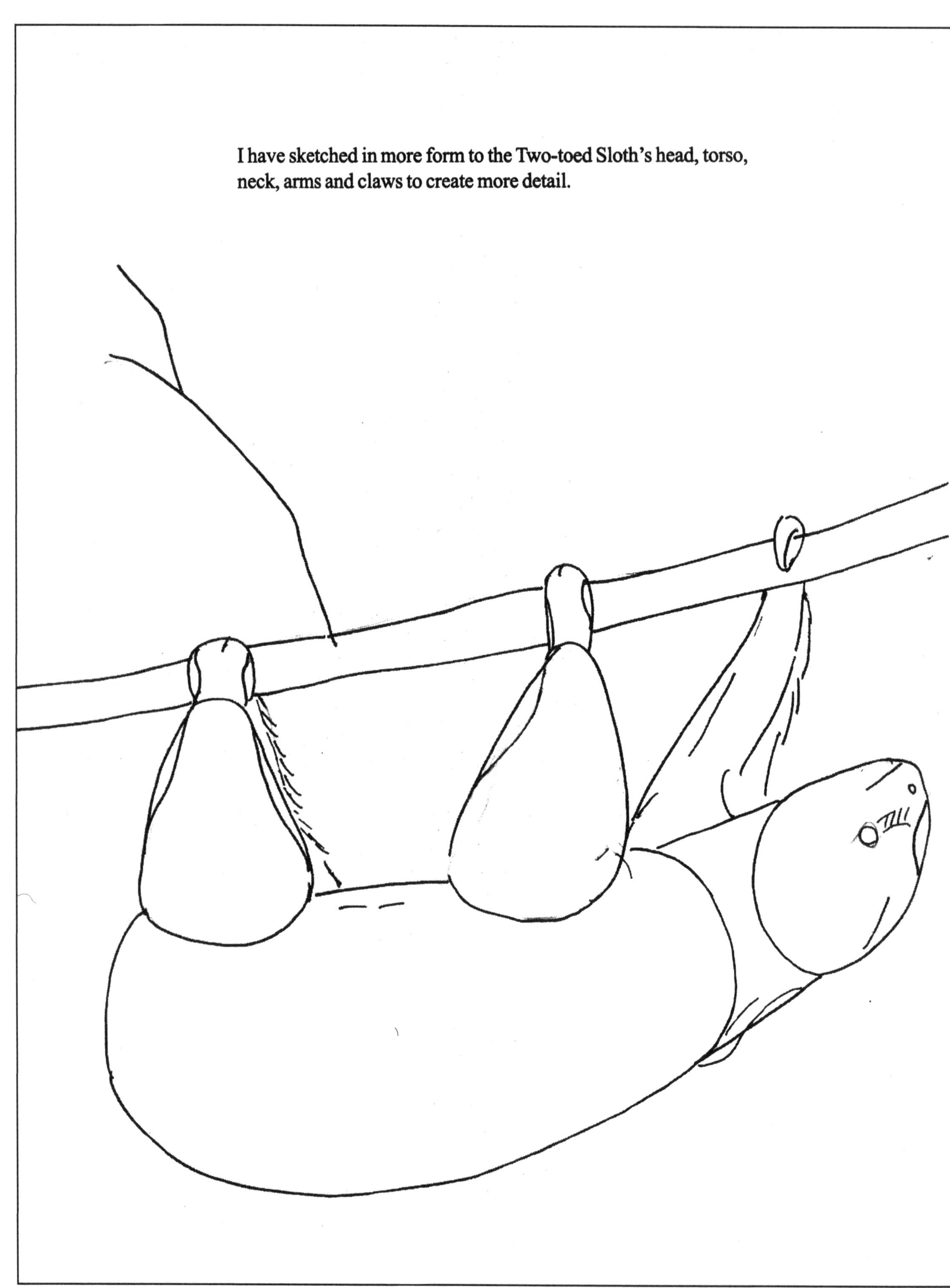
I have sketched in more form to the Two-toed Sloth's head, torso, neck, arms and claws to create more detail.

I have sketched in more form to the tree limb as well as adding hair to the Two-toed Sloth's head, torso, neck and arms to almost compete the drawing.

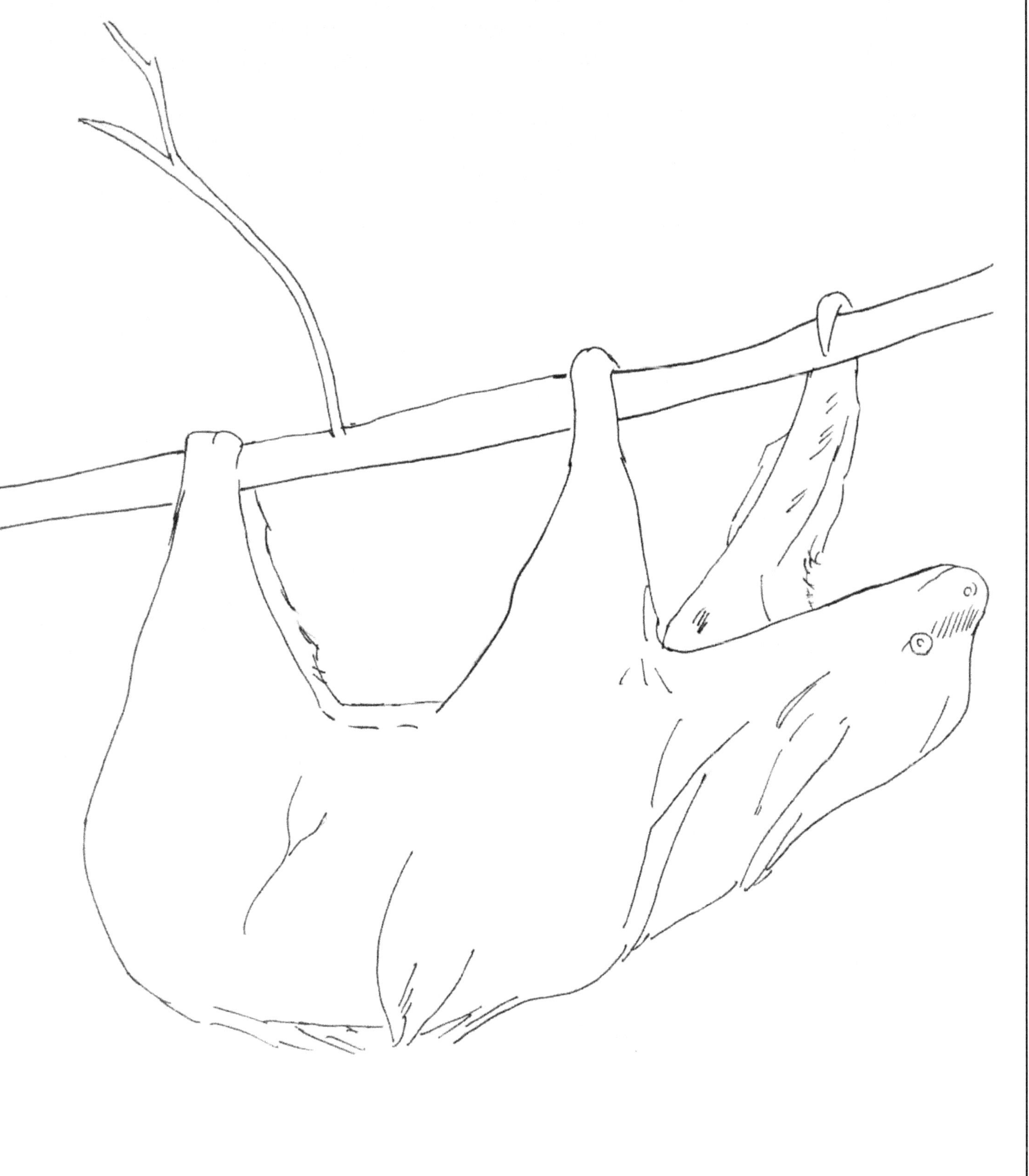

TWO-TOED SLOTH

TWO-TOED SLOTH the face is quite flatten and hairless, the eyes are small, set within black rings; the ears are also small and almost completely hidden beneath the long, gray-brown coat. The tail is a little more a stump. The front legs are slightly longer than the hind legs, and have feet with long curved claws. Length of head and body is about 25 inches, and weight is about 20 pounds.

This species has a vegetarian diet. It lives in tees, rarely descending to the ground, and spends much of its time hanging from branches, or resting in the fork between branches. A single offspring is born after a 5 to 6 month gestation period. In the first four weeks of its life the young sloth remains firmly attached to its mother, hidden in her coat. At 9 months it is almost completely independent, but does not reach full maturity until two of age.

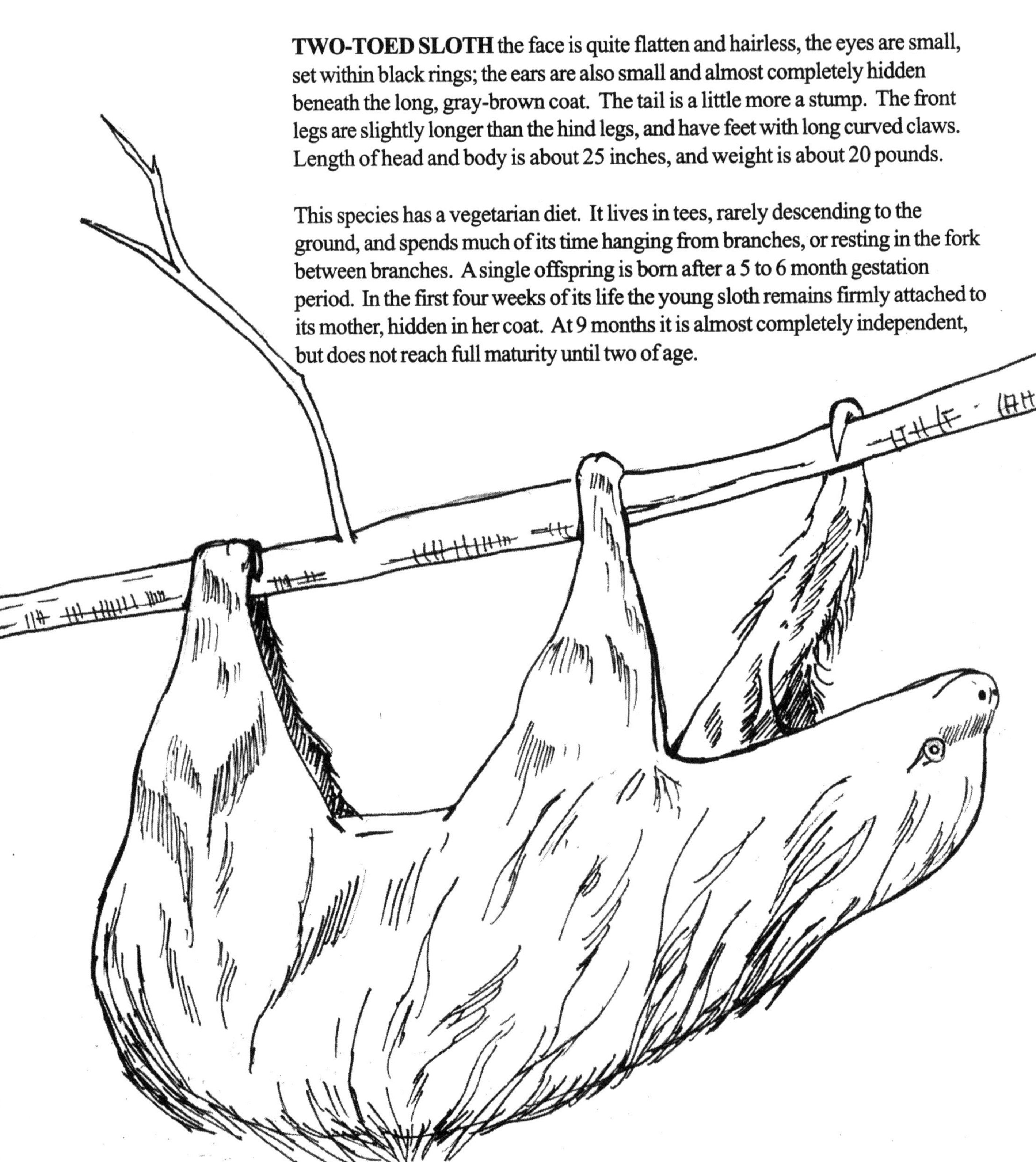

To start the show, I drew an outline of the Common Bat's head, torso, and wings.

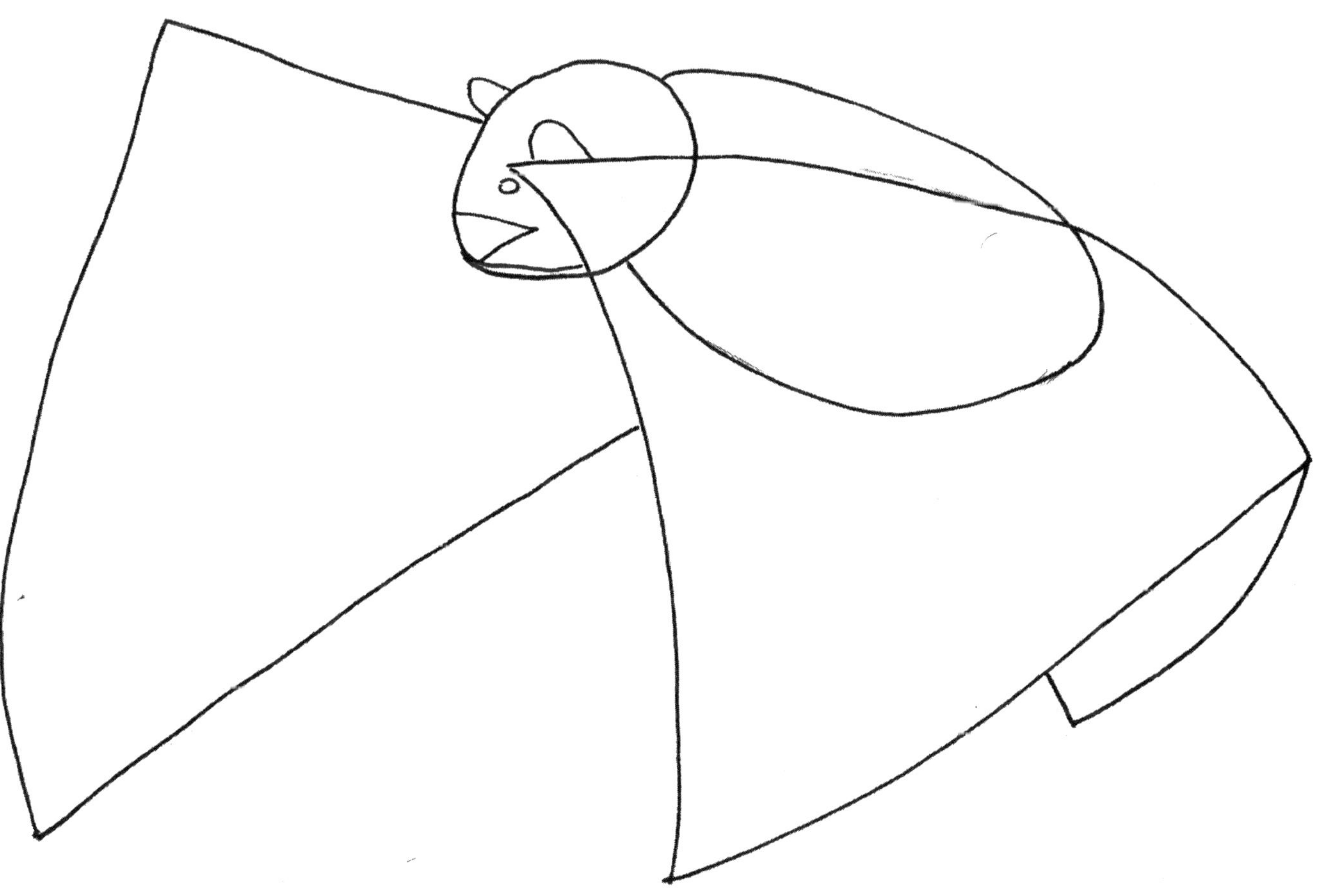

Now, you can sketch in some details to the Common Bat's head, torso, and wings.

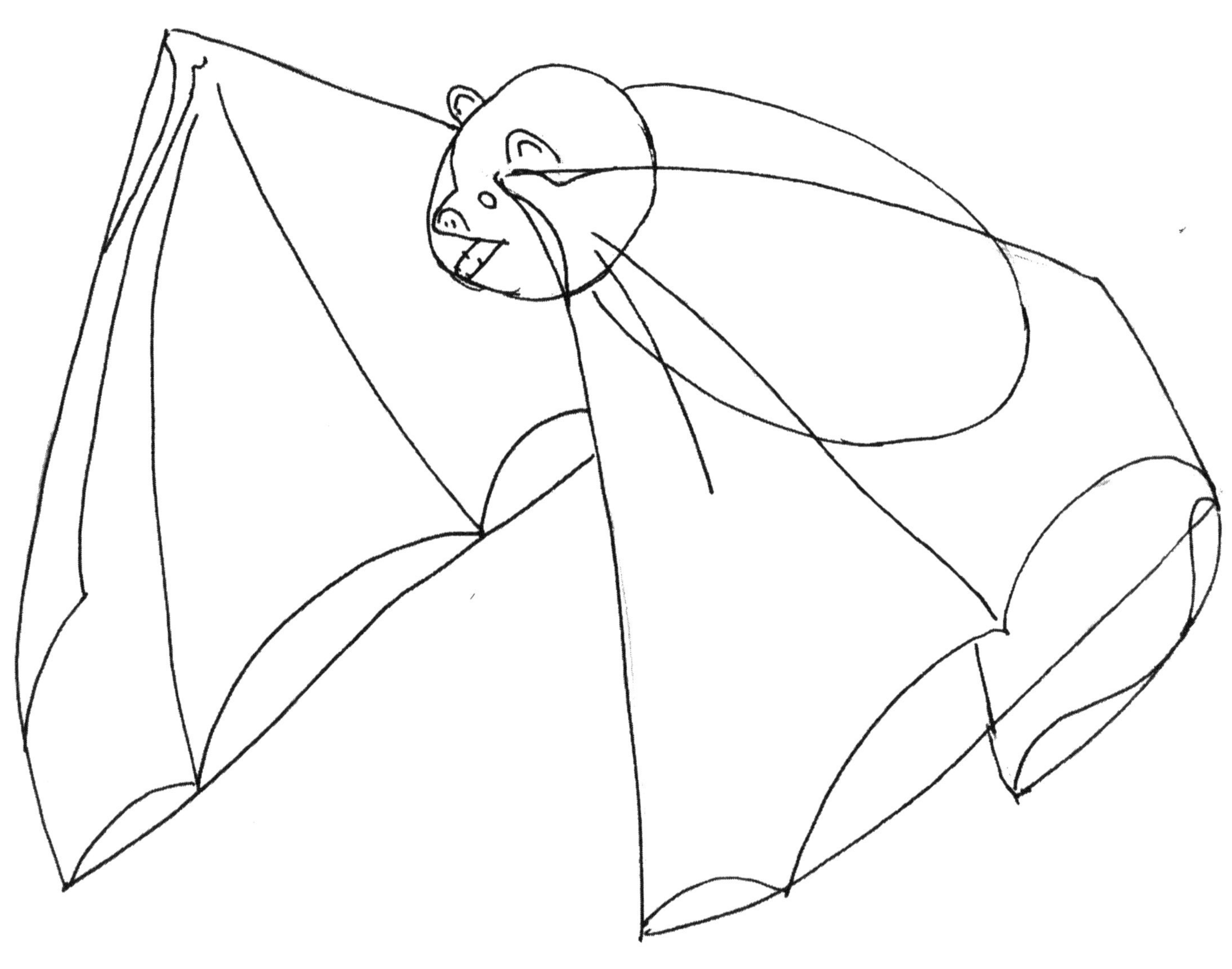

You've almost finished this drawing, just add more details to the Common Bat's head, torso, wings, and outline for shadows.

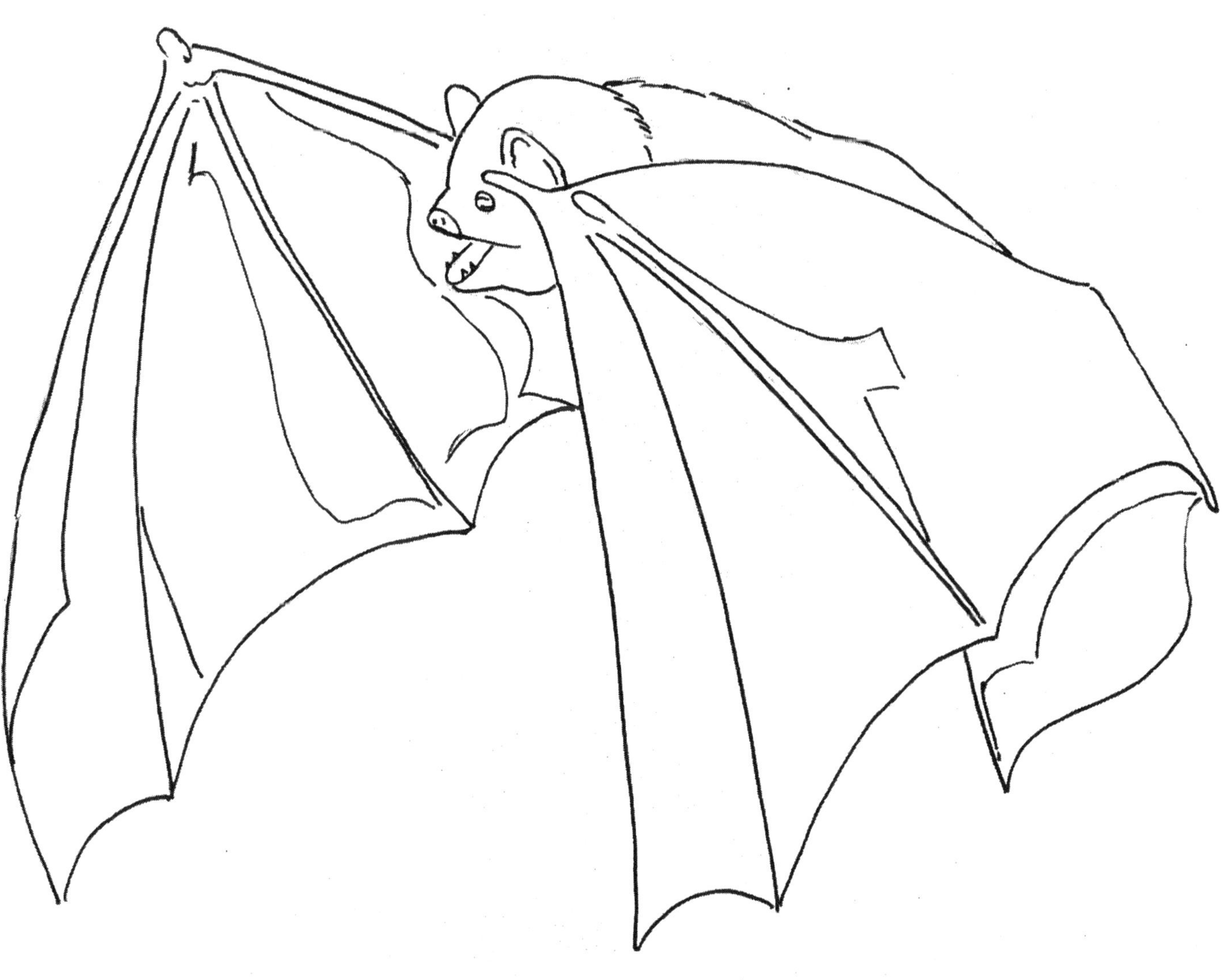

COMMON PIPISTRELLE BAT

COMMON PIPISTRELLE BAT small and robust, this bat has a short dark muzzle, small ears, with broadly rounded tip. Fur long, uniformly brown, may be slightly lighter beneath. Length of head and body about (1.6 in.), forearm about (1.2 in.), and weight (0.1 - 0.3 oz.).

This bat is found in Britain, southern Scandinavia, Western Europe to Caucasus; Morocco; Middle East to Kashmir. The most abundant bat in the British Isles and one of the most common in Europe, the tiny Pipistrelle roosts singly or in small colonies up to several hundred in number, often with other species. It favors hollow trees, or under loose bark, buildings, under roofs, but rarely found in caves. It forages throughout the night, and in spring and autumn may be seen flying about in midday as well, seeking small insects such as gnats. Common Pipistrelle hibernates in winter and sometimes migrates more than 1000 miles between seasonal roosting sites. Most young are born in July after a gestation period of about six weeks, and reach sexual maturity in two years. A single offspring is usual in Britain; twins are common in northern and central Europe.

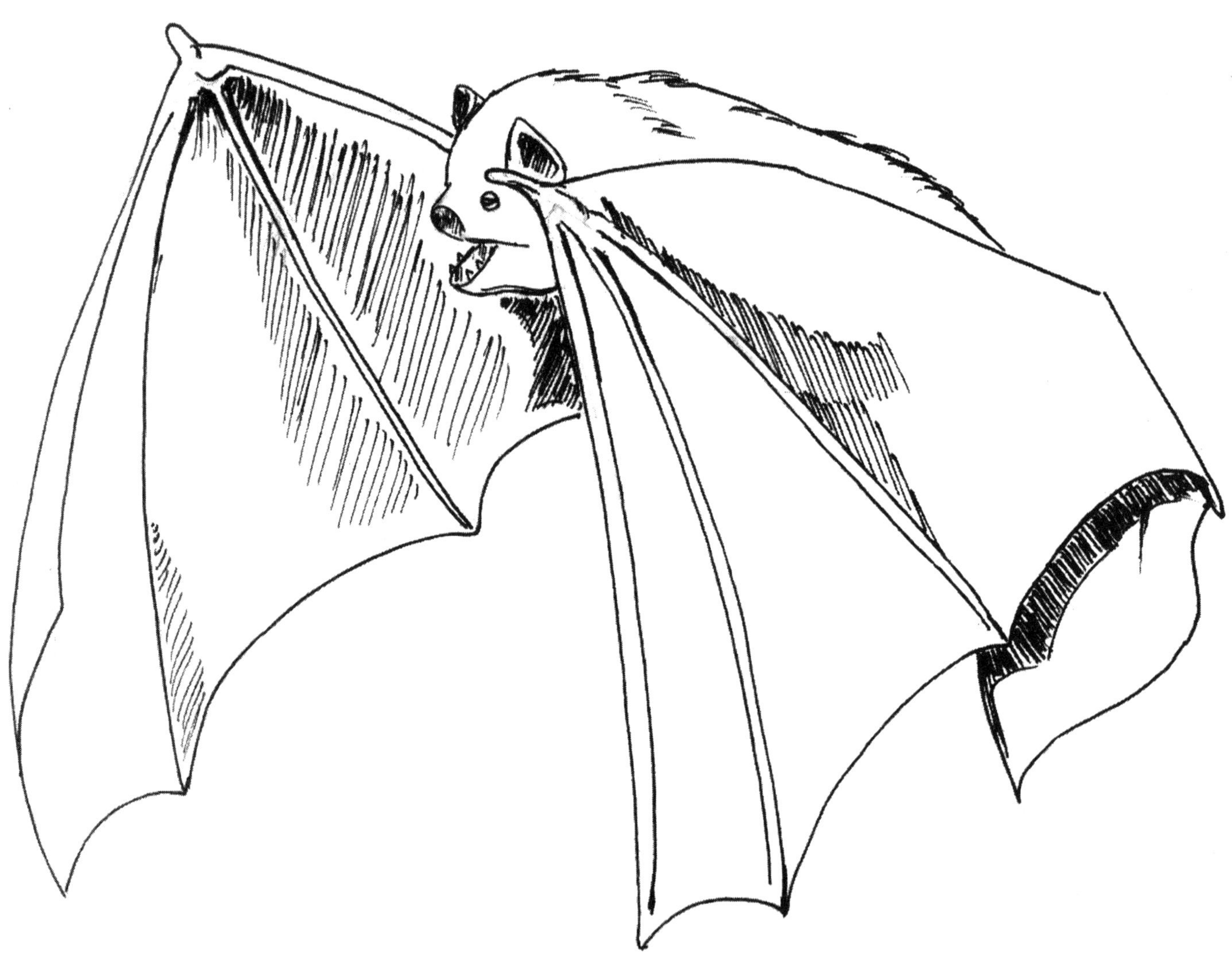

Let's first start drawing an outline of the Markhor's head, horns, neck, torso, tail, legs and hoofs.

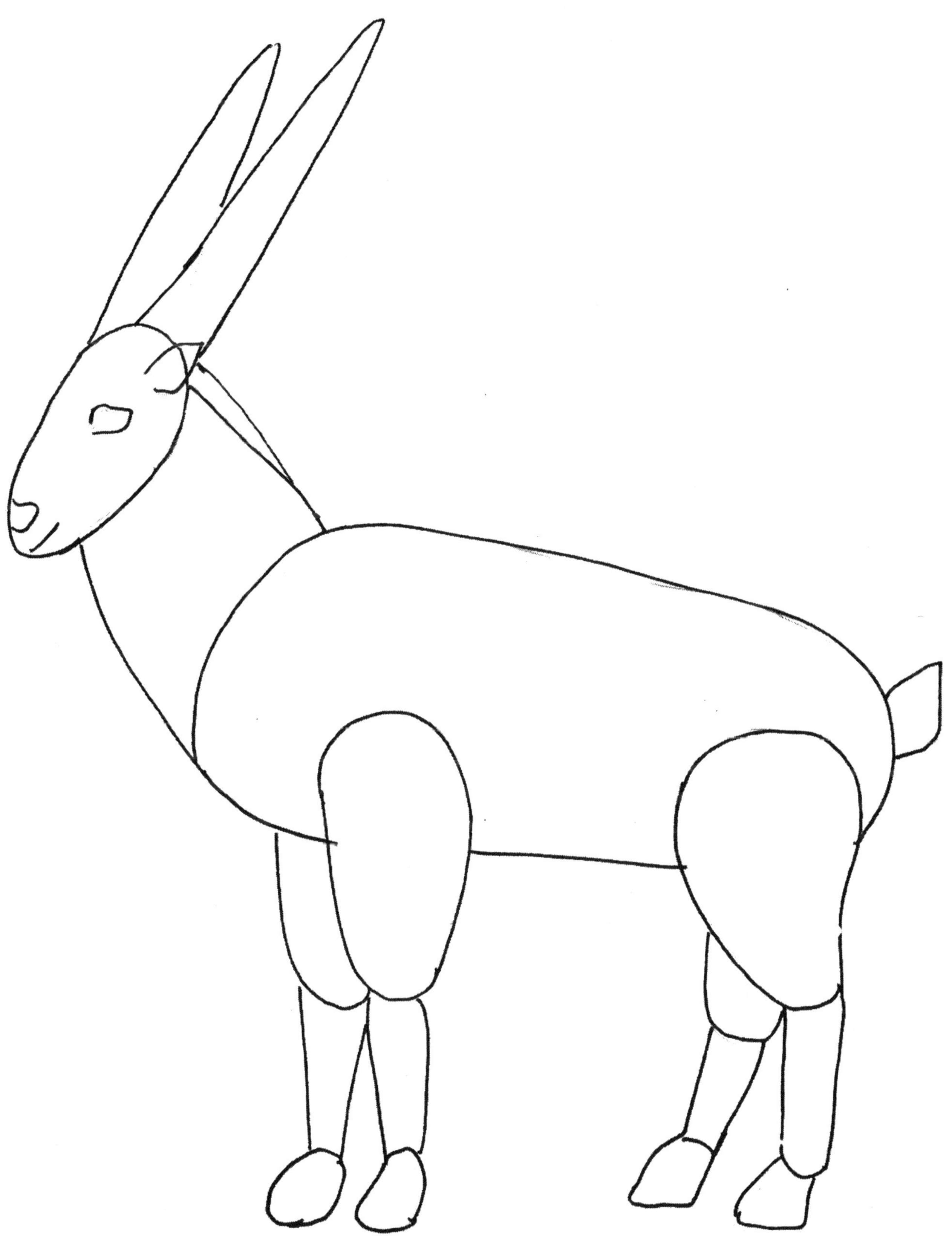

Sketch in more details of the Markhor's head, horns, neck, torso, tail, and hoofs.

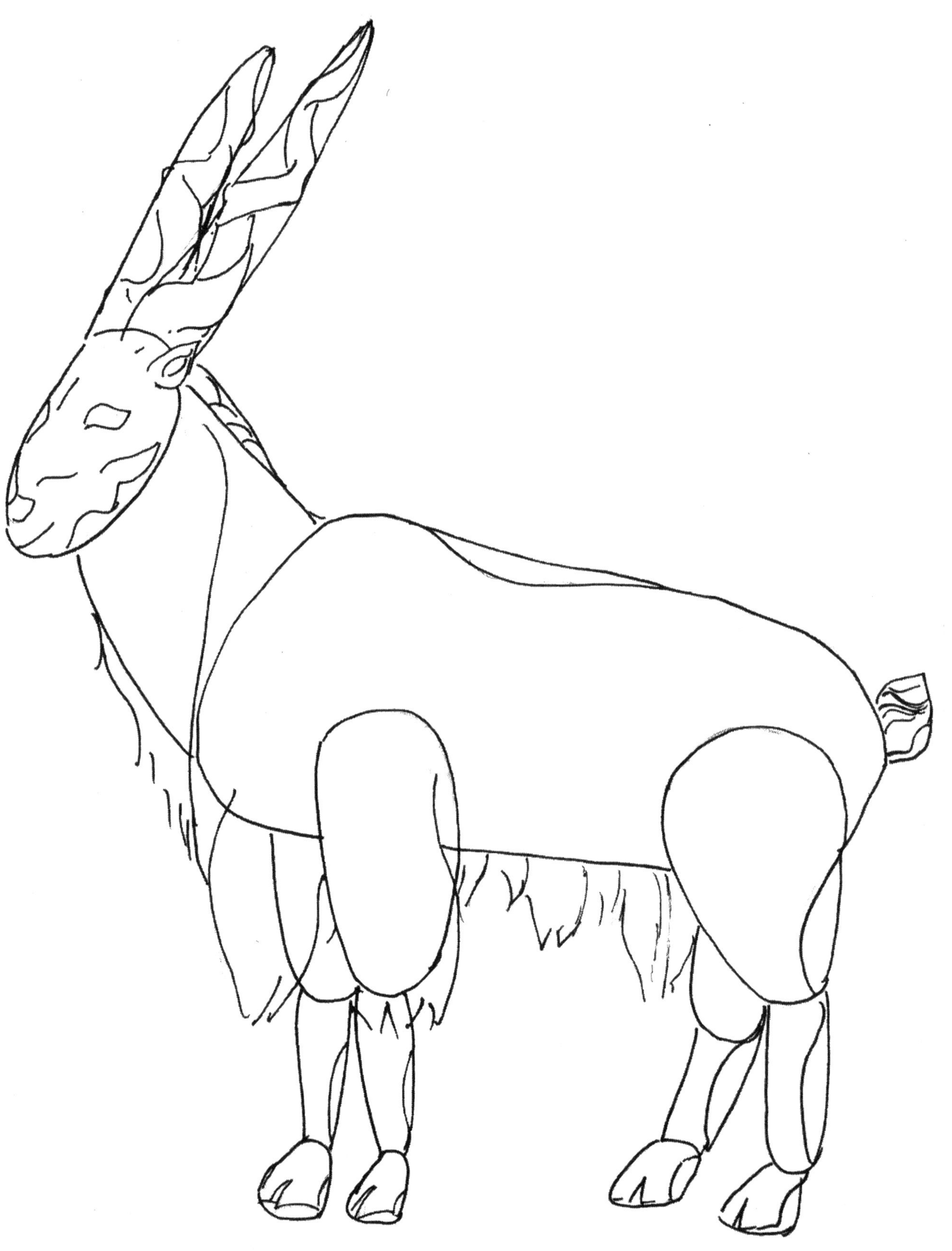

You can erase any lines not needed, draw in hair and add more details to the Markhor's head, horns, neck, torso, tail, and hoofs.

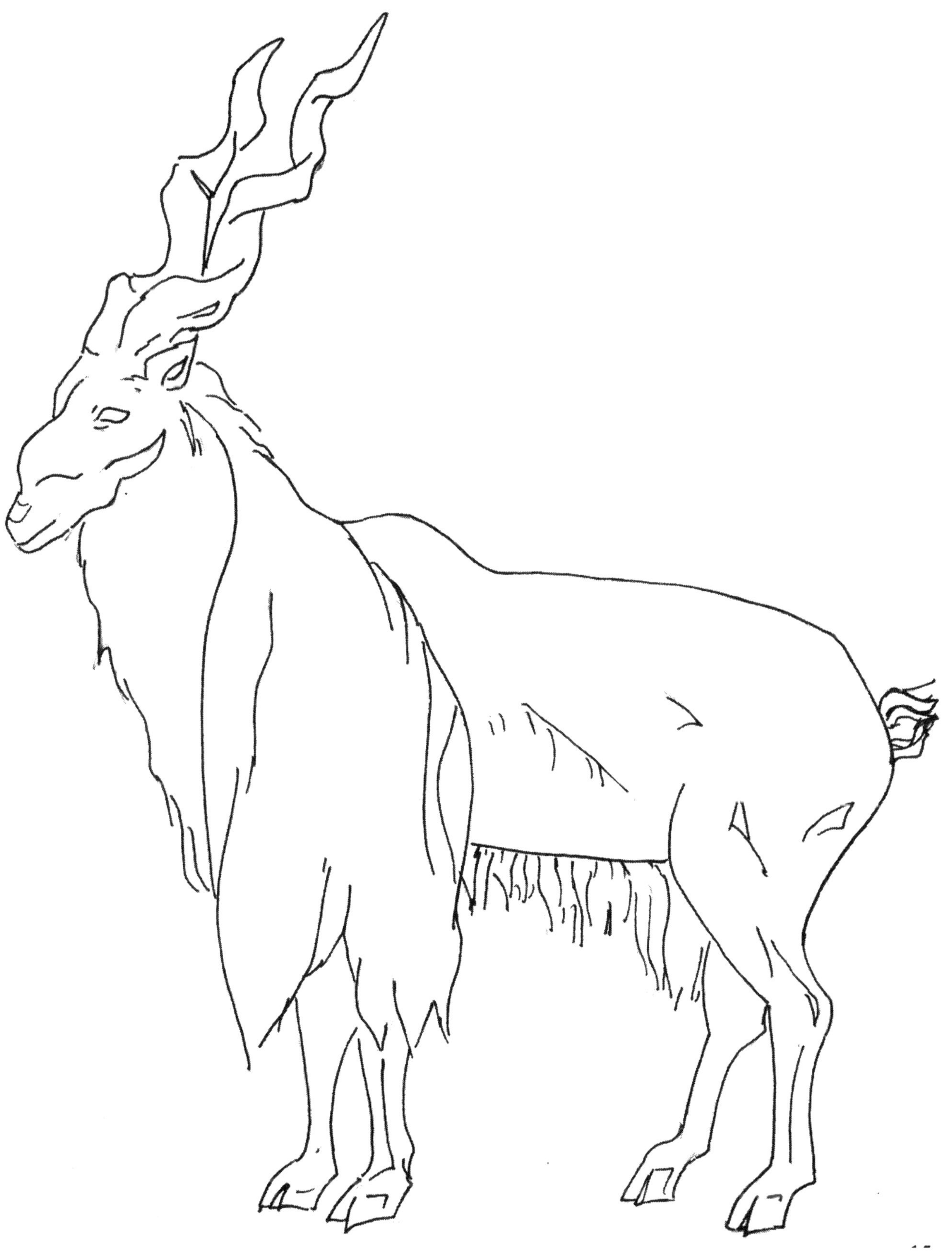

MARKHOR

MARKHOR the coat is short and smooth in summer and longer in winter, it is heavier in the northern part of its range. The males have a long beard on the chin and long hair on the throat, chest, and shanks; female have smaller fringes of long hair. The horns, which are present in both sexes, are spiral shaped, and are much smaller in the female. Length head and body is 64 to 67 inches, tail about 3 to 5 inches, and weight about 176 to 242 pounds; females smaller than males.

This creature is found in Afghanistan and the western Himalayas. Although one of the largest of the Caprinae, or wild goat, this usually solitary, nimble creature climbs and jumps over mountain terrain with ease. In the winter months it descends to lower altitudes to avoid extreme cold. Mating occurs in the winter. In the summer the females gather in small groups, which include the newborn. Gestation lasts for 5.5 months, and then the female delivers 1 or 2 kids. The numbers of this species has been considerably reduced because of hunting, and because of epidemics transmitted to them by domestic animals

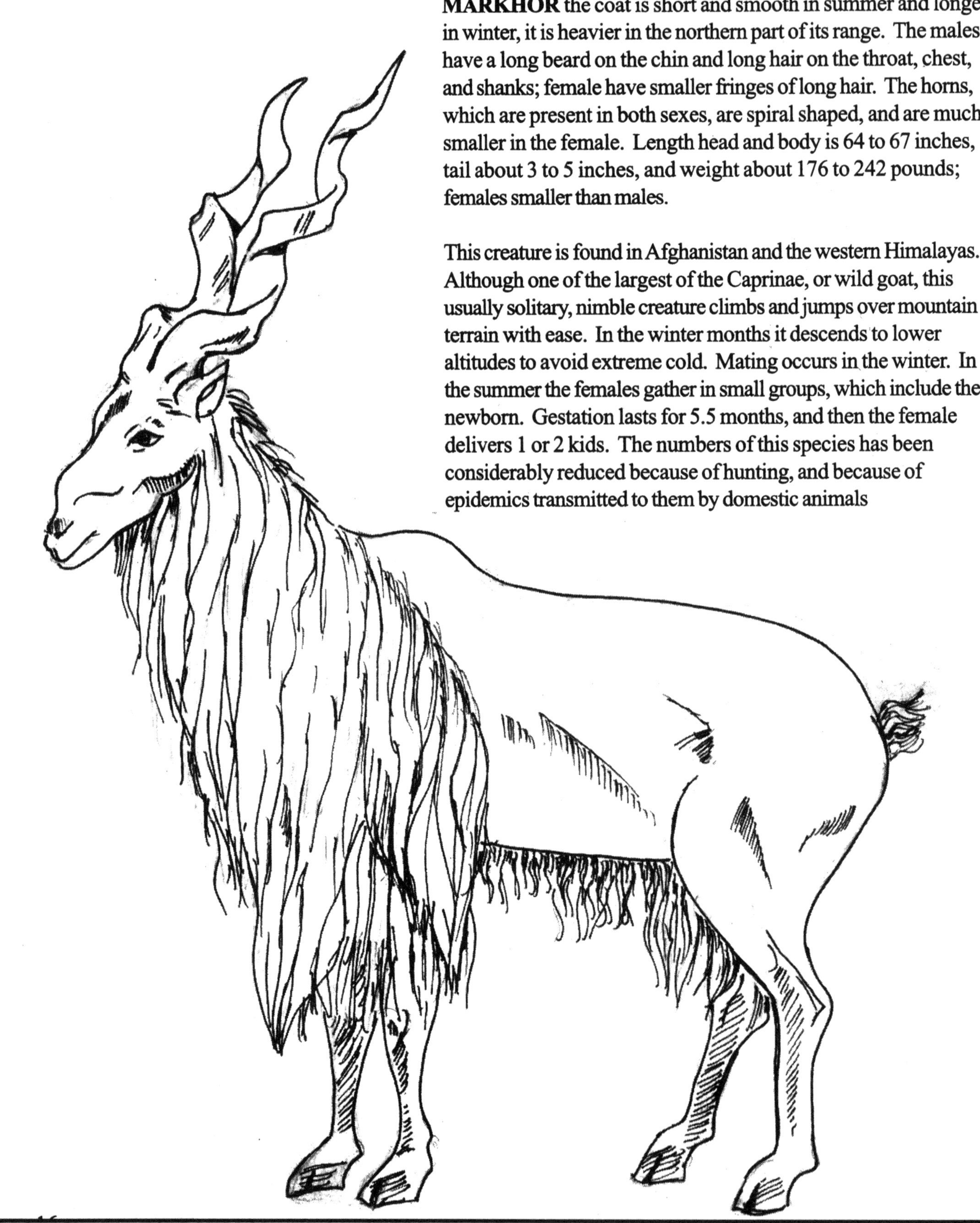

I started drawing an outline of the Walrus's head, neck, tusks, torso, and the rest of the body.

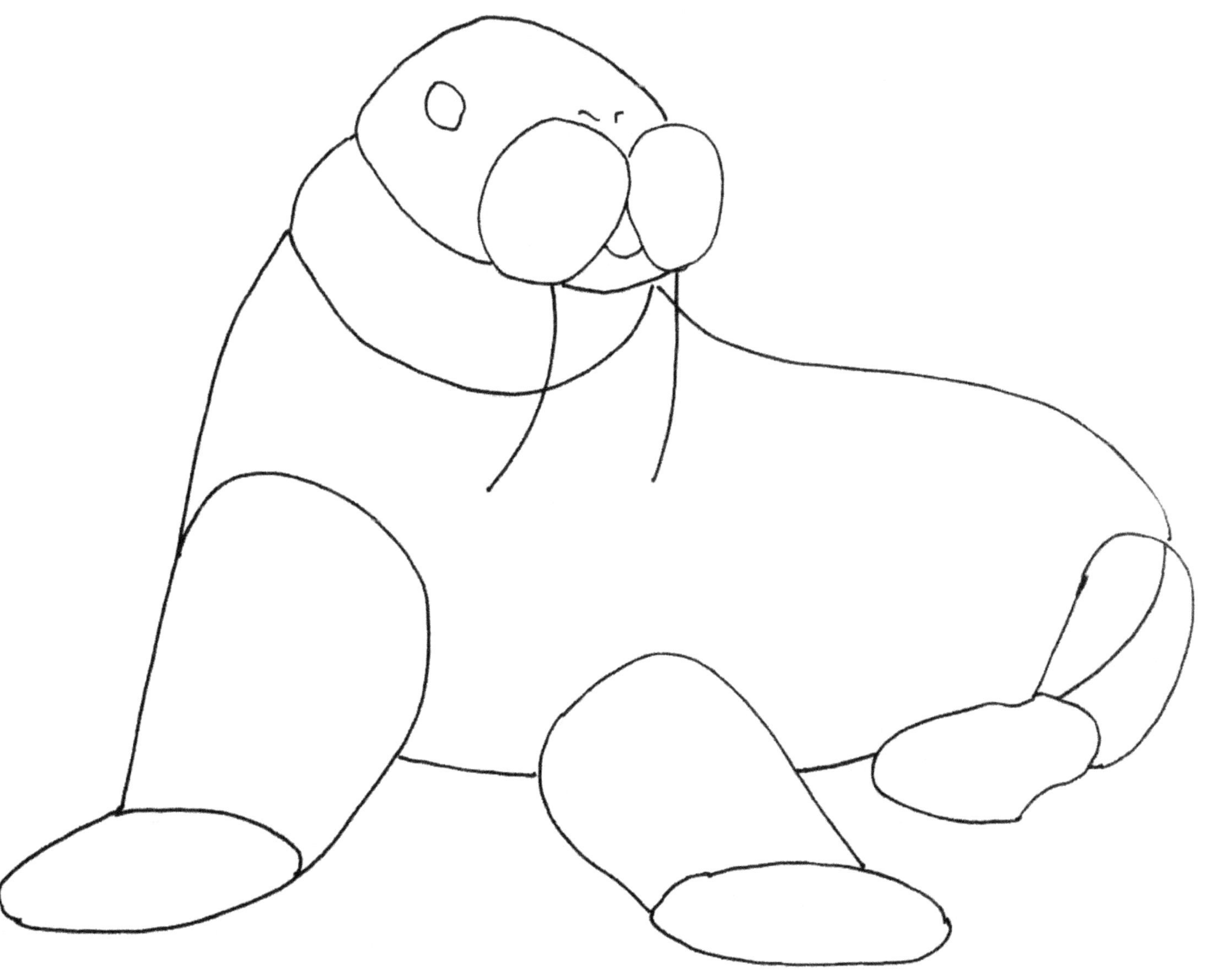

Sketch in more portions of the Walrus for a more precise description of the total body.

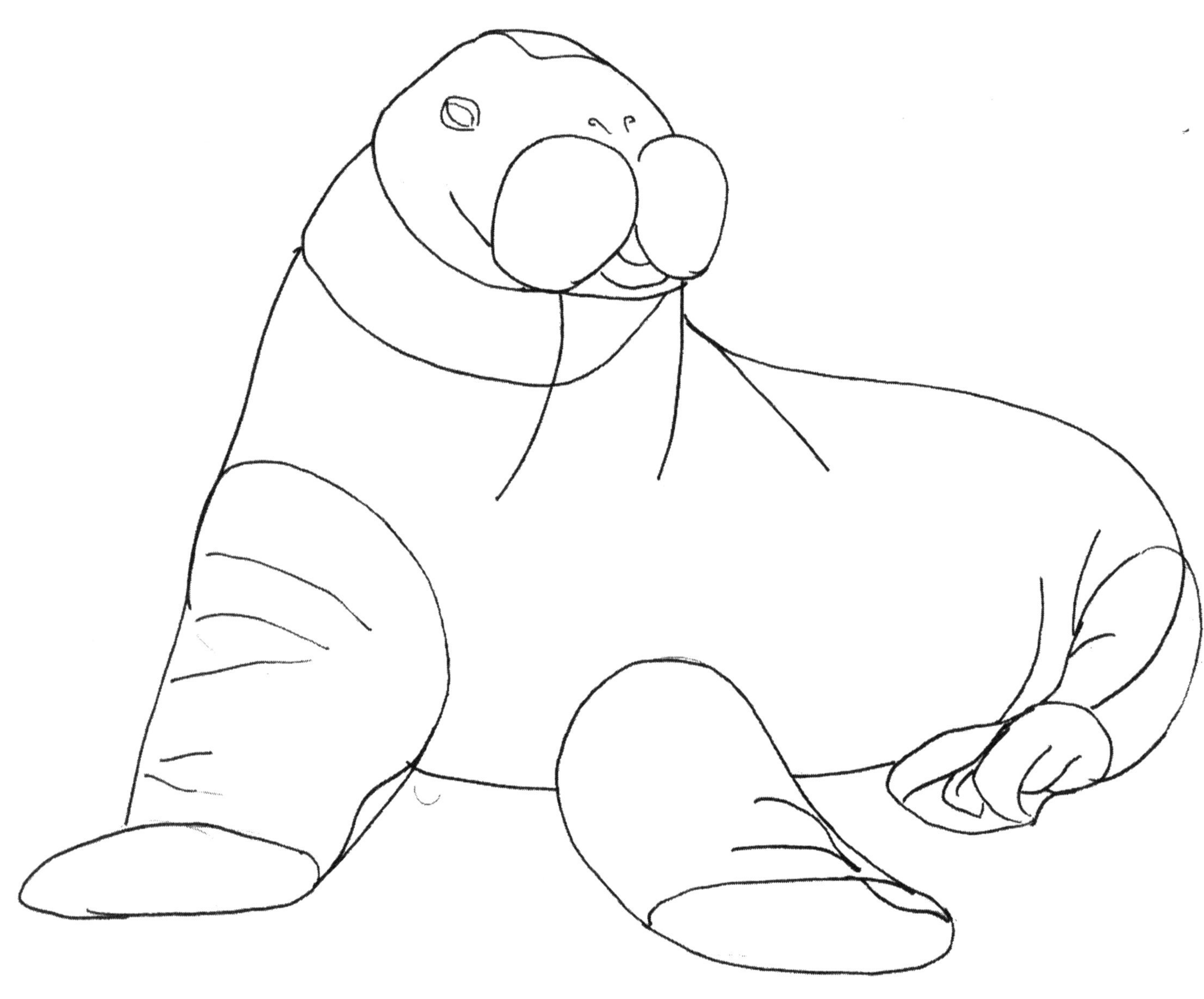

Add more details, such as forming the tusk, whiskers across the snout, wrinkles and you're almost there.

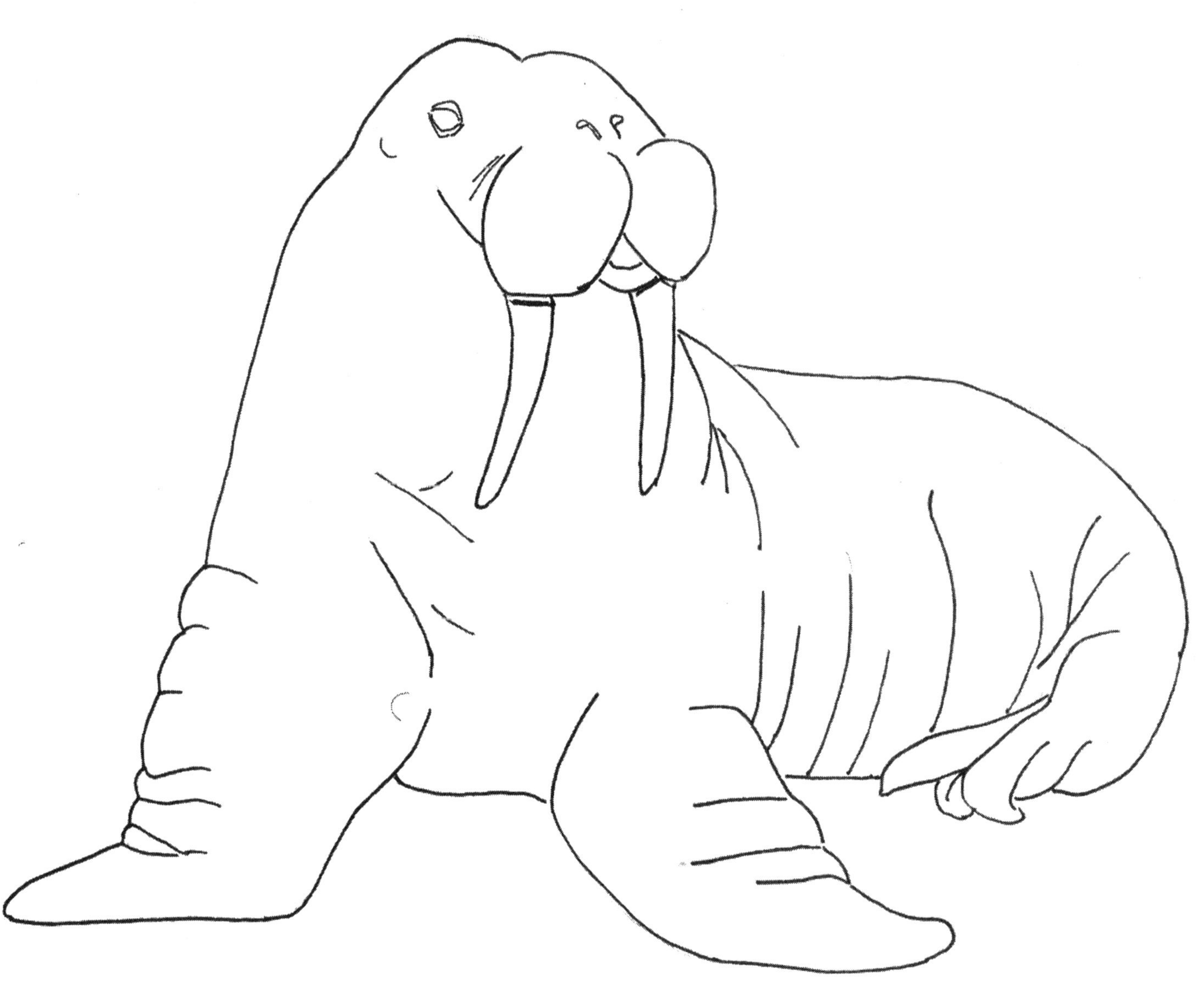

WALRUS

WALRUS the brown coat can be quite thin, and in older individuals the skin is completely bare. A layer of fat about 2-3 inches thick provides insulation. There are many stiff whiskers across the snout. There is no external ear. The upper canines form two tusks that can reach a length of 35 inches and which cause the entire structure of the cranium (skull) to be altered. The other 18 to 24 teeth are similar to each other. Total head to body length up to 12.5 feet, and weight over 2600 pounds with females being much smaller.

Founded in North circumpolar this gregarious species lives in large groups. It spends most of the day sleeping on ice. It usually flees if attacked, but there have been cases of walruses attacking the boats of Eskimos. A cow will vigorously defend her young. It feeds largely on mollusks, which it may wrench from the seabed with its tusks. Females breed every other year, and after an 11-12 month gestation, 1-2 young are born in April-June. The females become sexually mature at 4-5 years and the males at about 7 years.

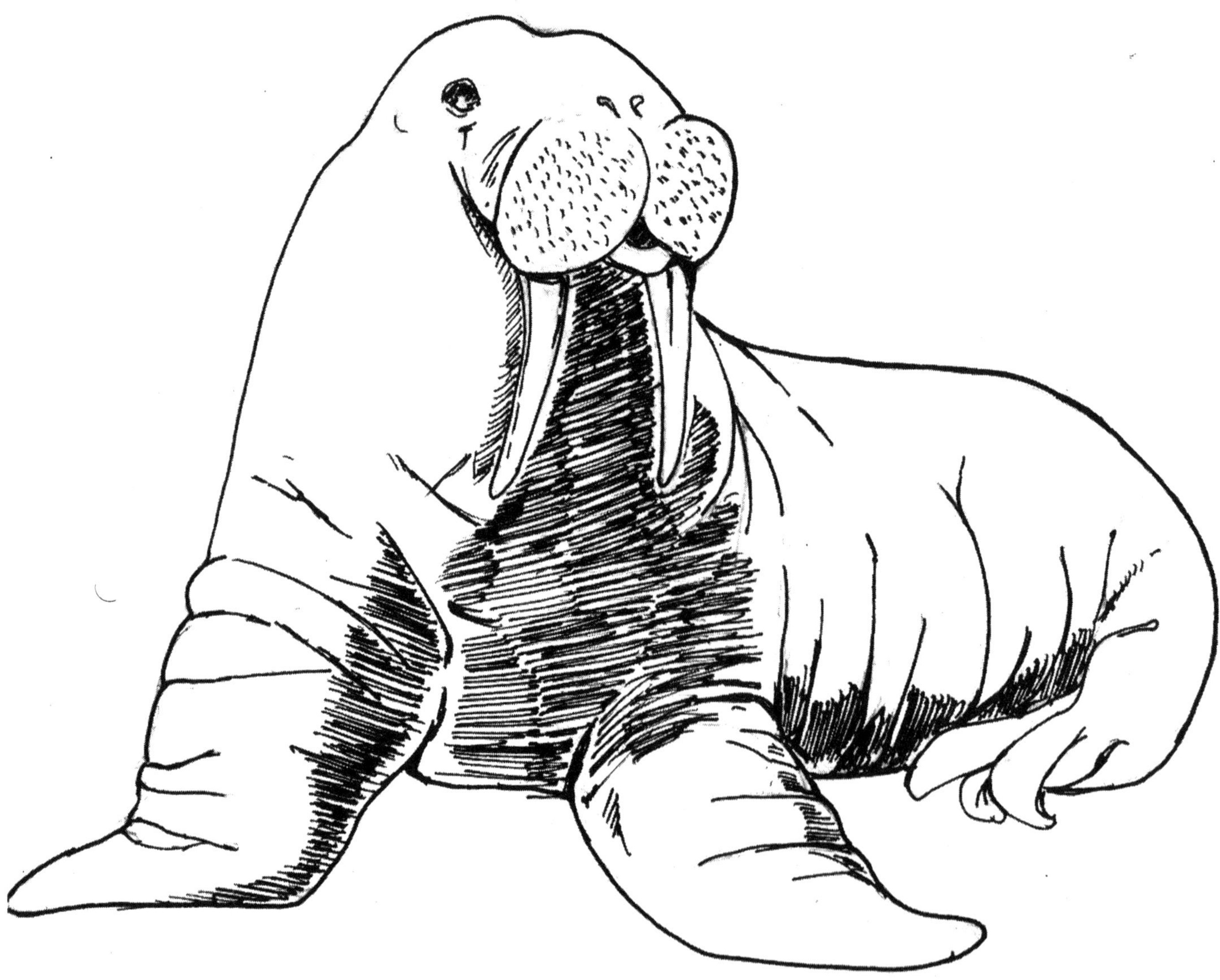

Let's start an outline of the Giraffe's head, neck, torso, tail, legs, and feet (hoofs).

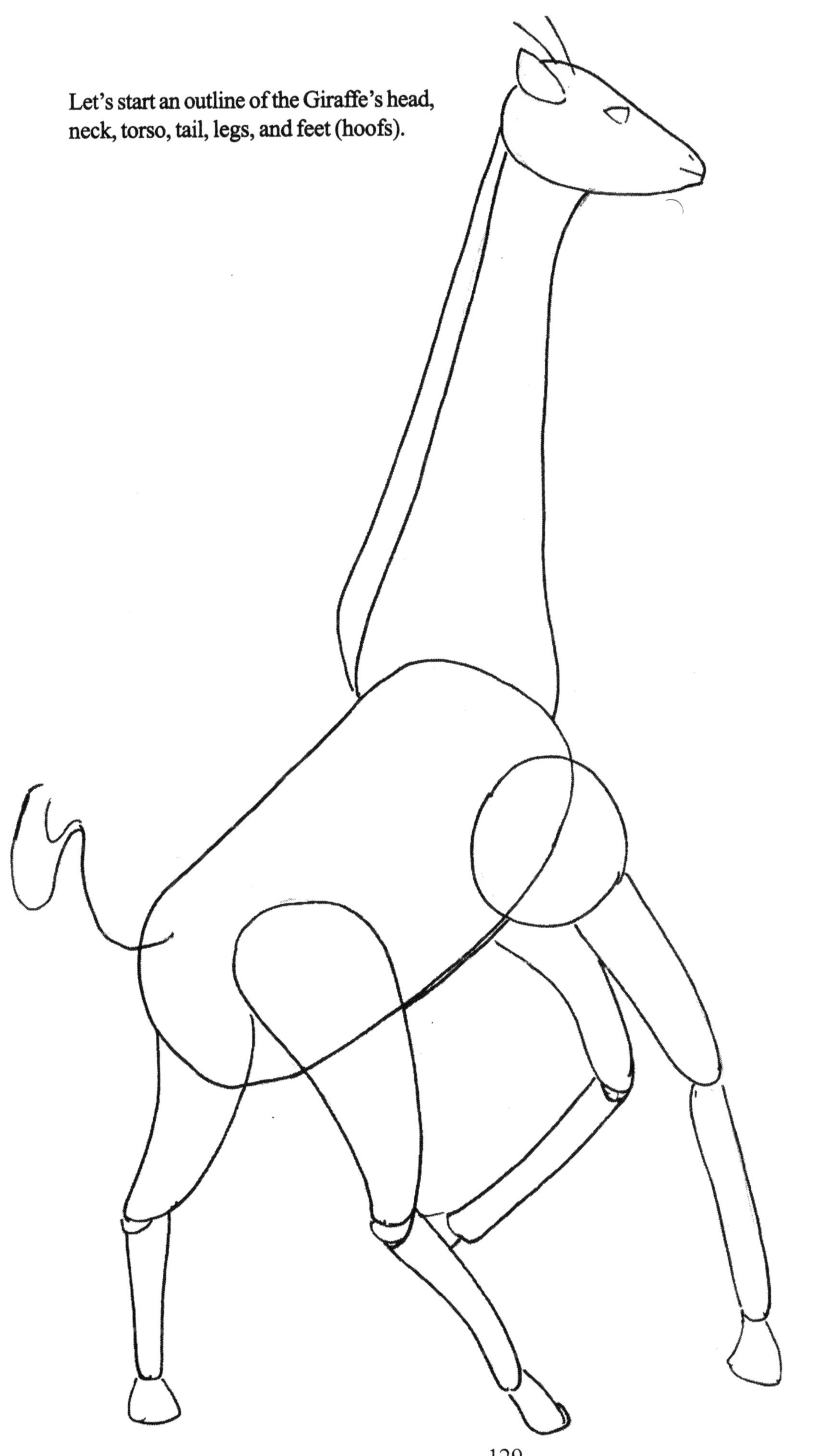

Now, you can sketch in some details to the Giraffe's head, neck, torso, tail, legs, and feet (hoofs).

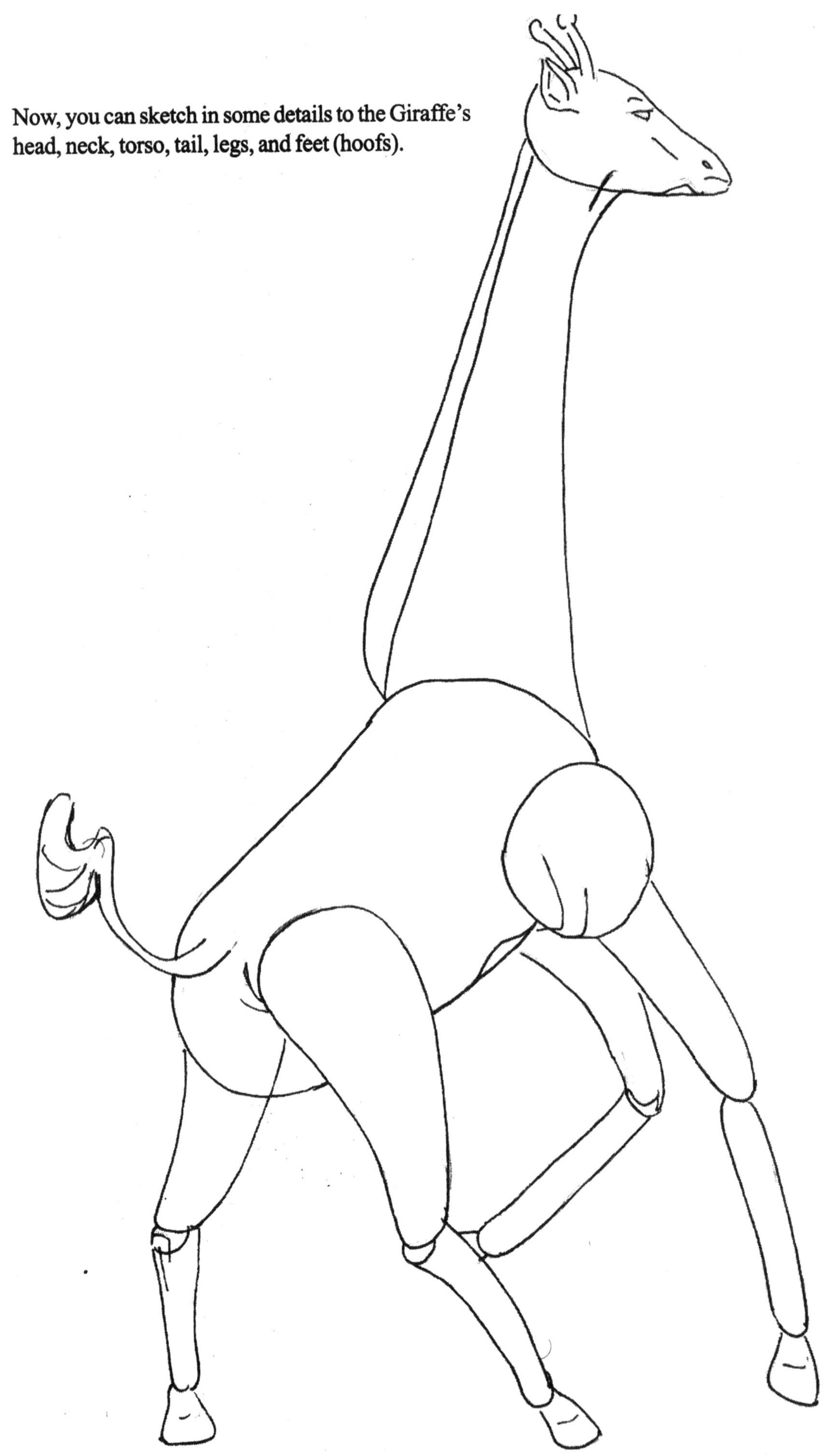

Continue to draw in more details including the coat pattern made up of brown spots.

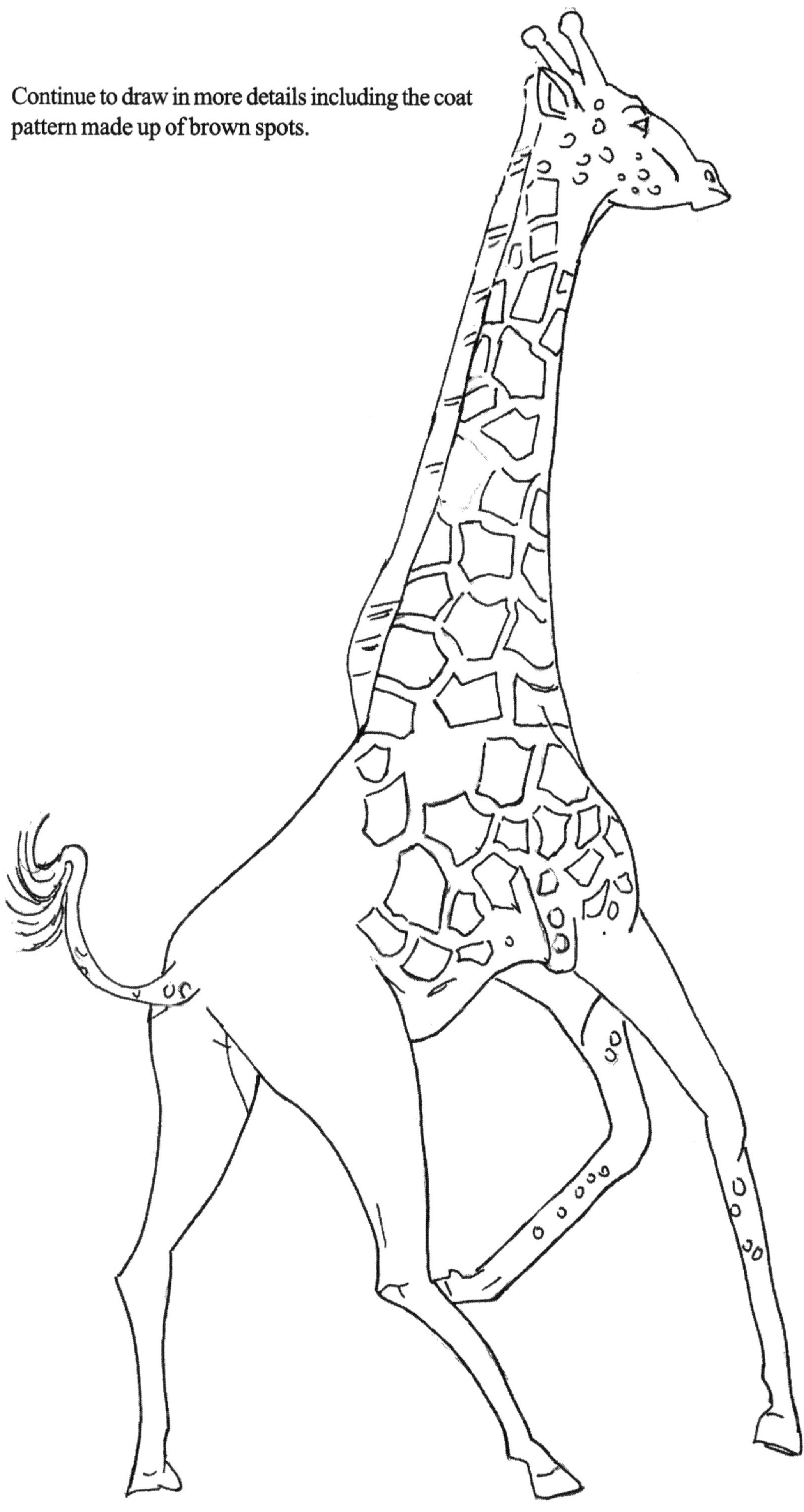

GIRAFFE

GIRAFFE is the tallest living animal. The coat pattern is made up of brown spots of varying sizes, separated by a network of light-colored lines. This pattern varies a great deal between the different geographical subspecies. The giraffe has two small horns and a medium bulge on its forehead, which is covered with skin and hair. Shoulder height about 11.5 feet, height to head up about 20 feet, and weight up to a little over a ton.

Found in sub-Sahara Africa this creature lives in herds, which can number up to 30 to 40 individuals. The group is dominated by an old bull giraffe, but is led by a female when on the move. Sometimes exclusively male groups are formed. The giraffe is vegetarian, and feeds on spiny or thorny plants, which it handles easily with prehensile upper lip and long tongue. When it walks it has an ambling gait, but when it runs it move its front legs together and its back legs together, in sequence. Giraffes breeds year round and give birth after a 15-month gestation to a single young. The offspring nurses for about a year, but begins to eat after a few weeks. The female reaches sexual maturity at 3.5 years of age, the male at about 4.5 years.

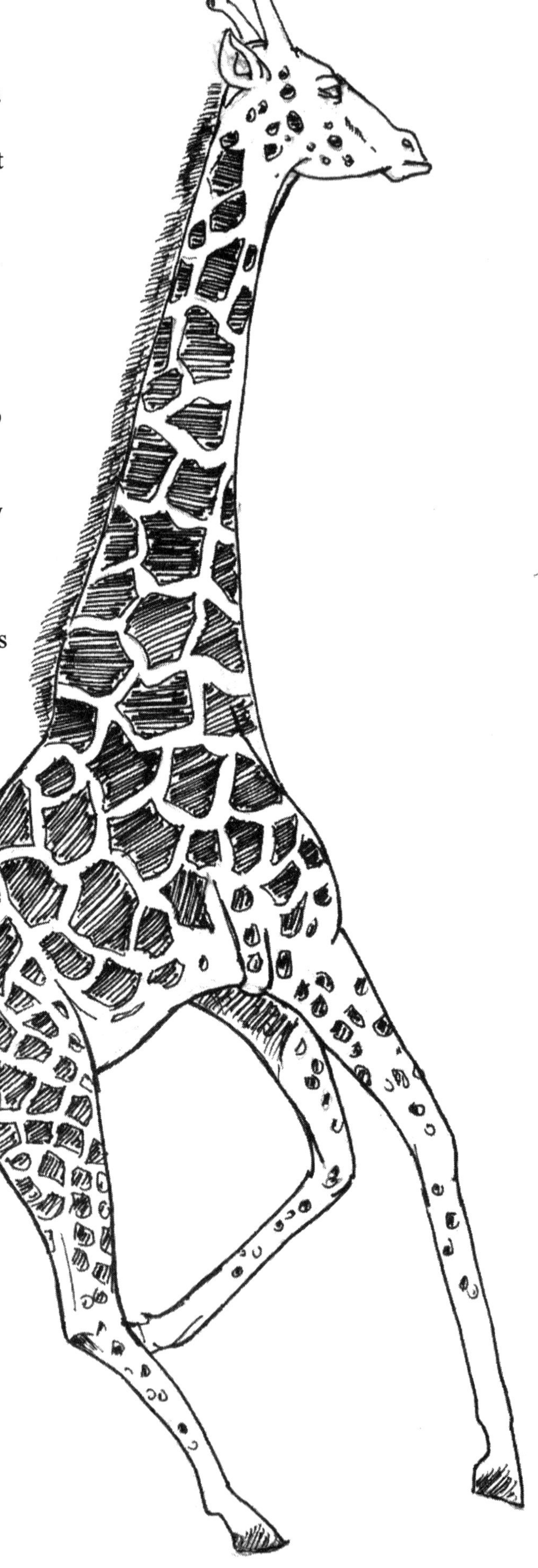

You can start an outline of the Laughing Hyena's head or torso with this figure, and then proceed with the tail, legs, and feet (paws).

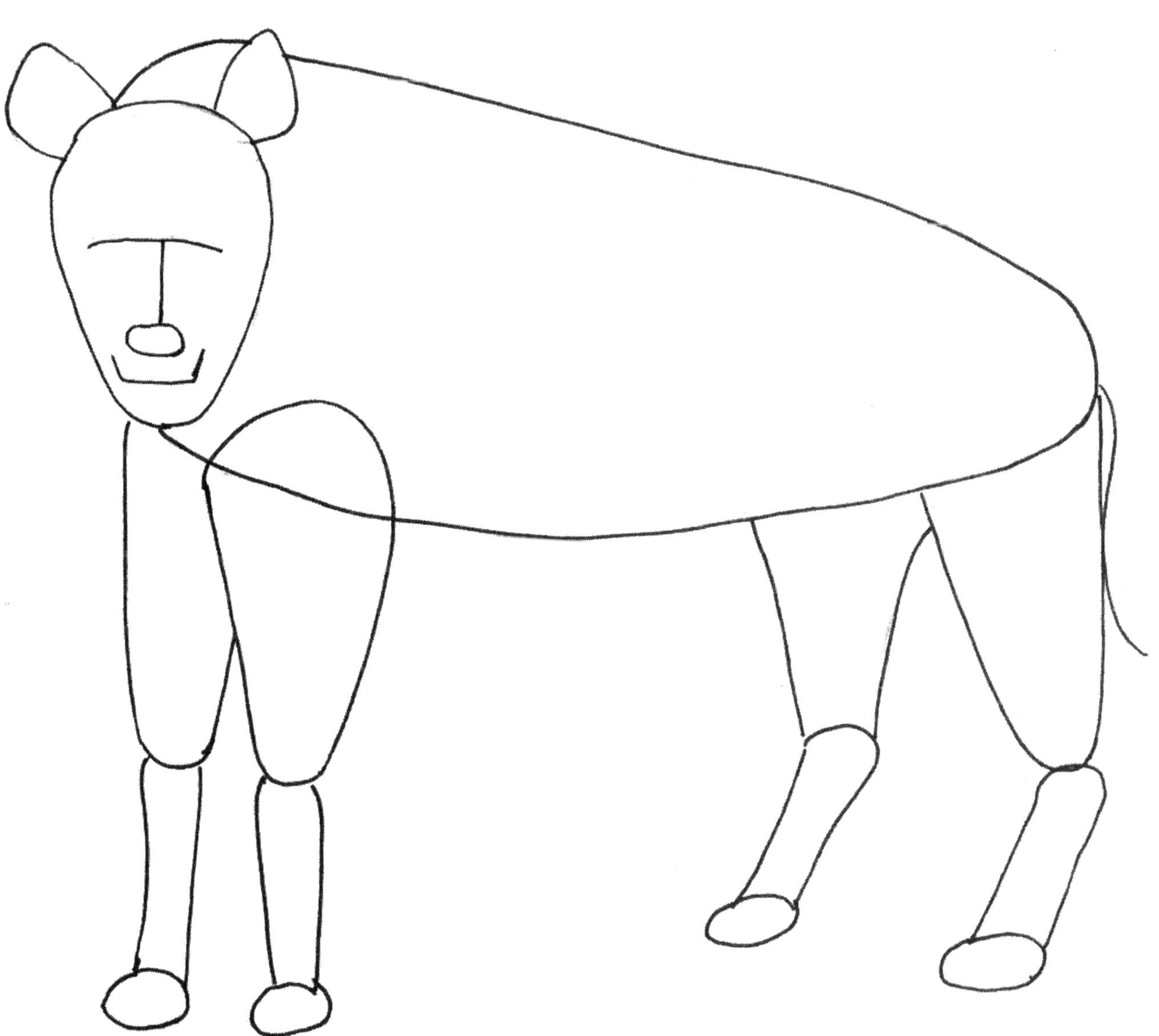

Shape the outline for a more precise figure of the head, torso, tail, legs, and feet.

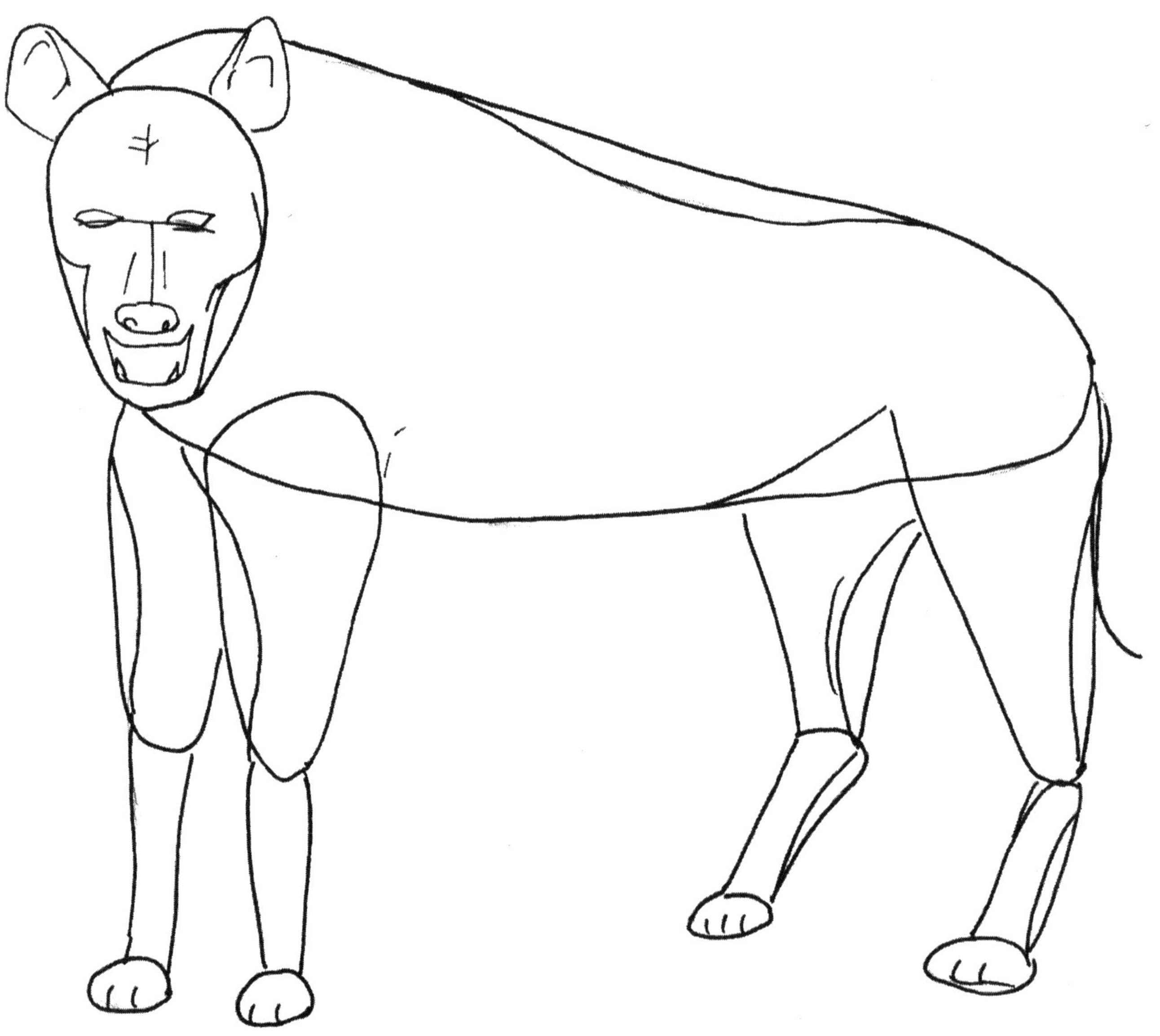

Erase any unneeded lines and put in more details including the Laughing Hyena's coat pattern made up of dark spots.

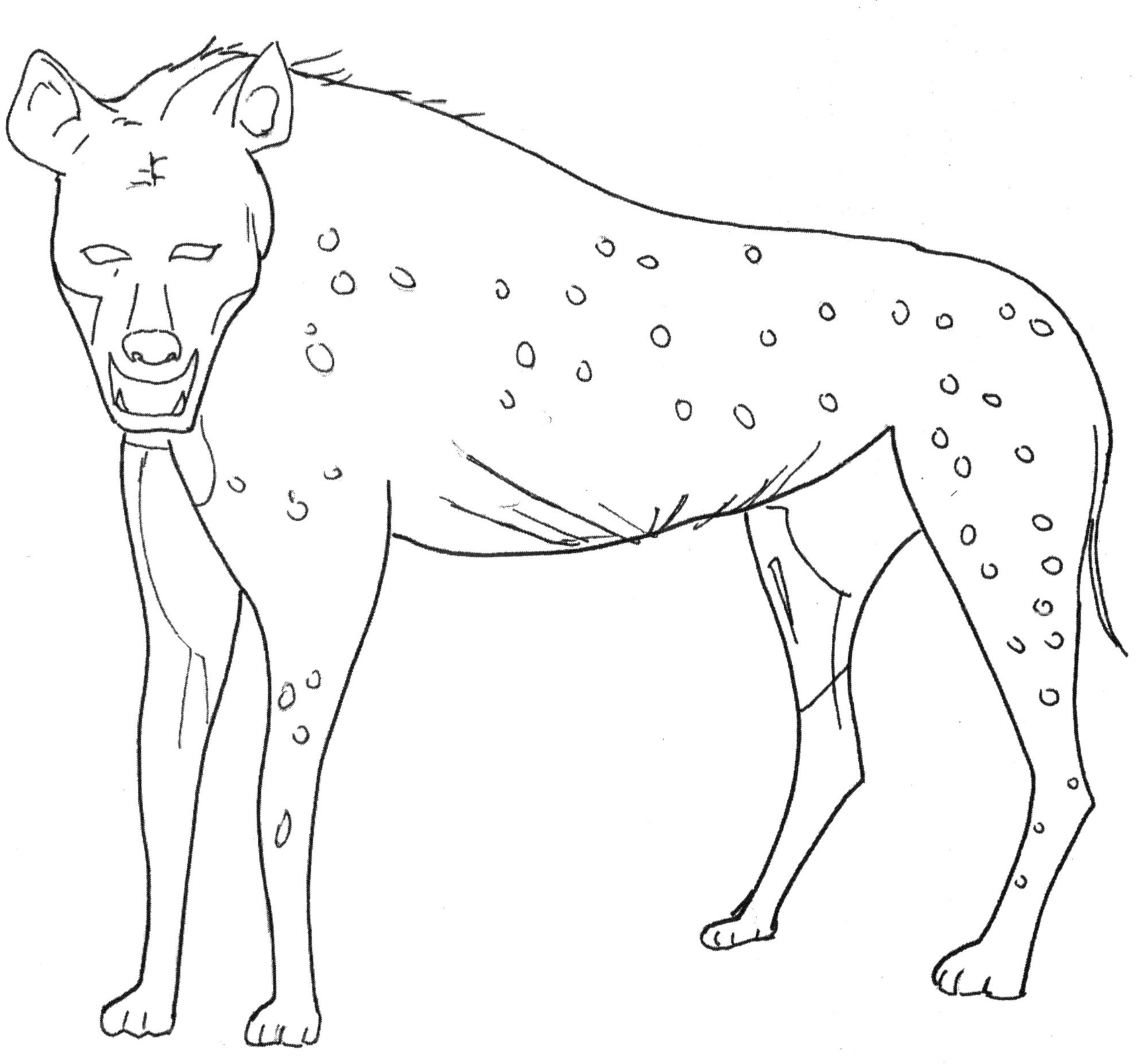

LAUGHING HYENA

LAUGHING HYENA is the largest of the hyenas, with powerful body, large head, large eyes, and rounded ears. The color of the coat is variable but tends to brown, yellow, and gray with numerous dark spots. They are found in Sub-Saharan Africa except densely forested areas and the southern tip of the continent. Length of head and body 4.3 - 5.3 feet, tail 10 - 12 inches, weight 130 - 180 pounds

This hyena is generally a night creature, but does move around during the day. It lives alone or pairs. It patrols a large territory and often follows large plant eating creatures. It feeds on carcasses, but can attack and tear apart animals the size of a gnu (wildebeest). During the courtship and mating period it sometimes gathers in large packs, which are quite noisy. The gestation period lasts for about 110 days, after which 1 or 2 young (rarely 3) are born. The offspring nurse for about 18 months.

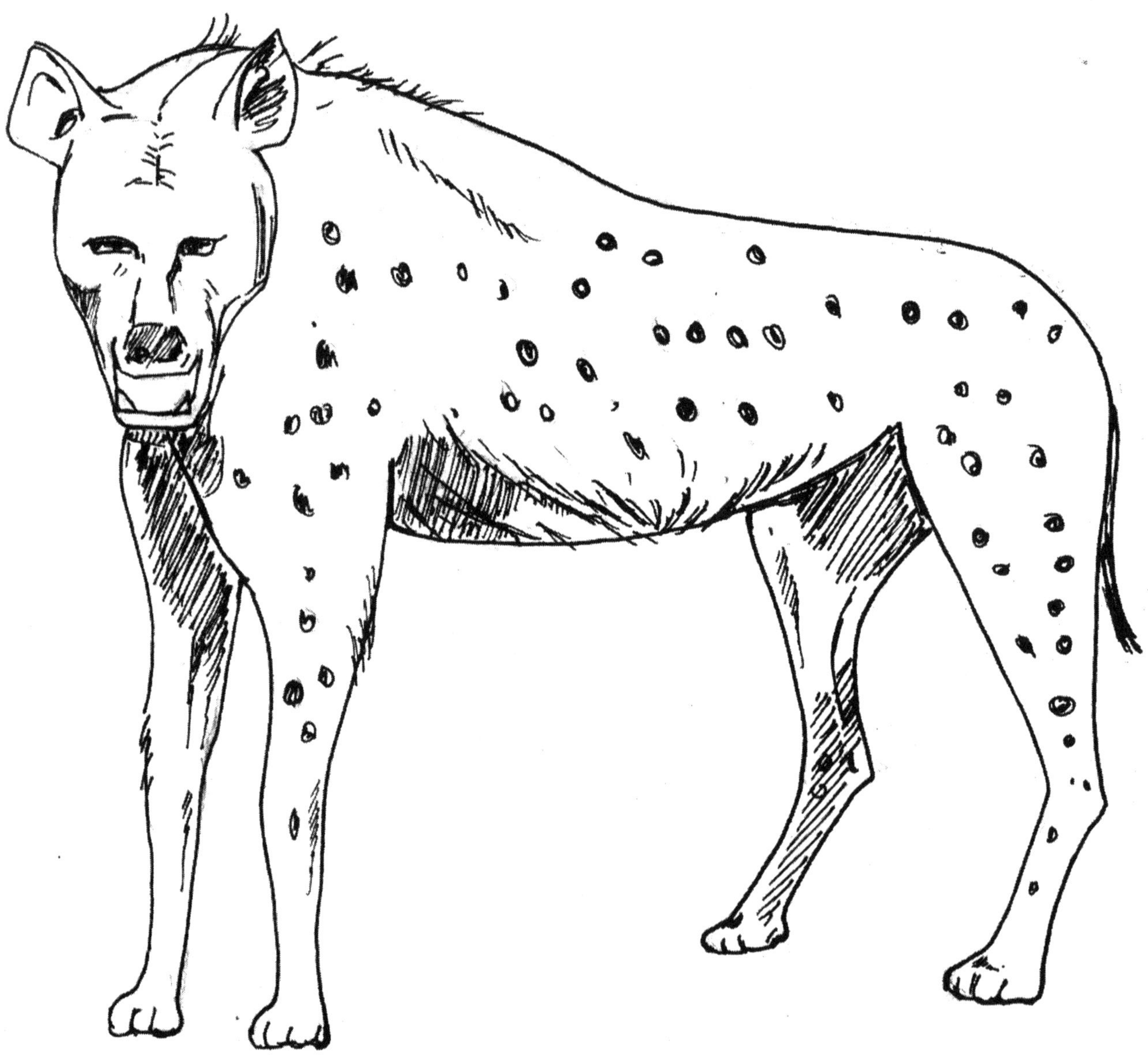

I'm sure you have figured out by now from the lessons of previous pages of this book, that when you start the drawing of a mammal most of the time you will start with head, unless it is in different position such as the backside of the mammal.

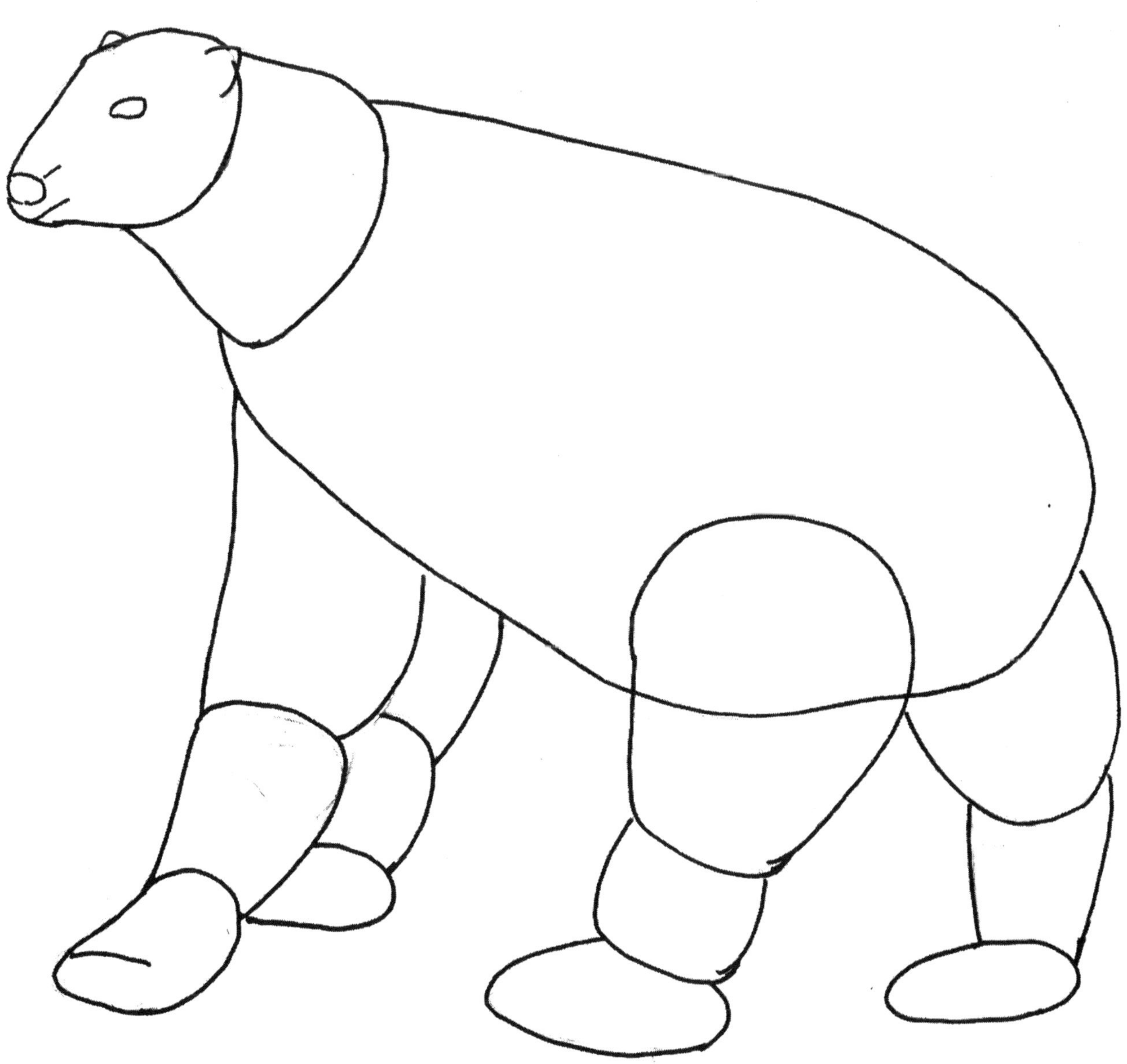

Shape the outline of the Polar Bear for a more precise figure of the head, torso, tail, legs, and feet.

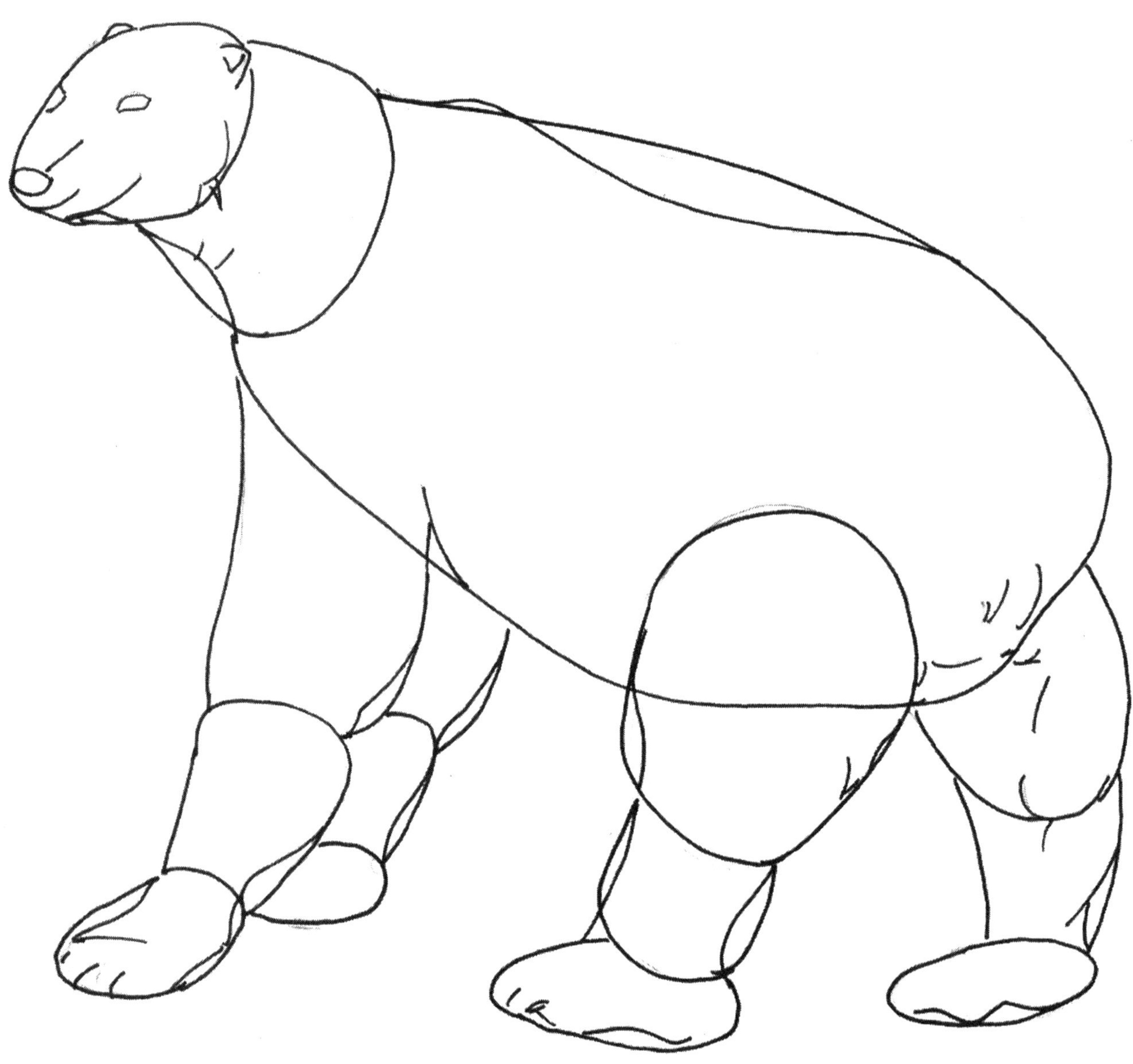

You can erase any lines not needed, draw in more details to the Polar Bear's head, neck, torso, tail, feet, and don't forget to put on its fur coat because it's cold out here.

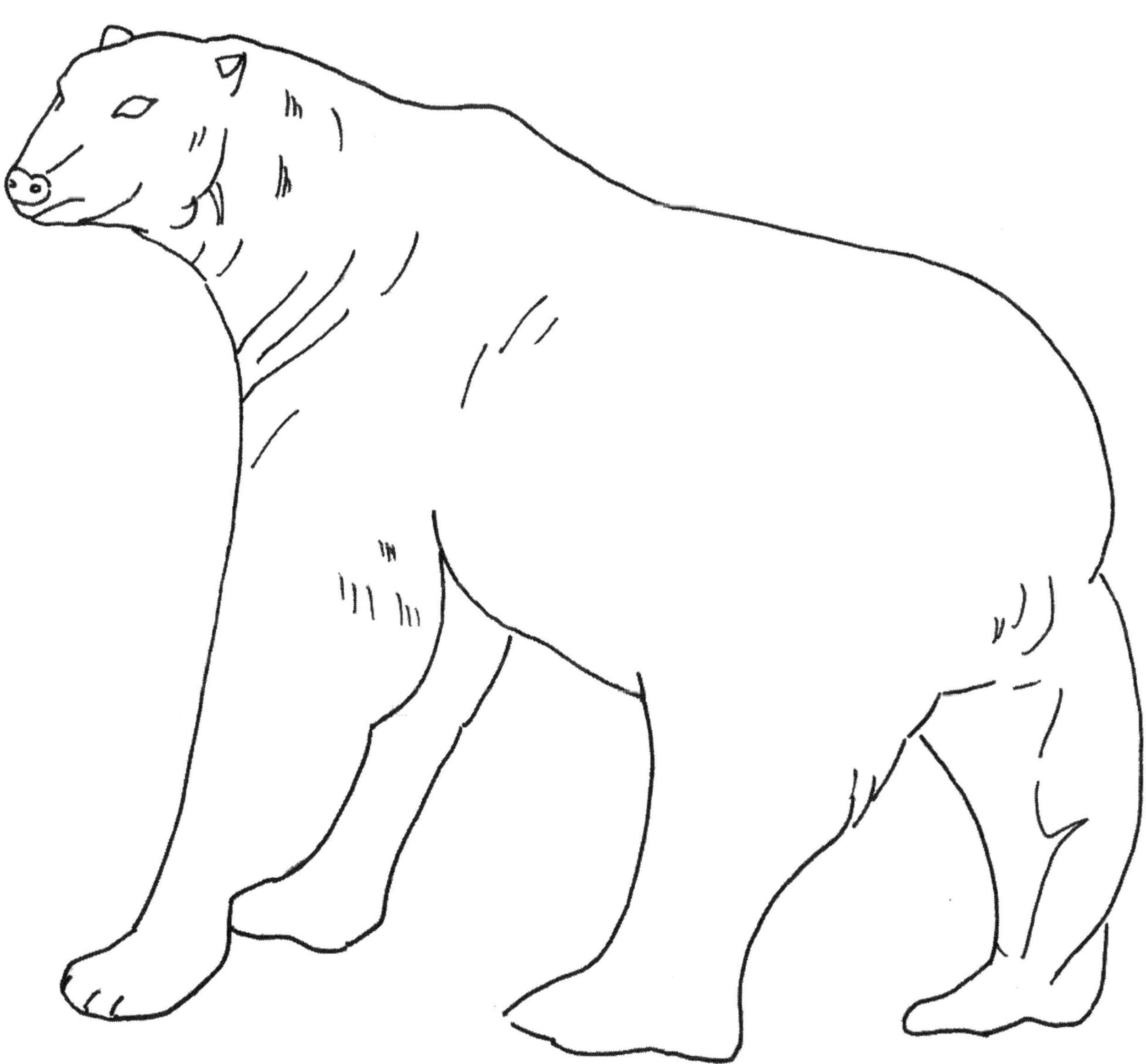

POLAR BEAR

POLAR BEAR may be the largest of land carnivore, but compared to other bears, the polar bear has a slender body covered with thick yellowish white fur, and a small head set on a long neck. The hind legs are longer than the front legs, which cause the back to slope forward. The length of head and body measures 7.2 - 8.2 feet, shoulder height up to 5.3 feet, weight over 1100 pounds.

The polar bear is solitary. Pairs are only formed for a few days while mating takes place from April to May. In October, the female leaves the floes and hides in a den dug out on ice on land. The young are born in December, but the mother and her cubs do not emerge from the den until April. The mother nurses her cubs (usually 1 - 3) for 18 months. Adult polar bears wander from ice floe to ice floe, but do seem to have a favorite hunting ground. It feeds on seals and fish. A good swimmer, it paddles with its front legs only.

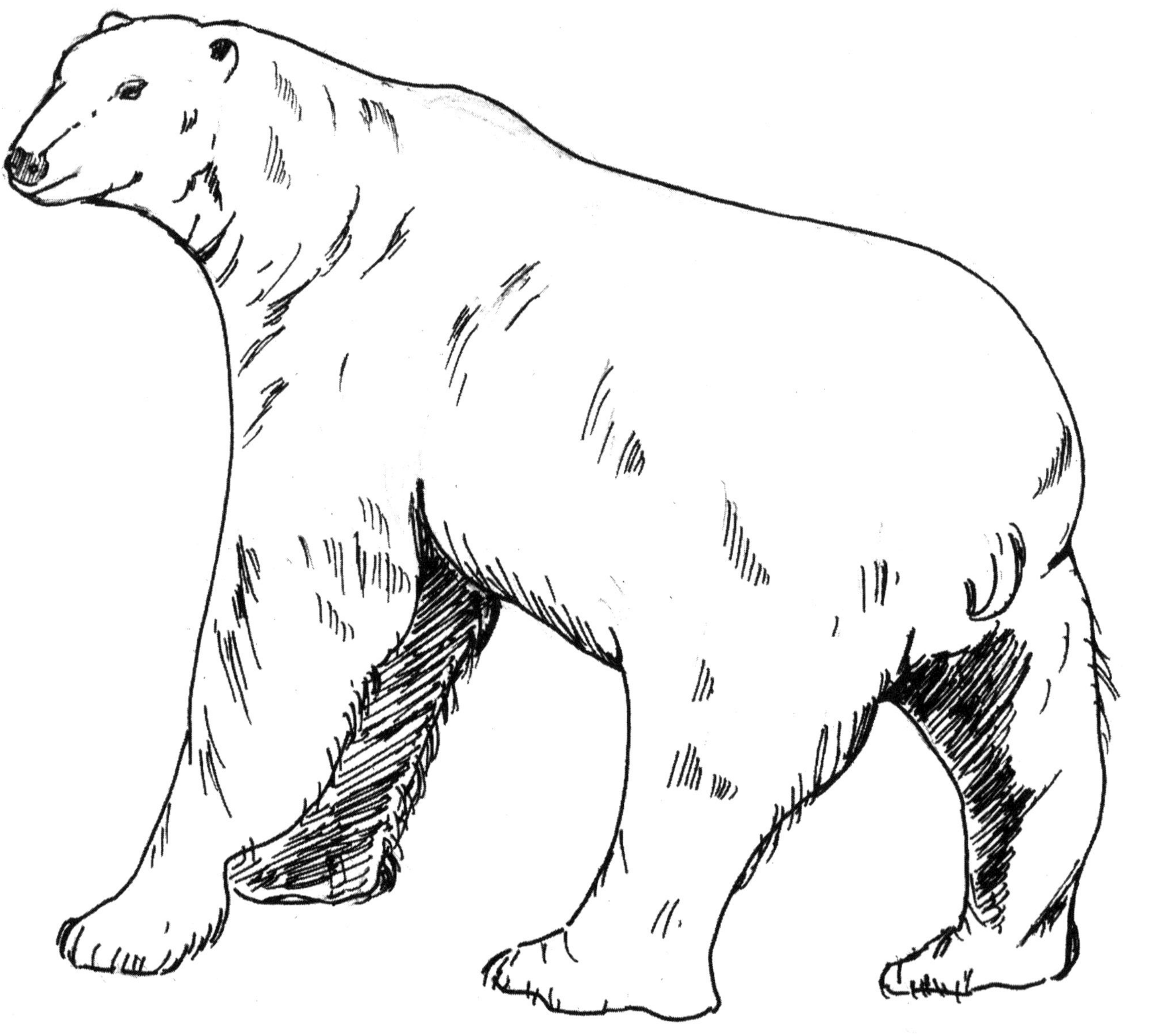

Let's get busy drawing this White Rhinoceros. Let's start with an outline of the head, horns, neck, torso, leg, and feet.

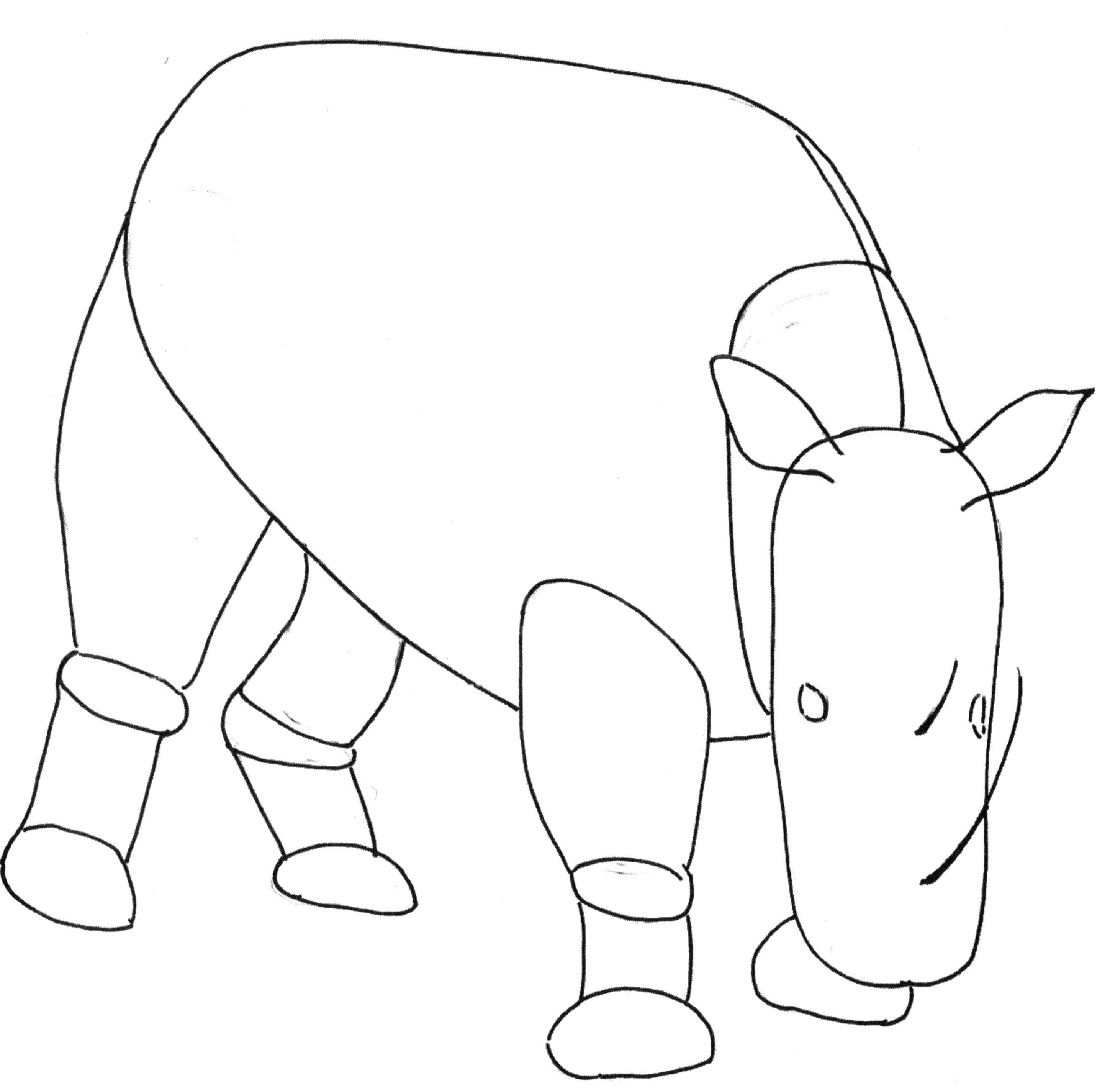

Now, let's define the various parts of the White Rhinoceros's body by drawing within the outlines.

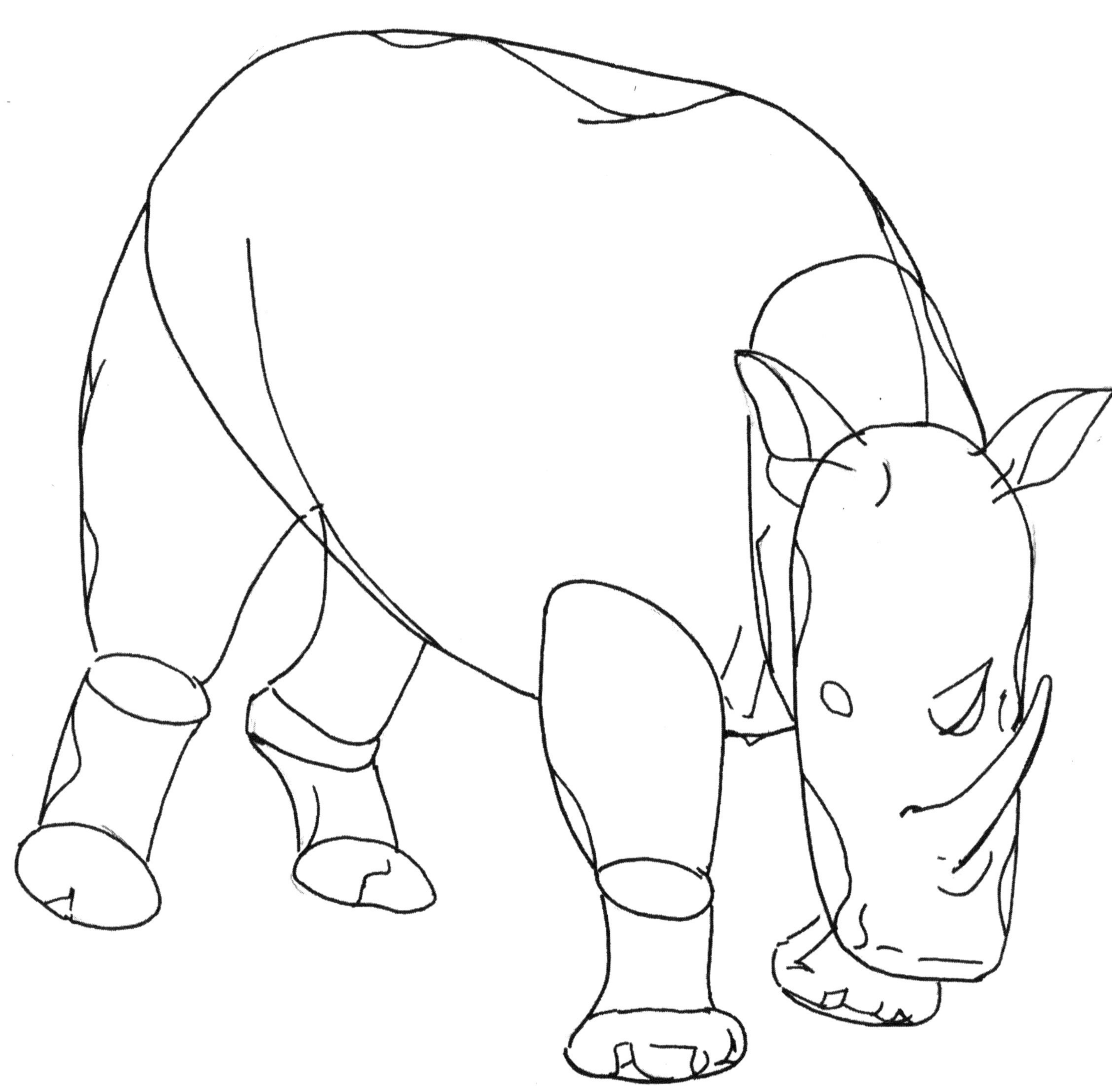

You can erase any lines not needed, draw in more details such as the wrinkles and shadows.

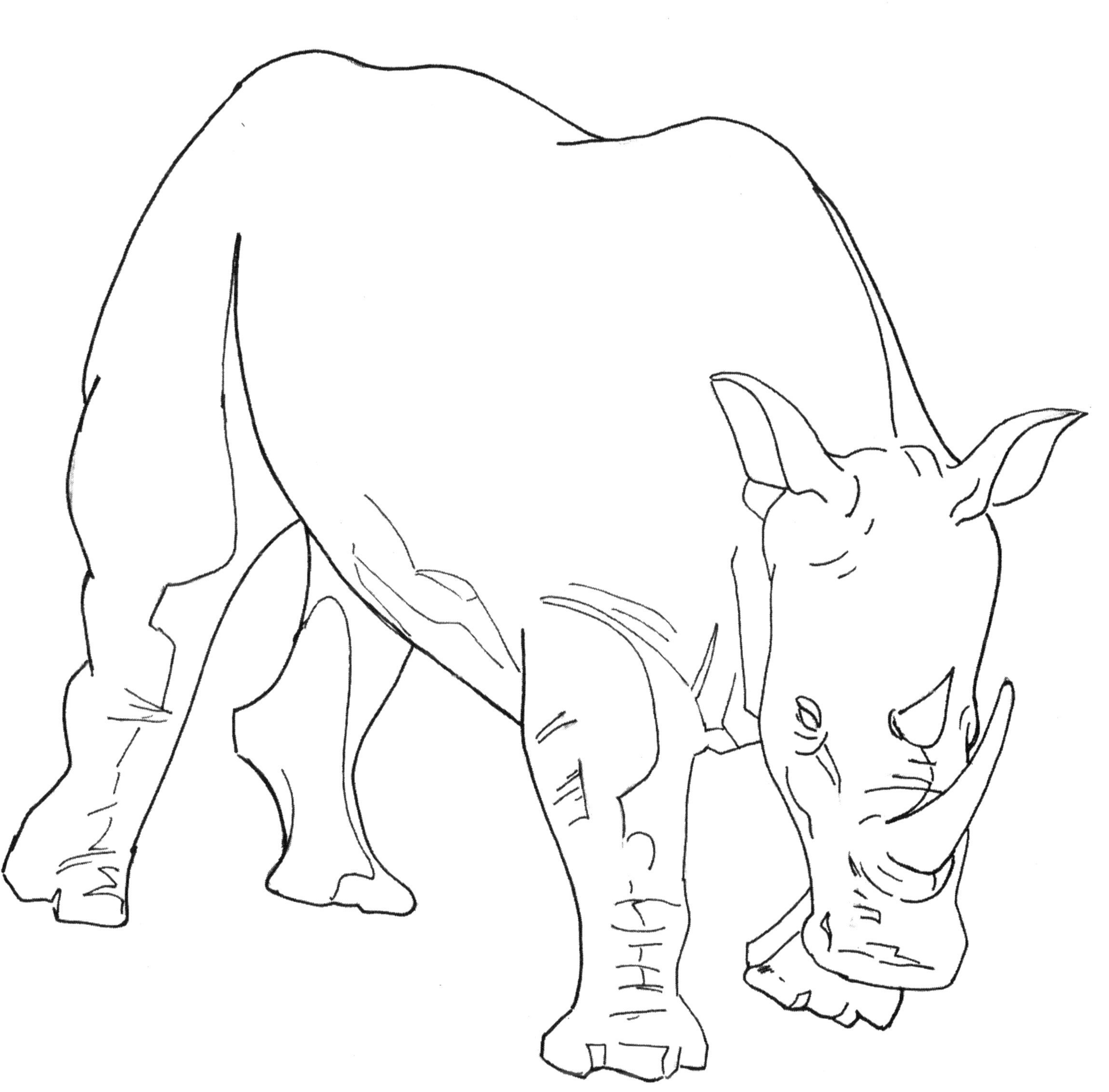

WHITE RHINOCEROS

WHITE RHINOCEROS is larger and heavier than the black rhinoceros and can be readily identified by the hump on the nape of its neck. The head is carried low. The horns are longer and thinner up to 65 inches. The ears are broad and have hairs on the edges. The upper lip is square shaped. Length of head and body up to 12.5 feet, shoulder height up to 6.1 feet, weight about 3.5 — 4 tons.

The white rhinoceros resides in the grasslands, swamps, and rivers of Southern Sudan and South Africa. This is the largest of land mammals other than the elephants. It is less aggressive than the black rhinoceros. It rarely charges and males only engage in combat during mating season. The males are usually solitary, but females with calves may be seen in groups. It feeds on grass and needs water daily, and often wallows at length. It moves slowly and always uses the same tracks and paths. It is active both during the day and at night. It has poor sight, but has acute hearing. The female has only one calf every 3 - 4 years after an estimated 17 - 18 month gestation.

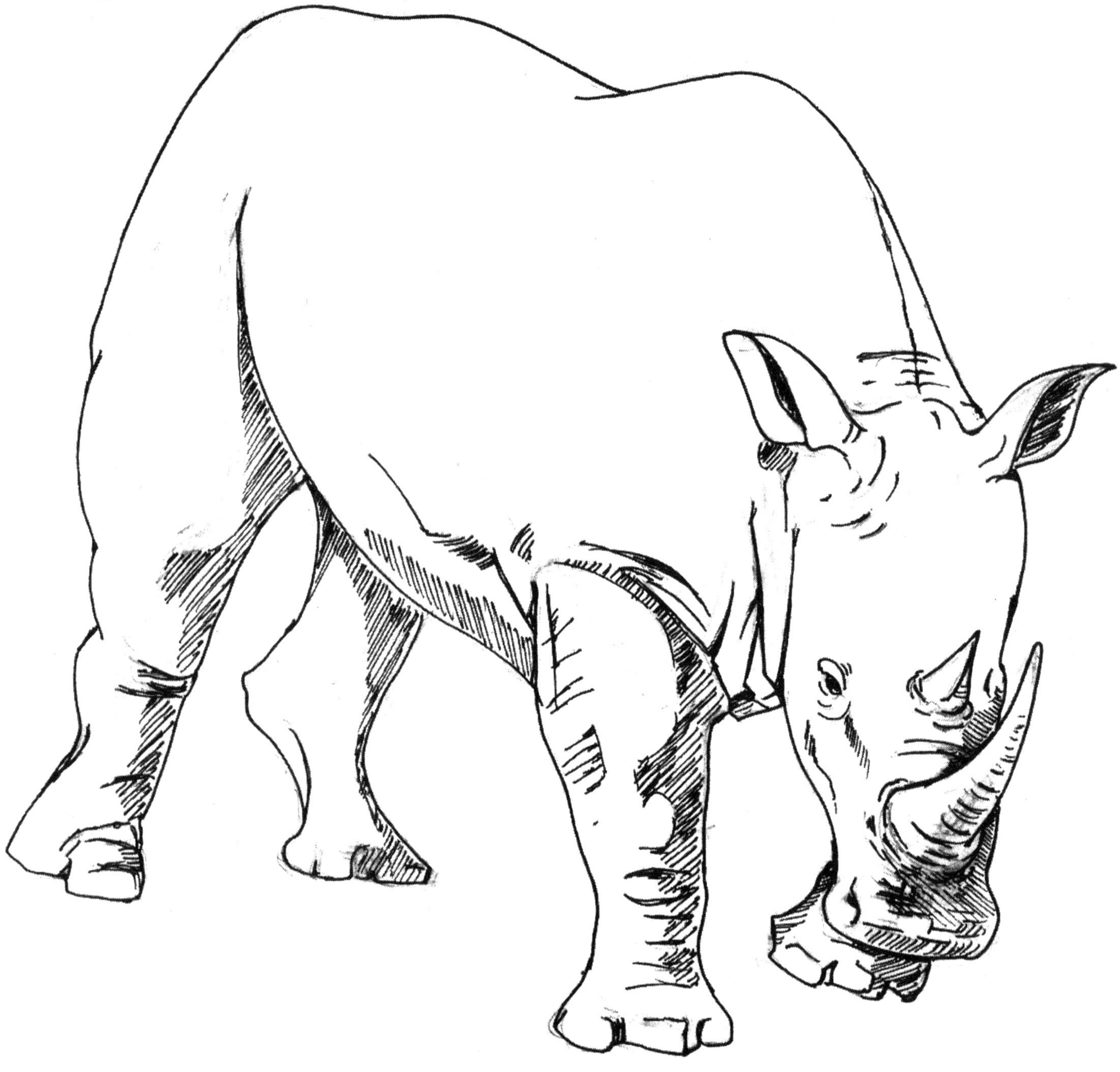

You can start to draw an outline of the Elephant's head, tusks, trunk, ears, torso, legs, and feet.

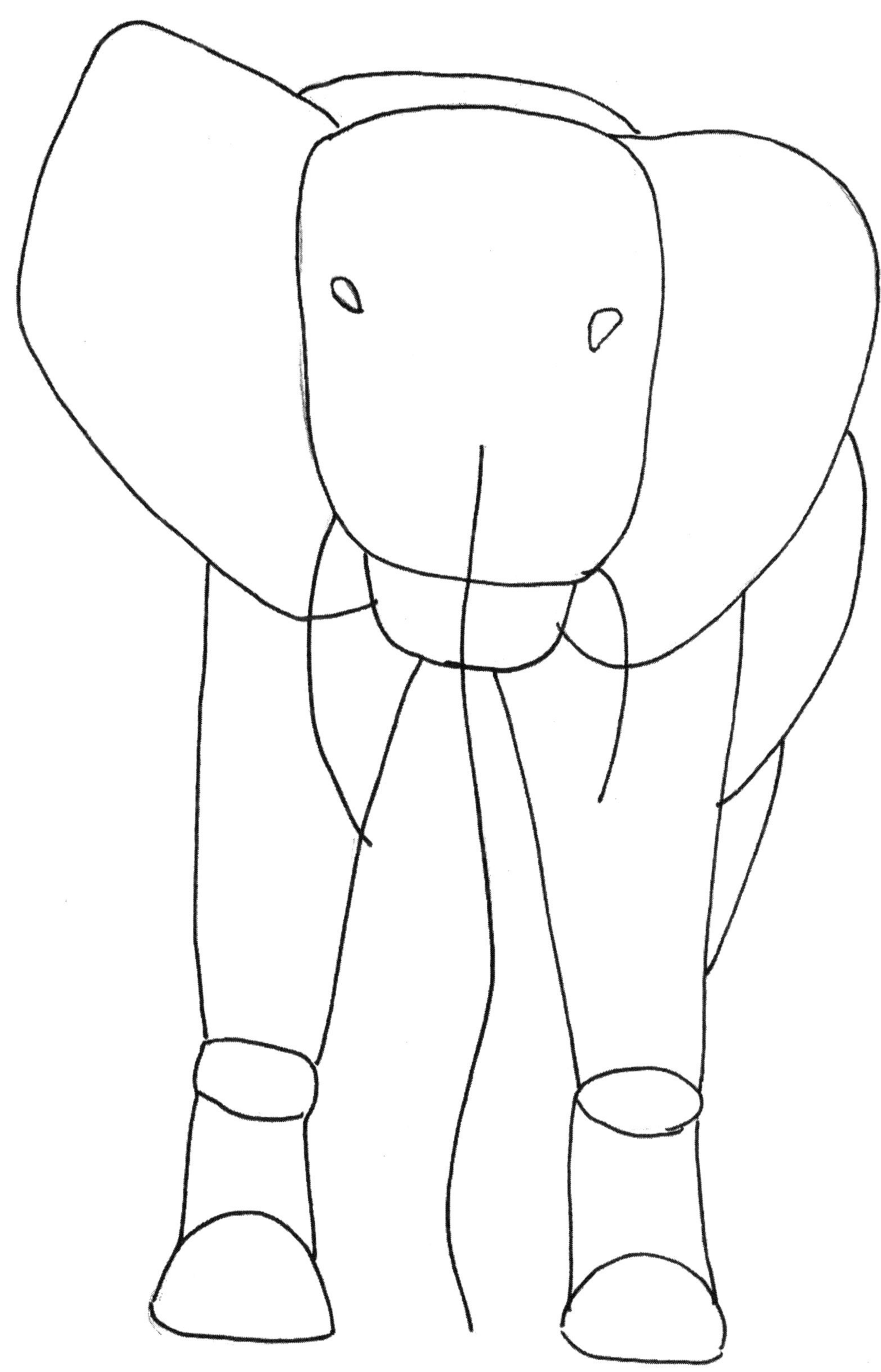

Sketch in more portions of the Elephant for a more precise description of the total body.

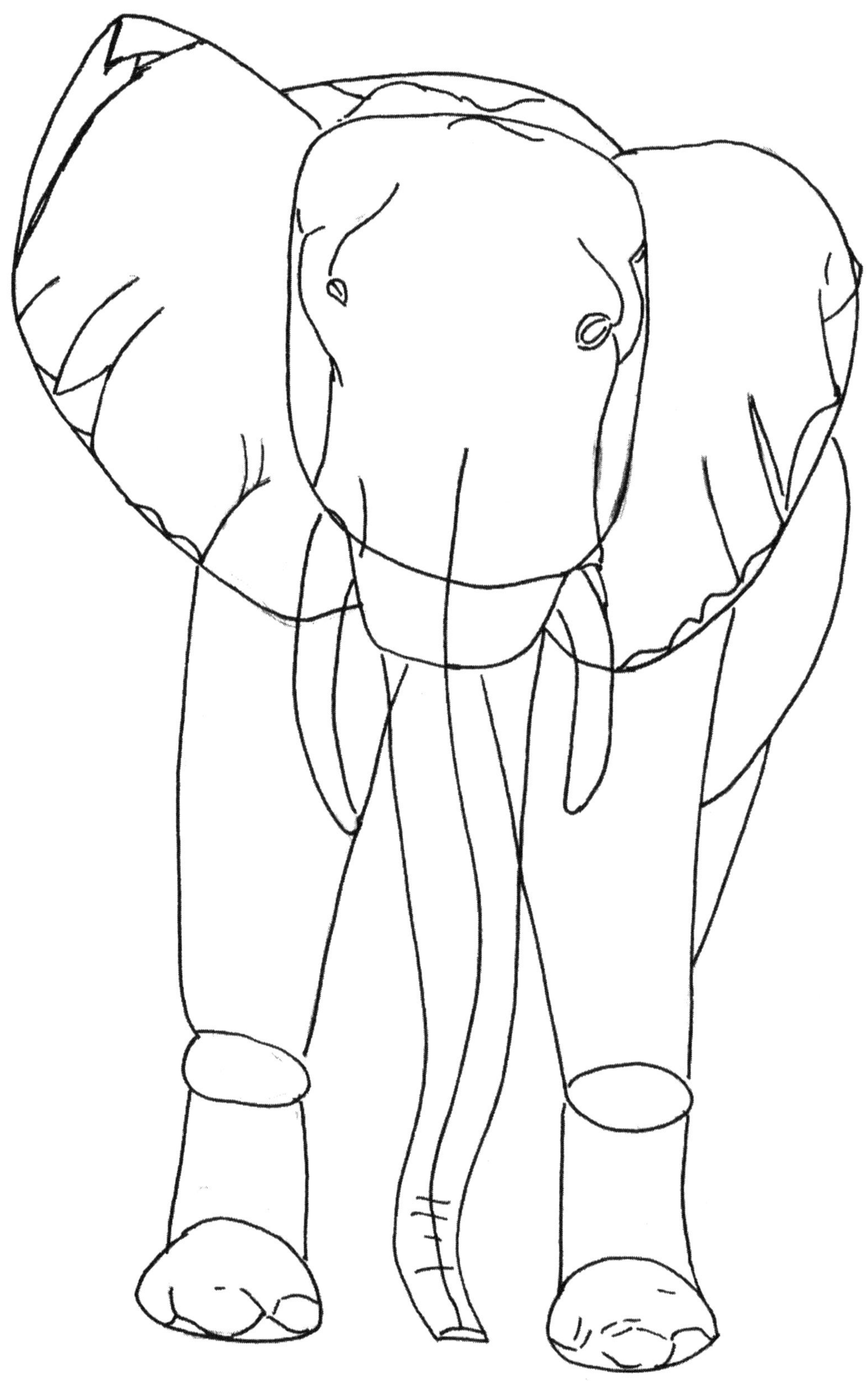

You can erase any lines not needed, draw in more details of the elephant such as the wrinkles and shadows.

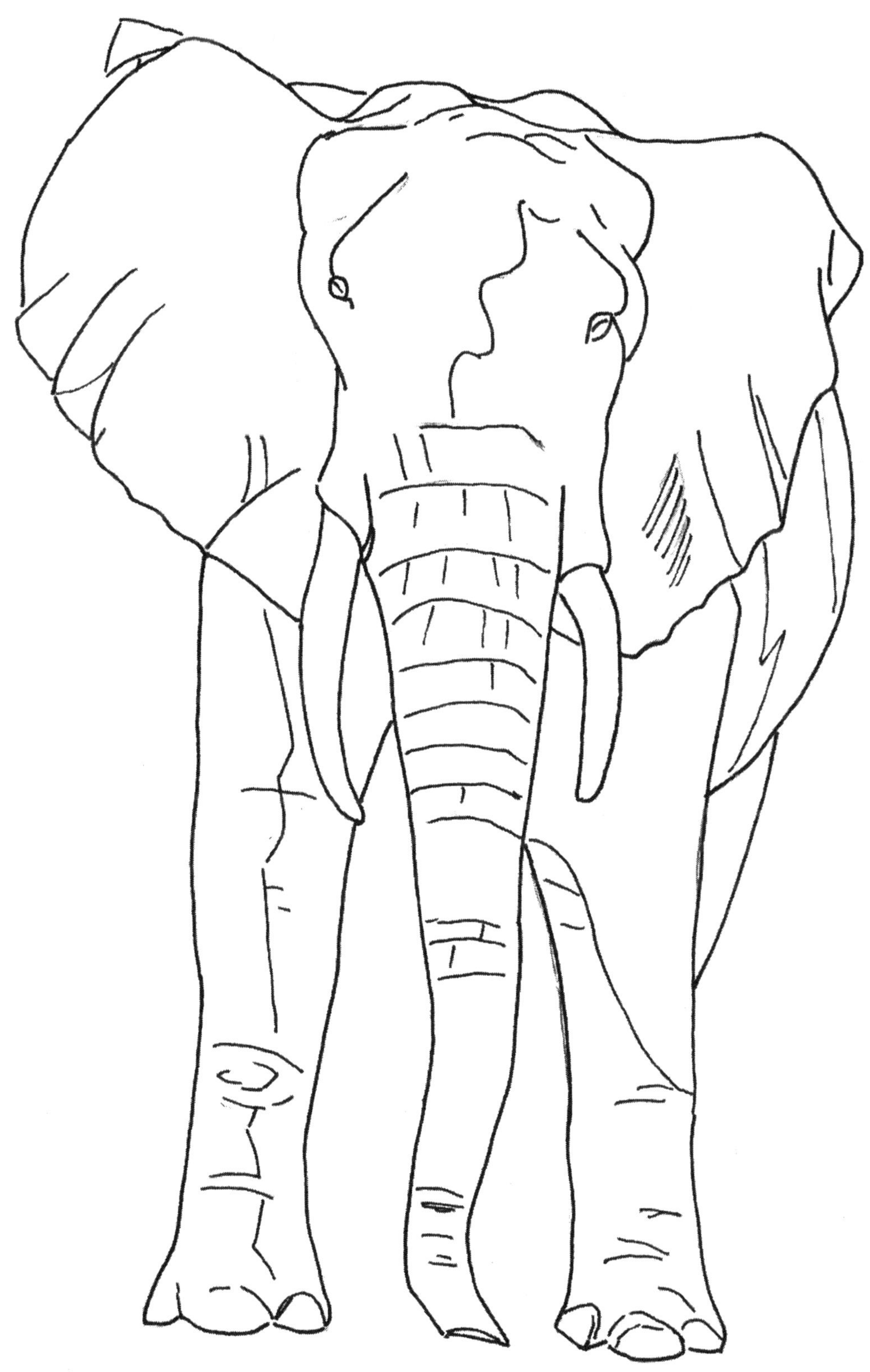

AFRICAN ELEPHANT

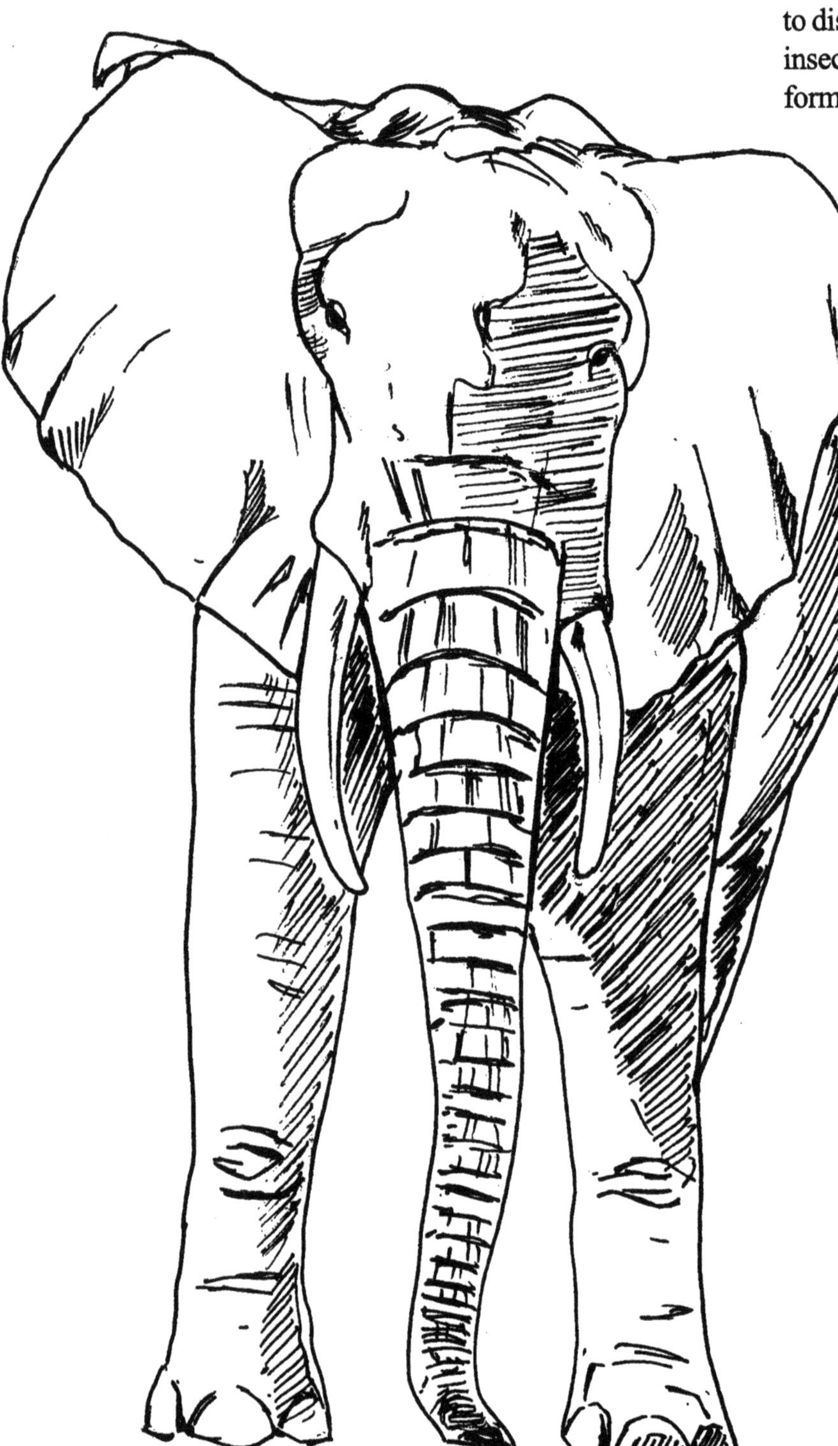

AFRICAN ELEPHANT this is the largest living land mammal. Its enormous ears serve to dissipate body heat and brush away insects from its eyes. The upper incisors form tusks, which average about 5 foot long and weigh about 35 pounds. Length of head and body including trunk up to 25 feet, shoulder height to 13 feet, weight may exceed 6000 tons.

This creature is found in Sub-Saharan Africa except southern Africa. This elephant is a social animal living in family groups, which have a matriarchal structure. The head of the group is an elderly female: she makes decisions about when and where to move, and keeps the peace. Groups of African elephants can number more 100 individuals in periods of drought. The groups are constantly moving when the animals are feeding. The elephant must drink daily, and enjoy bathing in waterholes. Breeding occurs all year, but a female will only give birth once every 4 years. Gestation lasts for 22 - 24 months, at the end of which a single offspring is born, weighing about 220 pounds. It nurses for 2 - 3 years.

Let's first start drawing an outline of the Wart Hog's head, ears, horns, neck, torso, tail, legs and hoofs.

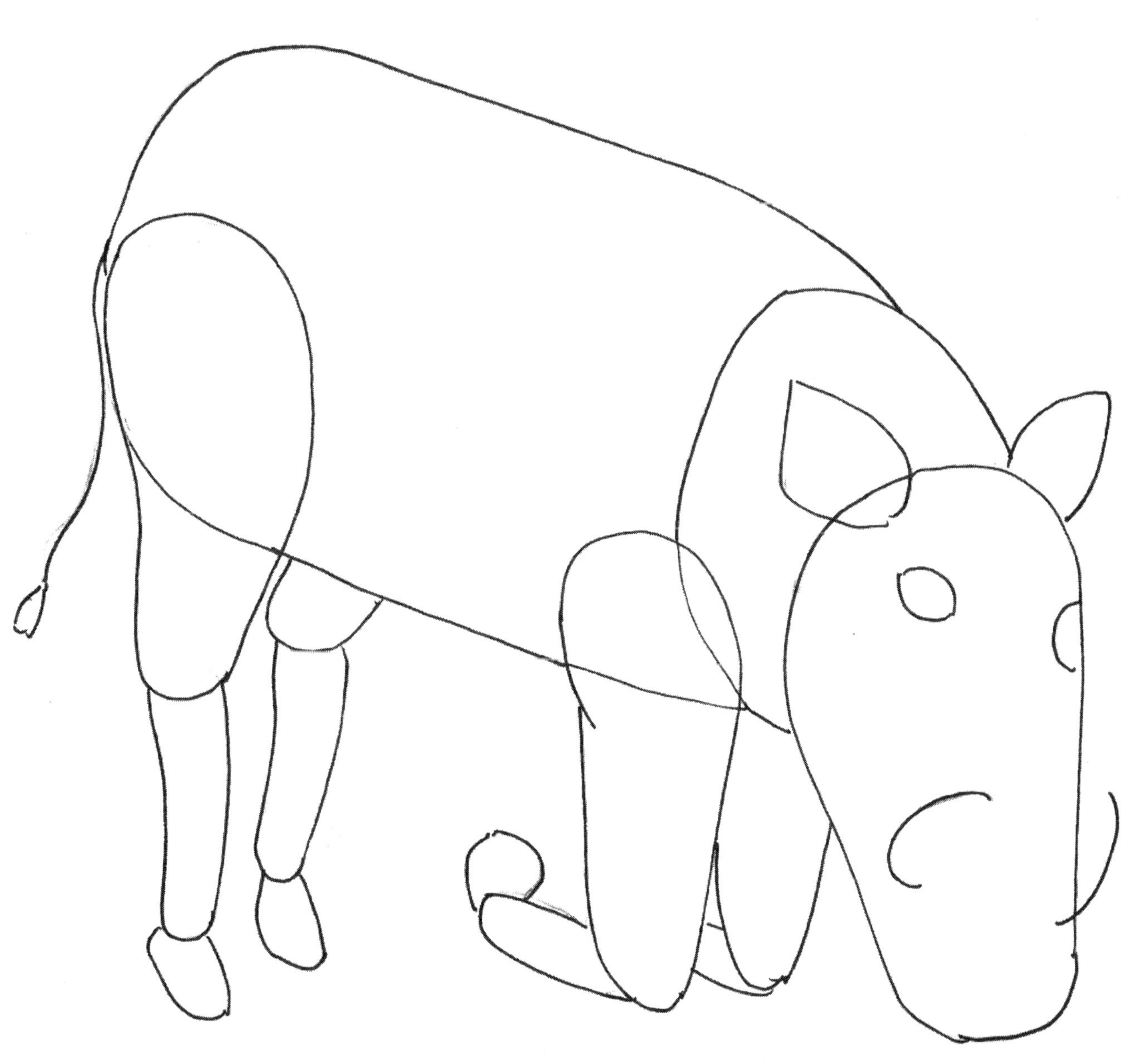

Sketch in more portions of the Wart Hog for a more precise description of the total body.

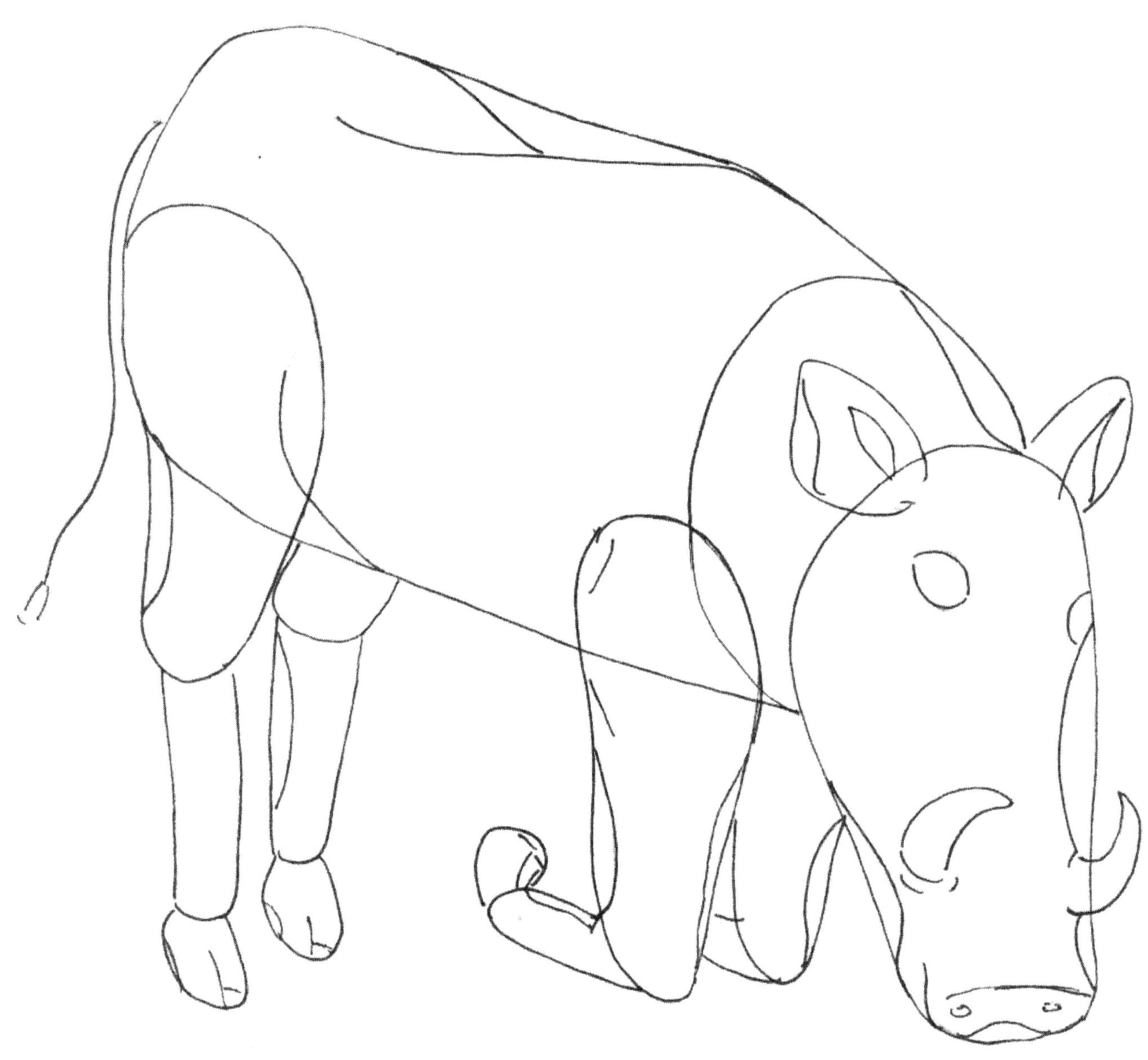

Now, let's define the various parts of the Wart Hog's body by drawing within the outlines.

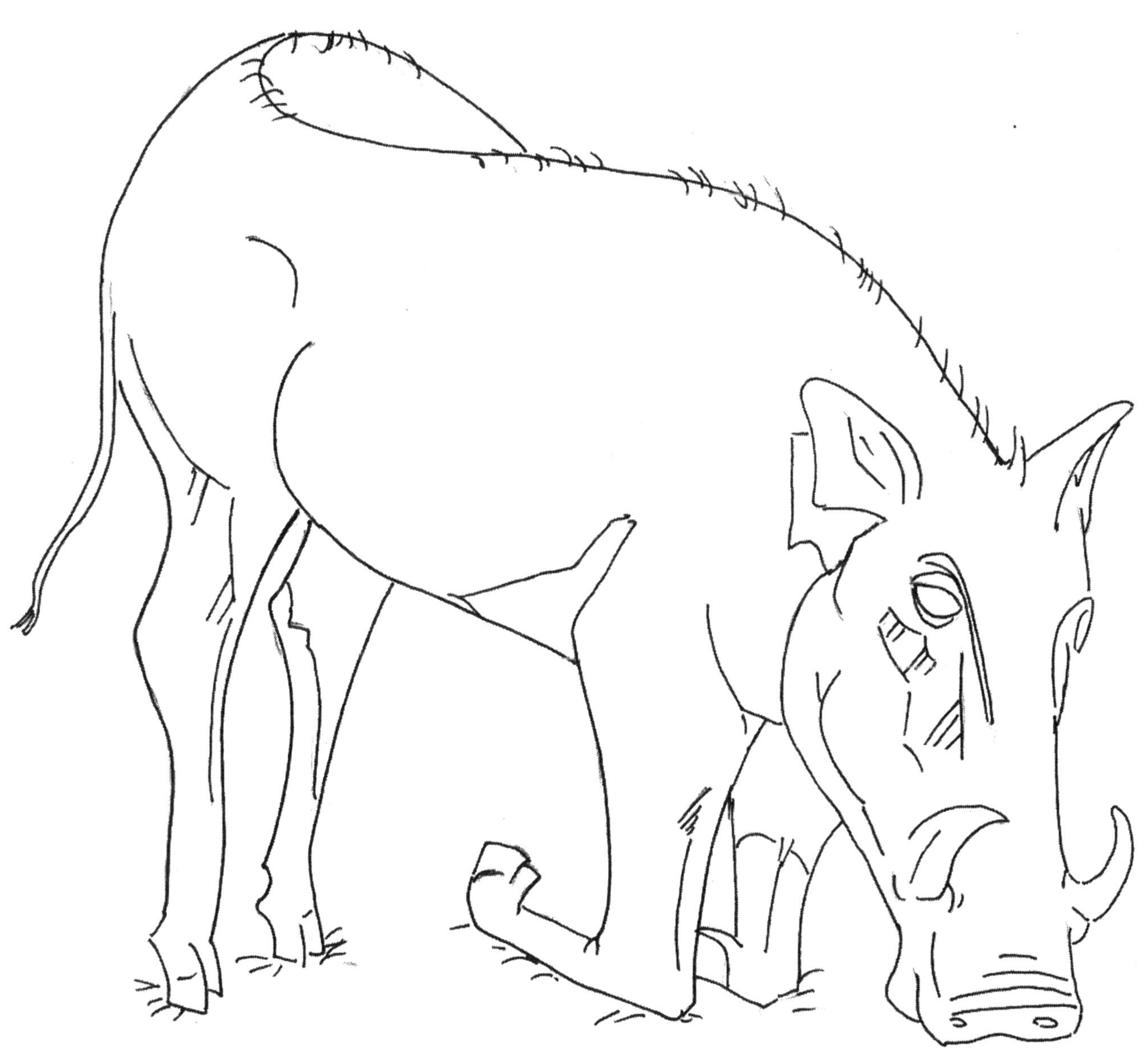

WART HOG

WART HOG the adult color is blackish, brownish, or grayish, the young are pinkish. The hide is almost hairless with only a few hairs present on the cheeks and on the back where they form a mane. The tail is long, has a tuft of hair at the end, and is carried in a distinctive vertical position when the animal is moving. The head is disproportionately large and has two pair of large warts. The tusk form a semicircle between them pointing forward and upward. The lower canines are extremely sharp. Length of head and body about 40 inches, shoulder height 25 - 30 inches, and weight 165 - 220 pounds with females somewhat smaller.

Found in the Sub-Saharan Africa the wart hog usually lives in small family groups, but several families will often band together temporally to form larger herds. They spend the hottest part of the day sheltered by vegetation or in its den. It is vegetarian and can often be seen grazing in a characteristic kneeling position. It feeds mostly on short grasses and herbs. It does not damage crops, and prefers to remain away from areas where there is human activity. Its main enemies are lion and leopards. After about 175 days of gestation 2 - 4 young are born which nurse for a few months and become independent about 1 year after birth

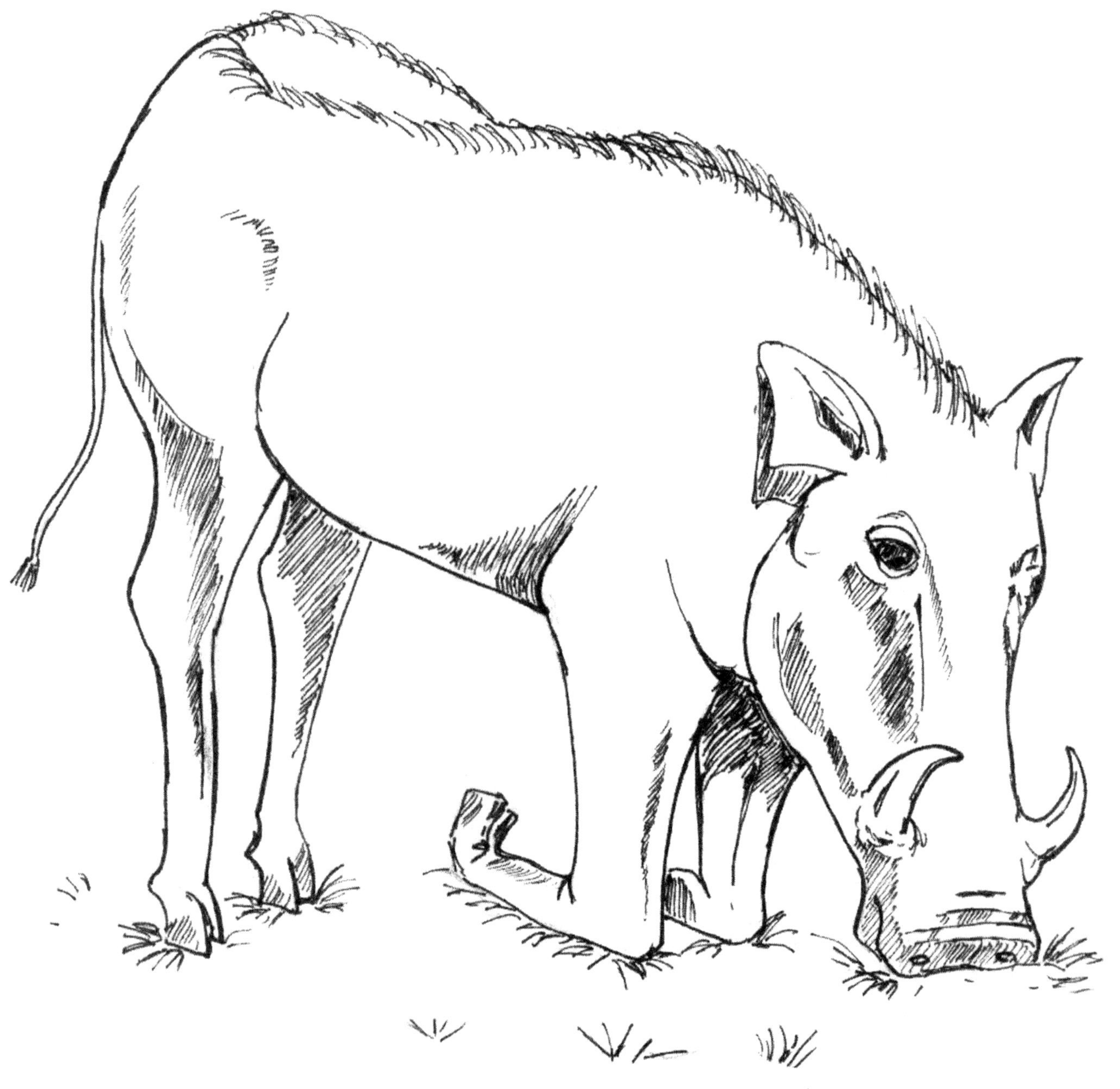

I started drawing the tree first then proceeded with drawing an outline of the Leopard's head, neck, torso legs, and claws.

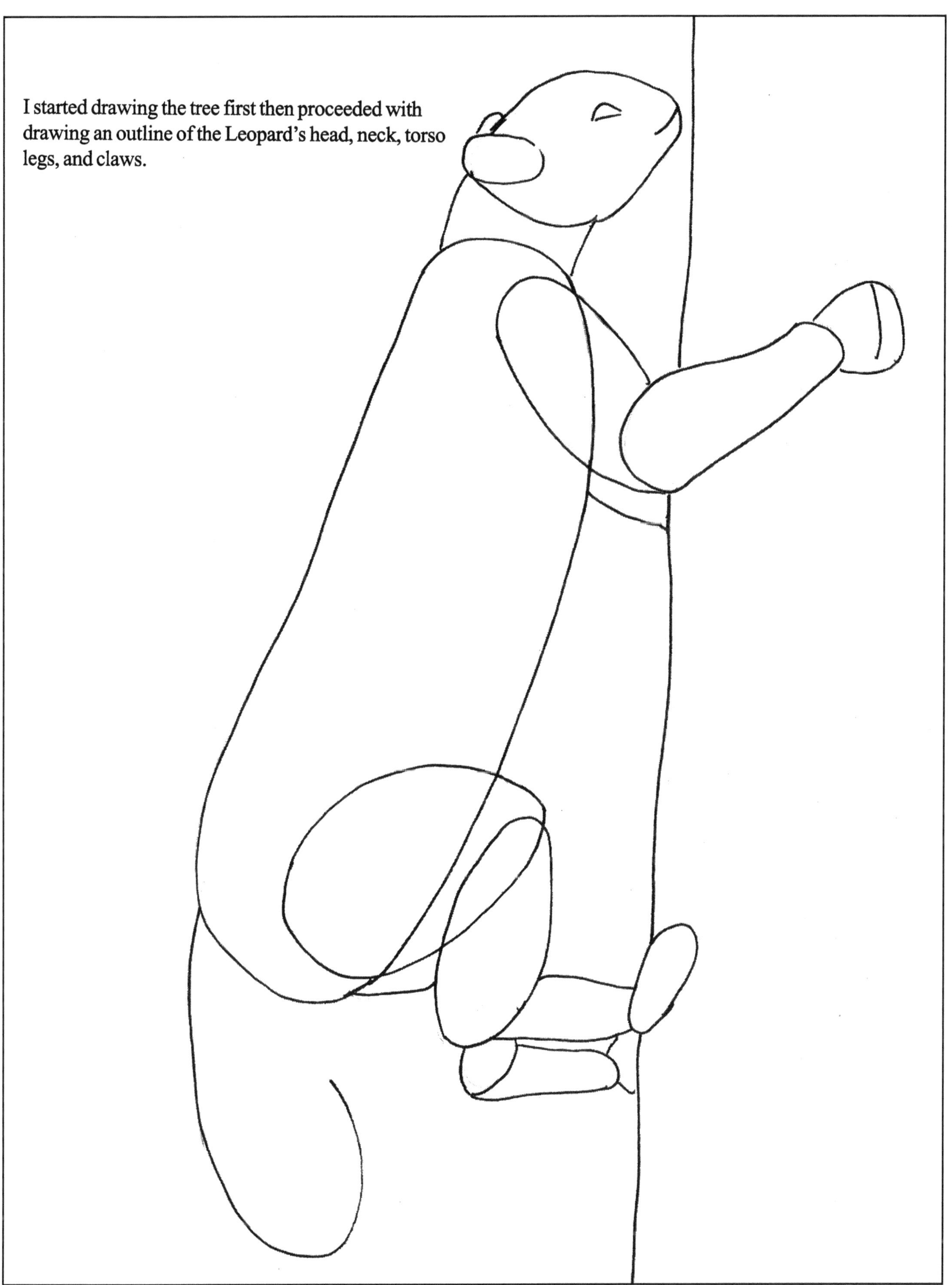

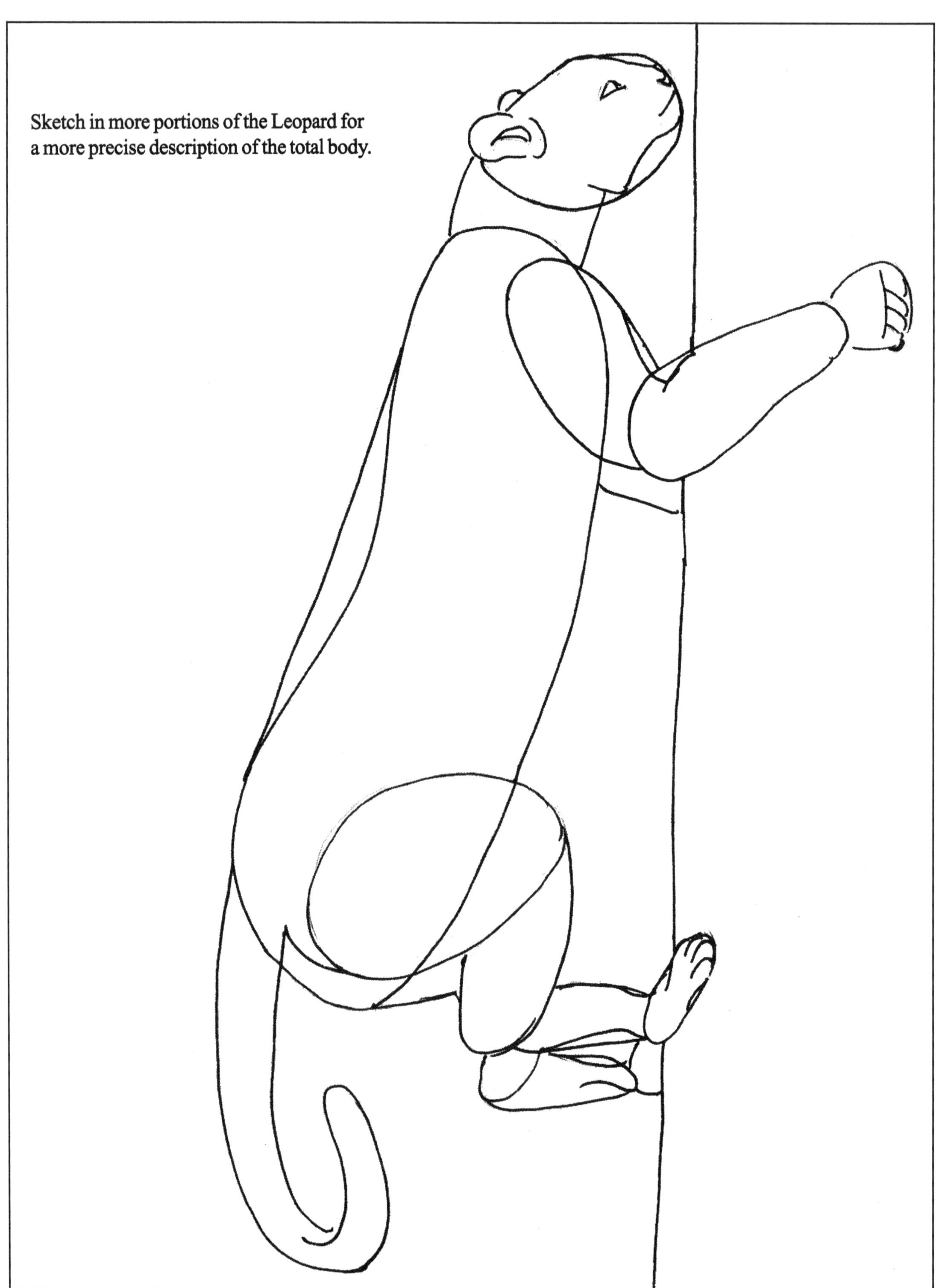
Sketch in more portions of the Leopard for
a more precise description of the total body.

Erase any unneeded lines and put in more details including the Leopard's coat pattern made up of dark spots.

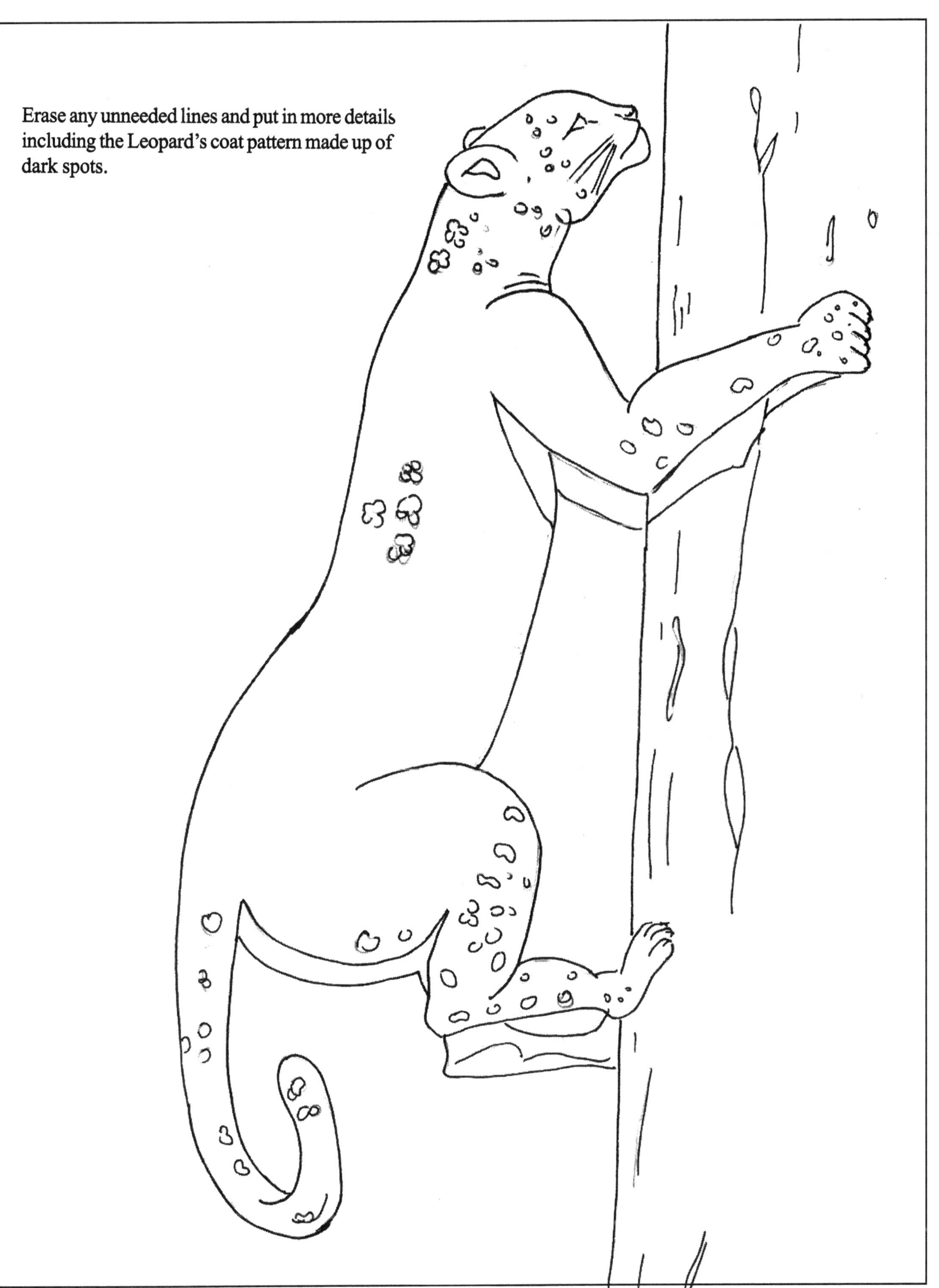

LEOPARD

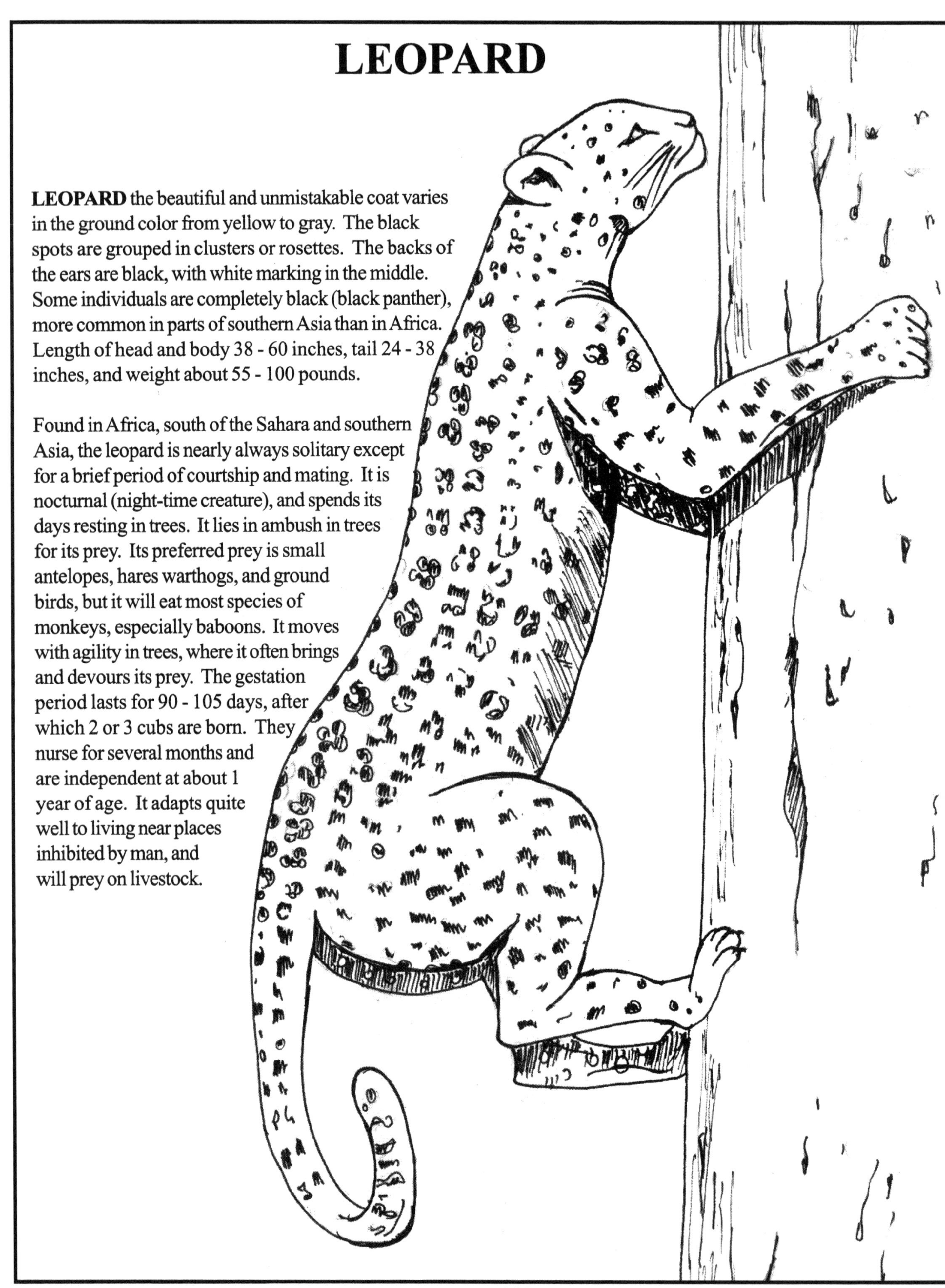

LEOPARD the beautiful and unmistakable coat varies in the ground color from yellow to gray. The black spots are grouped in clusters or rosettes. The backs of the ears are black, with white marking in the middle. Some individuals are completely black (black panther), more common in parts of southern Asia than in Africa. Length of head and body 38 - 60 inches, tail 24 - 38 inches, and weight about 55 - 100 pounds.

Found in Africa, south of the Sahara and southern Asia, the leopard is nearly always solitary except for a brief period of courtship and mating. It is nocturnal (night-time creature), and spends its days resting in trees. It lies in ambush in trees for its prey. Its preferred prey is small antelopes, hares warthogs, and ground birds, but it will eat most species of monkeys, especially baboons. It moves with agility in trees, where it often brings and devours its prey. The gestation period lasts for 90 - 105 days, after which 2 or 3 cubs are born. They nurse for several months and are independent at about 1 year of age. It adapts quite well to living near places inhibited by man, and will prey on livestock.

Start drawing an outline of the Dingo's head, ears, neck, torso, tail, legs, and paws.

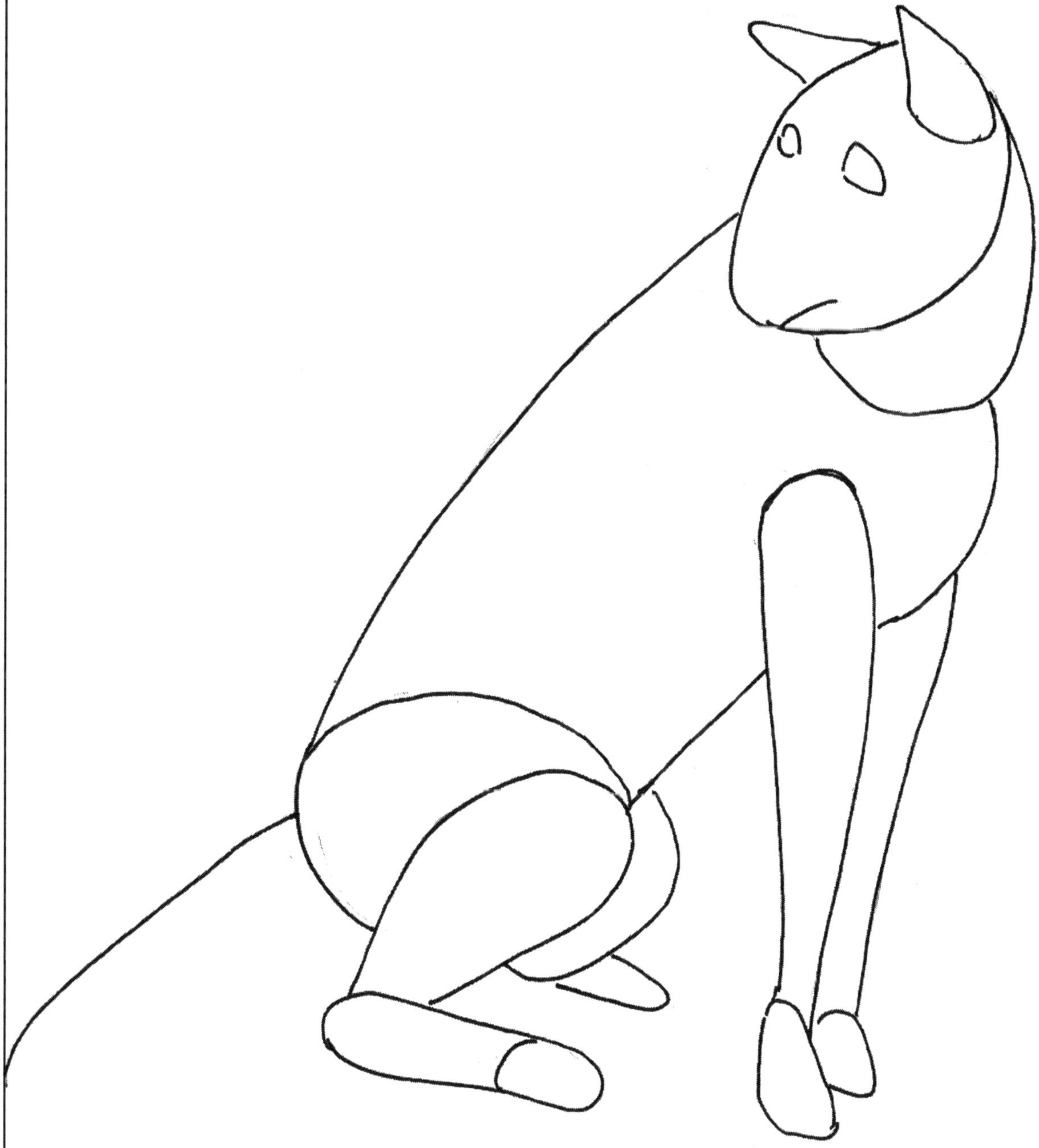

Begin shaping in the outline of the Dingo for a more precise description of the total body.

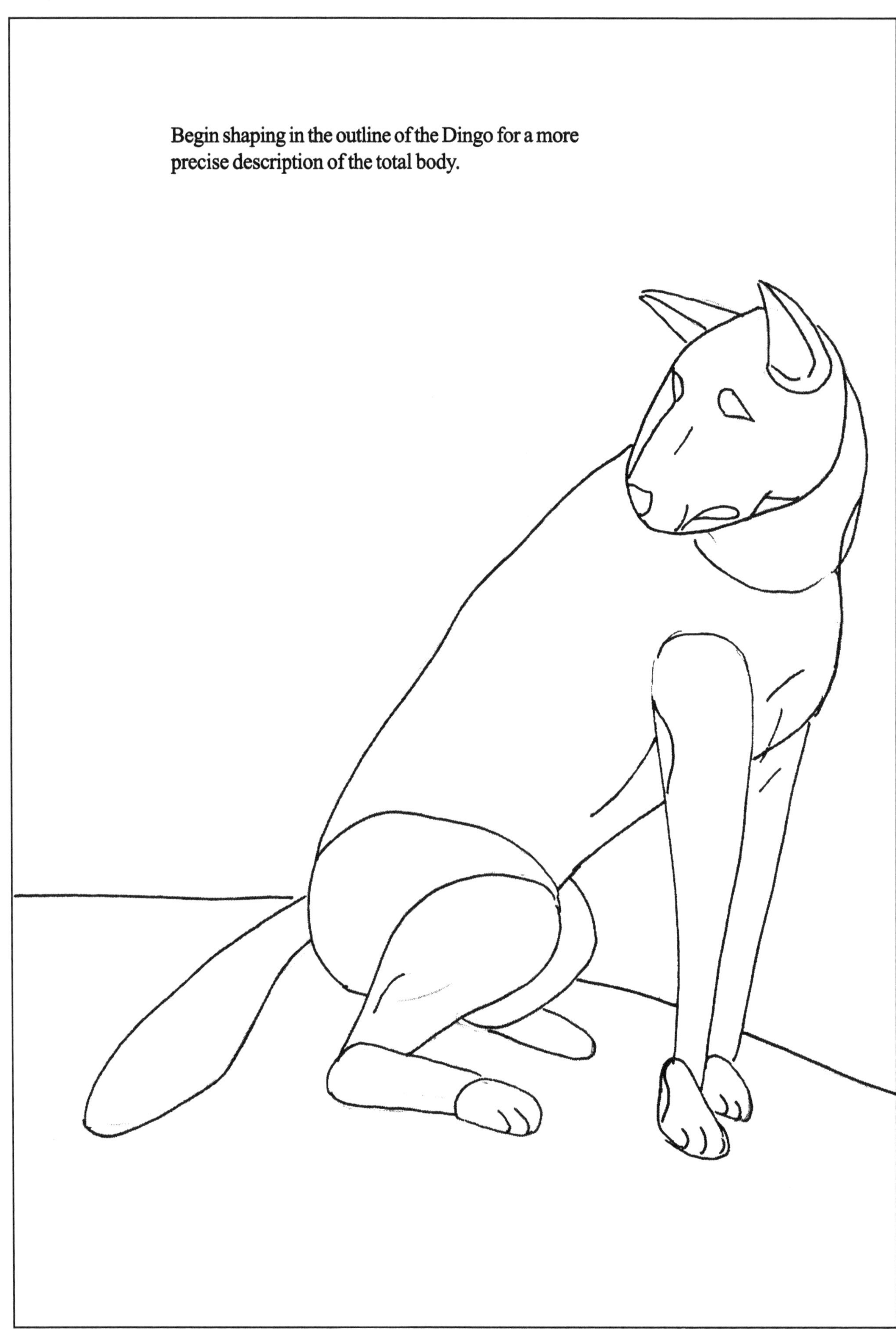

Get rid of any unnecessary lines to proceed to turn your drawing into a masterpiece.

DINGO

DINGO it resembles a large yellow dog: the color is more or less uniform, sometimes with reddish or beige highlights. The dingo is found in the scrub and semidesert environment of Australia. The dingo generally leads a solitary life or lives in pairs. Sometimes, but not regularly, large packs are formed, this is useful when hunting large kangaroos. Once the rabbit was introduced into Australia it became the dingo's primary prey, followed by smaller marsupials. The dingo reproduces once a year, and not twice like the domestic dog. Gestation lasts for 2 months and the female gives birth to 5 - 7 pups in early spring. The pups are reared by both parents, and within a pack, all adult members participate in their care. Length of head and body up to 44 inches, tail 10 to 16 inches, and they can weigh up to 77 pounds.

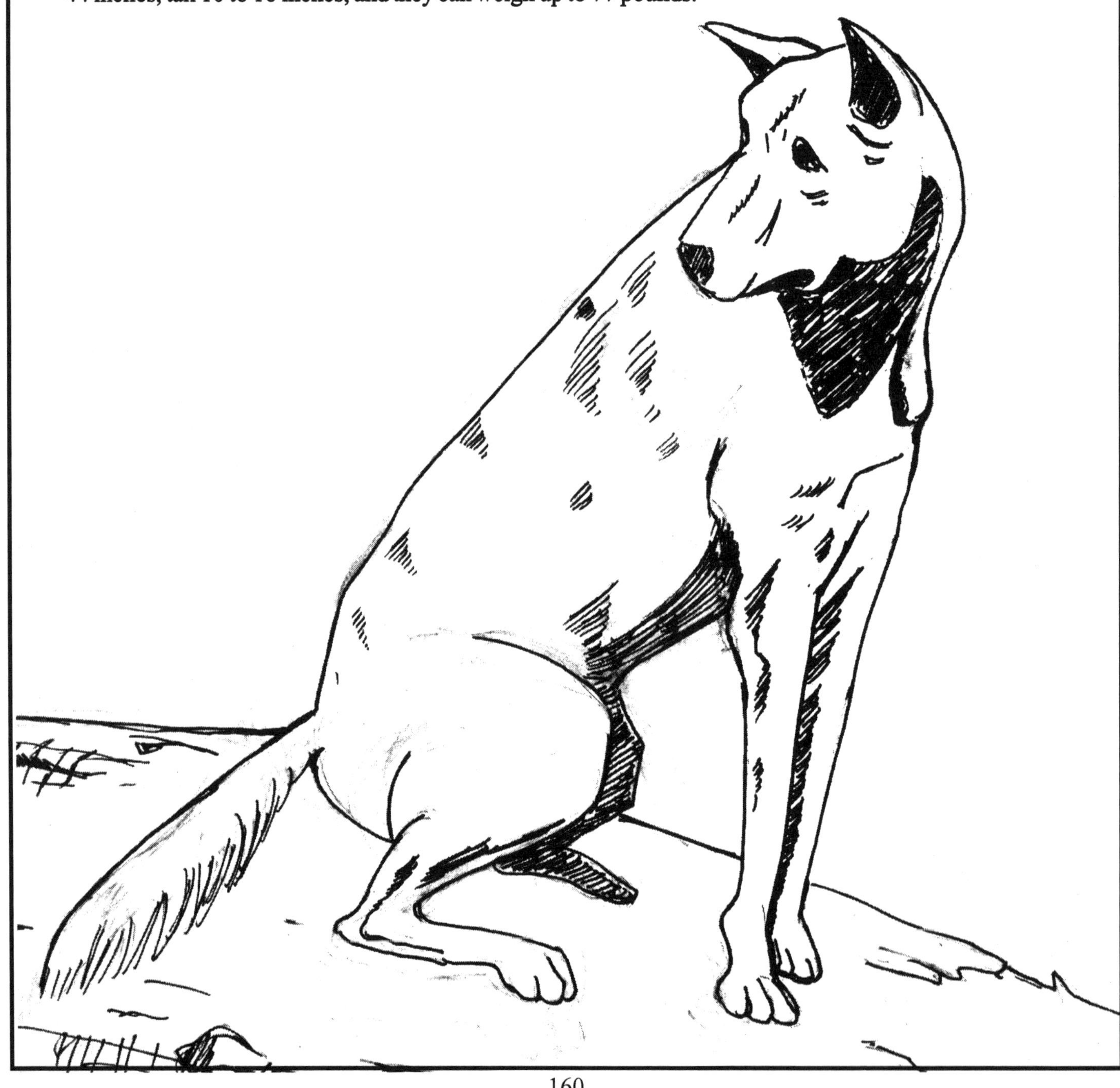

Start drawing an outline of the Baboon's head, ears, neck, torso, legs, and feet.

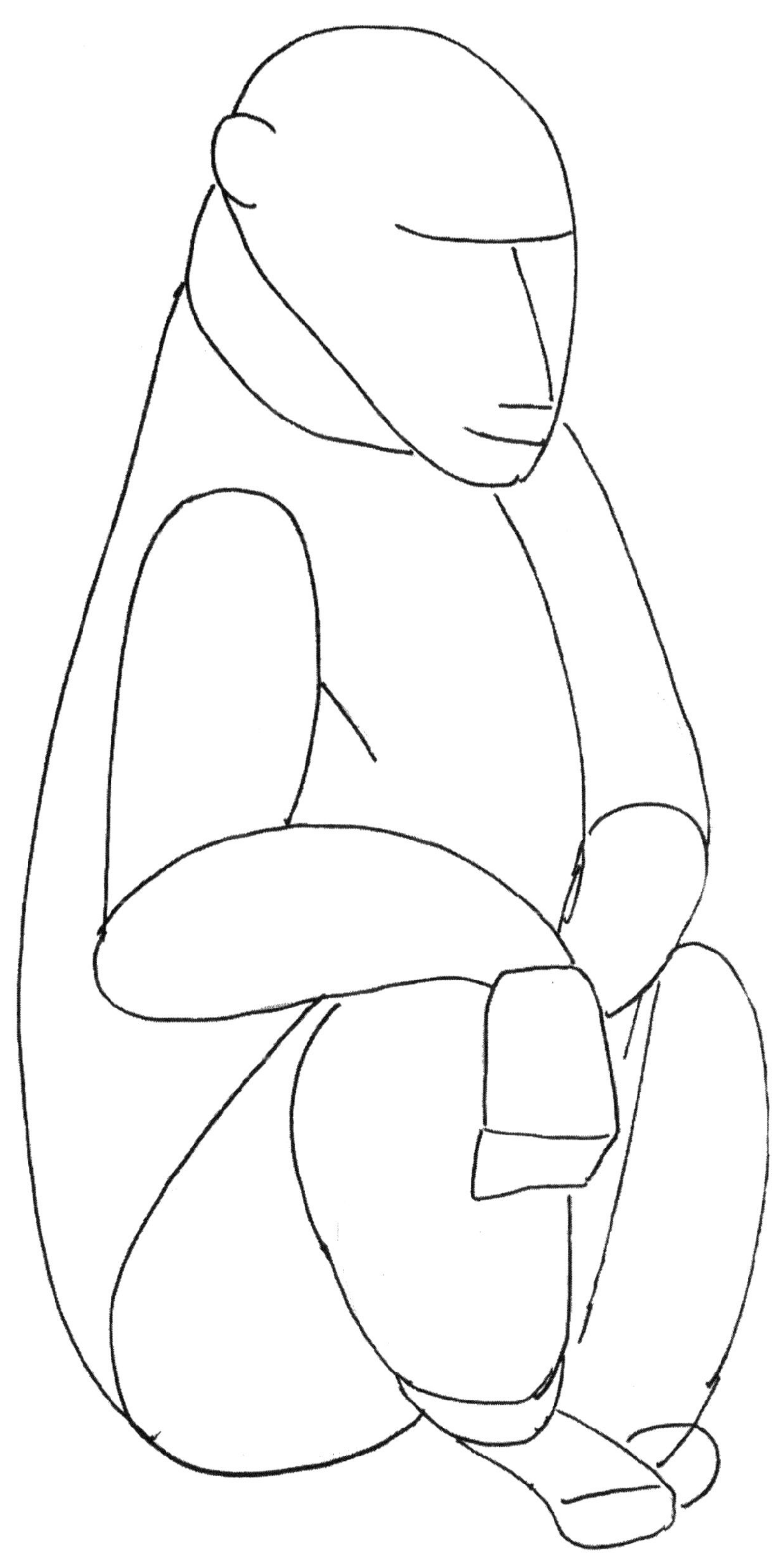

Begin shaping in the outline of the Baboon's head, ears, neck, torso, legs, and feet, for a more precise description of the total body.

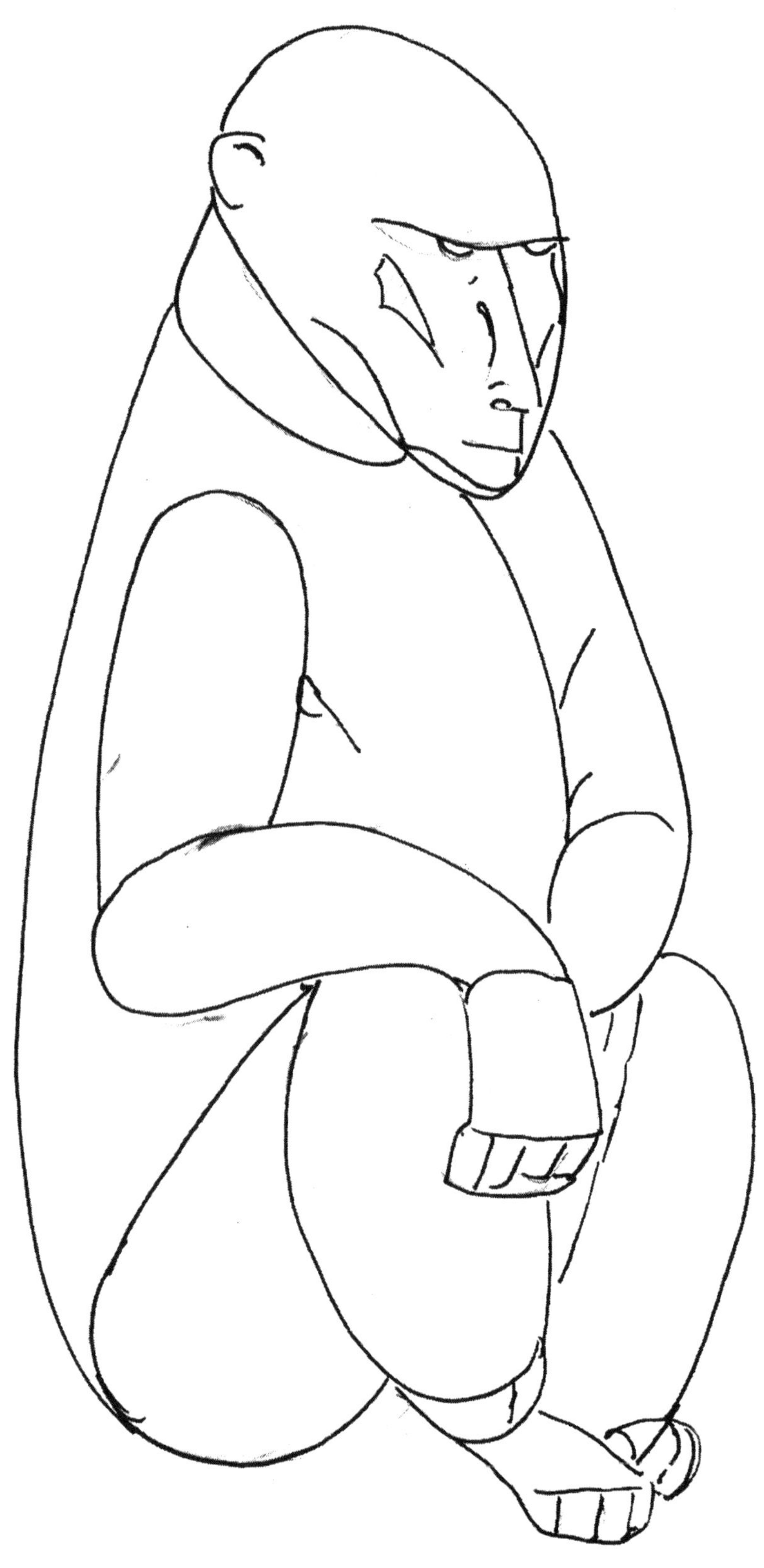

Get rid of any unnecessary lines add some hair, and then proceed to turn your drawing into another masterpiece.

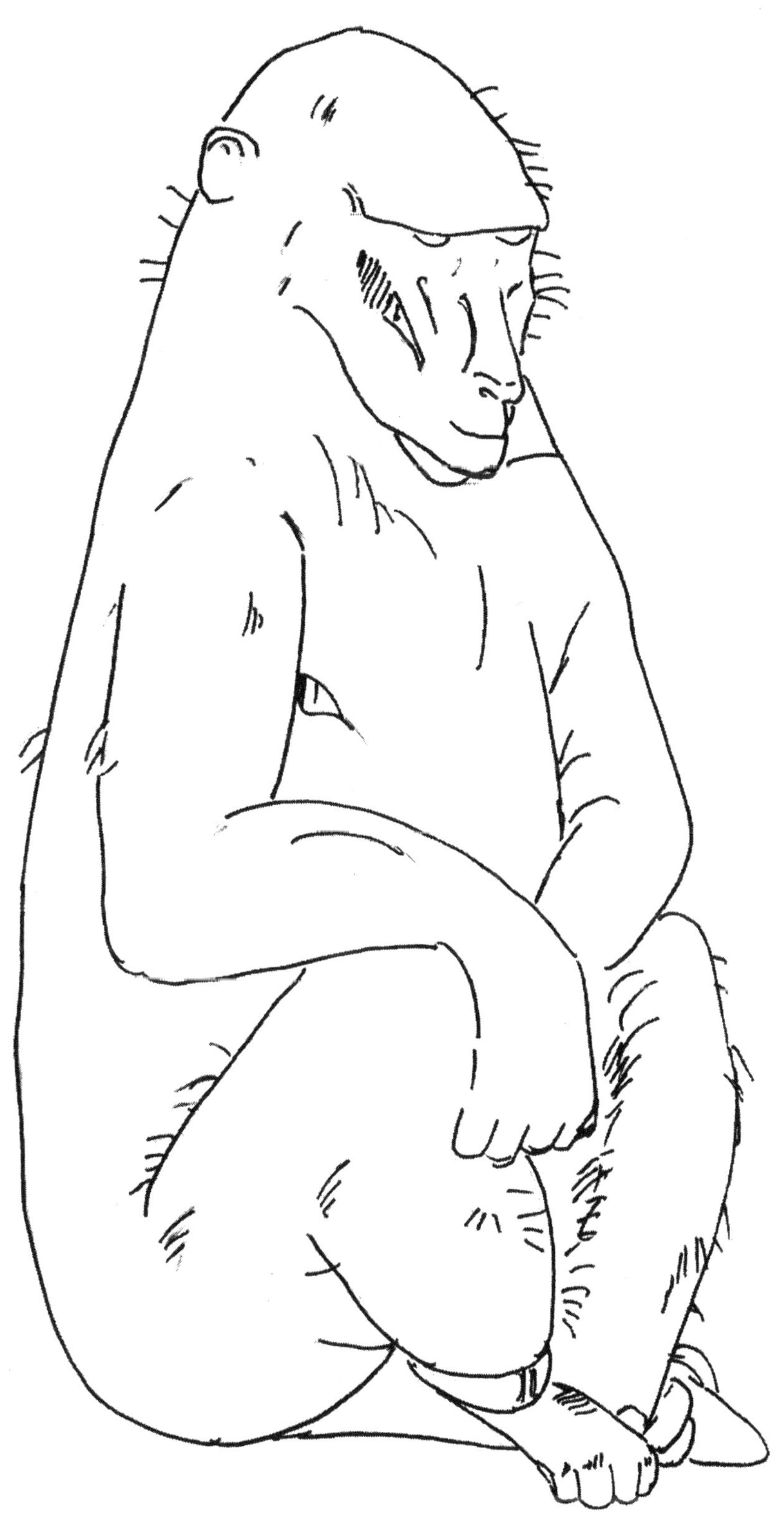

BABOON

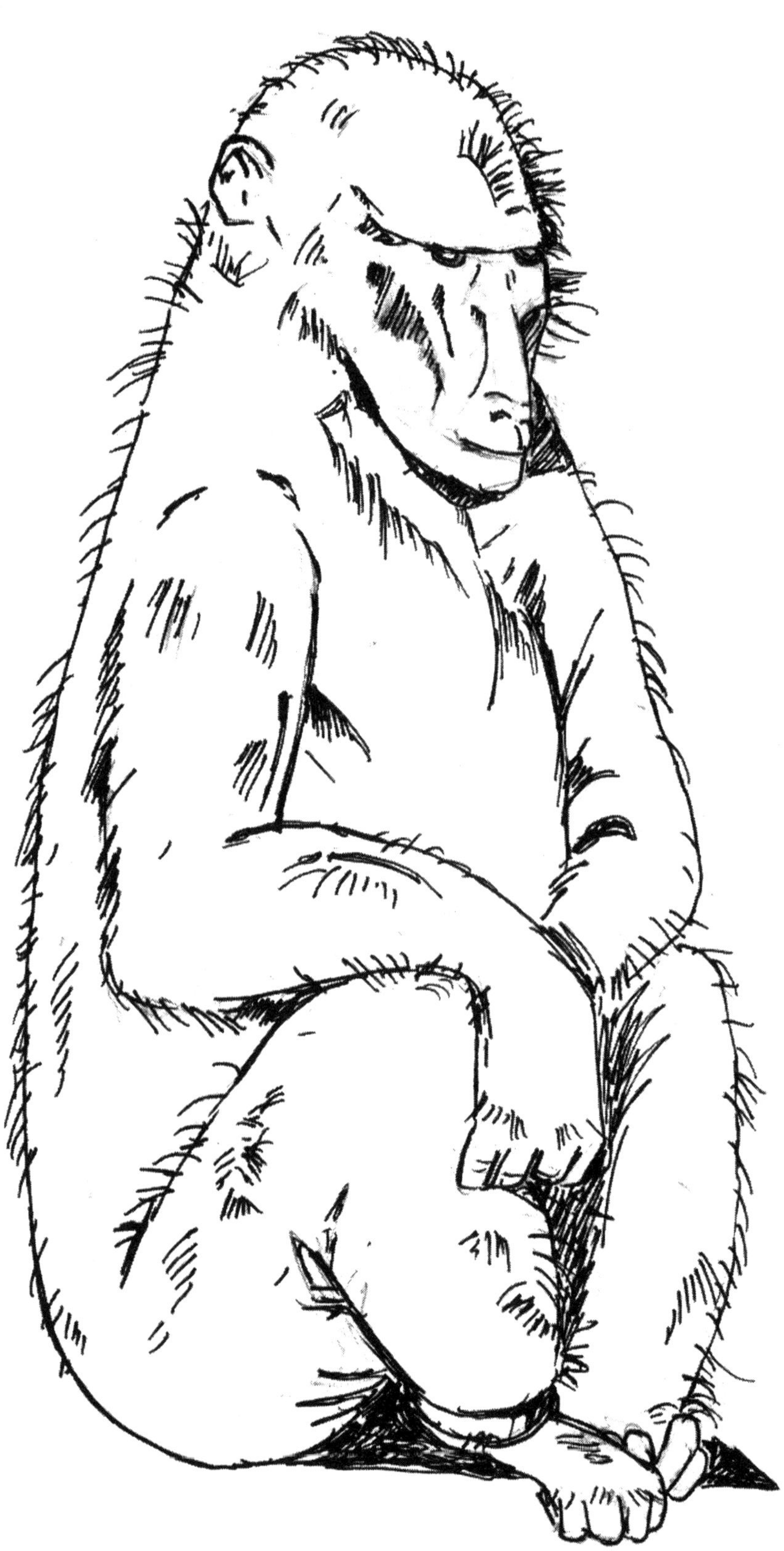

BABOON although a large monkey, is quite slender. Its coarse coat is dark olive-green, with the underside slightly paler and often bare. The length of head and body up to 40 inches, tail 27 inches, weight up to 100 pounds. They live in Senegal to Somalia and southward in Africa, and in southern Arabia.

Baboons live in large groups, numbering up to 150 - 200 individuals, in which is a strict hierarchical order. The size of the group depends on the availability of food and varies from habitat. When the group is on the move it can travel up to 6 miles a day. The young males take up positions in the front and rear of the group, with females, adult males, and young remaining in the middle. If attack, all the males will engage in fierce combat. Their last defense is to flee into trees. Baboons eat early in the day, feeding mainly on plant matter, but also eating small mammals and birds.

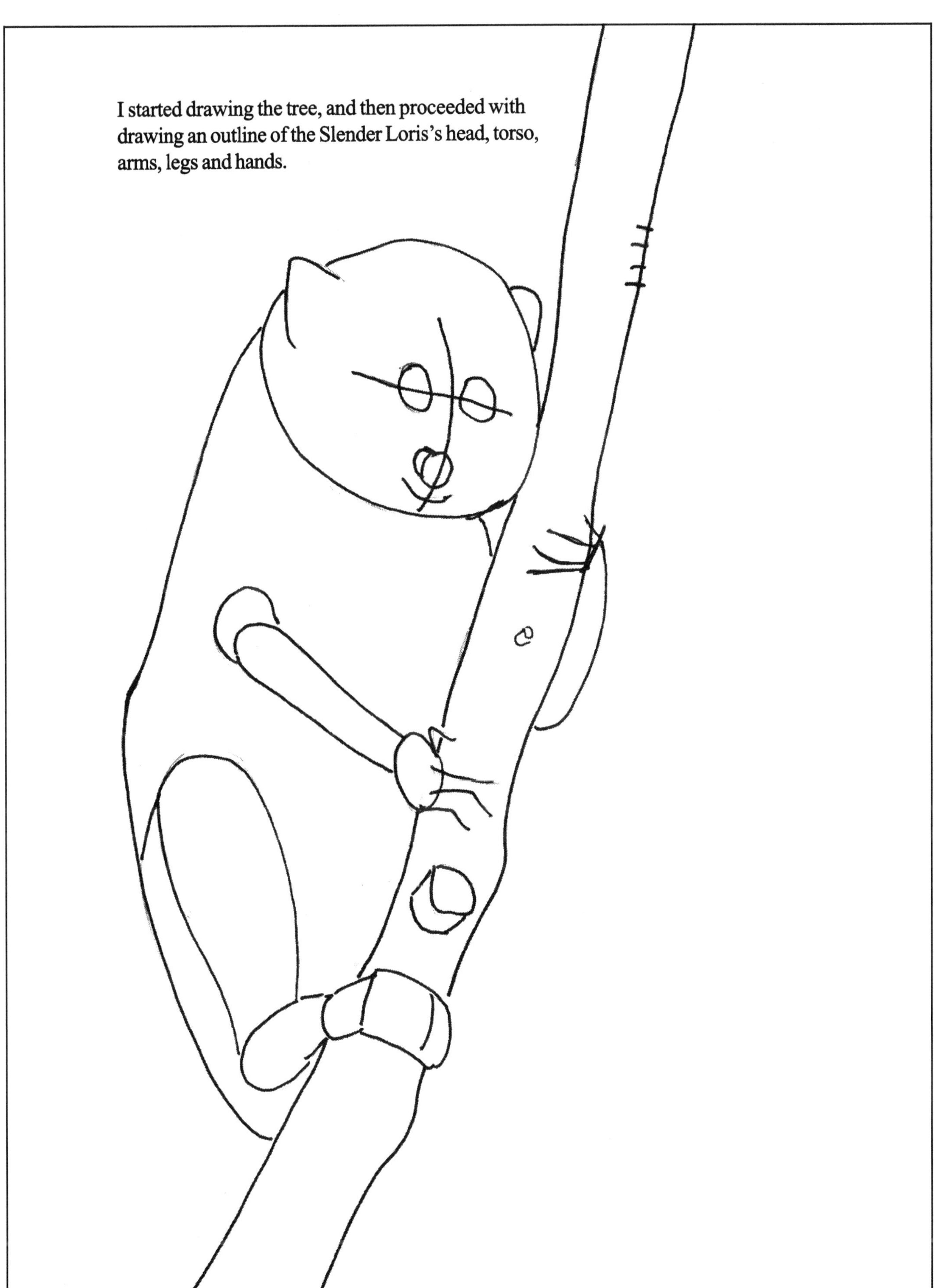
I started drawing the tree, and then proceeded with drawing an outline of the Slender Loris's head, torso, arms, legs and hands.

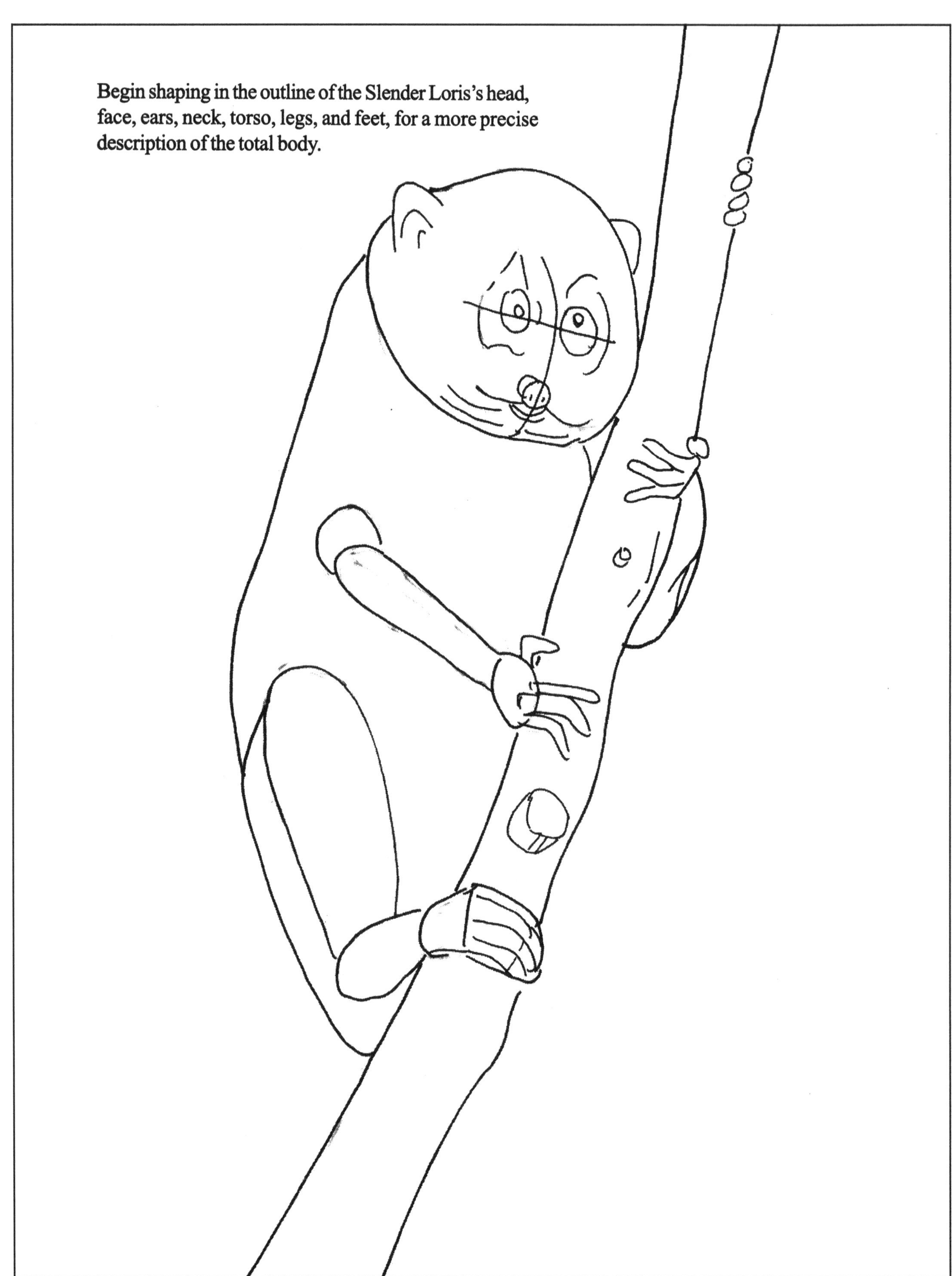
Begin shaping in the outline of the Slender Loris's head,
face, ears, neck, torso, legs, and feet, for a more precise
description of the total body.

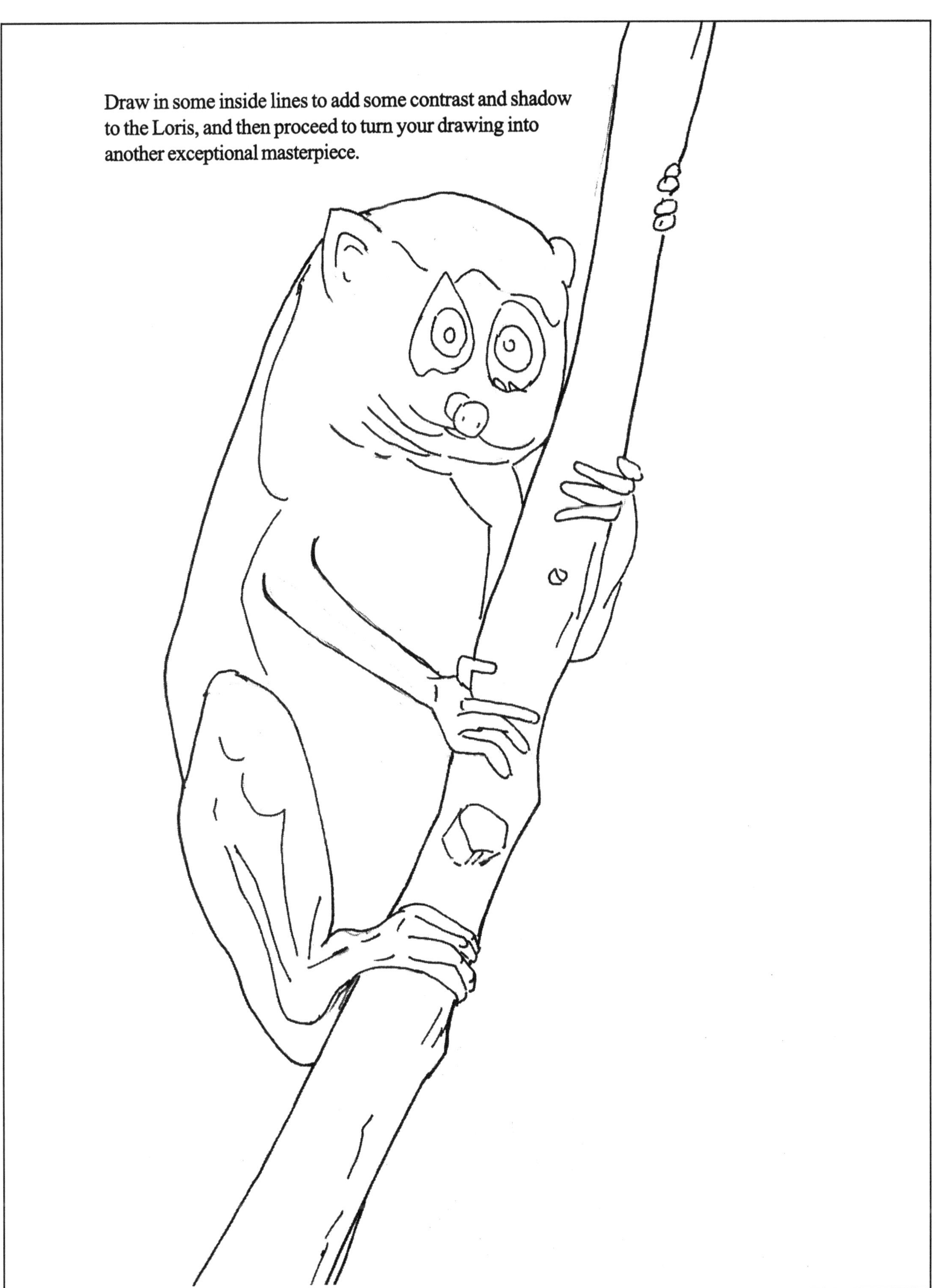

Draw in some inside lines to add some contrast and shadow to the Loris, and then proceed to turn your drawing into another exceptional masterpiece.

SLENDER LORIS

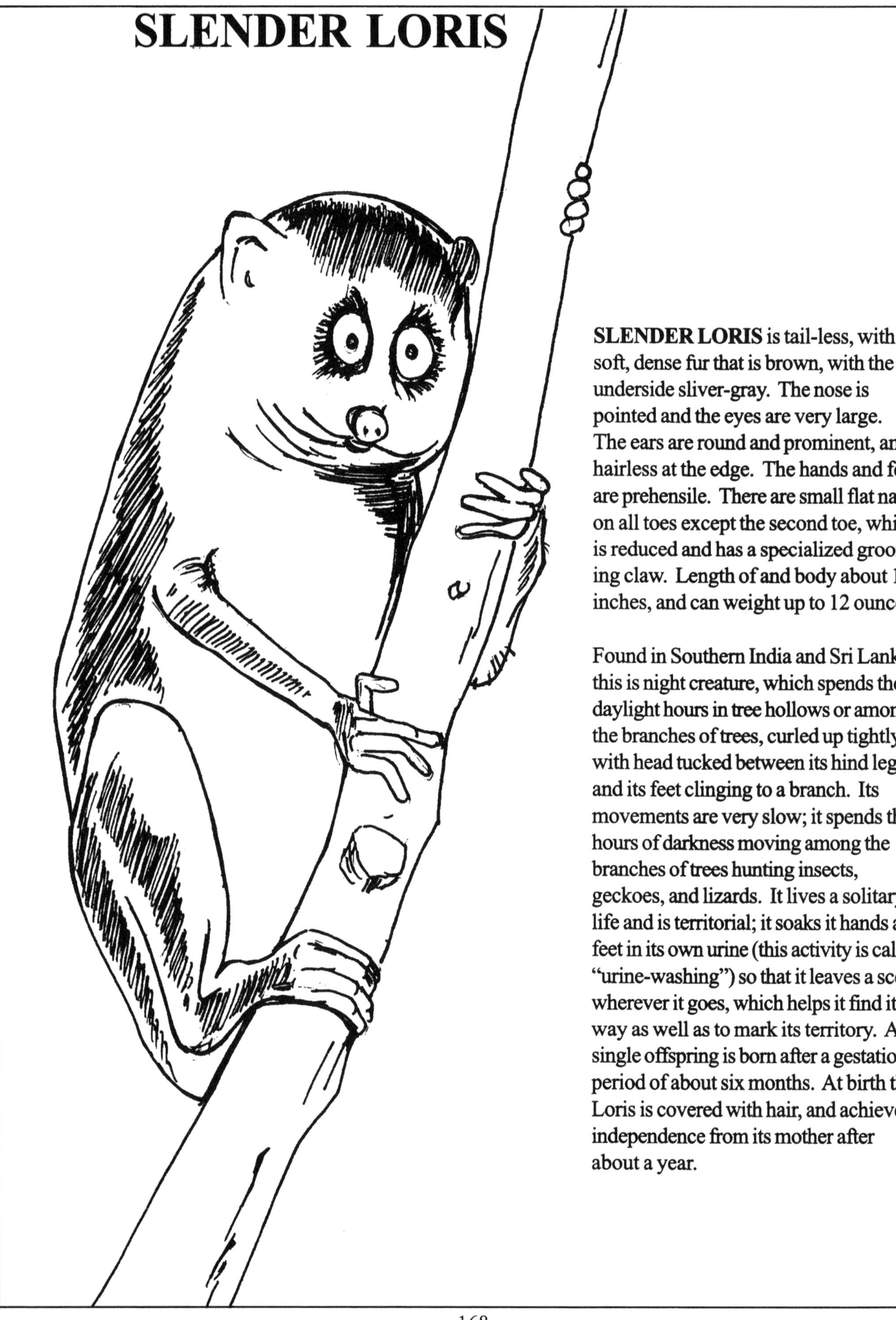

SLENDER LORIS is tail-less, with soft, dense fur that is brown, with the underside sliver-gray. The nose is pointed and the eyes are very large. The ears are round and prominent, and hairless at the edge. The hands and feet are prehensile. There are small flat nails on all toes except the second toe, which is reduced and has a specialized grooming claw. Length of and body about 10 inches, and can weight up to 12 ounces.

Found in Southern India and Sri Lanka, this is night creature, which spends the daylight hours in tree hollows or among the branches of trees, curled up tightly with head tucked between its hind legs, and its feet clinging to a branch. Its movements are very slow; it spends the hours of darkness moving among the branches of trees hunting insects, geckoes, and lizards. It lives a solitary life and is territorial; it soaks it hands and feet in its own urine (this activity is called "urine-washing") so that it leaves a scent wherever it goes, which helps it find its way as well as to mark its territory. A single offspring is born after a gestation period of about six months. At birth the Loris is covered with hair, and achieves independence from its mother after about a year.

Let's first start drawing an outline of the Red Kangaroo's head, ears, neck, torso, arms, legs, feet, and tail.

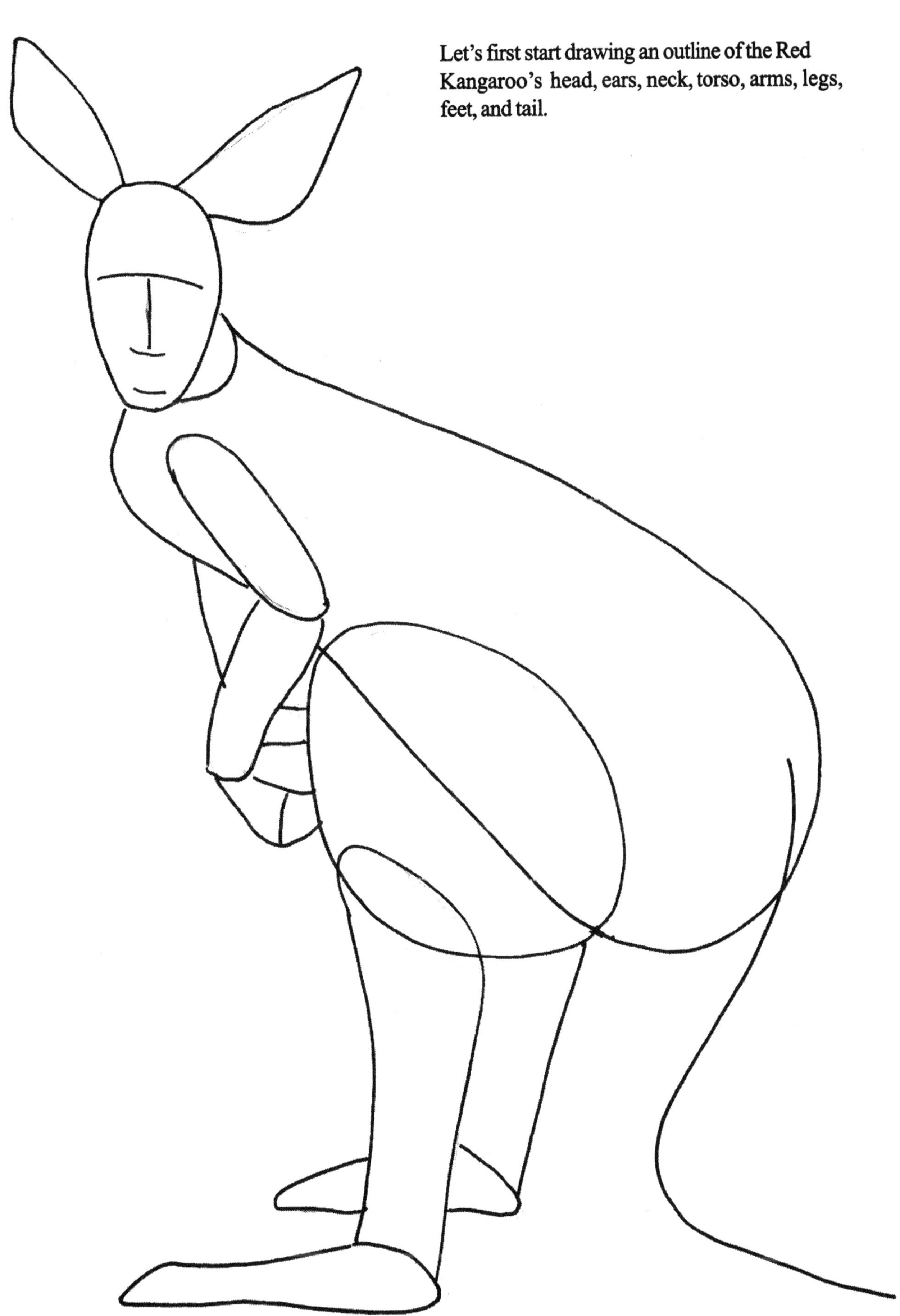

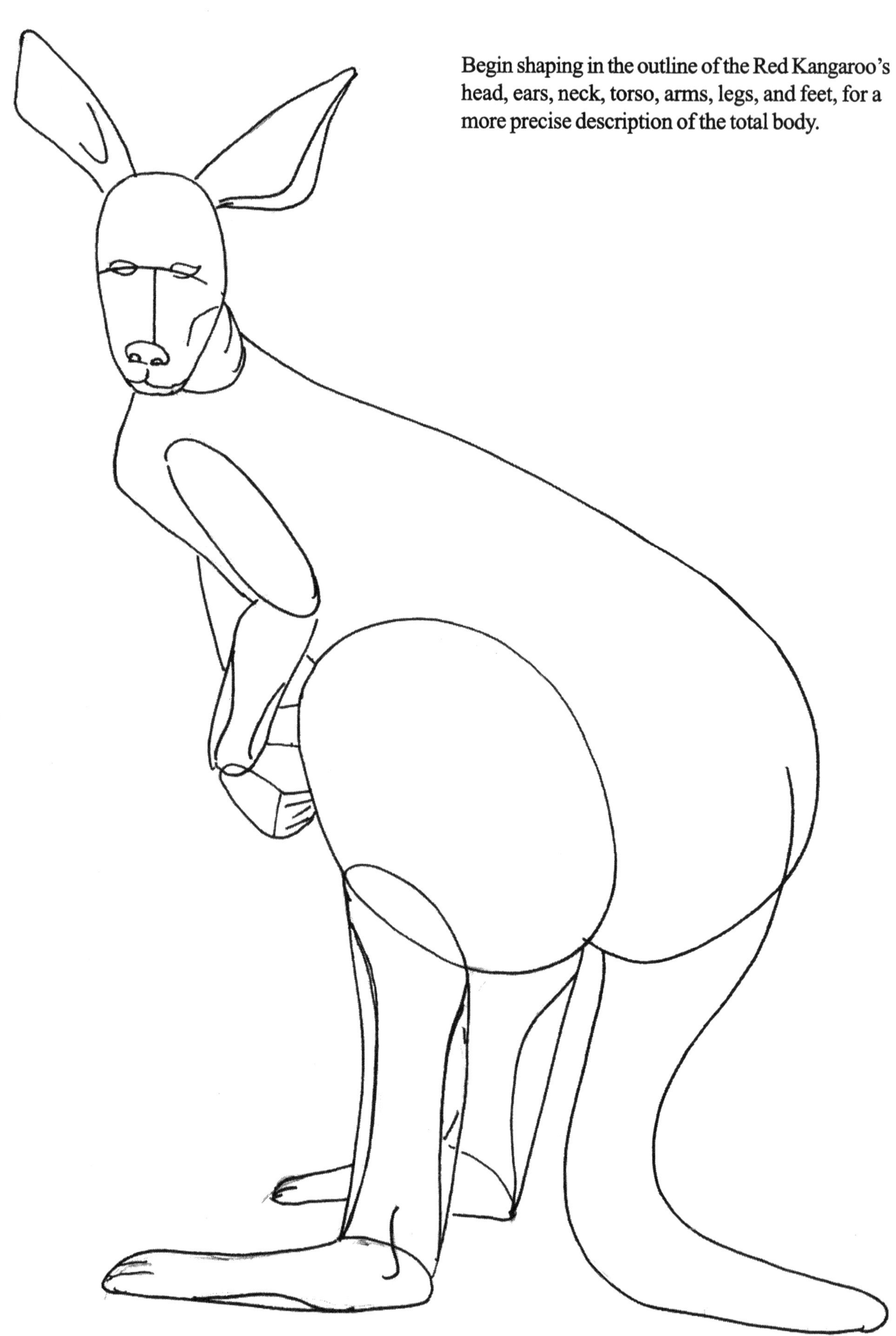

Begin shaping in the outline of the Red Kangaroo's head, ears, neck, torso, arms, legs, and feet, for a more precise description of the total body.

Draw in some inside lines to add some contrast and shadow to the Red Kangaroo's body to proceed to turn your drawing into an exceptional art piece.

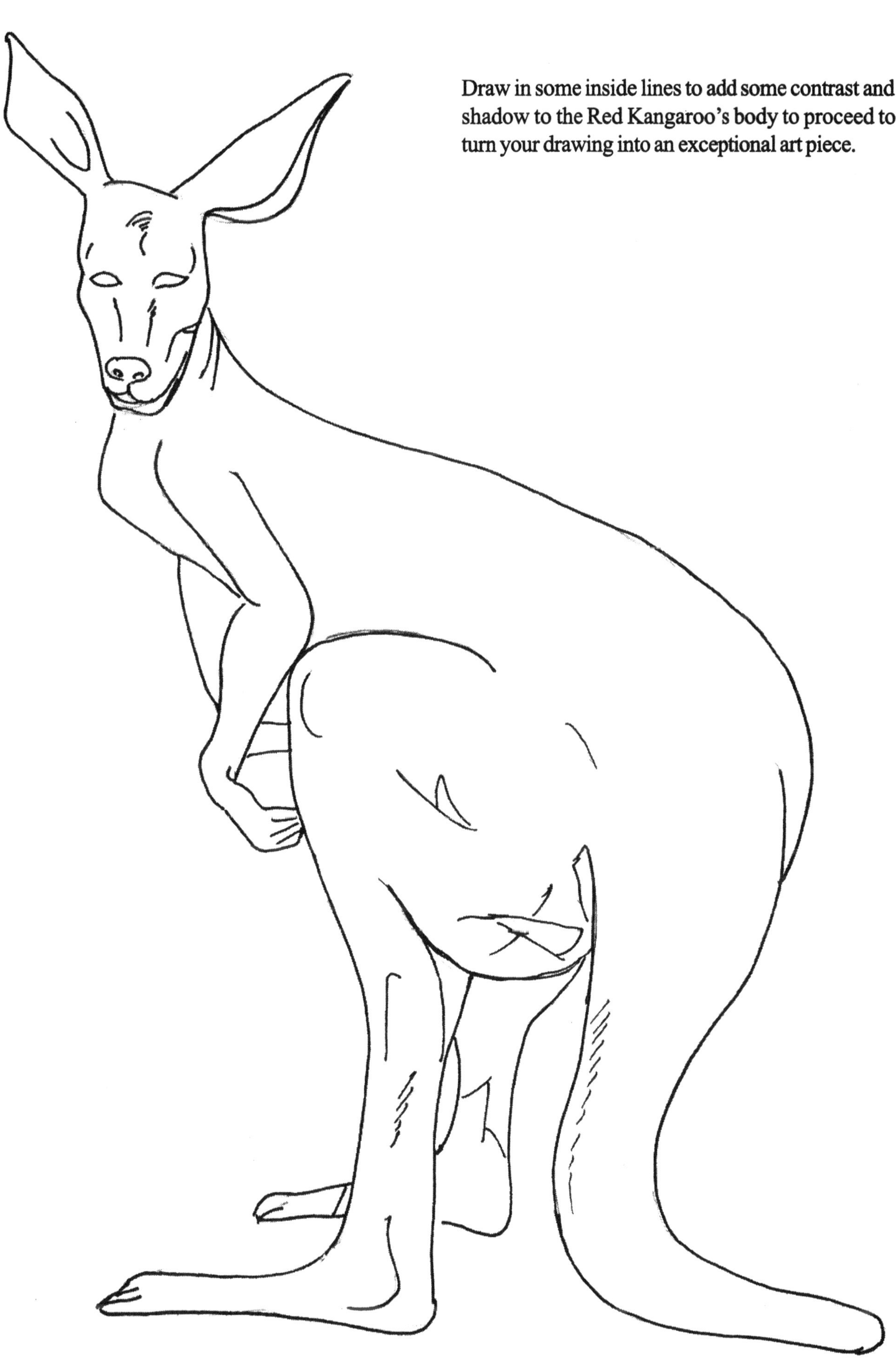

RED KANGAROO

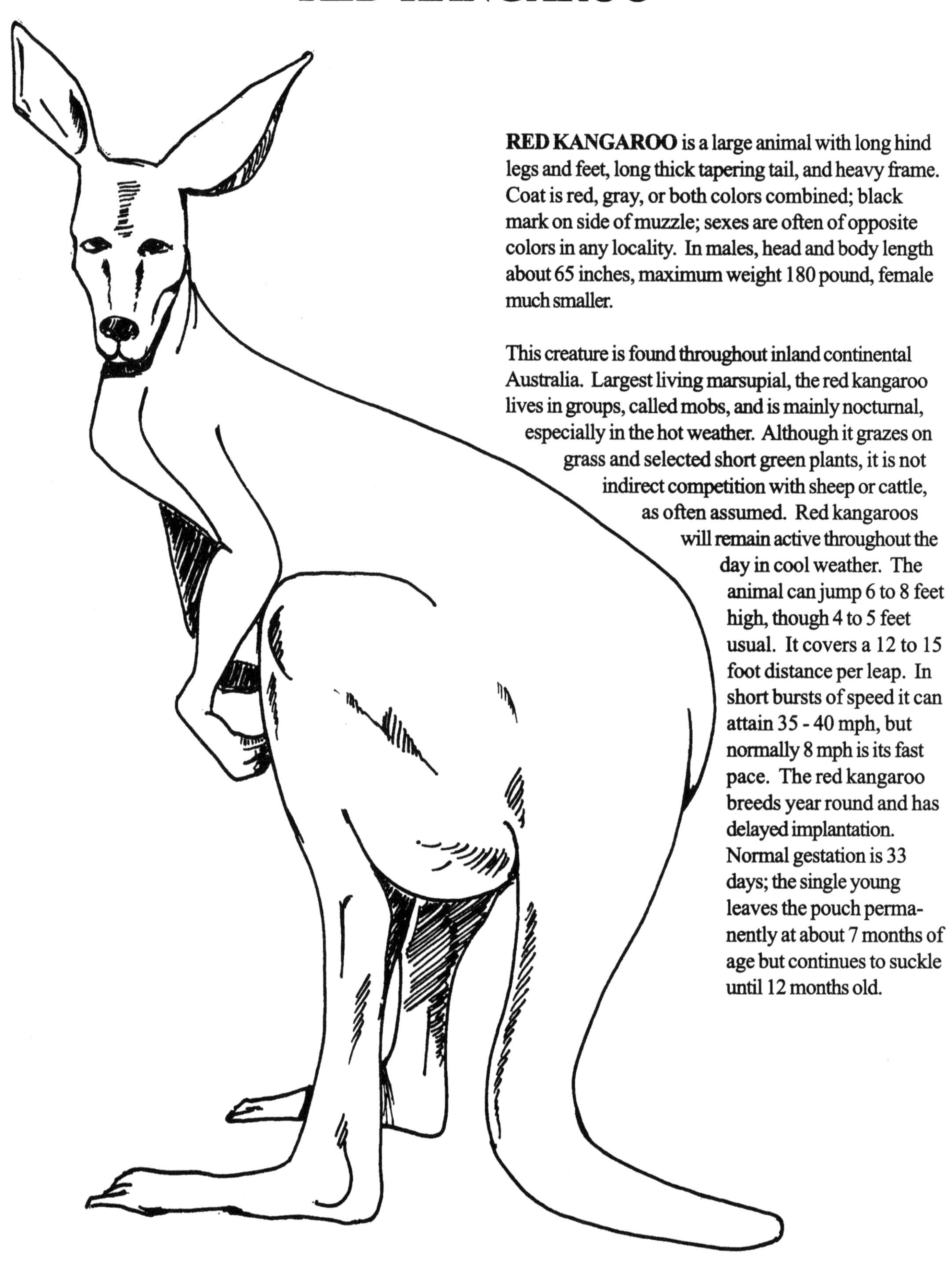

RED KANGAROO is a large animal with long hind legs and feet, long thick tapering tail, and heavy frame. Coat is red, gray, or both colors combined; black mark on side of muzzle; sexes are often of opposite colors in any locality. In males, head and body length about 65 inches, maximum weight 180 pound, female much smaller.

This creature is found throughout inland continental Australia. Largest living marsupial, the red kangaroo lives in groups, called mobs, and is mainly nocturnal, especially in the hot weather. Although it grazes on grass and selected short green plants, it is not indirect competition with sheep or cattle, as often assumed. Red kangaroos will remain active throughout the day in cool weather. The animal can jump 6 to 8 feet high, though 4 to 5 feet usual. It covers a 12 to 15 foot distance per leap. In short bursts of speed it can attain 35 - 40 mph, but normally 8 mph is its fast pace. The red kangaroo breeds year round and has delayed implantation. Normal gestation is 33 days; the single young leaves the pouch permanently at about 7 months of age but continues to suckle until 12 months old.

Let's get busy drawing this Llama. Let's start with an outline of the head, ears, neck, torso, leg, and hoofs.

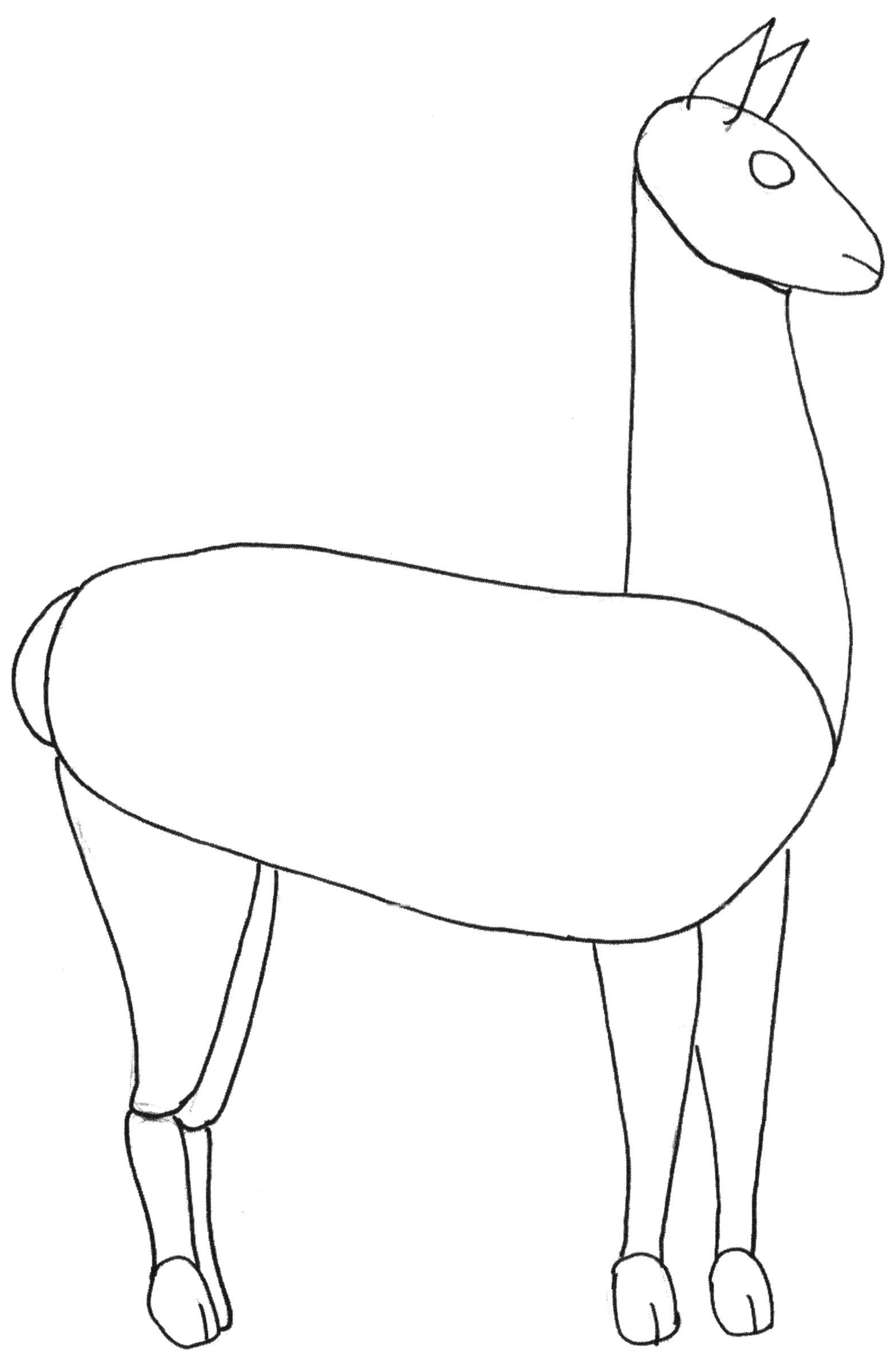

Begin shaping in the outline of the Red Llama's head, ears, neck, torso, arms, legs, and feet, for a more precise description of the total body.

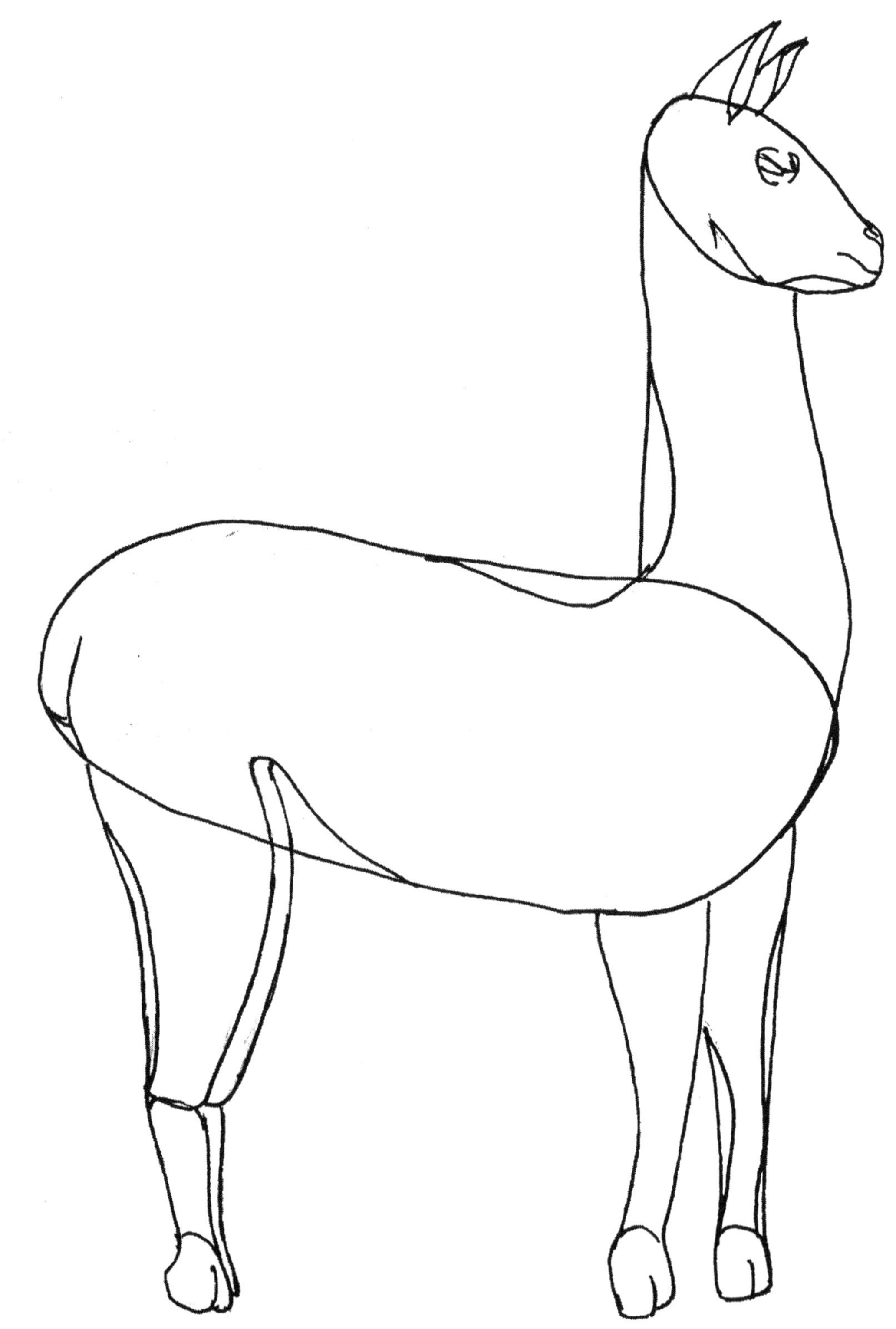

Get rid of any unnecessary lines add some hair, and then proceed to turn your drawing into one of your best works of art.

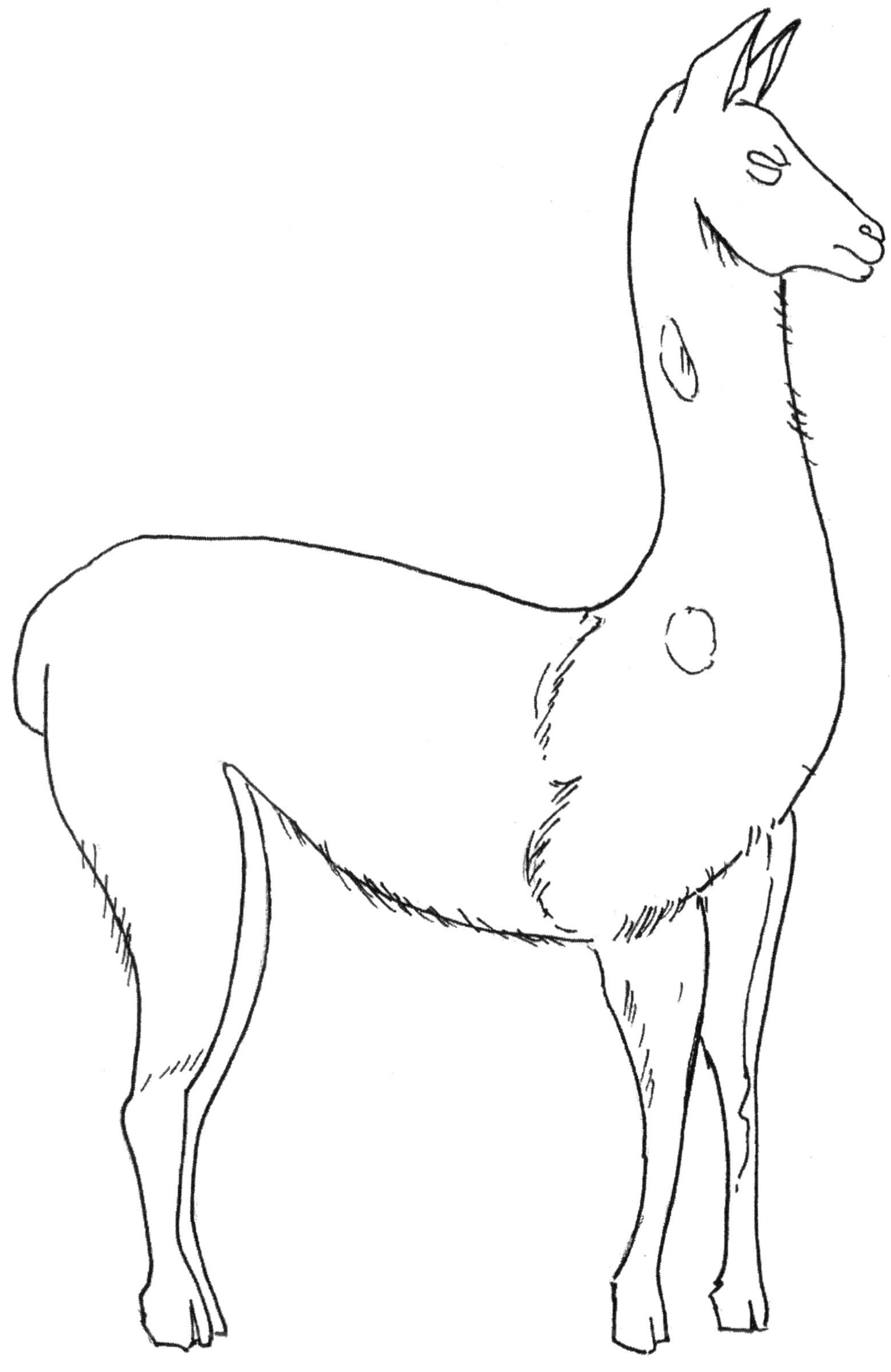

LLAMA

LLAMA the long shaggy coat varies in color from white all over through spotted or speckled, to brown black, or reddish brown all over. It is somewhat like the guanaco in appearance but stockier, with long and more varied coat texture and color. Length of head and body up to 6.6 feet, shoulder height 4 feet, weight over 290 pounds.

The llama is from South America, in the Andres and tends to live in small groups made up of a dominant male with a harem of about 5-10 females and their young. Young males are kept away the group and lead a bachelor existence. Breeding occurs in the spring, and after 10 months of gestation, the female gives birth to a single young. There no true wild llamas, all are domesticated and are used to transport goods at high altitudes.

As far as zoological systematics is concerned, this species still poses a problem. Some authors consider it to be a domesticated form of the guanaco.

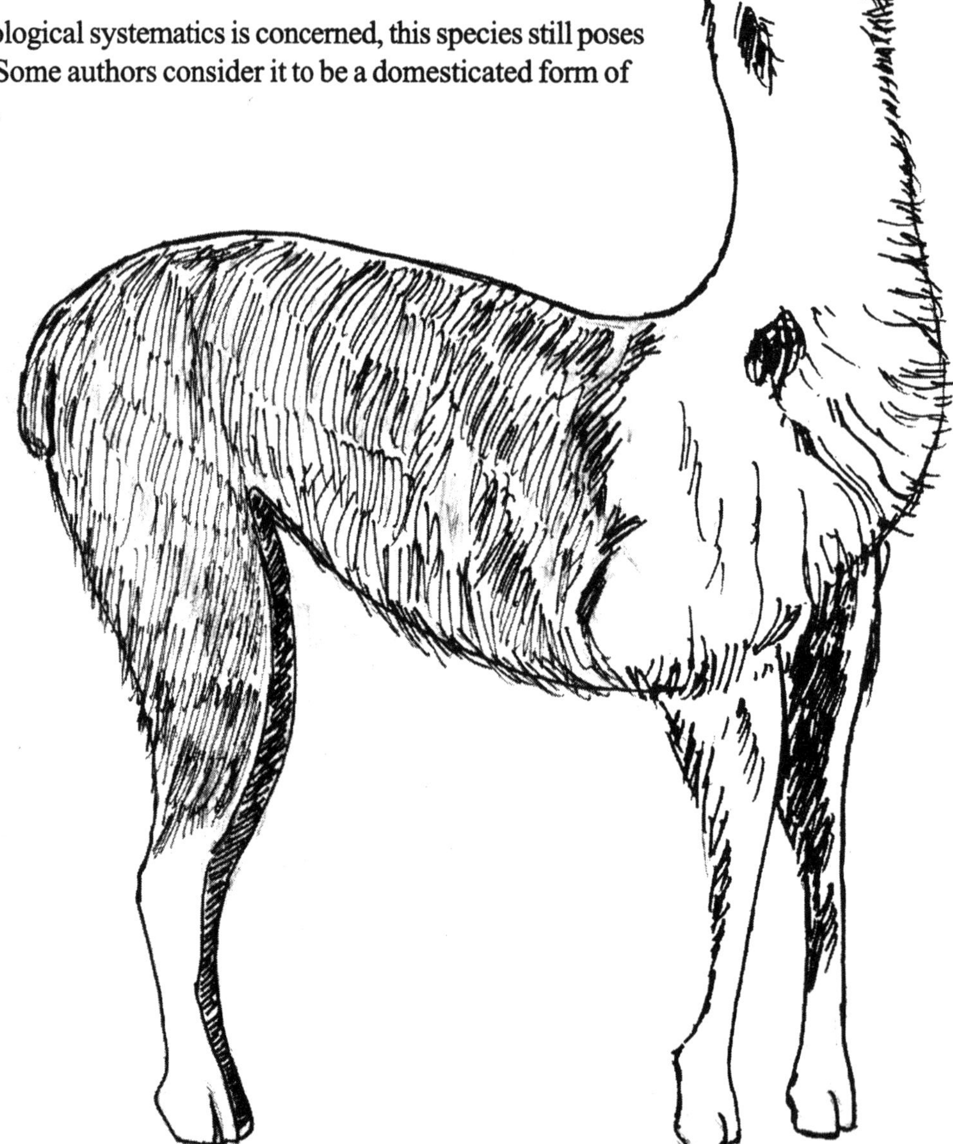

Let's start drawing an outline of the Aardvark, the first mammal in the dictionary. Begin drawing the head, ears, neck, torso, legs, and tail

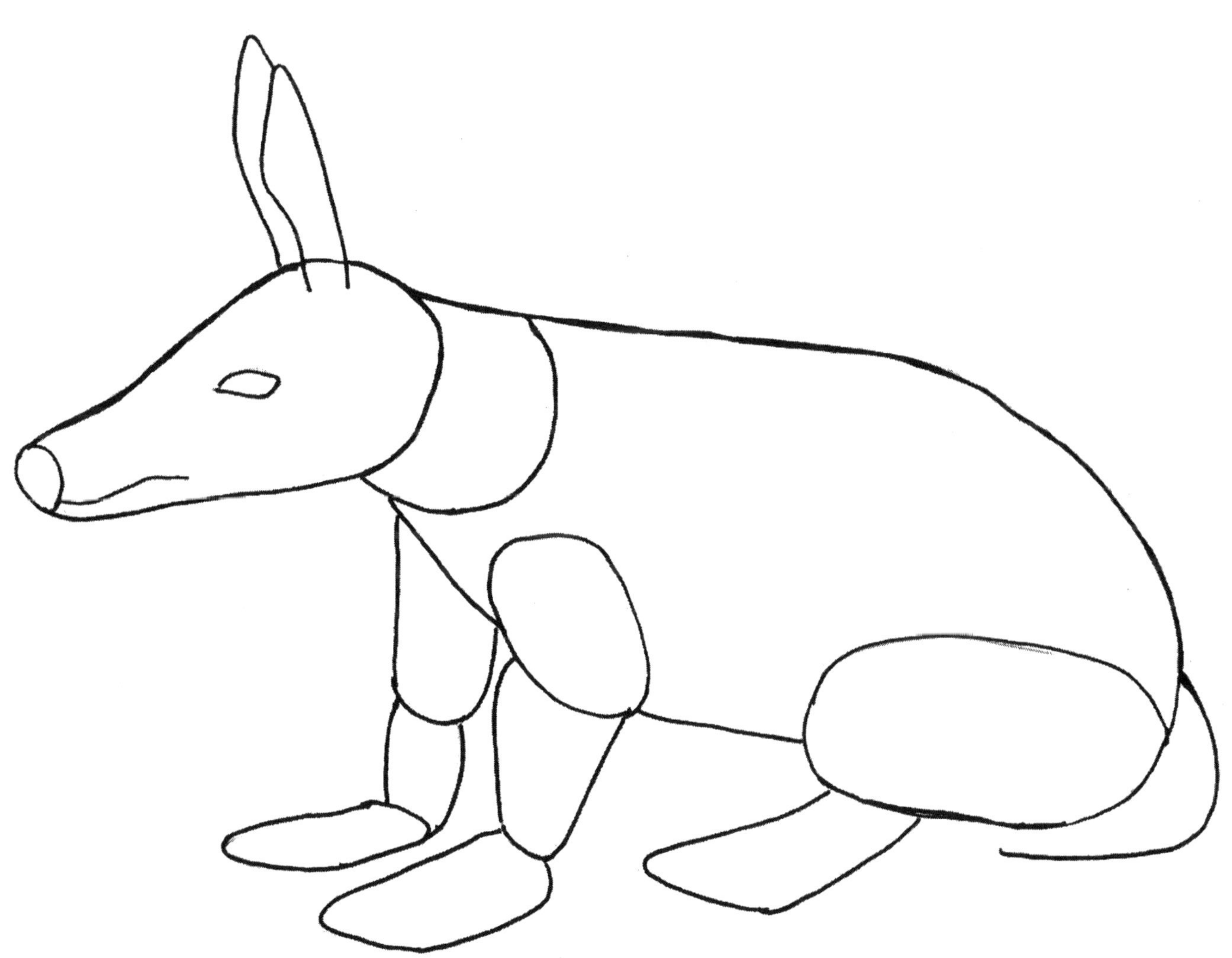

Now, let's define the various parts of the Aardvark's total body by drawing within the outlines.

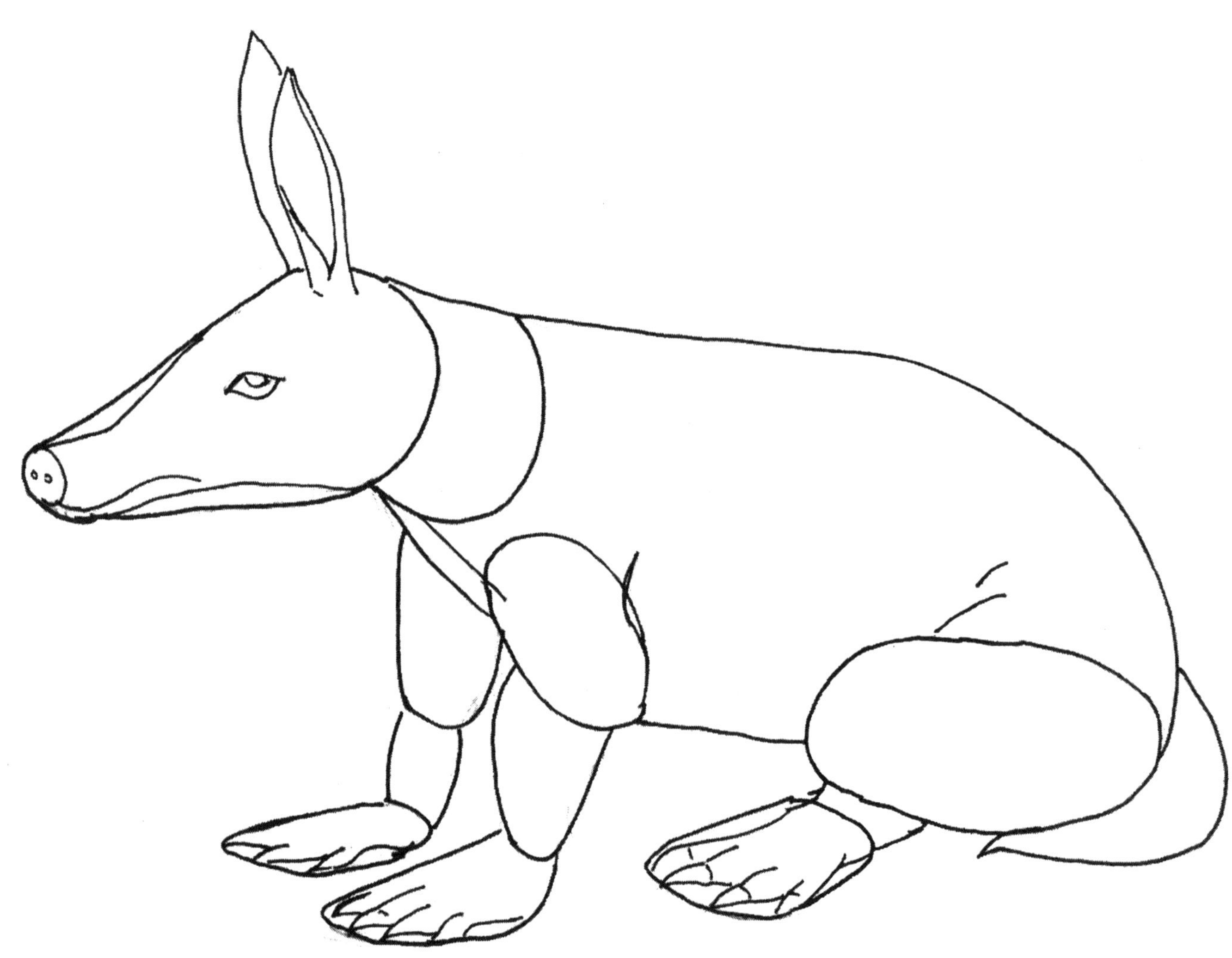

You can erase any lines not needed, draw in more details such as the hair and lines for shadows.

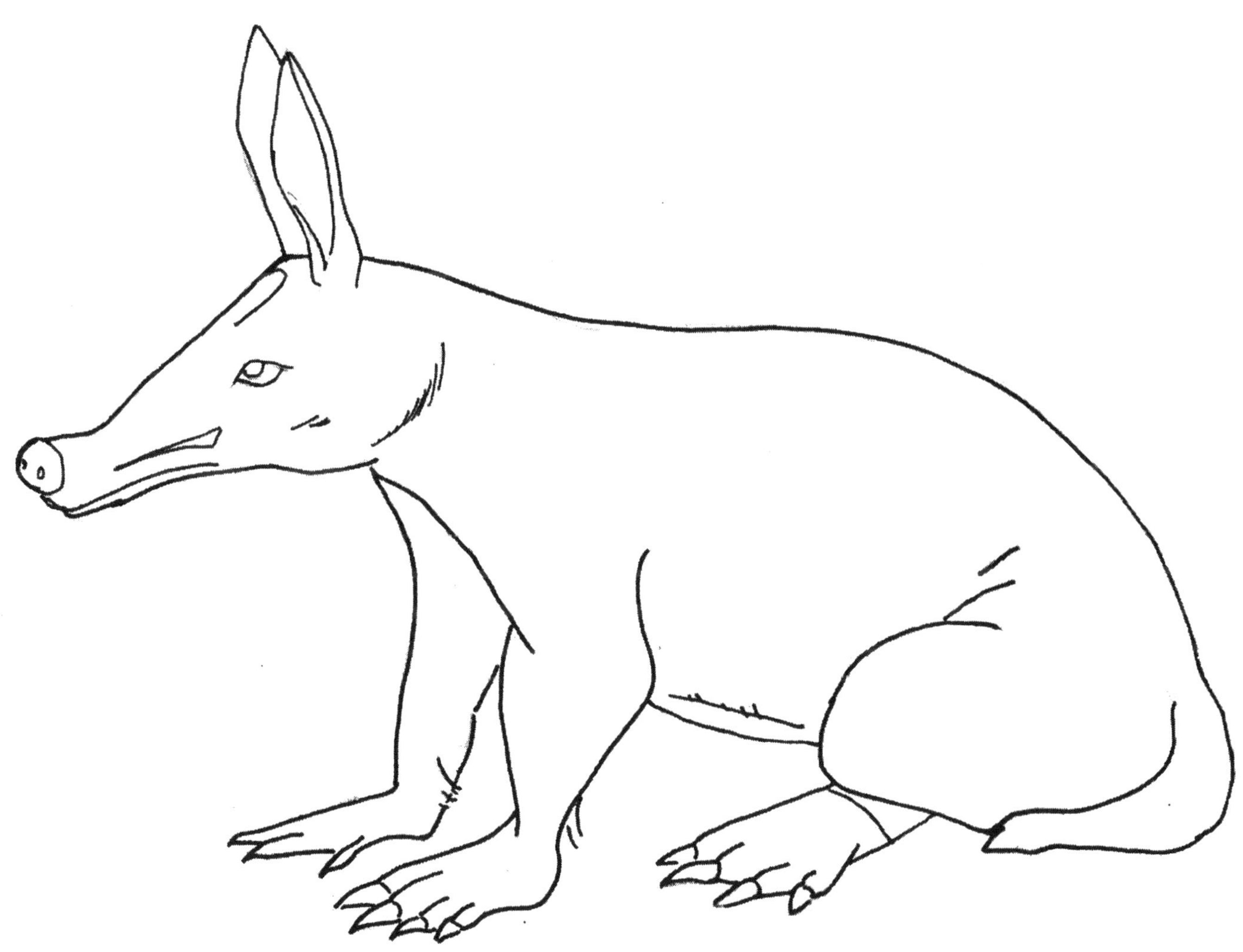

AARDVARK

AARDVARK this fairly large creature has a distinctive shape, with a curved back and a rather pig like snout. Its ears are long and tough; it has strong feet with four toes on the front foot and five on the back. All toes have large claws. The grayish skin is thick and bare except for a few hairs. Length of head and body is 40 - 60 inches, tail 18 - 24 inches, and weight 175 - 220 pounds.

The aardvark resides in Africa south of the Sahara. They inhabit the grasslands, and open forests where the ground is soft. The aardvark is a nocturnal creature and very difficult to observe. It spends the day in its burrow. It is a very efficient digger, and can disappear underground rapidly. The tunnels are sometimes very long and complex, with numerous openings, but they invariably end in a large chamber. It feeds on termites, which it sucks into the mouth with its sticky tongue. It is a solitary animal, except when the female is accompanied for a while by one or more young. Gestation lasts 7 months, after which a single offspring is born. Although the young is nursed for only a few months, it will often remain with its mother for many more months.

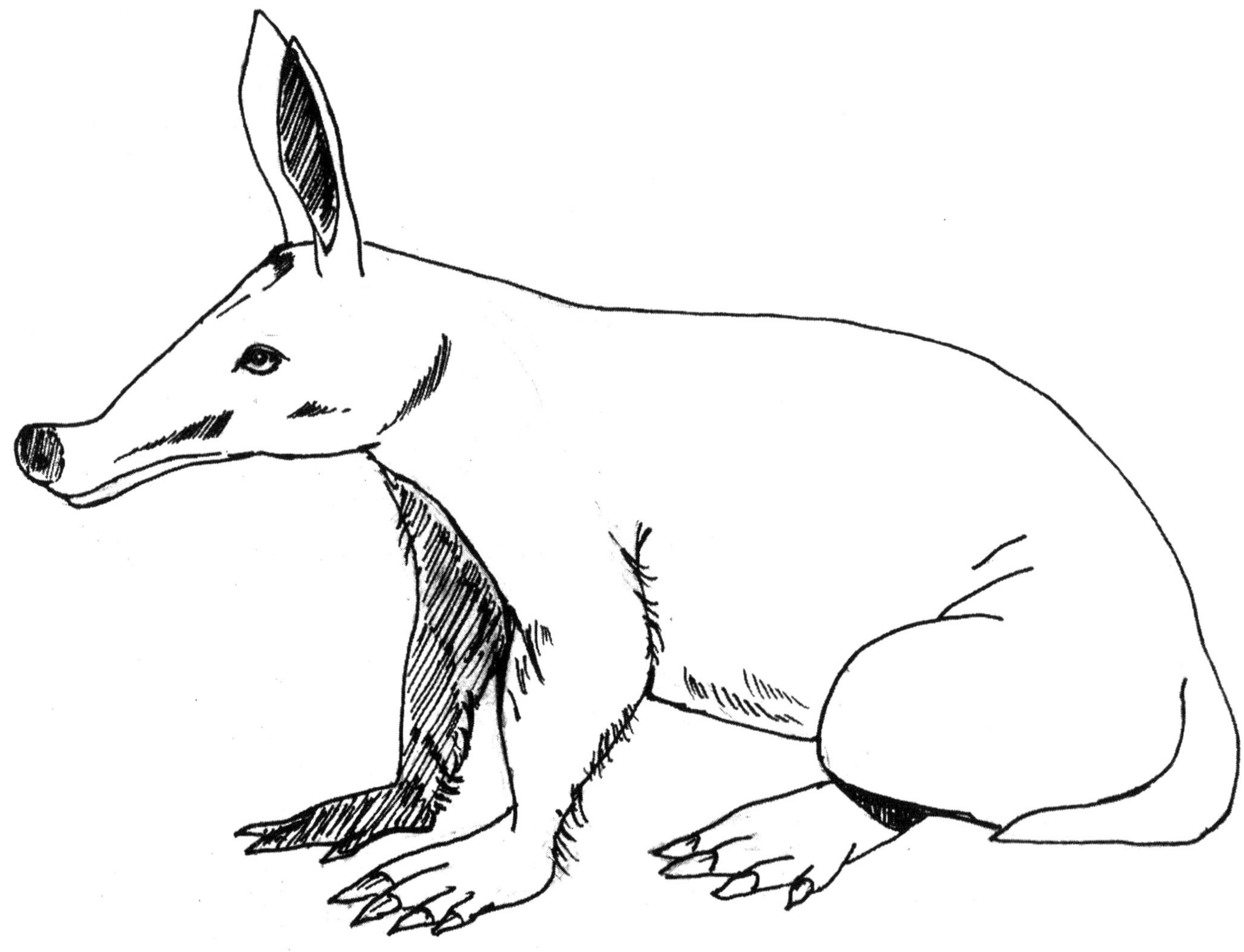

Start drawing an outline of the Gorilla's head, neck, torso, arms, legs, and feet.

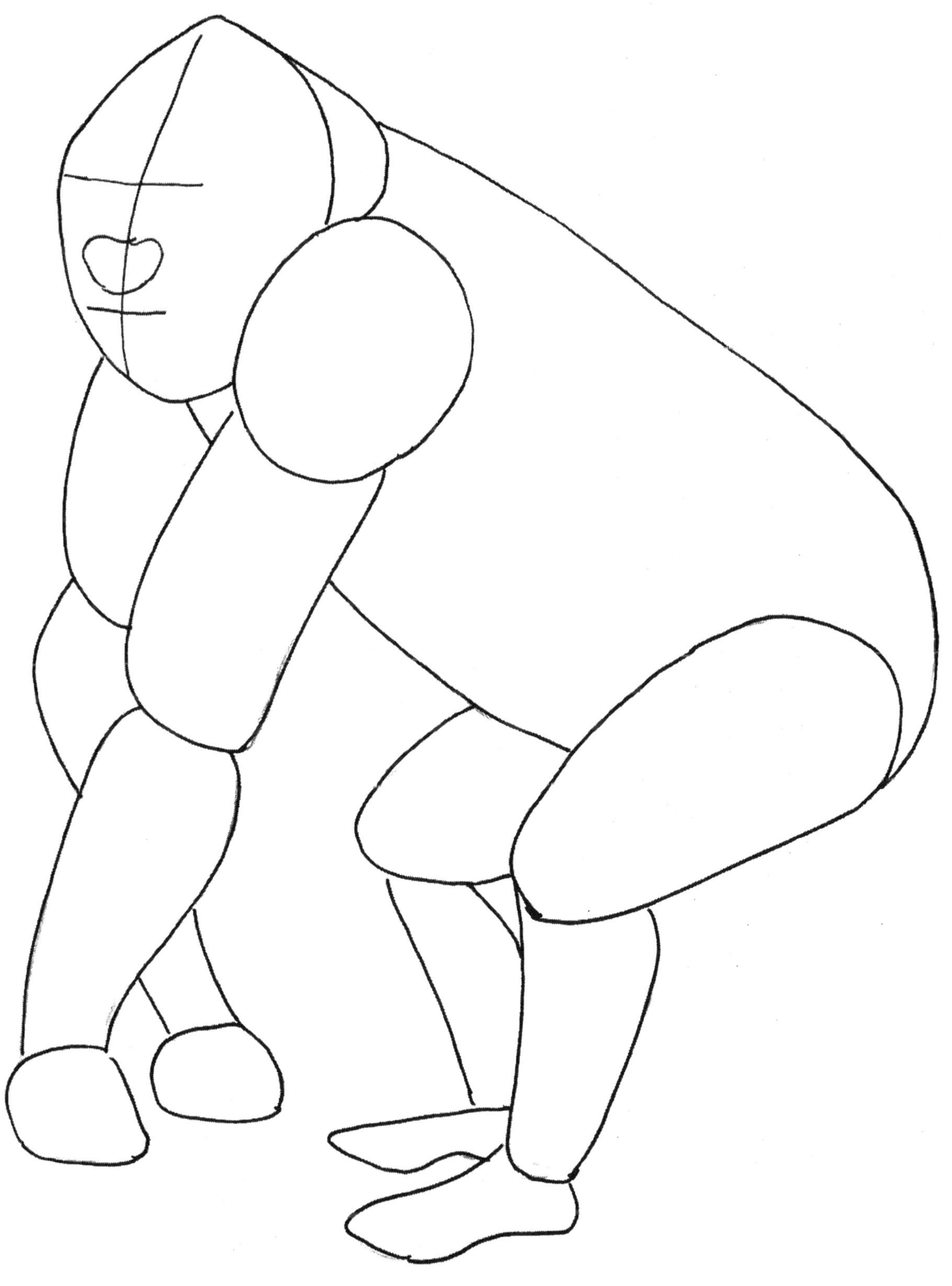

Begin shaping the Gorilla's body from head to toe for a more definitive look.

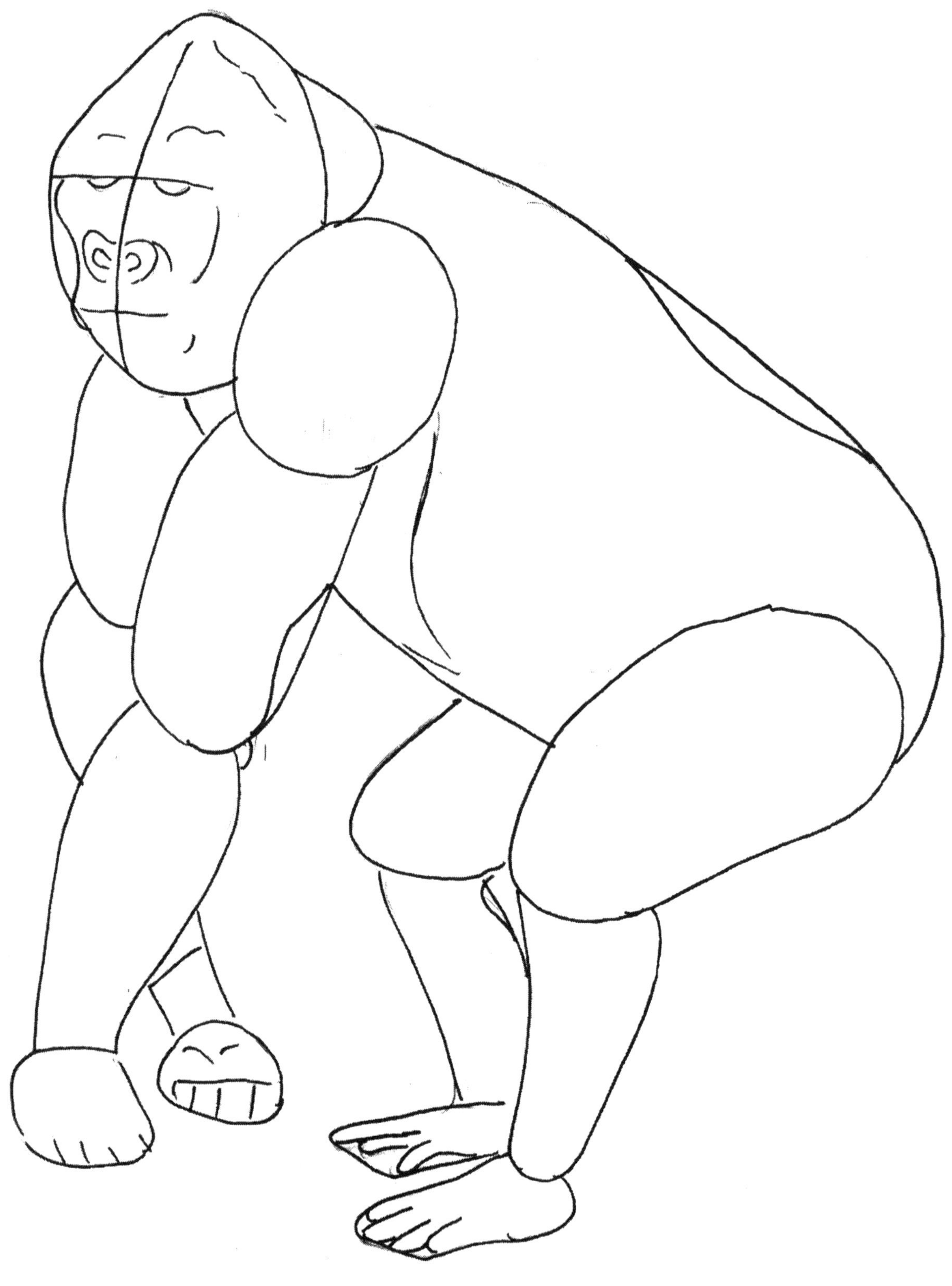

Now, let's define the various parts of the Gorilla's body by drawing within the outlines to create more detail.

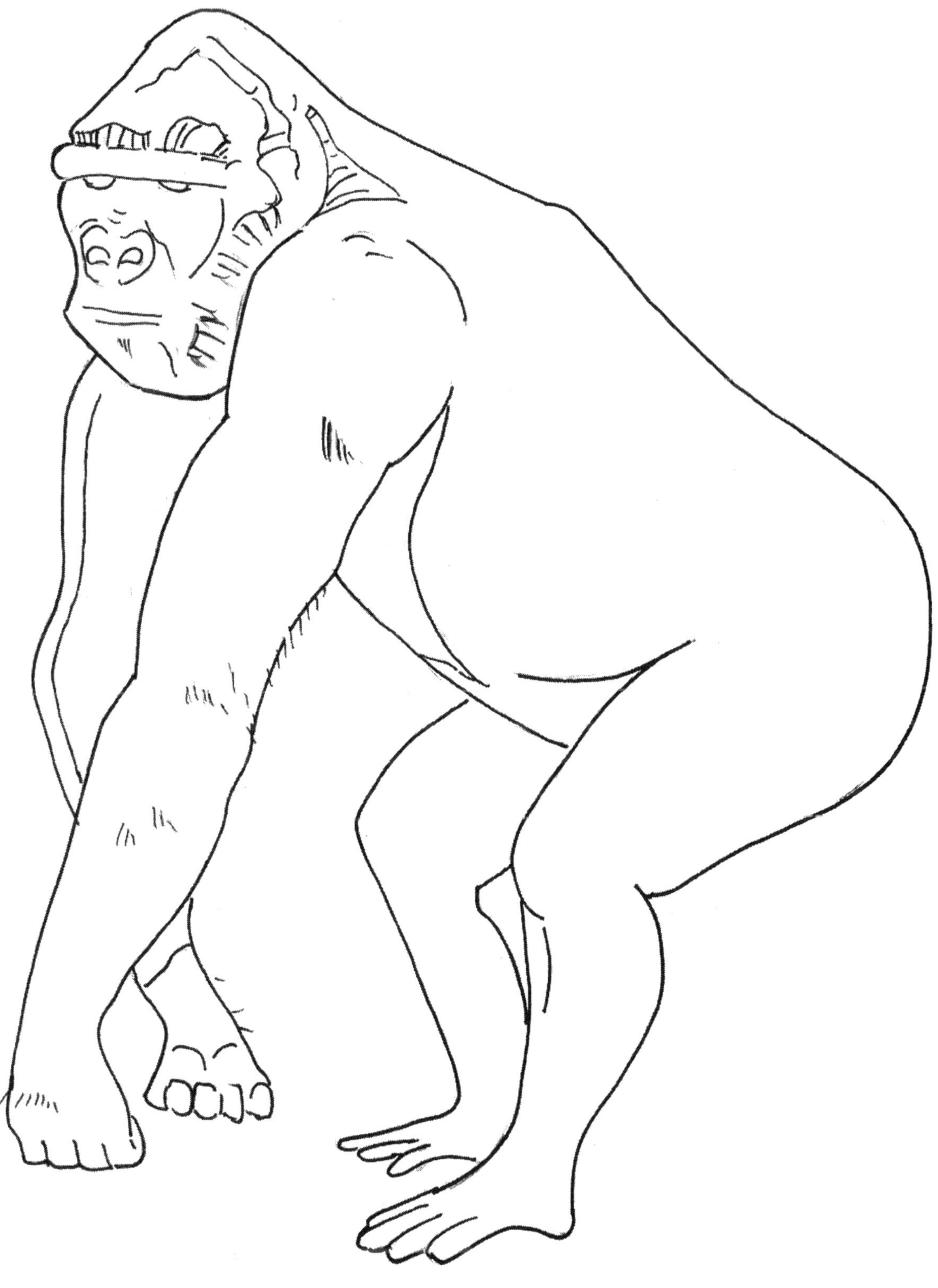

GORILLA

GORILLA The gorilla is the largest and heaviest of the primates; the head is especially large, and it has highly developed chest muscles. The shape of the face varies somewhat, as do its facial expressions. Its ears are relatively small, the nostrils are always flared. The coat is black, but has silver and gray highlights in adult males. When a gorilla is older than 10 years the whole coat turns gray. In colder parts of the gorilla's habitat, the coat tends to be shaggier, and longer. Length of head and body is 4.60 - 6.10 feet, standing up to 6.7 feet, weight up to 500 pounds, female are smaller.

Lowland gorilla is found in Cameroon, Gabon, and Zaire, and the mountain gorilla in Uganda, Rwanda, and Tanzania. The gorilla lives mainly on the ground, and adults only venture into trees to build nests, though young gorillas often play in trees. On the ground it is quadruped and the weight of the body rests at the front on the central small bones of the fingers in kind of locomotion called knuckle-walking. The gorilla is a peaceful creature, and will only attack if attacked. A vegetarian, it lives in groups of 2 - 30 individuals, always dominated by a large male. After a 251 - 289 day gestation, single offspring (rarely twins) is born.

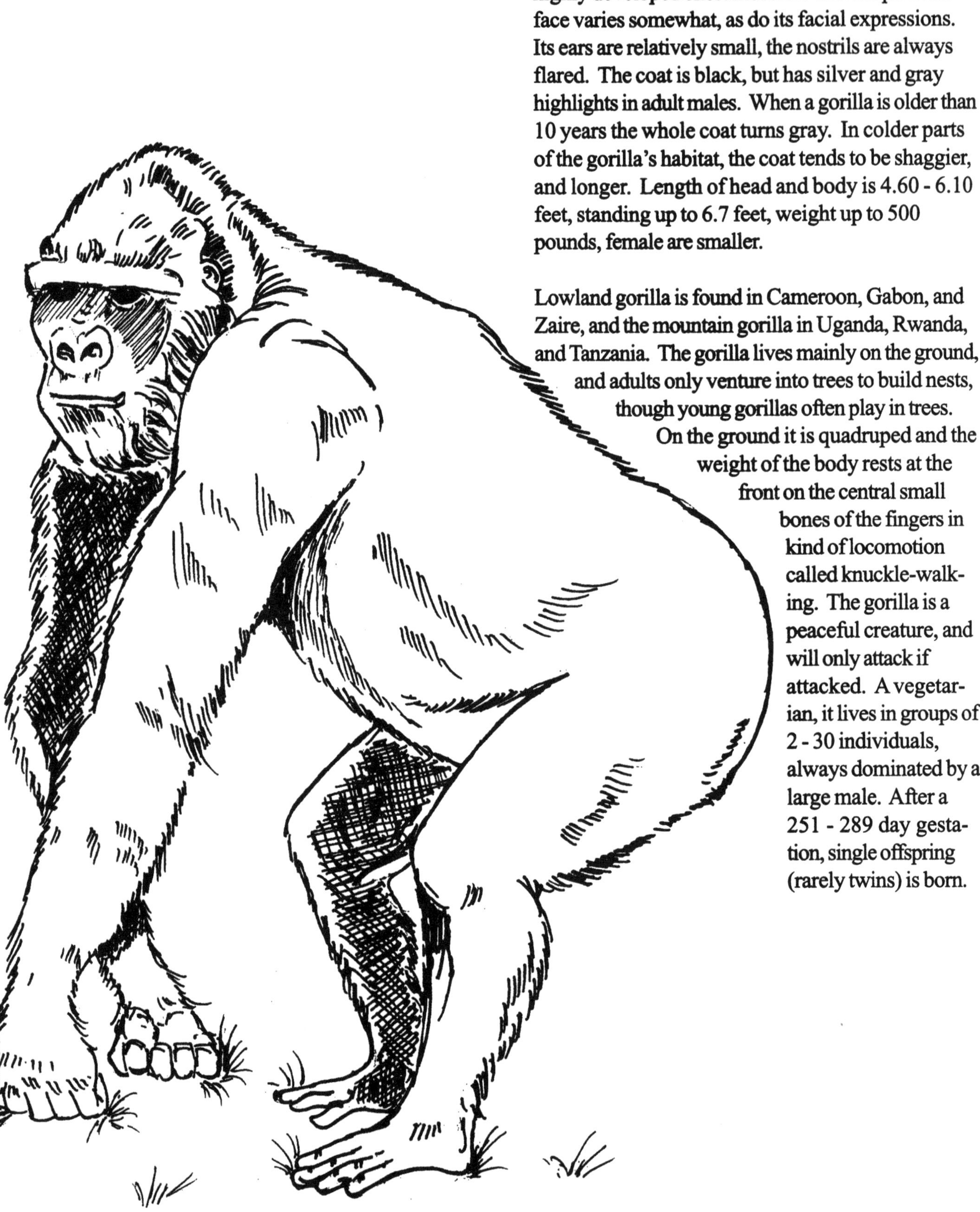

Let's start drawing an outline of the Loin, the king of the jungle. Let's begin with the head, ears, neck, torso, mane, legs, paws, and tail.

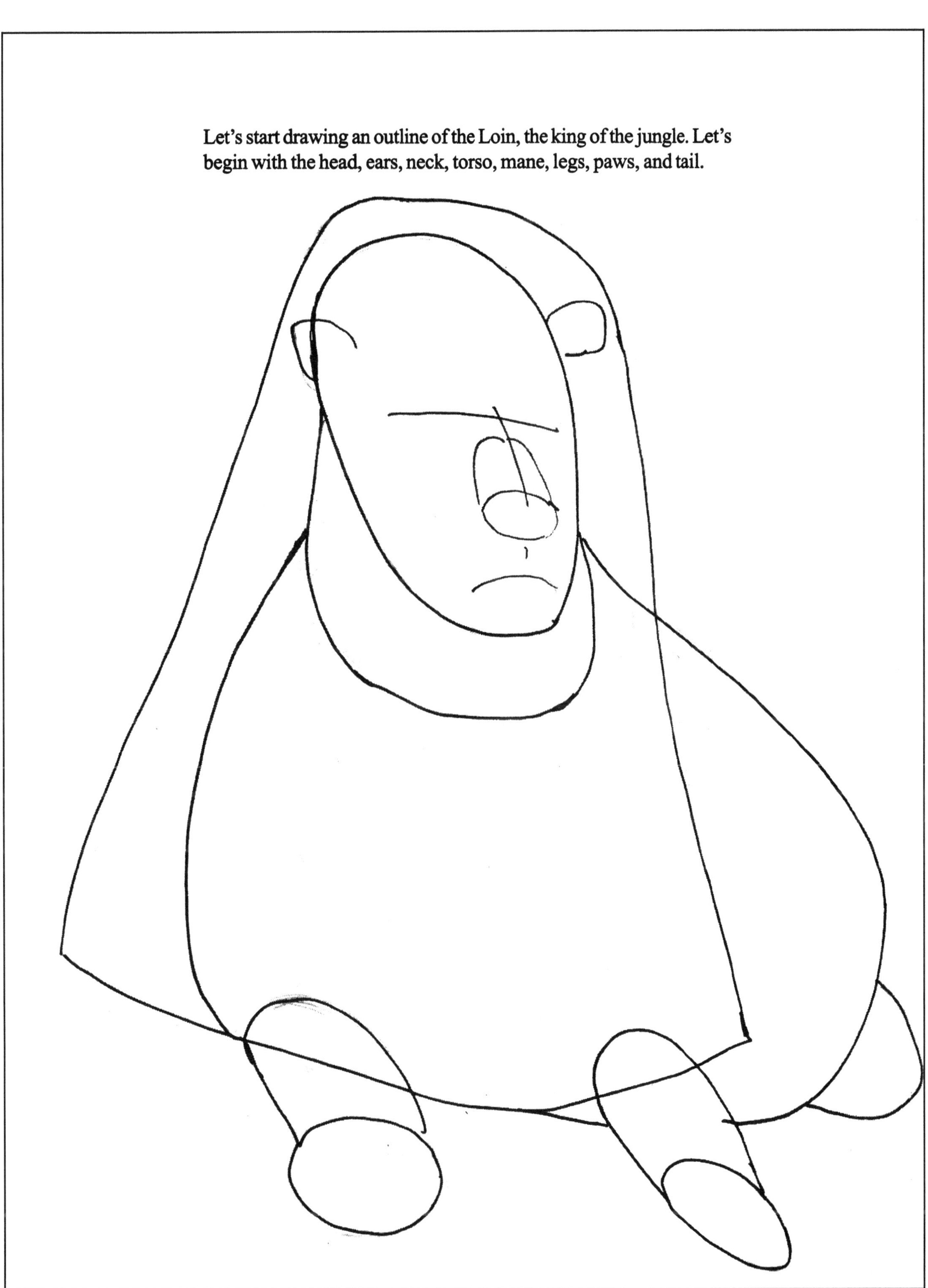

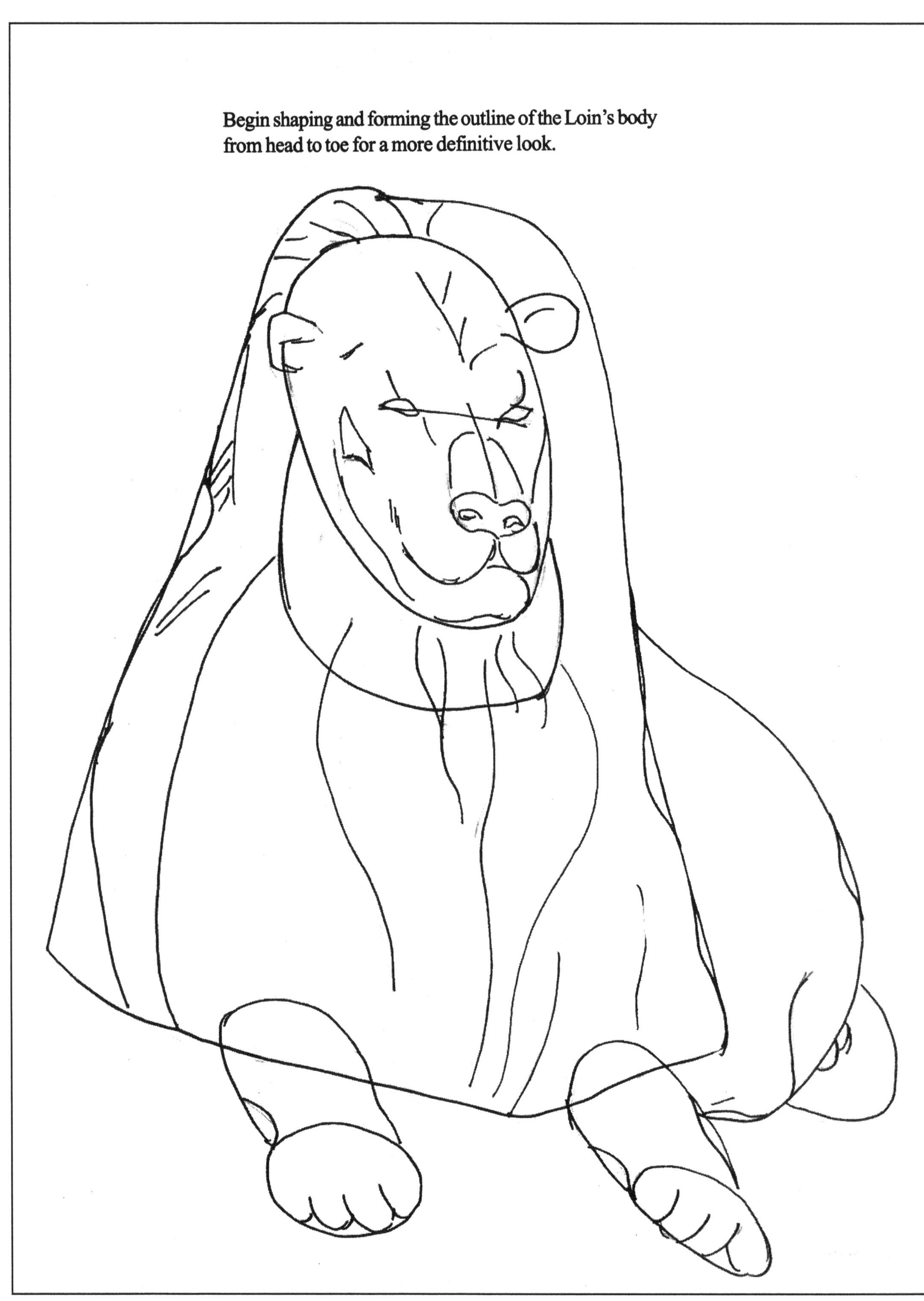
Begin shaping and forming the outline of the Loin's body
from head to toe for a more definitive look.

You can erase any lines not needed, draw in more details in the face, mane, and shadow lines.

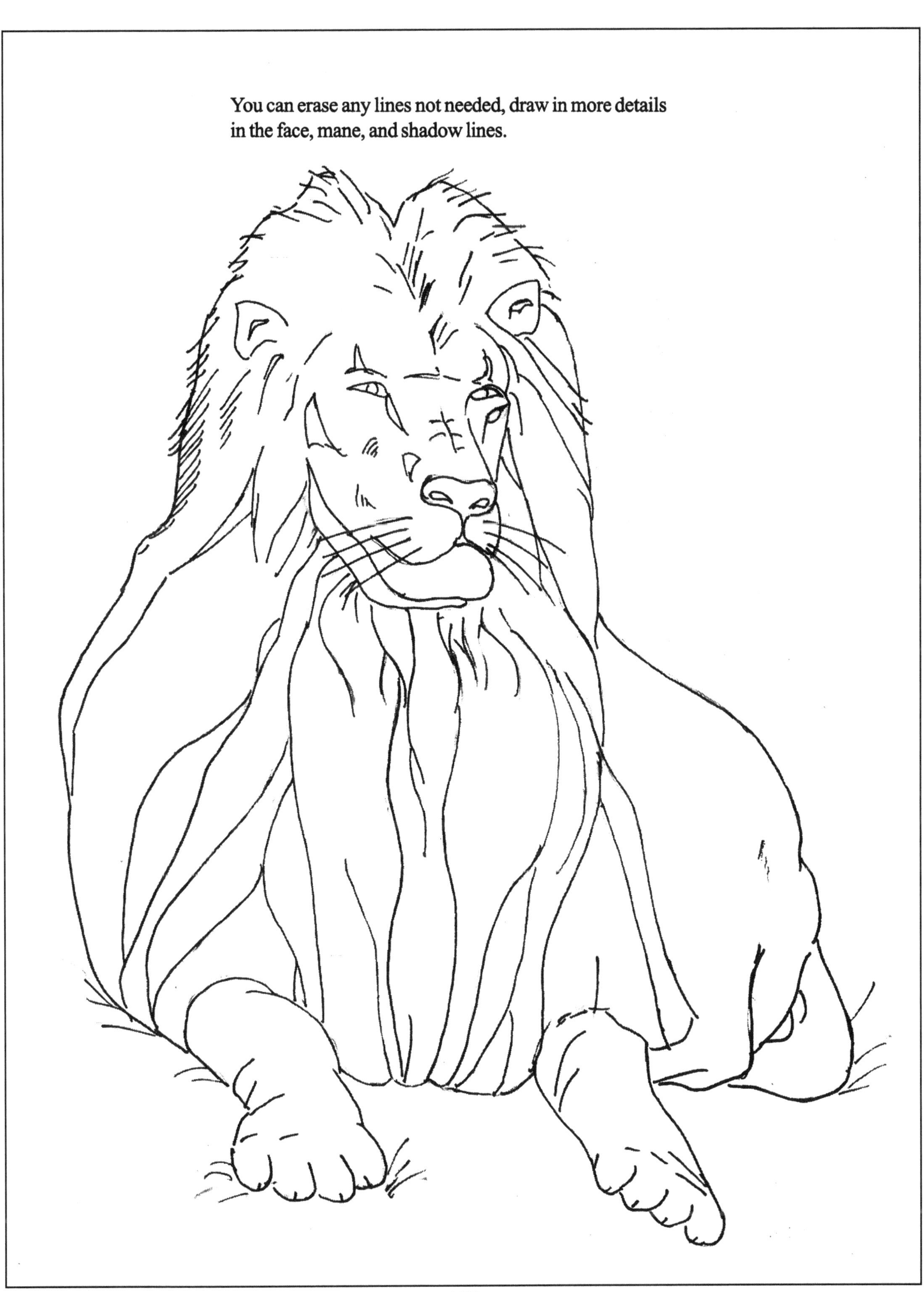

LION

LION the normal color is tawny yellow but varies from gray to ochre and can be blackish, the female has paler coloring, especially on the throat and on the underside of the body. The length of mane, found only in males, may be associated with harshness of the local climate. Length of head and body in males is 5.6 - 6.3 feet, tail about 3 feet, and weight 330 - 550 pounds. Female are much smaller than males.

Lions can be found throughout Africa and southern Asia to India. Lions are social animals, living in prides usually made of one or more adults males, two or more females, cubs, adolescents. It hunts mainly at night, but is also active during the cooler part of the day. It hunts by ambushing prey, and does not usually pursue it. The resources of several lions are often combined; while the group stalks the prey, a single lion, usually a lioness, may ambush it. Gestation lasts for 105 days, after which the female gives birth to 2 - 4 cubs that will remain with the group for at least 18 months.

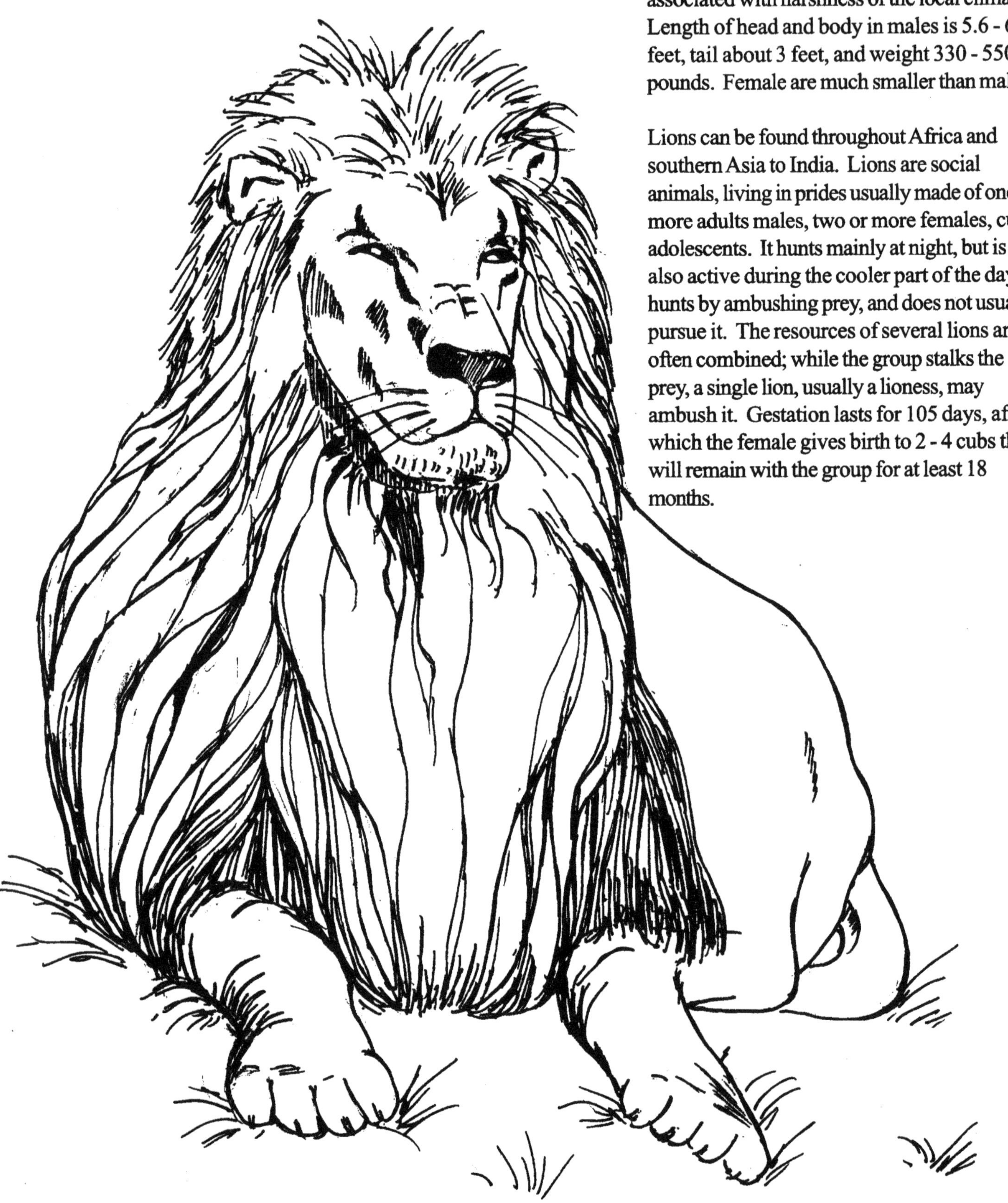

www.ingramcontent.com/pod-product-compliance
Ingram Content Group UK Ltd.
Pitfield, Milton Keynes, MK11 3LW, UK
UKHW051138260726
13967UKWH00010B/3120